eHealth Innovative Approaches and Applications

eHealth Innovative Approaches and Applications

Editors

Stefano Silvestri
Francesco Gargiulo

MDPI

Basel • Beijing • Wuhan • Barcelona • Belgrade • Novi Sad • Cluj • Manchester

Editors
Stefano Silvestri
National Research Council of Italy (CNR)
Rome
Italy

Francesco Gargiulo
National Research Council of Italy (CNR)
Rome
Italy

Editorial Office
MDPI
St. Alban-Anlage 66
4052 Basel, Switzerland

This is a reprint of articles from the Special Issue published online in the open access journal *Applied Sciences* (ISSN 2076-3417) (available at: https://www.mdpi.com/journal/applsci/special_issues/C2BUU28H91).

For citation purposes, cite each article independently as indicated on the article page online and as indicated below:

Lastname, A.A.; Lastname, B.B. Article Title. *Journal Name* **Year**, *Volume Number*, Page Range.

ISBN 978-3-7258-0921-9 (Hbk)
ISBN 978-3-7258-0922-6 (PDF)
doi.org/10.3390/books978-3-7258-0922-6

Contents

About the Editors

Stefano Silvestri

Stefano Silvestri, Ph.D., is a researcher at the Institute for High-Performance Computing and Networking of the National Research Council of Italy (CNR-ICAR) and is an adjunct professor of Computer Science at the University of Campania "L. Vanvitelli", and at University "G. Fortunato". He received his MSc in electrical engineering from the University of Naples "Federico II" and his Ph.D. in Information and Communication Technology and Engineering from the University of Naples "Parthenope". His main research interests are artificial intelligence, machine/deep learning, smart health, natural language processing, and big data analytics. He has participated in several national and international research projects and authored and co-authored more than 30 scientific articles in peer-reviewed journals and conference proceedings. Moreover, he has been a member of the program committee of several international conferences and workshops and has guest-edited international journals.

Francesco Gargiulo

Francesco Gargiulo is a technological researcher with the Institute for High Performance Computing and Networking, National Research Council, Italy (ICAR-CNR). He received his MSc degree (cum laude) in telecommunication engineering and his Ph.D. degree in information and automatic engineering from the University of Naples Federico II in 2006 and 2009, respectively. He has been involved in different national and European projects. He has authored numerous peer-reviewed articles in international journals and conference proceedings. His research interests include e-health, big data analytics, natural language processing, artificial intelligence, deep learning, and quantum computing. He has been on the program committee of international conferences and workshops and is currently a member of the editorial board of some international journals.

Preface

In the last few years, the rapid growth of the available ICT technologies and methodologies tailored for the e-health domain provided several innovations for physicians, patients, healthcare organizations, and policymakers but also opened new challenges for the scientific research community in the healthcare informatics field. The e-health systems leveraging the most recent ICT methods, such as artificial intelligence (IA), Internet of Medical Things (IoMT), large language models (LLMs), and others, are becoming widely adopted in daily medical practice. On the other hand, the awareness of physicians, medical professionals, patients, and other users must be increased, making them aware of the large number of possibilities provided by these technologies and, on the other side, to warn them about their threats and issues, such as the privacy of the digitized data, the cyber security issues, the explainability of AI models, and others.

In this scenario, it is very important to disseminate the most recent results achieved by the scientific community related to the use of innovative e-health approaches and applications in healthcare and medicine, promoting their effective adoption and highlighting their issues and limits.

For these reasons, this Special Issue collects articles that present e-health approaches and applications that exploit recent and innovative ICT technologies and techniques, such as IA, IoMT, and others, to implement advanced tools and methods. Therefore, this Special Issue article represents a useful resource targeted to a multidisciplinary audience. The topics of the published papers belong to several areas of e-health, such as artificial intelligence and machine learning, medical imaging, Internet of Medical Things (IoMT), e-health cyber security, and large language models.

Stefano Silvestri and Francesco Gargiulo
Editors

applied sciences

MDPI

Editorial

Special Issue on eHealth Innovative Approaches and Applications

Stefano Silvestri * and Francesco Gargiulo *

Institute for High Performance Computing and Networking, ICAR-CNR, Via Pietro Castellino 111, 80131 Naples, Italy
* Correspondence: stefano.silvestri@icar.cnr.it (S.S.); francesco.gargiulo@icar.cnr.it (F.G.)

1. Introduction

Innovative ICT technologies, approaches and applications are becoming increasingly pervasive in several domains, including in medicine and healthcare. In these latter cases, physicians and medical professionals can recently incorporated complex and advanced systems, based on the latest technologies, into their daily routines. Scientific research constantly proposes new approaches and applications with high potential for usage in the eHealth sector. For example, the advent of digitised images in pathology and advances in Artificial Intelligence (AI) have led to an explosion of innovation in the traditional field of pathology, creating what is now described as Computational Pathology [1], which defines new and increasingly effective AI approaches for digital image analysis. Similarly, the pervasive adoption of AI in other medical fields has allowed the definition and implementation of innovative systems to support the work of physicians, medical professionals and policy makers, such as recommender systems [2], smart patient support and remote monitoring systems [3,4]. Another technology that has become increasingly pervasive in medicine in recent years is the Internet of Medical Things (IoMT), which is currently largely adopted in healthcare; this technology is redefining smart healthcare systems and approaches to providing care [5].

Furthermore, the great recent improvements in the field of Natural Language Processing (NLP), with the release of Large Language Models (LLMs) such as ChatGPT, also impacted the biomedical domain, quickly leading to the widespread use of these models in medical research (as in other domains) or in healthcare. Recently, LLMs have provided functional eHealth applications ranging from the development of virtual medical assistants to the acceleration of various benchmarks of several biomedical information tasks, including document classification or relation extraction, exploiting closed-domain models such as BioBERT [6], or BERTMeSH [7]. Examples of further innovative eHealth technologies based on LLMs are smart assistants and question-answering systems, such as Med-PaLM 2 [8], ChatDoctor [9] or MedPrompt [10], which obtain very promising performances and results.

On the other hand, this current revolution in the medical domain, thanks to these new technologies and approaches, has some drawbacks and issues that must be taken into account in order to effectively exploit all its advantages without any risks or problems. eHealth approaches must guarantee the required levels of privacy and security [11–13] during the processing, transmission and sharing of medical and personal information, preventing violations or thefts of patients' sensitive medical data. The scarcity of medical and clinical datasets with high-quality annotations is also a limitation in the development and improvement of innovative eHealth approaches [14–16]. Furthermore, the increasing number of connected medical devices and the complex digital healthcare delivery systems cause several cyber security issues [17,18], due to the increased risk of surface attack. Thus, defining innovative cyber security techniques specifically tailored for the healthcare domain is required. The growing volume of medical data, and their complexity and heterogeneity, pose additional challenges for the effective extraction of valuable insights [19–21]. In

Citation: Silvestri, S.; Gargiulo, F. Special Issue on eHealth Innovative Approaches and Applications. *Appl. Sci.* **2024**, *14*, 2571. https://doi.org/10.3390/app14062571

Received: 11 March 2024
Accepted: 14 March 2024
Published: 19 March 2024

this case, tailored approaches are also required [22,23]. Moreover, physician, medical professional and patient awareness must be increased, and all parties must be warned of the possibilities and threats inherent to digital medicine [24,25].

In this scenario, it becomes crucial to disseminate the most recent results and enhancements achieved by research in the domain of eHealth. While taking full advantage of the latest advances in ICT approaches applied to the medical sector, their issues and limits must also be highlighted in order to, finally, facilitate the effective and widespread adoption and usage of the most innovative eHealth systems by patients, physicians and healthcare organisations.

This Special Issue presents innovative eHealth approaches and applications, which apply the most recent ICT technologies and techniques, such as IA, IoMT and others, to implement smart tools and methodologies to support the work of physicians and to promote the adoption of new eHealth tools in medicine and by healthcare organisations. At the same time, these contributions address the issues that usually affect this domain, like data privacy, the cyber security of the devices and healthcare infrastructures, the awareness and the involvement of medical personnel, etc. Therefore, the articles included in this Special Issue represent useful resources targeted to a multidisciplinary audience.

2. Published Articles

The main purpose of this Special Issue was to collect recent developments and research in the eHealth domain, presenting innovative approaches and applications while considering a multidisciplinary approach and multi-perspective views, including medicine, Information and Communication Technologies, Artificial Intelligence (AI), Internet of Things (IoT), Big Data Analytics, Cyber Security, and others. The focus of this Special Issue centres on the whole e-health domain.

In total, there were 13 contributions selected for this Special Issue (listed after Section 3), which propose innovative approaches and applications in the previously mentioned areas. These articles have been provided by researchers with broad expertise in different fields and backgrounds, such as medicine, informatics and engineering.

The published papers belong to the main specific areas of eHealth, while some papers present multidisciplinary approaches; therefore, they are included in more than one area: (i) COVID-19 classification; (ii) Artificial Intelligence; iii) Medical Imaging; (iv) Fractal Analysis; (v) Internet of Medical Things (IoMT); (vi) Machine Learning; (vii) Cyber Security; viii) Mobile Medical Apps; (ix) Scientific Literature Retrieval; and (x) Large Language Models. A summary of the papers published in this Special Issue is presented below.

Silvestri et al. (contribution 1) described a complex Deep Learning architecture, whose main aim is to improve the eXtreme Multilabel Text Classification problem [26] related to the classification and large-scale semantic indexing of scientific articles in PubMed [27]. In detail, the authors proposed an architecture called the Hierarchical Deep Neural Network (HDNN), which reproduces the same topology of the label set, in the case where this set is hierarchically organised (such as the MeSH adopted by PubMed). The experimental assessment performed by the authors compared the performances of the proposed HDNN with a classic flat CNN DL architecture for text classification when applied to task of semantically indexing PubMed articles. The results showed that the HDNN outperforms the CNN, in particular in the cases of hierarchical measures, demonstrating that, when a hierarchical label set is available, the reproduction of the label hierarchy directly into the DL architecture provides significant benefits. On the other hand, this complex and deep architecture has a high computational time, due to the need, during training, of propagating the weights calculated in a certain level to the next level before updating the weights of the next level of the HDNN architecture. Therefore, a more efficient parallel architecture is foreseen as an area of future work by the authors.

The contribution of Inigo Lopez-Gazpio (contribution 2) introduced an innovative Problem-Based Learning (PBL) methodology to enhance the teaching of Android programming education, specifically tailored for the development of nutritional applications.

The main novelty of the proposed approach is the integration of advanced programming concepts with practical application development, fostering deeper understanding and engagement among students. In detail, this application allows the programmers to access extensive and detailed nutritional information from different open-access food databases. The proposed approach was tested in a research project that involved third-year students of the Computer Science faculty at the University of Deusto in Spain. The students were engaged in the development of applications aimed at improving access to nutritional knowledge. The preliminary results of this research indicated a significant improvement in student engagement and learning outcomes compared to traditional teaching methods, underlining the possible use of this methodology in fostering research and advancing educational practices in computer science. The findings not only provided insights related to the unique challenges associated with Android programming, but also suggested possible customised educational strategies that can optimise the learning experience.

Alourani et al. (contribution 3) presented a framework for the efficient management of IoMT devices over an Information Centric Network (ICN). The current massive traffic growth generated by IoMT causes challenges related to the transmission of these data [12]. An approach to reduce IoMT traffic is the adoption of ICN [28], which leverages persistent naming multicast communication and thus reduces the response time. In this way, ICN used for IoMT can reduce the overhead due to the distribution of commonly accessed content. On the other hand, the excessive and unbalanced energy consumption of the IoMT devices that the ICN could cause can degrade the performance of the network. To address this issue, the authors presented a framework called the Dynamic Cache Scheme (DCS), which implements energy-efficient cache scheduling in IoMT over ICN with the aim of reducing network traffic and mitigating energy-related issues. This framework establishes a balance between multi-hop traffic and data item freshness by leveraging an effective use for caching in IoMT. The authors tested several parameters, such as the cache–hit ratio, stretch and content retrieval latency, comparing the obtained results with the current state of the art. The results demonstrated that the DCS approach outperforms the compared models in terms of the cache–hit ratio, stretch and content retrieval latency. The authors also assessed its possible adoption in other domains and scenarios.

Viana dos Santos Santana et al. (contribution 4) compared different ML models for the correct classification of COVID-19 and influenza (which present similar symptoms) during coexisting outbreaks in Brazil. In detail, they tested Decision Tree (DT), Multilayer Perceptron (MLP), Gradient Boosting Machine (GBM), Random Forest (RF), eXtreme Gradient Boosting (XGBoost), K-Nearest Neighbors, Support Vector Machine (SVM), and Logistic Regression algorithms on real COVID-19 and influenza datasets, which are openly available and were acquired by Brazilian healthcare. The obtained results were also assessed using a 10-fold cross-validation method, which increased their confidence. Finally, the authors analysed and commented on the obtained results, highlighting some specific features of each tested approach, and providing useful hints for the adoption of ML-based systems in the decision-making processes of physicians and policy makers.

The paper from Karagiannis et al. (contribution 5) discusses the cyber security issues related to the transmission of standard DICOM (Digital Imaging and Communications in Medicine) medical images. The universal adoption of DICOM images has revolutionised digital imaging in medicine, providing standard tools for the storage, sharing and transmission of both medical images and their related data (included, in a standard way, into the DICOM tags of the image). On the other hand, the implementation and deployment of the DICOM protocol often suffer from incomplete understanding, causing cyber security vulnerabilities within the healthcare ecosystem [29]. The authors of the paper proposed a specific implementation of DICOM for the communication of images and their related data to the PACS (Picture Archiving and Communication System) servers, whose main purpose is to address possible cyber threats. Moreover, they also implemented a simulation environment which is able to produce network traffic related to the use of the DICOM protocol. Overall, the resources provide the researchers with an advanced platform for the implementation of security control tests for evaluating the robustness of security measures, identifying vulnerabilities, and testing security configurations. In this way, they gain a comprehensive understanding of DICOM communication and its practical implementation. Finally, the generated traffic allowed for the creation of realistic datasets, which are useful for the development of ML, and anomaly detection techniques.

Suvirtat et al. (contribution 6) investigated the use of Large Language Models (LLMs) for coding inpatient diagnoses. ICD coding is very useful for several tasks, ranging from statistical analysis to clinical research or medical billing, as well as for ensuring and improving the interoperability of medical documents. Moreover, the application of ICD coding is often mandatory for several official documents in many countries. The automatic application of ICD coding is not an easy task due to the very large number of codes; moreover, the complexity of clinical and medical language, which is used in many documents that must be tagged with the corresponding ICD codes, makes this task more difficult. The paper presented an analysis of the performance of three LLMs (mBERT [30], Multilingual E5 [31] and MEDPSU-RoBERTa [32]), examining their performances on a very large Thai language dataset formed from inpatient admissions. The results showed satisfactory results and confirmed that MEDPSU-RoBERTa, which is a domain-specific model, is able to achieve the best results. The results also highlighted that the performances are strictly dependent on the datasets, obtaining more accurate results in the cases of codes with larger number of samples, while the rarity of certain diseases (and corresponding documents in the datasets) posed challenges to accurate coding. Finally, the results underlined the difficulties when the models are faced with long clinical documents.

Czekster et al. (contribution 7) produced work focused on the security of IoMT devices, presenting a systematic literature review of Risk Assessment approaches specifically devoted to the IoMT. IoMT devices can be very effective instruments in supporting the remote management and care of patients; on the other hand, as they are able to collect and transmit sensitive data, they have critical and strict security requirements. While classic cyber security Risk Assessment approaches can be exploited to identify and assess potential risks, they are not able to manage sophisticated cyber-attacks in near real time. In these latter cases, Dynamic Risk Assessment (DRA) approaches [33] are more suitable for tackling the risks to patients when using IoMT devices. The authors produced a detailed literature review of RA related to the IoMT, highlighting the current trends and the more recent approaches in this field. In more detail, the review first focused on the significant ways of mitigating the impact of unauthorised intrusions, protecting end-users from personal data leakage and ensuring the device usage continuity. Furthermore, the paper identified the main research directions for DRA, addressing the challenges related to the dynamic infrastructures and the uncertain attack surfaces, with the aim of improving user protection and preventing cyber attacks.

The contribution from Pervan et al. (contribution 8) described a DICOM-based medical image communication system named Medical Imaging and Diagnostics on the Move (MIDOM). The proposed system includes some enhancements based on evolutions of the custom lossless Classification and Blending Predictor Coder (CBPC) [34] compression method previously developed by the same authors. Moreover, the MIDOM system was also integrated with Orthanc [35], a lightweight DICOM server, and a medical images-storing PACS server. The proposed system was tested on five real-world anonymised medical image sets, evaluating compression ratios and latency reduction, with the aim of simulating scenarios where medical service availability might be severely limited. The obtained results in all scenarios demonstrated that MIDOM, exploiting the included compression methods, was able to lower the network latency by at least 60% with respect to the transmission of raw and uncompressed image sets, allowing, at the same time, the perfect reconstruction of medical images.

Karagiannis et al. (contribution 9) described Chidroid, a mobile Android application whose purpose is retrieving, collecting and distributing logs from smart healthcare devices in the domain of the IoMT. The growing adoption of IoMT-connected devices in healthcare has also caused an increase in cyber attacks [36], which could potentially provide attackers with access to patients' Personal Health Information (PHI) [37]. The approach described in this paper allows for the creation of datasets, semi-structured data or structured data from unstructured data. These datasets can be very useful for the development of AI methods for detecting cyber security threats and vulnerabilities and mitigating them. Moreover, Chidroid can be used as a policy-based tool to analyse the security issues in the most recent versions of Android. The tests performed demonstrated the effectiveness of the application, which retrieves logs and system metrics from several IoMT devices. Finally, the paper presented a method to perform a security analysis on Android devices that uses minimal system resources and reduces battery consumption.

The study from Fordellone et al. (contribution 10) focuses on an entropy-based fuzzy clustering technique for interval-valued data (EFC-ID) for cancer detection. The early detection of cancer can improve the chances of successful treatment, and screening techniques have the purpose of identifying possible signs of specific cancers or pre-cancers before symptoms have developed. On the other hand, precise detection mainly relies on human experience, and is thus affected by human and visual inspection errors. The authors tested the proposed clustering approach on the Breast dataset, demonstrating that EFC-ID can obtain better results compared to FKM in terms of several metrics (AUC, sensitivity and specificity). Moreover, further experiments on the Multiple Myeloma data demonstrated that EFC-ID outperforms the classic FKM in terms of Chi-squared, Accuracy rate and Adjusted Rand Indexes. The obtained results confirmed that the proposed EFC-ID is able to correctly identify the natural partition.

Contaldo et al. (contribution 11) presented a review paper that reports on the recent literature on the applications of fractal analysis devoted to the diagnosis of oral cancer and Oral Potentially Malignant Disorders. In the case of fractal analysis applied to diagnostics, the Fractal Dimension (FD) is usually calculated as a measure of the degree of regularity of a tissue or structure [38]. This feature can be applied to the analysis of lesions (such as oral lesions) to determine the degree of irregular tissue/vascularisation derailment; physicians correlate this with the nature of the lesion with the aim of identifying possible cancerous lesions. This paper evaluates the recent published literature on the fractal analysis of oral cancer and its precursors, namely Oral Potentially Malignant Disorders (OPMDs), investigating the specific FD that can be predictive of cancer and OPMDs. The authors only considered articles from three literature databases (Scopus, PubMed and Web of Science), and investigated according to the PRISMA checklist to analyse if fractal analysis can support the diagnosis of oral cancer and, moreover, if it can distinguish it from its precursors. The results of this review highlighted that fractal analysis, when applied to oral oncology, is promising, because it can be adopted as an effective and noninvasive diagnostic and prognostic tool for various premalignant lesions, especially for measuring the progression of premalignant lesions and OPMDs [39].

Kioskli et al. (contribution 12) framed the current state of cyber hygiene, explaining the related context and habits of end-users. They then proposed several best practices that should be adopted by healthcare organisations and professionals in order to achieve a high level of cyber hygiene, particularly regarding human-centric approach. Currently, critical healthcare infrastructures are very vulnerable to cyber attacks [40], as demonstrated by the several successful cyber attacks in recent years. Many of these are caused by a lack of awareness and incorrect behaviours on the part of end-users, who do not adopt the required level of cyber hygiene, i.e, regularly and promptly applying software updates, or adopting unique and strong passwords. Thus, the issues faced in this paper are of great importance and urgency, considering the large and increasing number of cyber attacks in the healthcare domain; these are very often caused by human errors. Therefore, cyber education can prevent many of the issues caused by poor cyber hygiene. On the other hand, cyber security and hygiene eduction for non-expert users (such as in the case of the healthcare domain) should adopt human-centric approaches to be more effective. Therefore, this paper firstly reports the best practices that should be adopted by healthcare organisations and professionals to achieve a high level of cyber hygiene. Moreover, it explains how these best practises could be applied in a use-case scenario with the aim of improving awareness about privacy and cyber security. Finally, the authors presented their long-term vision based on human-centric approaches, which aims to facilitate the development of efficient practices and education associated with cyber hygiene, leveraging a flexible, adaptable and practical framework.

The article from Junaid et al. (contribution 13) is a review of the more recent advances in Artificial Intelligence and Wearable Sensors in Healthcare Delivery. The combined use of AI and IoT in healthcare allows for defining frameworks and solutions for the smart analysis of health and clinical data, improving the work of physicians and providing additional evidence for clinical decisions. Therefore, the authors highlighted how the application of AI and the IoT has changed healthcare service delivery from the traditional hospital-centred model to a personal portable device-centred model. In detail, this literature review highlights how recent research describes the advantages of embracing AI techniques and wearable sensors in tasks related to innovating and optimising the analysis of health and clinical data. Moreover, the review also discusses some challenges related to the issues of using AI and the IoT applied to healthcare data analysis. Finally, it identifies some issues and opportunities for future work.

3. Future of eHealth Applications and Approaches

This Special Issue gathered several studies in the field of eHealth, and the results of the published research describe interesting innovative approaches and applications from this domain. This Special Issue also underlines some of the issues that remain, as well as some risks and limits, proposing possible solutions.

In detail, some of the presented papers focused on Artificial Intelligence and Machine Learning applied to medicine and care applications, such as COVID-19 classification (contribution 4), biomedical scientific literature semantic indexing (contribution 1), the early detection of breast cancer (contribution 10) and reviewing the more recent combined use of Artificial Intelligence and IoMT wearable sensors in healthcare (contribution 13). Other papers considered eHealth cyber security, proposing a simulation environment to test DICOM communication and evaluate the related risks (contribution 5), producing a literature review of the cyber security issues of IoMT devices (contribution 7) and framing the current state of cyber hygiene in the eHealth domain, proposing a human-centric approach for the effective education of non-expert users on the best cyber security practises (contribution 12). One published paper reviewed the application of a Fractal Analysis methodology for oral cancer diagnosis (contribution 11). Another paper proposed a traffic and energy optimisation for IoMT devices (contribution 3). A study that describes the use of LLMs for automatic ICD-10 classification was presented in contribution 6, comparing them on a very large Thai language dataset formed from inpatient admissions. Two applications were, respectively, described in contribution 8 and contribution 9, presenting, in the first case, a DICOM-based medical image communication system enhanced with advanced compression methods, and, in the latter case, an Android application for the collection and distributions of logs from IoMT devices, tailored to analyse their cyber security issues. Finally, an approach to support the development of applications related to the nutritional domain has been presented in contribution 2.

The eHealth domain, thanks to evolutions in its technologies and the methods, is constantly evolving, and, therefore, new volumes of this Special Issue have been planned for the future.

Funding: This work is supported by European Union - NextGenerationEU - National Recovery and Resilience Plan (Piano Nazionale di Ripresa e Resilienza, PNRR) - Project: "SoBigData.it - Strengthening the Italian RI for Social Mining and Big Data Analytics" - Prot. IR0000013 - Avviso n. 3264 del 28/12/2021, and by the European Commission, grant number 101083563, DS4HEALTH—Digital skills for Healthcare Transformation.

Acknowledgments: This Special Issue would not have been possible without the contributions of the authors and the reviewers. We congratulate all authors. Moreover, we would like to take this opportunity to express our sincere gratitude to all the reviewers. Finally, we place on record our gratitude to Simona Sada and to Giuseppe Trerotola for their technical and administrative supports.

Conflicts of Interest: The authors declare no conflicts of interest.

List of Contributions

1. Silvestri, S.; Gargiulo, F.; Ciampi, M. Integrating PubMed Label Hierarchy Knowledge into a Complex Hierarchical Deep Neural Network. *Appl. Sci.* **2023**, *13*, 13117. https://doi.org/10.3390/app132413117
2. Lopez-Gazpio, I. Bridging Theory and Practice: An Innovative Approach to Android Programming Education through Nutritional Application Development and Problem-Based Learning. *Appl. Sci.* **2023**, *13*, 12140. https://doi.org/10.3390/app132212140.
3. Alourani, A.; Sardaraz, M.; Tahir, M.; Khan, M.S. Dynamic and Energy Efficient Cache Scheduling Framework for IoMT over ICN. *Appl. Sci.* **2023**, *13*, 11840. https://doi.org/10.3390/app132111840
4. Santana, I.V.d.S.; Sobrinho, A.; da Silva, L.D.; Perkusich, A. Machine Learning for COVID-19 and Influenza Classification during Coexisting Outbreaks. *Appl. Sci.* **2023**, *13*, 11518. https://doi.org/10.3390/app132011518
5. Karagiannis, S.; Magkos, E.; Ntantogian, C.; Cabecinha, R.; Fotis, T. Cybersecurity and Medical Imaging: A Simulation-Based Approach to DICOM Communication. *Appl. Sci.* **2023**, *13*, 10072. https://doi.org/10.3390/app131810072
6. Suvirat, K.; Tanasanchonnakul, D.; Chairat, S.; Chaichulee, S. Leveraging Language Models for Inpatient Diagnosis Coding. *Appl. Sci.* **2023**, *13*, 9450. https://doi.org/10.3390/app13169450
7. Czekster, R.M.; Grace, P.; Marcon, C.; Hessel, F.; Cazella, S.C. Challenges and Opportunities for Conducting Dynamic Risk Assessments in Medical IoT. *Appl. Sci.* **2023**, *13*, 7406. https://doi.org/10.3390/app13137406
8. Pervan, B.; Tomic, S.; Ivandic, H.; Knezovic, J. MIDOM-A DICOM-Based Medical Image Communication System. *Appl. Sci.* **2023**, *13*, 6075. https://doi.org/10.3390/app13106075
9. Karagiannis, S.; Ribeiro, L.L.; Ntantogian, C.; Magkos, E.; Campos, L.M. Chidroid: A Mobile Android Application for Log Collection and Security Analysis in Healthcare and IoMT. *Appl. Sci.* **2023**, *13*, 3061. https://doi.org/10.3390/app13053061
10. Fordellone, M.; Benedictis, I.D.; Bruzzese, D.; Chiodini, P. A Maximum-Entropy Fuzzy Clustering Approach for Cancer Detection When Data Are Uncertain. *Appl. Sci.* **2023**, *13*, 2191. https://doi.org/10.3390/app13042191
11. Contaldo, M.; Spirito, F.D.; Palo, M.P.D.; Amato, A.; Fiori, F.; Serpico, R. Fractal Analysis Applied to the Diagnosis of Oral Cancer and Oral Potentially Malignant Disorders: A Comprehensive Review. *Appl. Sci.* **2024**, *14*, 777. https://doi.org/10.3390/app14020777
12. Kioskli, K.; Fotis, T.; Nifakos, S.; Mouratidis, H. The Importance of Conceptualising the Human-Centric Approach in Maintaining and Promoting Cybersecurity-Hygiene in Healthcare 4.0. *Appl. Sci.* **2023**, *13*, 3410. https://doi.org/10.3390/app13063410
13. Junaid, S.B.; Imam, A.A.; Abdulkarim, M.; Surakat, Y.A.; Balogun, A.O.; Kumar, G.; Shuaibu, A.N.; Garba, A.; Sahalu, Y.; Mohammed, A.; et al. Recent Advances in Artificial Intelligence and Wearable Sensors in Healthcare Delivery. *Appl. Sci.* **2022**, *12*, 10271. https://doi.org/10.3390/app122010271

References

1. Hosseini, M.S.; Bejnordi, B.E.; Trinh, V.Q.H.; Chan, L.; Hasan, D.; Li, X.; Yang, S.; Kim, T.; Zhang, H.; Wu, T.; et al. Computational pathology: A survey review and the way forward. *J. Pathol. Inform.* **2024**, *15*, 100357. [CrossRef] [PubMed]
2. Etemadi, M.; Bazzaz Abkenar, S.; Ahmadzadeh, A.; Haghi Kashani, M.; Asghari, P.; Akbari, M.; Mahdipour, E. A systematic review of healthcare recommender systems: Open issues, challenges, and techniques. *Expert Syst. Appl.* **2023**, *213*, 118823. [CrossRef]
3. Wen, M.H.; Bai, D.; Lin, S.; Chu, C.J.; Hsu, Y.L. Implementation and experience of an innovative smart patient care system: A cross-sectional study. *BMC Health Serv. Res.* **2022**, *22*, 126. [CrossRef] [PubMed]
4. Ciampi, M.; Coronato, A.; Naeem, M.; Silvestri, S. An intelligent environment for preventing medication errors in home treatment. *Expert Syst. Appl.* **2022**, *193*, 116434. [CrossRef]

5. Ajagbe, S.A.; Awotunde, J.B.; Adesina, A.O.; Achimugu, P.; Kumar, T.A., Internet of Medical Things (IoMT): Applications, Challenges, and Prospects in a Data-Driven Technology. In *Intelligent Healthcare: Infrastructure, Algorithms and Management*; Springer Nature Singapore: Singapore, 2022; pp. 299–319. _14. [CrossRef]
6. Lee, J.; Yoon, W.; Kim, S.; Kim, D.; Kim, S.; So, C.H.; Kang, J. BioBERT: A pre-trained biomedical language representation model for biomedical text mining. *Bioinformatics* **2019**, *36*, 1234–1240. [CrossRef] [PubMed]
7. You, R.; Liu, Y.; Mamitsuka, H.; Zhu, S. BERTMeSH: Deep contextual representation learning for large-scale high-performance MeSH indexing with full text. *Bioinformatics* **2020**, *37*, 684–692. [CrossRef] [PubMed]
8. Singhal, K.; Tu, T.; Gottweis, J.; Sayres, R.; Wulczyn, E.; Hou, L.; Clark, K.; Pfohl, S.; Cole-Lewis, H.; Neal, D.; et al. Towards Expert-Level Medical Question Answering with Large Language Models. *arXiv* **2023**, arXiv:cs.CL/2305.09617.
9. Li, Y.; Li, Z.; Zhang, K.; Dan, R.; Jiang, S.; Zhang, Y. ChatDoctor: A Medical Chat Model Fine-Tuned on a Large Language Model Meta-AI (LLaMA) Using Medical Domain Knowledge. *Cureus* **2023**, *15*, e40895. [CrossRef]
10. Ahmed, A.; Zeng, X.; Xi, R.; Hou, M.; Shah, S.A. MED-Prompt: A novel prompt engineering framework for medicine prediction on free-text clinical notes. *J. King Saud Univ. Comput. Inf. Sci.* **2024**, *36*, 101933. [CrossRef]
11. Ciampi, M.; Sicuranza, M.; Silvestri, S. A Privacy-Preserving and Standard-Based Architecture for Secondary Use of Clinical Data. *Information* **2022**, *13*, 87. [CrossRef]
12. Pradyumna, G.R.; Hegde, R.B.; Bommegowda, K.B.; Jan, T.; Naik, G.R. Empowering Healthcare With IoMT: Evolution, Machine Learning Integration, Security, and Interoperability Challenges. *IEEE Access* **2024**, *12*, 20603–20623. [CrossRef]
13. Thapa, C.; Camtepe, S. Precision health data: Requirements, challenges and existing techniques for data security and privacy. *Comput. Biol. Med.* **2021**, *129*, 104130. [CrossRef] [PubMed]
14. Chatterjee, P.; Das Sharma, K.; Chakrabarti, A. Weakly supervised learning in domain transfer scenario for brain lesion segmentation in MRI. *Multimed. Tools Appl.* **2024**, 1–17. [CrossRef]
15. Zhang, Y.; Chen, J.; Ma, X.; Wang, G.; Bhatti, U.A.; Huang, M. Interactive medical image annotation using improved Attention U-net with compound geodesic distance. *Expert Syst. Appl.* **2024**, *237*, 121282. [CrossRef]
16. Silvestri, S.; Gargiulo, F.; Ciampi, M. Iterative Annotation of Biomedical NER Corpora with Deep Neural Networks and Knowledge Bases. *Appl. Sci.* **2022**, *12*, 5775. [CrossRef]
17. Islam, S.; Papastergiou, S.; Kalogeraki, E.M.; Kioskli, K. Cyberattack Path Generation and Prioritisation for Securing Healthcare Systems. *Appl. Sci.* **2022**, *12*, 4443. [CrossRef]
18. Silvestri, S.; Islam, S.; Amelin, D.; Weiler, G.; Papastergiou, S.; Ciampi, M. Cyber threat assessment and management for securing healthcare ecosystems using natural language processing. *Int. J. Inf. Secur.* **2024**, *23*, 32–50. [CrossRef]
19. Karatas, M.; Eriskin, L.; Deveci, M.; Pamucar, D.; Garg, H. Big Data for Healthcare Industry 4.0: Applications, challenges and future perspectives. *Expert Syst. Appl.* **2022**, *200*, 116912. [CrossRef]
20. Luchini, C.; Pea, A.; Scarpa, A. Artificial intelligence in oncology: Current applications and future perspectives. *Br. J. Cancer* **2022**, *126*, 4–9. [CrossRef]
21. Busnatu, S.; Niculescu, A.G.; Bolocan, A.; Petrescu, G.E.D.; Păduraru, D.N.; Năstasă, I.; Lupușoru, M.; Geantă, M.; Andronic, O.; Grumezescu, A.M.; Martins, H. Clinical Applications of Artificial Intelligence—An Updated Overview. *J. Clin. Med.* **2022**, *11*, 2265. [CrossRef]
22. Wang, Y.; Wang, L.; Rastegar-Mojarad, M.; Moon, S.; Shen, F.; Afzal, N.; Liu, S.; Zeng, Y.; Mehrabi, S.; Sohn, S.; Liu, H. Clinical information extraction applications: A literature review. *J. Biomed. Inform.* **2018**, *77*, 34–49. [CrossRef] [PubMed]
23. Gargiulo, F.; Silvestri, S.; Ciampi, M. A Big Data architecture for knowledge discovery in PubMed articles. In Proceedings of the 2017 IEEE Symposium on Computers and Communications (ISCC), Heraklion, Greece, 3–6 July 2017; pp. 82–87. [CrossRef]
24. Sezgin, E.; Özkan Yildirim, S.; Yildirim, S. Investigation of physicians' awareness and use of mHealth apps: A mixed method study. *Health Policy Technol.* **2017**, *6*, 251–267. [CrossRef]
25. Affinito, L.; Fontanella, A.; Montano, N.; Brucato, A. How physicians can empower patients with digital tools: A joint study of the Italian Scientific Society of Internal Medicine (FADOI) and the European Federation of Internal Medicine (EFIM). *J. Public Health* **2022**, *30*, 897–909. [CrossRef]
26. Liu, J.; Chang, W.; Wu, Y.; Yang, Y. Deep Learning for Extreme Multi-label Text Classification. Proceedings of the 40th International ACM SIGIR Conference on Research and Development in Information Retrieval; ACM: Shinjuku, Tokyo, Japan, 2017; pp. 115–124. [CrossRef]
27. Nentidis, A.; Krithara, A.; Paliouras, G.; Gasco, L.; Krallinger, M. BioASQ at CLEF2022: The Tenth Edition of the Large-scale Biomedical Semantic Indexing and Question Answering Challenge. In *Advances in Information Retrieval*; Hagen, M., Verberne, S., Macdonald, C., Seifert, C., Balog, K., Norvaag, K., Setty, V., Eds.; Springer International Publishing: Cham, Switzerland, 2022; pp. 429–435.
28. Vasilakos, A.V.; Li, Z.; Simon, G.; You, W. Information centric network: Research challenges and opportunities. *J. Netw. Comput. Appl.* **2015**, *52*, 1–10. [CrossRef]
29. Eichelberg, M.; Kleber, K.; Kämmerer, M. Cybersecurity Challenges for PACS and Medical Imaging. *Acad. Radiol.* **2020**, *27*, 1126–1139. [CrossRef] [PubMed]

30. Devlin, J.; Chang, M.W.; Lee, K.; Toutanova, K. BERT: Pre-training of Deep Bidirectional Transformers for Language Understanding. In Proceedings of the 2019 Conference of the North American Chapter of the Association for Computational Linguistics: Human Language Technologies, Volume 1 (Long and Short Papers); Burstein, J., Doran, C., Solorio, T., Eds.; Association for Computational Linguistics: Minneapolis, MN, USA, 2019; pp. 4171–4186. [CrossRef]
31. Wang, L.; Yang, N.; Huang, X.; Jiao, B.; Yang, L.; Jiang, D.; Majumder, R.; Wei, F. Text embeddings by weakly-supervised contrastive pre-training. *arXiv* **2022**, arXiv:2212.03533.
32. Suvirat, K.; Chairat, S.; Horsiritham, K.; Kongkamol, C.; Chaichulee, S. De-identification of Thai Free-text Clinical Notes. In Proceedings of the 2023 15th Biomedical Engineering International Conference (BMEiCON), Pittsburgh, PA, USA, 5–18 October 2023; pp. 1–5. [CrossRef]
33. Cheimonidis, P.; Rantos, K. Dynamic Risk Assessment in Cybersecurity: A Systematic Literature Review. *Futur. Internet* **2023**, *15*, 324. [CrossRef]
34. Knezovic, J.; Kovac, M.; Mlinaric, H. Classification and blending prediction for lossless image compression. In Proceedings of the MELECON 2006-2006 IEEE Mediterranean Electrotechnical Conference, Malaga, Spain, 16–19 May 2006; pp. 486–489. [CrossRef]
35. Jodogne, S.; Bernard, C.; Devillers, M.; Lenaerts, E.; Coucke, P. Orthanc—A lightweight, restful DICOM server for healthcare and medical research. In Proceedings of the 2013 IEEE 10th International Symposium on Biomedical Imaging, San Francisco, CA, USA, 7–11 April 2013; pp. 190–193. [CrossRef]
36. Thomasian, N.M.; Adashi, E.Y. Cybersecurity in the Internet of Medical Things. *Health Policy Technol.* **2021**, *10*, 100549. [CrossRef]
37. Hatzivasilis, G.; Soultatos, O.; Ioannidis, S.; Verikoukis, C.; Demetriou, G.; Tsatsoulis, C. Review of Security and Privacy for the Internet of Medical Things (IoMT). In Proceedings of the 2019 15th International Conference on Distributed Computing in Sensor Systems (DCOSS), Santorini Island, Greece, 29–31 May 2019; pp. 457–464. [CrossRef]
38. Bayrak, E.A.; Kirci, P., Fractal Analysis Usage Areas in Healthcare. In *System Analysis & Intelligent Computing: Theory and Applications*; Springer International Publishing: Cham, Switzerland, 2022; pp. 377–406. [CrossRef]
39. Spyridonos, P.; Gaitanis, G.; Bassukas, I.D.; Tzaphlidou, M. Evaluation of vermillion border descriptors and relevance vector machines discrimination model for making probabilistic predictions of solar cheilosis on digital lip photographs. *Comput. Biol. Med.* **2015**, *63*, 11–18. [CrossRef]
40. Rees, D. Cyber Attacks in Healthcare: The Position across Europe. Available online: https://www.pinsentmasons.com/out-law/analysis/cyber-attacks-healthcare-europe (accessed on 8 March 2024).

applied sciences

MDPI

Article

Integrating PubMed Label Hierarchy Knowledge into a Complex Hierarchical Deep Neural Network †

Stefano Silvestri *,‡, Francesco Gargiulo ‡ and Mario Ciampi

Institute for High Performance Computing and Networking, National Research Council of Italy (ICAR-CNR), Via Pietro Castellino 111, 80131 Naples, Italy; francesco.gargiulo@icar.cnr.it (F.G.); mario.ciampi@icar.cnr.it (M.C.)
* Correspondence: stefano.silvestri@icar.cnr.it
† This paper is an extended, improved version of the paper: F. Gargiulo, S. Silvestri and M. Ciampi, Exploit Hierarchical Label Knowledge for Deep Learning. In 2019 IEEE 32nd International Symposium on Computer-Based Medical Systems (CBMS) 2019, Cordoba, Spain, 5–7 June 2019.
‡ These authors contributed equally to this work.

Abstract: This paper proposes an innovative method that exploits a complex deep learning network architecture, called Hierarchical Deep Neural Network (HDNN), specifically developed for the eXtreme Multilabel Text Classification (XMTC) task, when the label set is hierarchically organized, such as the case of the PubMed article labeling task. In detail, the topology of the proposed HDNN architecture follows the exact hierarchical structure of the label set to integrate this knowledge directly into the DNN. We assumed that if a label set hierarchy is available, as in the case of the PubMed Dataset, forcing this information into the network topology could enhance the classification performances and the interpretability of the results, especially related to the hierarchy. We performed an experimental assessment of the PubMed article classification task, demonstrating that the proposed HDNN provides performance improvement for a baseline based on a classic flat Convolution Neural Network (CNN) deep learning architecture, in particular in terms of hierarchical measures. These results provide useful hints for integrating previous and innate knowledge in a deep neural network. The drawback of the HDNN is the high computational time required to train the neural network, which can be addressed with a parallel implementation planned as a future work.

Keywords: extreme multilabel text classification; hierarchical deep neural network; natural language processing; BioBERT; PubMed MeSH

Citation: Silvestri, S.; Gargiulo, F.; Ciampi, M. Integrating PubMed Label Hierarchy Knowledge into a Complex Hierarchical Deep Neural Network. *Appl. Sci.* **2023**, *13*, 13117. https://doi.org/10.3390/app132413117

Academic Editor: Alessandro L. Koerich

Received: 31 October 2023
Revised: 27 November 2023
Accepted: 6 December 2023
Published: 9 December 2023

1. Introduction

The most recent studies in the field of artificial intelligence, and in particular in the Natural Language Processing (NLP) area, have proposed innovative deep learning (DL) network architectures, which were able to sensibly improve the previous state-of-the-art systems. Examples of these topologies are the Attention and Transformer-based Deep Neural Network architectures [1,2], which have provided a breakthrough in several application domains of medicine and healthcare, such as medical imaging or biomedical information extraction tasks [3–6].

On the other hand, among the various open issues related to DNNs, there is a need to incorporate prior and external knowledge directly into the neural architectures, allowing exploitation of predefined rules or knowledge by the neural architecture independently from its training [7]. Recently, some contributions to address this issue have been provided by Graph Neural Networks (GNNs) [8,9]. Moreover, it has been demonstrated that incorporating innate structures into artificial intelligence (AI) systems could provide substantial benefits [10].

Following these results, this paper presents a solution for incorporating an external innate structure into AI systems to integrate this kind of external knowledge within the DNN architecture. We applied the proposed approach to a specific difficult task: the *eXtreme Multilabel Text Classification* (XMTC) [11,12]. This task consists of the labeling of textual documents with a variable number of labels belonging to a very large set, formed by thousands or more elements. In many real-world applications, the labels lie in a hierarchical tree-like structure, and in this case, the task can be called *hierarchical multilabel text classification*.

An example of a hierarchical XMTC task is the automatic assignment of the MeSH (Medical Subject Headings) terms to the biomedical scientific articles indexed by PubMed (https://www.ncbi.nlm.nih.gov/pubmed/ (accessed on 5 December 2023)), the official indexing and search engine for the biomedical scientific literature provided and maintained by the US National Library of Medicine (NLM). Domain experts manually tag each paper in PubMed for indexing and searching purposes. The classes used in PubMed belong to a large set called MeSH, where each label lies in a hierarchical tree structure. The manual annotation task is very long and difficult, and several methods have been proposed in the literature to support this process and implement a hierarchical extreme multilabel text classifier, like the ones described in the more recent BioASQ distributed tasks results [13–16]. The large-scale MeSH indexing task has previously been faced with hybrid DNNs and classic machine learning techniques [17], BERT-based solutions [18–20], or by adopting GNN-based approaches [21], improving the obtained performances over the years and often combining the integration of more approaches to exploit their respective advantages. Anyway, the complexity of this task and the need for more innovative and performing architectures is supported by the recent works presented in the literature, as well as by the distributed task proposed every year by BioASQ.

In this context, this paper proposes an innovative approach for the XMTC problem based on a Hierarchical Deep Neural Network (HDNN). This network topology internally reproduces the hierarchy of the labels within its structure. In this way, each node is specialized for the classification of its children nodes labels, considering both the results of the parent nodes and a representation of the input text. The network topology is dynamically and automatically obtained by an algorithm, which implements the network topology by iterating basic DNN blocks, following the hierarchical graph of the labels. In addition, to remove the hierarchical inconsistencies of the label set associated with each training sample, where some labels of the hierarchy could not be included [12], we also defined a methodology able to overcome this problem, expanding the label set following the hierarchy and adding the missing labels. We also evaluated the behavior and performances of the proposed HDNN approach applied to the PubMed MeSH indexing task, extending previous experiments presented in [22] and further demonstrating its effectiveness. In particular, this paper extends the previous results, first by including and testing the BioBERT model [18] as the initial layer of the proposed architecture for text encoding. BioBERT is a BERT-based architecture pretrained on a large biomedical domain document collection extracted from PubMed, which has been successfully adopted in many complex biomedical domain NLP tasks. Moreover, we more deeply analyzed the complexity of the algorithm, in particular with respect to the distribution of the number of nodes and the corresponding children nodes. Finally, we extended the number of experiments performed to further investigate the behavior of the proposed architecture.

The main novelty of the proposed approach is the development of a technique specifically devoted to incorporating hierarchical innate knowledge into the neural network architecture, able to dynamically adapt to any label set and capable of dealing with huge label numbers, such as the PubMed MeSH.

As mentioned above, the most recent best-performing approaches for large-scale PubMed indexing integrate more methodologies and techniques. Therefore, the proposed HDNN, combined with other approaches, can further improve the results obtained in this complex task. This paper extends and improves the research previously presented in [22], first integrating the BioBERT model [18] (a BERT model pretrained on a very large scientific biomedical article collection extracted from PubMed) within the HDNN architecture; moreover, it extends and more deeply investigates the preliminary experiments previously presented. Finally, it provides a more accurate analysis of the performances of the proposed architecture, especially in terms of the depth of the label hierarchy.

This paper is structured as follows: The next Section 2 is devoted to a review of the most recent related works in the fields of integrating external knowledge into DNNs, hierarchical text classification, and PubMed large-scale indexing. In Section 3, the details of the methodology are described, and in Section 4, the experiments and results are illustrated and then discussed. Section 5 concludes the paper and presents some possible future works.

2. Related Works

Some interesting approaches to integrating prior knowledge have recently been presented in the literature. The work of [9] proposed a graph convolutional network that fuses external knowledge related to sentiment lexicon and part-of-speech information, with the purpose of improving the sentiment classification task. In detail, the authors exploited an external sentiment lexicon specifically developed for this purpose and used it to calculate a sentiment score for each word of the sentences of the dataset, building in this way a sentiment score matrix that weights the most important words for sentiment classification. The idea is to use this lexicon to compensate for the fact that the syntactic dependency trees cannot usually capture edge labels. Their experiments confirmed the effectiveness of the proposed model and also verified that the integration of external knowledge can support aspect-based sentiment analysis. In [8], the authors proposed a model to capture and exploit global dependencies among these sentences based on a graph neural network. Specifically, they first represented the input sentences as a graph, including various relations (entity–entity, sentence–sentence, and entity–sentence) to increase the information represented in the graph. After that, they introduced a graph recurrent network, which learns the semantic representations of the sentences. The experimental assessment showed significant performance improvements over the existing state-of-the-art models.

The research presented by [23] proposed to leverage preexisting class hierarchies, such as WordNet, to integrate additional domain knowledge into a DL classifier. They fitted the hierarchy of the classes into a probabilistic model and then derived a novel encoding of the labels and a corresponding loss function. Experiments on ImageNet and NABirds confirmed the effectiveness of this method.

In [24], a model named *KHGCN* is proposed, which is able to learn the entity relationship in the knowledge graph, removing the noisy information at the same time. This model is devoted to a personalized recommendation system. In detail, it extracts node embeddings in graphs and learns its hierarchical structure, also introducing an attentive mechanism to strengthen the knowledge graph aggregation. The experiments validated this on real-world datasets, demonstrating its effectiveness.

The authors of [25] presented a method for incorporating a label hierarchy into a DNN architecture, reproducing the same hierarchy in the neural network topology, to improve multiclass text classification tasks. In detail, the authors proposed an architecture named *HDLTex*, whose parent and child layers are connected following the exact topology of the hierarchical set of labels. The authors tested this method on a dataset composed of papers indexed on Web Of Science, comparing the results obtained by different combinations of neural network architectures (DNN, CNN, RNN) as nodes of the HDLTex model, demonstrating that this method can outperform baseline systems.

The idea of incorporating hierarchical class relations into a neural network has also been investigated by [26], where the authors applied a structured learning procedure incorporating hierarchical information using the labels, in addition to hierarchical distance, to successfully improve subpopulation shift modeling. The authors of [27] proposed a Topic-aware Hierarchical Multiple Attention Network for a hierarchical text classification model based on multihead self-attention integrated with convolutional filters to the end of capturing long-range dependencies. Moreover, this model also combines topic distributions generated by (LDA) Latent Dirichlet Allocation with sentence-level and document-level inputs in a hierarchical architecture. The experimental results prove that this approach improves on the current state-of-the-art hierarchical models.

The application of DL to the medical domain can support the analysis of huge document collections but must face several problems, such as data acquisition, conservation and exchanging, imbalanced datasets, the need of explainability of the models, quality assurance, privacy preservation, respect of local laws, and other ethical issues [28].

The article presented by [29] describes a BiLSTM deep learning model based on a decision tree combined with a data balancing strategy, with the purpose of supporting automated diagnosis tasks from the analysis of questionnaires, also ensuring a secure data exchange between patients and their medical teams. The model also adopts a preliminary data preprocessing module, based on classic balancing algorithms to prepare the data for the network training to overcome imbalanced dataset issues. This issue has been also considered by [30], who proposed a DL method based on CNN combined with SMOTE to the end of effectively handling imbalanced data related to breast cancer. Their results demonstrate that this approach sensibly improves the binary classification of imbalanced datasets.

In [31], the XMTC task is tackled by a hybrid approach, which leverages two stages. The first one is devoted to the retrieval task and exploits two approaches, a Point Mutual Information method and a Unified Label-Semantic Embedding method, to the end of extracting hundreds of candidate labels from a huge label set. Then, the latter stage performs a ranking task, using a model based on a pretrained Transformer architecture, which is capable of distinguishing the true labels from the candidate ones and also providing an explainability mechanism. The experimental assessment showed performance improvements over the state-of-the-art methods.

The authors of [32] introduced a hierarchical Transformer-based architecture, specifically designed for the automatic diagnosis of eye diseases in textual ophthalmology electronic medical records. The proposed model includes a hierarchical Transformer architecture that learns the contextualized representations of each sentence in each document of the dataset, recognizing through an attention-based predictor the diagnosis parts of the documents and effectively extracting the required information related to the diseases.

The main difference between the proposed method here and the previously presented related works is the possibility of reproducing the hierarchical structure directly into the neural network architecture, dynamically adapting with any label hierarchy and also introducing prior knowledge into the neural network.

3. Methodology

The proposed HDNN for XMTC task is based on a neural network topology designed to reproduce the same hierarchical structure of the label set. To this end, we defined a recursive algorithm that automatically builds the network topology by iterating a basic DNN block, which corresponds to each node of the label hierarchy. In addition, we also exploited a methodology to expand the labels of each sample document of the training set, adding all missing ancestors in the label tree and obtaining a more consistent training dataset. In this section, the details of both these methods are described.

3.1. Hierarchical Deep Neural Network

The main purpose of the proposed methodology is the automatic creation of a DNN topology whose structure and interconnections reproduce the label hierarchy. To this end, a recursive algorithm is defined. This algorithm iterates basic neural network blocks, connecting them to each other following the label hierarchy, creating, as a result, the schema depicted in Figure 1. As shown in the figure, the nodes of the HDNN can be classified into three main groups:

- *Preprocessing node:* Where textual data in the input are converted into a word-embedding based representation (the green ones in the upper left part of the figure);
- *Internal node*: A DNN basic block whose inputs are word-embeddings-based and the classification result is obtained as the output of its parent node. In the same way, its output is connected in input to the corresponding children node;
- *Root Node*: A special internal node that corresponds to the root of the hierarchy. It differs from the other internal nodes because its input is directly and only connected to the output of the preprocessing node.

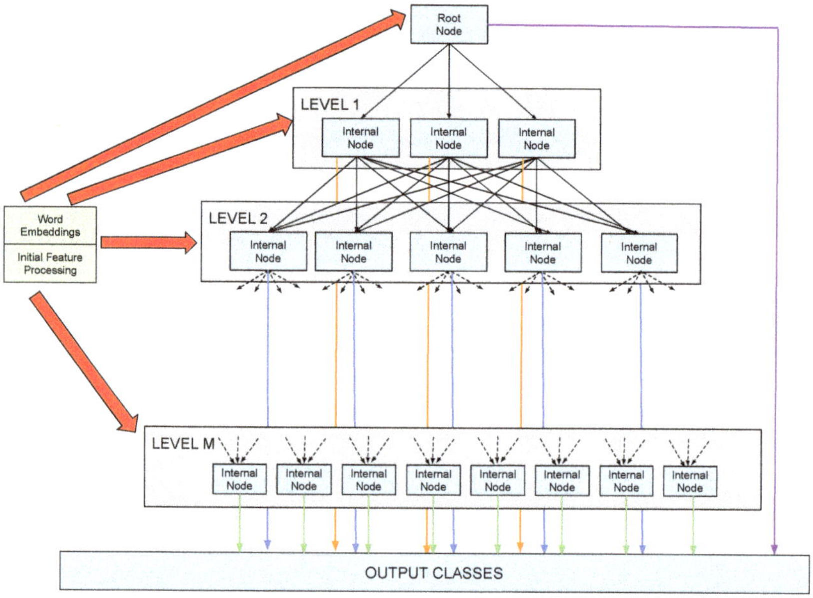

Figure 1. Schema of the internal architecture of an HDNN: The green blocks represent the mapping of the text into its own encoded version, provided to the root and all internal nodes (red arrows). The black arrows represent the outputs of each node, connected to the internal nodes of the next hierarchy level. The outputs of these nodes are also used to build the final classification output classes (depicted as colored arrows).

The preprocessing nodes create an encoded-word representation, exploiting static or dynamic word embedding models [2,33], exploiting in both cases models pretrained on biomedical document collections, to improve the final results [18,34]. The word vectors that represent the words of a document in input are extracted and then concatenated and convoluted in the block named *Initial Feature Processing*, producing a set of features extracted from the text representation, and sending it to each node of the HDNNs.

Figure 2a,b shows the details of the latter two aforementioned node types. These nodes have two main purposes: (i) specializing the features extracted for the corresponding level of labels in the hierarchy tree and (ii) predicting the classes and providing this information to their children nodes, in addition to the final complete prediction. The internal blocks of these nodes include a CNN layer, whose inputs are the results of the preprocessing block, followed by max-pooling and flattened layers; only in the case of internal nodes, the flattened output is concatenated with the output coming from its father node. Finally, the last layer is a dense fully connected layer devoted to label classification. As mentioned, the prediction is also sent to the children of that node in the topology. In summary, the nodes of one level specialize and extract the features for the same level of the hierarchy and provide as output the classifications, which are used as input by their corresponding children nodes.

The only structural difference between the root node and the internal nodes is that the latter concatenates the output of other directly connected internal nodes with the output of their own convolution layer. Furthermore, the convolution layer of the root node has a higher number of filters in order to capture more information at the top level of the topology.

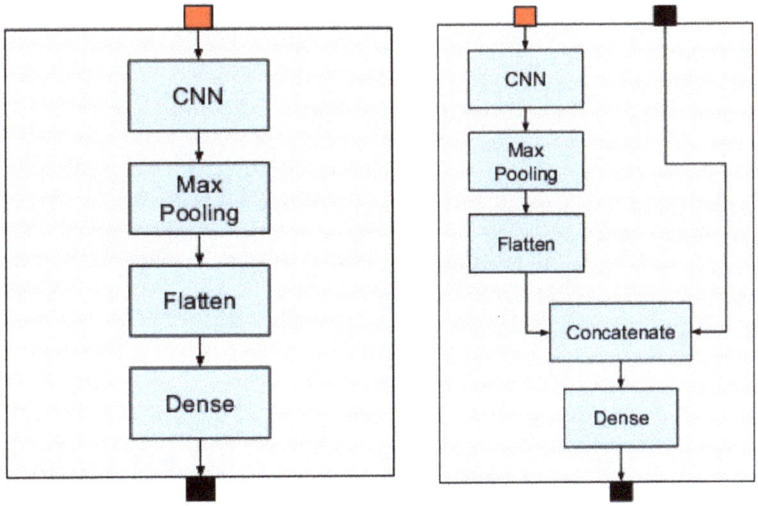

(**a**) (**b**)

Figure 2. In (**a**), the **Root Node Structure** is depicted. The node inputs the encoded text (red input), which is processed using a CNN-dense internal structure. The result is the prediction of the first-level node children (black output). In (**b**), the **Internal Node Structure** is represented. The node takes in the encoded text (red input) and its parent node prediction (black input). The result is the prediction related to the subclassification problem corresponding to the node children (black output).

The topology of the HDNN can be fully automatically generated by iterating the aforementioned basic blocks, reproducing the same exact structure of the hierarchical graph of the labels. To this end, we specifically defined a recursive algorithm, whose details are shown in the next pseudocode in Algorithm 1. The pseudocode implements a recursive function whose input is the representation of the hierarchical label tree; the algorithm iterates the internal node layers blocks, connecting each node with both input text representation and all other children nodes, following the same structure of the hierarchy of the labels, obtaining in this way the architecture represented in Figure 1. The proposed algorithm can be used in any case where a predefined known hierarchical label structure is defined, allowing for the automatic network topology generation starting from the basic internal elements and the representation of the label hierarchy.

Algorithm 1 Pseudocode for HDDN generation

```
function MAKEMODEL(TREE, X1, X2)
    while tree : do
        children = tree.getChildren()
        if len(children)! = 0 then
            x2 = node(x1, x2, len(children))
            out = concatenate(out, x2)
            for child in children do
                makeModel(child, x1, x2)
```

3.2. Hierarchical Label Set Expansion

In real-world applications, it often happens that domain experts manually tag documents with labels belonging to a hierarchy without considering all the labels along a full path. In other words, a label set consistent with the hierarchy should be formed with all ancestors of each label in the corresponding tree, starting from the root. Manual tagging has mainly summary and indexing purposes and, thus, a more compact label set that does not consider all the labels along a whole path of the tree can better synthesize the document content. On the other hand, a machine learning (ML) system trained with a dataset with incomplete labeling in the perspective of the hierarchy can lead to unpredictable results. PubMed is an example of such a document collection: each manually assigned label belongs to a hierarchically organized set (MeSH), and the documents are not labeled with all the classes lying along the tree path formed by all the ancestors of the classes used as labels.

To improve the performances of machine learning systems trained on datasets like the ones described above, we proposed a methodology for the automatic expansion of the label set of each sample document of the training set, which adds any missing class along the hierarchy path for each label. We called this methodology *Hierarchical Label Set Expansion* (HLSE) [12]. Several experiments performed in previous studies confirmed the utility of the HLSE for the classification task, improving the final results. Moreover, considering the hierarchical network topology of the HDNN, it is necessary to include all the labels to reproduce a standard topology for each possible depth without missing some classes along the label set path. Therefore, it is necessary to apply the HLSE to all documents of the training set and test set before creating the corresponding HDNN when the data miss, in some cases, some labels along the hierarchy.

To better explain the HLSE, it is also important to describe more in detail the MeSH hierarchical tree. As mentioned above, the MeSH is a thesaurus provided and constantly updated by the NLM (National Library of Medicine), whose terms are hierarchically organized and controlled, as well as encoded with an alphanumeric code. The MeSH vocabulary is specifically designed to support the indexing of the biomedical scientific literature in PubMed, MEDLINE, and in the other NLM databases, as well as of any document belonging to the same area.

The MeSH terms are structured as 16 hierarchical trees, each one identified by a letter. These hierarchical trees have different levels, which include one or more subheadings, identified with their name and a numerical code, which starts with the same letter as their root node. Each deeper level in the same branch adds another numerical code to the higher-level code, separated by a period. Figure 3 shows an example of a part of this tree structure (the MeSH hierarchy is available and can be interactively browsed at https://meshb.nlm.nih.gov/treeView (accessed on 5 December 2023)) starting from the tree *Diseases* [C], with the corresponding class names and codes.

The colors of the blocks in Figure 3 can help us better clarify the issue that HLSE addresses, as well as better illustrate how it works. The right part of Figure 3 shows the full path from the root to the leaf *Edema, Cardiac*, also including both class names and MeSH codes (the code of the leaf is [C14.280.434.482]).

Usually, the MeSH tagging of the documents in PubMed does not include the full path, as shown in the Figure, but only some parts of it. For example, a human expert could tag a paper whose main topic is cardiac edema with the leaf *Edema, Cardiac* [C14.280.434.482] and another more generic label from a higher level, such as *Cardiovascular Diseases* [C.14] (in light blue in the figure). The expert could omit the other labels depicted in orange in the figure, namely *Diseases* [C], *Heart Diseases* [C.14.280], and *Heart Failure* [C.14.280.434], considering them unnecessary. While these missing labels might not be very useful for a human user, conversely, they could be very important in the training phase of a supervised machine learning model. If other papers on cardiac edema are tagged with the leaf *Edema, Cardiac* [C14.280.434.482] but with different labels along the hierarchy path, there will be high variability in the labels of documents with a very similar topic, making the correct training of an ML classifier very difficult.

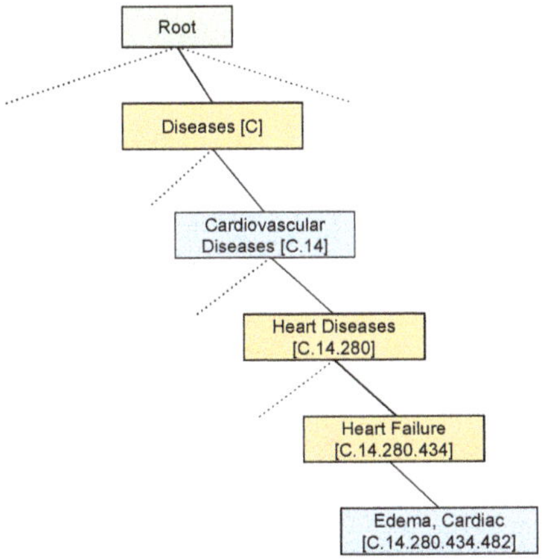

Figure 3. Example of a part of the MeSH label tree hierarchy that shows the full path from the root to the leaf *Edema, Cardiac*.

The HLSE has the purpose of removing this kind of noise from the training set, adding any missing label along the path from the root to each lower-level leaf in the labels of each document. Therefore, in the example in Figure 3, the labels in orange are added to the classes of that document. In this way, all the samples of the training set will have more uniform labeling. The drawback is an increase in the number of labels per document, but it was already demonstrated in [22] that this additional information improves hierarchical classification.

4. Experimental Assessment and Discussion

In this Section, we first describe the details and the features of the datasets used in the experimental assessment. Then, we illustrate the tools required to implement the proposed methods and the hardware used in the experiments. Then, an overview of the multilabel measures is provided, distinguishing flat and hierarchical measures. Finally, the obtained results are shown and discussed to try to investigate the behavior of the proposed HDNN in improving hierarchical classification when applied to the PubMed large-scale indexing XMTC problem.

4.1. Dataset

The experimental assessments have been performed on a subset of PubMed abstracts. We exploited the big data architecture described in [35] to download and extract from PubMed a collection of 11,075,577 abstracts, including the corresponding titles and their MeSH labels. Each document is tagged with a variable number of MeSHs, which currently counts more than 30,000 different labels. We also processed the labels of each document before applying HLSE (see Section 3.2) to complete the hierarchical label set of each document. It is important to underline that the same MeSH could be located in more branches of the tree, making the number of nodes of the tree higher than the total MeSH number, as shown in Table 1, obtaining 57,859 nodes after the use of the HLSE on the dataset. The automatic classification of a text collection with the above-described features is a hierarchical multiclass multilabel problem, as defined in Section 1. The dataset has been divided into a training set and a test set, respectively, randomly selecting 99% and 1% of the documents.

To simplify this complex problem, we decided to consider a maximum tree depth equal to five, substituting all the MeSHs that belong to a deeper level of the original hierarchy with the corresponding ancestor of the fifth level. In this way, we obtained 23,255 different tree nodes, distributed as shown in Figure 4, where it is possible to observe that a very high number of nodes have few children and very few nodes have more than 90 children. We evaluated the average number of children per node to be 5.18, with a standard deviation of 7.30.

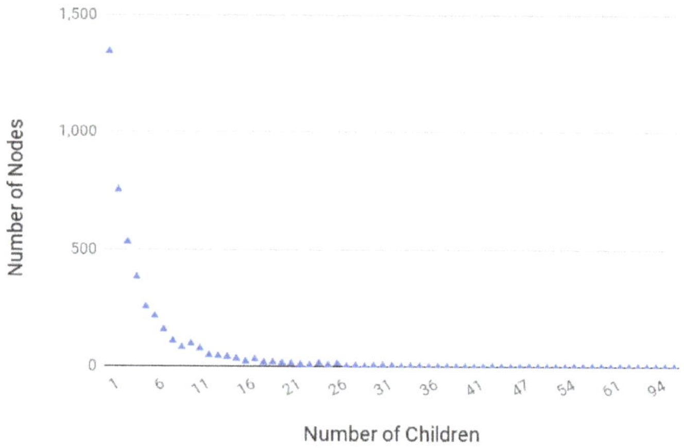

Figure 4. Distribution of the number of nodes per children node.

Table 1 summarizes the details of the datasets, showing the number of nodes, the average number of labels per document, and the average number of documents per label, and it compares these parameters considering a tree depth reduction to five and the original dataset with all levels, applying in both cases the HLSE.

Table 1. Dataset statistics: L is the number of tree nodes, L^* is the average labels count per document, and L^o is the average documents count per label.

MeSHDepth	L	L^*	L^o
5	23,255	39.18	18,740.05
All	57,859	50.57	19,614.76

The automatic classification of PubMed articles is included in the tasks of BioASQ (http://bioasq.org/ (accessed on 5 December 2023)), a research challenge on biomedical semantic indexing and question answering. A discussion of the experimental results can provide further details for improving the BioAsq results [13] and solving large XMTC problems.

4.2. Word Embedding Models

We tested two different embedding models to represent the input text. The first one is a classical static word embedding model [33] pretrained on a large biomedical-domain corpus formed by abstracts from PubMed articles, which is also provided as an additional resource for the BioASQ challenge (the model is publicly available at http://bioasq.org/news/bioasq-releases-continuous-space-word-vectors-obtained-applying-word2vec-pubmed-abstracts (accessed on 5 December 2023)). The latter model, namely the BioBERT model [18], leverages the dynamic word embedding representation extracted from a biomedical BERT model pretrained on a corpus formed by PubMed abstracts and PMC full-text articles, in addition to general-domain English Wikipedia and BooksCorpus data. The features of these models and the corresponding pretraining corpora details are reported in Tables 2 and 3.

Table 2. BioASQ word embedding features.

Vector Size	Training Algorithm	Window Size	Training Set Size	Vocabulary Size
200	CBOW	5	10,876,004	1,701,632

Table 3. BioBERT features.

BERT Model	Training Corpus Word Count	Biomedical Domain Corpus Word Count
BERT-large-cased	≈21.3 Billion words	≈18 Billion words

4.3. Tools and Hardware

Focusing on the tools used for the implementation and execution of the experimental assessment, the preprocessing phase (tokenization and sentence splitting) was performed using Apache Spark and Stanford CoreNLP wrappers for Spark (https://github.com/databricks/spark-corenlp (accessed on 5 December 2023)). The obtained NLP preprocessed text is the input of the word embedding layers, which converts the words into a vectorial representation. For this purpose, we used the Gensim Python library [36] version 4.2 in the case of static word embeddings, while we adopted the Hugging Face Python library (https://huggingface.co/ (accessed on 5 December 2023)) to obtain dynamic embeddings from the BioBERT model, providing a whole sentence as input.

The proposed HLSE and HDNN algorithms were also implemented in Python. In detail, we exploited Keras (https://keras.io (accessed on 5 December 2023)) version 2.11, with Tensorflow 2 backend for the definition, training, and testing of the HDNN. Moreover, the implementation requires the pyTree library, which provides a list-derived tree structure for Python, which is exploited to represent the label hierarchy. Finally, the Numpy, Pandas, and Pickle libraries were required to run the code. We underline that the code is publicly available on SoBigData research infrastructure (the code is publicly available at https://data.d4science.net/RgXa (accessed on 5 December 2023)).

All the experiments were performed on a deep learning cluster based on an IBM Power9 architecture, where each node was equipped with 2 Power9 CPUs at 3.7 GHz, 512 GB of RAM and 4 Nvidia Tesla V100 GPUs with 16 GB of dedicated VRAM. The operating system is Red Hat Enterprise Linux Server release 7.6. The current implementation of the HDNN runs on a single node and on a single GPU (the parallel implementation is not ready yet).

4.4. Evaluation Metrics

Different evaluation measures for multilabel text classification were proposed in the literature. These measures can be grouped into two classes: *flat* and *hierarchical* [37]. The flat measures base evaluates each single result obtained for each label in terms of Precision P_i, Recall R_i, and F1 score F_i for each class c_i, which equals

$$P_i = \frac{tp_{c_i}}{tp_{c_i} + fp_{c_i}}; \tag{1}$$

$$R_i = \frac{tp_{c_i}}{tp_{c_i} + fn_{c_i}} \tag{2}$$

$$F_i = \frac{2 \cdot P_i \cdot R_i}{P_i + R_i} \tag{3}$$

where tp_{c_i}, fp_{c_i}, and fn_{c_i} are, respectively, the true positives, false positives, and false negatives of the class c_i. These values are then averaged, obtaining the measures for the text classification task. The microaverage, which gives equal weight to each per-document classification result [38], is obtained by averaging over all labels each member of the fraction of the previous equations, respectively, obtaining the micro-Precision MiP, micro-Recall MiR, and micro-F1 MiF, defined as

$$MiP = \frac{\sum_{i=1}^{L} tp_{c_i}}{\sum_{i=1}^{L}(tp_{c_i} + fp_{c_i})} \tag{4}$$

$$MiR = \frac{\sum_{i=1}^{L} tp_{c_i}}{\sum_{i=1}^{L}(tp_{c_i} + fn_{c_i})} \tag{5}$$

$$MiF = \frac{2 \cdot MiP \cdot MiR}{MiP + MiR} \tag{6}$$

with L equal to the total class number.

To complete the flat-measure-based evaluation, Accuracy Acc must be considered, which is calculated as

$$Acc = \frac{\sum_{i=i}^{M} \frac{t_{p_i}+t_{n_i}}{t_{p_i}+t_{f_i}+f_{p_i}+f_{n_i}}}{M} \tag{7}$$

where t_{n_i} are the true negatives for the class c_i.

Another flat measure is the example-based metrics, which evaluate bipartitions calculated on the average differences in the true label and the predicted label sets over all examples of the evaluation dataset. If we have a dataset with M multilabel examples and if $Y_i, i = 1 \ldots M$ is the set of true labels for each example and Z_i is the set of predicted labels for ith example, the example-based Precision, Recall, and F1 score, respectively, indicated as EBP, EBR, and EBF, are defined as

$$EBP = \frac{1}{M}\sum_{i=i}^{M}\frac{|Y_i \cap Z_i|}{|Z_i|} \tag{8}$$

$$EBR = \frac{1}{M}\sum_{i=i}^{M}\frac{|Y_i \cap Z_i|}{|Y_i|} \tag{9}$$

$$EBF = \frac{1}{M}\sum_{i=i}^{M}\frac{|Y_i \cap Z_i|}{|Y_i| + |Z_i|} \tag{10}$$

The EBP metric estimates how many predicted labels for the ith example are correct, while the EBR estimates the number of assigned labels correctly retrieved; EBF combines both measures for a global evaluation.

Furthermore, when the classification problem has a hierarchically organized label set, it is also possible to adopt the hierarchical measures that consider the label hierarchy in the classification results, taking into account the full path of the exact concepts in the class hierarchy and measuring whether parts of the path have been correctly classified. The definition of hierarchical measures is based on the augmented set of the true and predicted classes, respectively, Y_{aug} and $\hat{Y}_{aug}$, which are equal to

$$Y_{aug} = Y \cup An(y_1) \cup \cdots \cup An(y_N) \tag{11}$$

$$\hat{Y}_{aug} = \hat{Y} \cup An(\hat{y}_1) \cup \cdots \cup An(\hat{y}_M) \tag{12}$$

where $An(y_n)$ and $An(\hat{y}_m)$ are the ancestors of the true and predicted classes.

Starting from them, it is possible to define the hierarchical Precision, Recall, and F1 score (called HiP, HiR, and HiF). These measures consider the classifications result of a single document as a subtree path in the hierarchy as

$$HiP = \frac{|\hat{Y}_{aug} \cap Y_{aug}|}{|\hat{Y}_{aug}|} \quad (13)$$

$$HiR = \frac{|\hat{Y}_{aug} \cap Y_{aug}|}{|Y_{aug}|} \quad (14)$$

$$HiF = \frac{2 \cdot HiP \cdot HiR}{HiP + HiR} \quad (15)$$

The Y_{aug} and $\hat{Y}_{aug}$ identify two subtrees, respectively, representing the path of the true classifications and the path of the predicted classifications. The intersection of these two subtree paths is their similarity. Therefore, the HiP is the ratio between the subtree intersection and the predicted classifications paths, and the HiR is the ratio between the intersection and true classifications paths.

Adding all the ancestors in the sets, as in the previous case, overestimates the error if the hierarchy tree has nodes with many ancestors. To account for this behavior, the LCA-based measures [13] were defined. These kinds of measures are based on the *Lowest Common Ancestor* (LCA) concept from the graph theory [39]. The $LCA(n_1, n_2)$ of two nodes, n_1 and n_2, of a tree T is the node in T the furthest from the root that is an ancestor of both n_1 and n_2. To obtain LCA-based measures, the LCA concerning the set of predicted classes $\hat{Y}$ for each class y in the set of true classes Y, called $LCA(y, \hat{Y})$, and LCA for the set of true classes Y for each class $\hat{y}$ in the set of predicted classes $\hat{Y}$, named $LCA(\hat{y}, Y)$, must be calculated as

$$LCA(y, \hat{Y}) = \underset{m}{argmin} \cdot \gamma(m, y) \quad (16)$$

$$LCA(\hat{y}, Y) = \underset{m}{argmin} \cdot \gamma(m, \hat{y}) \quad (17)$$

where $\gamma(u, v)$ is the distance between the nodes u and v in the tree. Now, it is possible to define two graphs G_t and G_p, respectively, formed by the shortest paths from each $y \in Y$ to $LCA(y, \hat{Y})$ and the shortest path from each $\hat{y} \in \hat{Y}$ to $LCA(\hat{y}, Y)$. Then, the set Y_{aug_L} formed by all the nodes in the graph G_t and the set $\hat{Y}_{aug_L}$, which contains all the nodes in the graph G_p, must be constructed. Finally, LCA Precision $LCaP$, LCA Recall $LCaR$, and LCA F1 score $LCaF$ are defined as

$$LCaP = \frac{|\hat{Y}_{aug_L} \cap Y_{aug_L}|}{|\hat{Y}_{aug_L}|}; \quad (18)$$

$$LCaR = \frac{|\hat{Y}_{aug_L} \cap Y_{aug_L}|}{|Y_{aug_L}|} \quad (19)$$

$$LCaF = \frac{2 \cdot LCaP \cdot LCaR}{LCaP + LCaR} \quad (20)$$

In our experiments, whose main purpose is the contribution of the proposed HDNN to the incorporation of the label hierarchy knowledge directly into the neural network, the information provided by the hierarchical measures is very important.

4.5. Results and Discussion

In order to investigate the capability of the HDNN in incorporating the hierarchical label knowledge into the neural network, we compared it with a classic CNN architecture, such as the one described in [40], where the same CNN layers of the HDNN are implemented but organized in a flat topology. In detail, considering that we simplified the problem using at least the fifth level of the MeSH tree in our experimental assessment, as described in Section 4.1, each internal node corresponding to an element of the hierarchy is formed by a cascade of two DNN layers (CNN and dense layers) for the two preprocessing CNN layers in the *Initial Feature Processing* block (see Figure 1). In this case, it is possible to estimate 17 layers for the deepest tree branch and 4 layers for the flat CNN architecture.

Tables 4 and 5, respectively, show the flat and hierarchical measures obtained with a simple CNN architecture and the proposed HDNN approach, using static (WE) or dynamic word embeddings (BioBERT). As expected, it is possible to note a performance improvement in the case of the HDNN, in both terms of flat and hierarchical measures. Moreover, the use of dynamic BioBERT-based embedding provides further improvement compared with the classic static word embedding approach in the first layer of the neural network. In more detail, the MiF and the EBF scores obtained by HDNN are, respectively, improved by 24.7% and 30.8% in the case of static WE and by 23.7% and 35.8% using BioBERT embeddings. Moreover, the increment in the HiF score is equal to 19.8% for HDNN WE and 35.9% for HDNN BioBERT. The higher impact of the HDNN is obtained in terms of LCA-based hierarchical measures: the LCa-F improves by 58.6% when static WEs are used and by 65.2% when exploiting the BioBERT model to encode input text.

In summary, the HDNN obtains improvements in overall performances in terms of all the considered measures (with the slight exception of HiP for HDNN WE, probably caused by the overestimation of the error provided by this measure in the case of nodes with many ancestors). More importantly, the results show a significant increment in the case of LCA-based hierarchical measures. The information related to this score considers the correct classification of the label hierarchy, giving a higher weight in the case of the assignment of a label that lies in the same hierarchy path. This behavior demonstrates that the HDNN is able to assign more correct labels with respect to a flat CNN architecture, but in many cases, other labels, although not originally included in the manual annotation, could be a reasonable assignment. The next examples can better clarify this result.

Referring to Figure 3, if a document related to cardiac edema is tagged with the label *Heart Failure* (the higher-level label in the hierarchy path), a flat measure will consider this result completely wrong, while the hierarchical measure will suggest that the result is not perfect but a good result. For our purposes, this information is very important because an improvement in the hierarchical measures shows that the neural network has improved the correct classification of the labels along the hierarchy path, demonstrating that some information about the hierarchy has been embedded within the HDNN.

More in detail, considering as an example a paper from the dataset, the article *Myocardial Edema: A Translational View* has been manually tagged with several MeSHs by NLM human experts (for simplicity, we focus on a single example). Among them, there is the label *Cell Enlargement* [G07.345.249.410.500]. The flat DNN architectures were not able to correctly predict it. On the other hand, the HDNN BioBERT, although it also did not find this label, identified a set of ancestors of this MeSH, namely *Physiological Phenomena* [G07], *Growth and Development* [G07.345], *Growth* [G07.345.249], and *Cell Growth Processes* [G07.345.249.410], which is the father node of the correct label. Analyzing the content of the paper, all these labels would not be considered wrong by a human annotator, as they are related to the topics of the scientific article. More importantly, the *Cell Growth Processes* [G07.345.249.410] MeSH is semantically very similar to its child *Cell Enlargement* [G07.345.249.410.500]. In summary, the HDNN approach suggested a set of possible correct candidate labels, and, moreover, these labels lie in the same tree of the correct MeSH, providing, as expected, an increment in hierarchical scores.

The obtained results demonstrate that the HDNN can support the integration of innate information and prior knowledge into a DNN and can be used to improve the performance in complicated tasks like XMTC.

Table 4. Performances of HDNN and CNN with static and dynamic embeddings in terms of flat measures.

Test	FLAT Measures						
	Acc	EBP	EBR	EBF	MiP	MiR	MiF
CNN WE	0.1353	0.7528	0.1398	0.2324	0.7522	0.1336	0.2268
CNN BioBERT	0.2344	0.7828	0.1619	0.2684	0.7810	0.1592	0.2644
HDNN WE	**0.1719**	**0.7578**	**0.1828**	**0.2894**	**0.7578**	**0.1739**	**0.2829**
HDNN BioBERT	**0.3015**	**0.8213**	**0.2187**	**0.3453**	**0.8191**	**0.2041**	**0.3270**

Table 5. Performances of HDNN and CNN with static and dynamic embeddings in terms of hierarchical measures.

Test	Hierarchical Measures					
	HiP	HiR	HiF	LCa-P	LCa-R	LCa-F
CNN WE	0.7839	0.1635	0.2665	0.5530	0.0738	0.1273
CNN BioBERT	0.8117	0.1775	0.2899	0.5824	0.1113	0.1819
HDNN WE	0.7820	**0.2052**	**0.3194**	**0.6350**	**0.1239**	**0.2020**
HDNN BioBERT	**0.8229**	**0.2573**	**0.3941**	**0.7177**	**0.1944**	**0.3005**

On the other hand, a limitation of the proposed approach is related to its high computational time. The training time required in our experiments is approximately three days for each model, while the prediction on the test set and the calculation of the evaluation measure need approximately 15 min. The flat CNN model requires approximately 1 h to be trained on the same dataset and a few minutes for the prediction task. More in detail, we measured the training times of both flat CNN and HdNN approaches, observing in the case of HDNN 15,000 s for each epoch formed by 100,000 document samples, whereas the CNN training time for the same epoch is about 100 s, using the hardware described in Section 4.1. The HDNN training time is very high, especially if compared with the other flat CNN architecture, although both network topologies are characterized by a comparable number of parameters: 40,079,550 in the case of CNN and 45,194,480 in the case of HDNN. The very high training time of the HDDN is caused by the complexity of the graph topology, where a large number of interconnections among all the nodes are involved in reproducing the label tree structure. Moreover, each internal node of the HDNN has to wait for the outputs of its ancestor nodes before proceeding to execute forward and backward passes during the Stochastic Gradient Descent of the training of the model.

We compared the training time of a CNN and an HDNN with an increasing depth of labels in the training set for a deeper analysis of this behavior. We observed a comparable training time for CNN and HDNN in the case of labels belonging only to the first layer of the hierarchy. On the other hand, the training time of the HDNN increases in an exponential way at each deeper level of the hierarchy we included in the training set, while the CNN does not show substantial increases in training time.

5. Conclusions

This paper presented an innovative deep learning network architecture based on a hierarchical structure, named *Hierarchical Deep Neural Network* (HDNN), specifically devoted to the hierarchical XMTC problem. The topology of the HDNN reproduces the same hierarchical structure of the labels. This general concept can be applied in all multilabel classification problems where the labels are organized in a hierarchical structure.

After an introduction to the problem and a related works section, we described the details of the HDNN and a methodology for the automatic creation of this DNN, starting from the label hierarchy structure, based on a recursive algorithm that iterates basic DNN blocks. We also defined a method for the regularization of the training set, named Hierarchical Label Set Expansion (HLSE), which adds to each document label set the corresponding ancestors if they are not present, obtaining a training set consistent with the predefined hierarchy.

The experimental assessment focused on the automatic labeling of the biomedical scientific literature indexed in PubMed, which adopts the MeSHs (Medical Subjects Headings) hierarchical label set. The obtained results can be useful for the improvement of the large biomedical indexing task, integrating it in more complex methodologies, as proposed by the most recent methodologies in the BioASQ distributed challenges [13–16], which usually integrate more methodologies to obtain state-of-the-art performances.

A limit of the proposed methodology is its high computation time, mainly required to update the network weights, caused by the need to wait for the complete update of the upper layers' weights before the calculation of the corresponding children nodes' new neural network weights. This issue can be addressed by adopting more powerful GPU architecture, such as the newer Nvidia H100 architecture, as well as implementing a parallel version of the HDNN training routine, capable of distributing the computational complexity among different nodes and GPUs. We envisage the development of a parallel version of the HDNN code as a future work. A possible strategy for the parallel implementation includes the development of a multi-GPU code, which runs each internal node of the same level of the HDNN on separate GPUs in parallel. Another possibility is to adapt some GNN parallel approaches, such as the ones proposed in [41–43], allowing better exploitation of the features of modern multi-GPU hardware architectures.

On the other hand, the results obtained in our experiments show performance improvements, especially in the cases of hierarchical measures. These results confirm that the HDNN is capable of improving the correct classification of the hierarchy of the assigned labels.

In future work, in addition to the parallel implementation of the code, we are planning to perform more complex experiments with more depth classification cases. We also want to formalize the network complexity correlated to the number of connections and parameters and the network depth to better define the problem and analyze its complexity. We are also studying methods to reduce the complexity of the network by changing the interconnections of the layers and adopting alternative training strategies. We are also planning new experiments considering different kinds of internal nodes of the HDNN, such as attention-based networks and other DNN architectures. Finally, given the complexity involved, we are also considering evaluating how this methodology can fit the newest context of quantum computing [44].

Author Contributions: Conceptualization, S.S. and F.G.; methodology, S.S. and F.G.; software, S.S. and F.G.; validation, S.S., F.G. and M.C.; formal analysis, S.S. and F.G.; investigation, S.S. and F.G.; resources, S.S., F.G. and M.C.; data curation, S.S. and F.G.; writing—original draft preparation, S.S. and F.G.; writing—review and editing, S.S., F.G. and M.C.; visualization, S.S. and F.G.; supervision, M.C.; project administration, M.C.; funding acquisition, M.C. All authors have read and agreed to the published version of the manuscript.

Funding: This work is supported by European Union—NextGenerationEU—National Recovery and Resilience Plan (Piano Nazionale di Ripresa e Resilienza, PNRR)—Project: "SoBigData.it—Strengthening the Italian RI for Social Mining and Big Data Analytics"—Prot. IR0000013—Avviso n. 3264 del 28/12/2021.

Data Availability Statement: The HDNN model code and the dataset are shared on the SoBigData research infrastructure https://data.d4science.net/RgXa (accessed on 5 December 2023).

Acknowledgments: We thank Giuseppe Trerotola and Simona Sada for the administrative support they provided.

Conflicts of Interest: The authors declare no conflict of interest.

References

1. Vaswani, A.; Shazeer, N.; Parmar, N.; Uszkoreit, J.; Jones, L.; Gomez, A.N.; Kaiser, L.; Polosukhin, I. Attention is All you Need. In Proceedings of the Advances in Neural Information Processing Systems 30: Annual Conference on Neural Information Processing Systems 2017, Long Beach, CA, USA, 4–9 December 2017; pp. 5998–6008.
2. Devlin, J.; Chang, M.W.; Lee, K.; Toutanova, K. BERT: Pre-training of Deep Bidirectional Transformers for Language Understanding. In Proceedings of the 2019 Conference of the North American Chapter of the Association for Computational Linguistics: Human Language Technologies, Minneapolis, MN, USA, 2–7 June 2019; ACL: Minneapolis, MN, USA, 2019; Volume 1, pp. 4171–4186. [CrossRef]
3. Shamshad, F.; Khan, S.; Zamir, S.W.; Khan, M.H.; Hayat, M.; Khan, F.S.; Fu, H. Transformers in medical imaging: A survey. *Med. Image Anal.* **2023**, *88*, 102802. [CrossRef]
4. Yang, X.; Bian, J.; Hogan, W.R.; Wu, Y. Clinical concept extraction using transformers. *J. Am. Med. Inform. Assoc.* **2020**, *27*, 1935–1942. [CrossRef]
5. Xiao, H.; Li, L.; Liu, Q.; Zhu, X.; Zhang, Q. Transformers in medical image segmentation: A review. *Biomed. Signal Process. Control* **2023**, *84*, 104791. [CrossRef]
6. Stylianou, N.; Vlahavas, I. TransforMED: End-to-End transformers for evidence-based medicine and argument mining in medical literature. *J. Biomed. Inform.* **2021**, *117*, 103767. [CrossRef]
7. Alicante, A.; Benerecetti, M.; Corazza, A.; Silvestri, S. A distributed architecture to integrate ontological knowledge into information extraction. *Int. J. Grid Util. Comput.* **2016**, *7*, 245–256. [CrossRef]
8. Yin, Y.; Lai, S.; Song, L.; Zhou, C.; Han, X.; Yao, J.; Su, J. An External Knowledge Enhanced Graph-based Neural Network for Sentence Ordering. *J. Artif. Intell. Res.* **2021**, *70*, 545–566. [CrossRef]
9. Gu, T.; Zhao, H.; He, Z.; Li, M.; Ying, D. Integrating external knowledge into aspect-based sentiment analysis using graph neural network. *Knowl.-Based Syst.* **2023**, *259*, 110025. [CrossRef]
10. Marcus, G. Deep Learning: A Critical Appraisal. *arXiv* **2018**, arXiv:abs/1801.00631.
11. Liu, J.; Chang, W.; Wu, Y.; Yang, Y. Deep Learning for Extreme Multi-label Text Classification. In Proceedings of the 40th International ACM SIGIR Conference on Research and Development in Information Retrieval, Tokyo, Japan, 7–11 August 2017; ACM: Tokyo, Japan, 2017; pp. 115–124. [CrossRef]
12. Gargiulo, F.; Silvestri, S.; Ciampi, M.; De Pietro, G. Deep neural network for hierarchical extreme multi-label text classification. *Appl. Soft Comput.* **2019**, *79*, 125–138. [CrossRef]
13. Nentidis, A.; Bougiatiotis, K.; Krithara, A.; Paliouras, G.; Kakadiaris, I. Results of the fifth edition of the BioASQ Challenge. In Proceedings of the BioNLP 2017 Workshop, Vancouver, BC, Canada, 4 August 2017; ACL: Vancouver, BC, Canada, 2017; pp. 48–57.
14. Nentidis, A.; Krithara, A.; Bougiatiotis, K.; Paliouras, G. Overview of BioASQ 8a and 8b: Results of the Eighth Edition of the BioASQ Tasks a and b. In Proceedings of the Working Notes of CLEF 2020—Conference and Labs of the Evaluation Forum, Thessaloniki, Greece, 22–25 September 2020; CEUR Workshop Proceedings; Cappellato, L., Eickhoff, C., Ferro, N., Névéol, A., Eds.; CEUR-WS.org: Aachen, Germany, 2020; Volume 2696.
15. Nentidis, A.; Katsimpras, G.; Vandorou, E.; Krithara, A.; Paliouras, G. Overview of BioASQ Tasks 9a, 9b and Synergy in CLEF2021. In Proceedings of the Working Notes of CLEF 2021—Conference and Labs of the Evaluation Forum, Bucharest, Romania, 21–24 September 2021; CEUR Workshop Proceedings; Faggioli, G., Ferro, N., Joly, A., Maistro, M., Pirpi, F., Eds.; CEUR-WS.org: Aachen, Germany, 2021; Volume 2936.
16. Nentidis, A.; Krithara, A.; Paliouras, G.; Gasco, L.; Krallinger, M. BioASQ at CLEF2022: The Tenth Edition of the Large-scale Biomedical Semantic Indexing and Question Answering Challenge. In *Advances in Information Retrieval*; Hagen, M., Verberne, S., Macdonald, C., Seifert, C., Balog, K., Norvaag, K., Setty, V., Eds.; Springer International Publishing: Cham, Switzerland, 2022; pp. 429–435.
17. Peng, S.; You, R.; Wang, H.; Zhai, C.; Mamitsuka, H.; Zhu, S. DeepMeSH: Deep semantic representation for improving large-scale MeSH indexing. *Bioinformatics* **2016**, *32*, 70–79. [CrossRef] [PubMed]
18. Lee, J.; Yoon, W.; Kim, S.; Kim, D.; Kim, S.; So, C.H.; Kang, J. BioBERT: A pre-trained biomedical language representation model for biomedical text mining. *Bioinformatics* **2019**, *36*, 1234–1240. [CrossRef] [PubMed]
19. You, R.; Liu, Y.; Mamitsuka, H.; Zhu, S. BERTMeSH: Deep contextual representation learning for large-scale high-performance MeSH indexing with full text. *Bioinformatics* **2020**, *37*, 684–692. [CrossRef] [PubMed]
20. Gu, Y.; Tinn, R.; Cheng, H.; Lucas, M.; Usuyama, N.; Liu, X.; Naumann, T.; Gao, J.; Poon, H. Domain-Specific Language Model Pretraining for Biomedical Natural Language Processing. *ACM Trans. Comput. Health* **2022**, *3*, 1–23. [CrossRef]
21. Mustafa, F.E.; Boutalbi, R.; Iurshina, A. Annotating PubMed Abstracts with MeSH Headings using Graph Neural Network. In Proceedings of the Fourth Workshop on Insights from Negative Results in NLP, Dubrovnik, Croatia, 5 May 2023; Association for Computational Linguistics: Dubrovnik, Croatia, 2023; pp. 75–81. [CrossRef]
22. Gargiulo, F.; Silvestri, S.; Ciampi, M. Exploit Hierarchical Label Knowledge for Deep Learning. In Proceedings of the 2019 IEEE 32nd International Symposium on Computer-Based Medical Systems (CBMS), Córdoba, Spain, 5–7 June 2019; pp. 539–542. [CrossRef]

23. Brust, C.A.; Denzler, J. Integrating Domain Knowledge: Using Hierarchies to Improve Deep Classifiers. In *Pattern Recognition*; Palaiahnakote, S., Sanniti di Baja, G., Wang, L., Yan, W.Q., Eds.; Springer International Publishing: Cham, Switzerland, 2020; pp. 3–16.
24. Chen, F.; Yin, G.; Dong, Y.; Li, G.; Zhang, W. KHGCN: Knowledge-Enhanced Recommendation with Hierarchical Graph Capsule Network. *Entropy* **2023**, *25*, 697. [CrossRef] [PubMed]
25. Kowsari, K.; Brown, D.E.; Heidarysafa, M.; Meimandi, K.J.; Gerber, M.S.; Barnes, L.E. HDLTex: Hierarchical Deep Learning for Text Classification. In Proceedings of the 2017 16th IEEE International Conference on Machine Learning and Applications (ICMLA), Cancun, Mexico, 18–21 December 2017; pp. 364–371. [CrossRef]
26. Mukherjee, A.; Garg, I.; Roy, K. Encoding Hierarchical Information in Neural Networks Helps in Subpopulation Shift. *IEEE Trans. Artif. Intell.* **2023**, 1–2. [CrossRef]
27. Jiang, Y.; Wang, Y. Topic-aware hierarchical multi-attention network for text classification. *Int. J. Mach. Learn. Cybern.* **2023**, *14*, 1863–1875. [CrossRef]
28. Aminizadeh, S.; Heidari, A.; Toumaj, S.; Darbandi, M.; Navimipour, N.J.; Rezaei, M.; Talebi, S.; Azad, P.; Unal, M. The applications of machine learning techniques in medical data processing based on distributed computing and the Internet of Things. *Comput. Methods Programs Biomed.* **2023**, *241*, 107745. [CrossRef]
29. Woźniak, M.; Wieczorek, M.; Siłka, J. BiLSTM deep neural network model for imbalanced medical data of IoT systems. *Future Gener. Comput. Syst.* **2023**, *141*, 489–499. [CrossRef]
30. Joloudari, J.H.; Marefat, A.; Nematollahi, M.A.; Oyelere, S.S.; Hussain, S. Effective Class-Imbalance Learning Based on SMOTE and Convolutional Neural Networks. *Appl. Sci.* **2023**, *13*, 4006. [CrossRef]
31. Xiong, J.; Yu, L.; Niu, X.; Leng, Y. XRR: Extreme multi-label text classification with candidate retrieving and deep ranking. *Inf. Sci.* **2023**, *622*, 115–132. [CrossRef]
32. Ye, X.; Xiao, M.; Ning, Z.; Dai, W.; Cui, W.; Du, Y.; Zhou, Y., NEEDED: Introducing Hierarchical Transformer to Eye Diseases Diagnosis. In Proceedings of the 2023 SIAM International Conference on Data Mining (SDM), Minneapolis, MN, USA, 27–29 April 2023; SIAM: Philadelphia, PA, USA, 2023; pp. 667–675. [CrossRef]
33. Mikolov, T.; Chen, K.; Corrado, G.; Dean, J. Efficient Estimation of Word Representations in Vector Space. In Proceedings of the 1st International Conference on Learning Representations, ICLR 2013, Scottsdale, AZ, USA, 2–4 May 2013; Workshop Track Proceedings; Bengio, Y., LeCun, Y., Eds.; ICLR: Scottsdale, AZ, USA, 2013.
34. Silvestri, S.; Gargiulo, F.; Ciampi, M. Improving Biomedical Information Extraction with Word Embeddings Trained on Closed-Domain Corpora. In Proceedings of the 2019 IEEE Symposium on Computers and Communications (ISCC), Barcelona, Spain, 29 June–3 July 2019; pp. 1129–1134. [CrossRef]
35. Gargiulo, F.; Silvestri, S.; Ciampi, M. A Big Data architecture for knowledge discovery in PubMed articles. In Proceedings of the 2017 IEEE Symposium on Computers and Communications, ISCC 2017, Heraklion, Greece, 3–6 July 2017; IEEE: Heraklion, Greece, 2017; pp. 82–87. [CrossRef]
36. Řehůřek, R.; Sojka, P. Software Framework for Topic Modelling with Large Corpora. In Proceedings of the LREC 2010 Workshop on New Challenges for NLP Frameworks, La Valleta, Malta, 22 May 2010; ELRA: Luxemburg, 2010; pp. 45–50. [CrossRef]
37. Tsoumakas, G.; Katakis, I.; Vlahavas, I. Mining multi-label data. In *Data Mining and Knowledge Discovery Handbook*, 2nd ed.; Springer: Berlin/Heidelberg, Germany, 2010; pp. 667–685. [CrossRef]
38. Manning, C.D.; Raghavan, P.; Schütze, H. *Chetion to Information Retrieval*; Cambridge University Press: Cambridge, UK, 2010. [CrossRef]
39. Aho, A.V.; Hopcroft, J.E.; Ullman, J.D. On finding lowest common ancestors in trees. *SIAM J. Comput.* **1976**, *5*, 115–132. [CrossRef]
40. Gargiulo, F.; Silvestri, S.; Ciampi, M. Deep Convolution Neural Network for Extreme Multi-label Text Classification. In Proceedings of the 11th International Joint Conference on Biomedical Engineering Systems and Technologies (BIOSTEC 2018)—Volume 5: HEALTHINF, Funchal, Madeira, Portugal, 19–21 January 2018; SciTePress: Madeira, Portugal, 2018; pp. 641–650. [CrossRef]
41. Zaman, S.; Moon, T.; Benson, T.; Jacobs, S.A.; Chiu, K.; Van Essen, B. Parallelizing Graph Neural Networks via Matrix Compaction for Edge-Conditioned Networks. In Proceedings of the 2022 22nd IEEE International Symposium on Cluster, Cloud and Internet Computing (CCGrid), Taormina, Italy, 16–19 May 2022; pp. 386–395. [CrossRef]
42. Petit, Q.R.; Li, C.; Emad, N. Distributed and Parallel Sparse Computing for Very Large Graph Neural Networks. In Proceedings of the 2022 IEEE International Conference on Big Data (Big Data), Osaka, Japan, 17–20 December 2022; pp. 6796–6798. [CrossRef]
43. Fu, Q.; Ji, Y.; Huang, H.H. TLPGNN: A Lightweight Two-Level Parallelism Paradigm for Graph Neural Network Computation on GPU. In Proceedings of the 31st International Symposium on High-Performance Parallel and Distributed Computing, Minneapolis, MN, USA, 27 June–1 July 2022; Association for Computing Machinery: New York, NY, USA, 2022; pp. 122–134. [CrossRef]
44. Buonaiuto, G.; Gargiulo, F.; De Pietro, G.; Esposito, M.; Pota, M. Best practices for portfolio optimization by quantum computing, experimented on real quantum devices. *Sci. Rep.* 2023, *in press*. [CrossRef] [PubMed]

applied sciences

MDPI

Article

Bridging Theory and Practice: An Innovative Approach to Android Programming Education through Nutritional Application Development and Problem-Based Learning

Inigo Lopez-Gazpio

Computer Science and Artificial Intelligence Department (CSAI), University of the Basque Country (UPV/EHU), Manuel Lardizabal Pasealekua, No. 1, 20018 Donostia, Spain; inigo.lopez@ehu.eus

Abstract: This study introduces an innovative Problem-Based Learning (PBL) methodology to enhance the teaching of Android programming, focusing on addressing nutritional challenges. Conducted within the Computer Science degree at the University of Deusto, this research engages third-year students in developing applications aimed at improving access to nutritional knowledge. The novelty of this approach lies in its integration of advanced programming concepts with practical application development, fostering a deeper understanding and engagement among students. The applications enable users to access detailed nutritional information from open-access food databases, catering to individuals with specific dietary constraints. Preliminary results indicate a significant improvement in student engagement and learning outcomes compared to traditional teaching methods, underscoring the potential of this methodology in fostering future researchers and advancing educational practices in computer science. This research contributes to the field by demonstrating the efficacy of combining PBL with application development in enhancing learning experiences and outcomes in programming education. Our findings not only contribute valuable insights into the unique challenges and motivators associated with Android programming but also pave the way for tailored educational strategies that can optimize the learning experience in this domain.

Keywords: action research; active learning computing education; cross-disciplinary skills; engagement; nutrition; project-based learning (PBL)

Citation: Lopez-Gazpio, I. Bridging Theory and Practice: An Innovative Approach to Android Programming Education through Nutritional Application Development and Problem-Based Learning. *Appl. Sci.* **2023**, *13*, 12140. https://doi.org/10.3390/app132212140

Academic Editors: Juan A. Gómez-Pulido, Stefano Silvestri and Francesco Gargiulo

Received: 10 October 2023
Revised: 25 October 2023
Accepted: 30 October 2023
Published: 8 November 2023

1. Introduction

The evolution of educational methodologies is pivotal in cultivating the future researchers and innovators of tomorrow [1,2], necessitating a relentless pursuit of innovative and effective teaching approaches [3–5]. This investigation is at the forefront of educational innovation, introducing a novel Problem-Based Learning (PBL) methodology to instruct Android programming, merging it with practical and socially relevant challenges in human nutrition.

Conducted within the structured environment of the programming lectures at the University of Deusto, this study involves third-year students enrolled in the Computer Science degree. The setting and the demographic are crucial in understanding the impact and the applicability of the introduced methodology, which focuses on an immersive learning experience. The proposed methodology challenges students to be active participants in their learning journey, developing Android applications that address pressing nutritional problems, a growing concern in today's health-conscious society [6]. This methodology not only deepens the comprehension of intricate programming concepts but also nurtures critical and reflective thinking and practical problem-solving skills, elements that are indispensable for budding researchers [7,8]. As argued in these investigations, it is necessary to establish a challenging learning atmosphere that enables students to acquire new knowledge, skills, and competencies. To this aim, alternatives for increasing student engagement far beyond traditional and inflexible teaching approaches must be offered in the classroom.

The applications conceptualized and developed during this research endeavor are designed to augment access to nutritional knowledge. They specialize in delivering detailed, user-specific nutritional information sourced from reliable, open-access food databases. This feature is a boon for individuals with specialized dietary needs, enabling them to make informed dietary choices, a need that is increasingly becoming paramount in our diverse societies [9]. The initial outcomes of this research are promising and indicative of a substantial enhancement in student engagement and learning outcomes, a significant stride compared to the outcomes of conventional, more rigid teaching methodologies. These encouraging findings accentuate the transformative potential and the versatility of amalgamating PBL with practical application development in the realm of programming education.

By intertwining advanced programming with real-world application development, this study makes a contribution to the evolving landscape of educational methodologies in computer science. It underscores the imperative of incorporating practical application and real-world problem-solving in the learning process, a strategy that is corroborated by several studies investigating meaningful learning [1,10]. The primary objective of this investigation is to methodically measure and analyze student engagement levels in Android programming, particularly within the initial stages of their developmental journey. While numerous studies have explored the broader realm of programming engagement [11], our research stands distinct in its sharp focus on Android-specific development. Our findings not only contribute valuable insights into the unique challenges and motivators associated with Android programming for beginners but also pave the way for tailored educational strategies that can optimize the learning experience in this domain. This study, therefore, serves as both a diagnostic tool and a foundation for future pedagogical advancements in the field of Android development education.

In the application of the methodology, students work all semester long in an active style, trying to investigate or respond to complex challenges. As a result, PBL is a challenge not only for students but also for lecturers as it moves away from the more traditional teaching practices. PBL implies a change of roles, work methodology, and evaluation in which students actively form teams and face complex challenges. Moreover, PBL invites students to identify what they should learn, to become involved in the search for information, to define strategies to be used, and to agree on common solutions.

2. Detailed Context of the Problem

The contemporary landscape of education is witnessing a paradigm shift, with an increasing emphasis on methodologies that transcend traditional lecture-based learning. In this transformative era, the integration of Problem-Based Learning (PBL) [12] in teaching Android programming emerges as a revolutionary approach, addressing the multifaceted challenges in human nutrition.

The problem's context is deeply rooted in the growing complexities of nutritional needs and the escalating demand for personalized dietary information [9]. Individuals with specific dietary constraints often grapple with the inherent difficulty of accessing appropriate and reliable nutritional information, a challenge that is accentuated by the plethora of unverified and generic information available [13]. Problem-Based Learning (PBL) thrives on real-world challenges that resonate with students, prompting them to apply theoretical knowledge in practical scenarios. In this study, the choice of a problem centered around healthy nutrition is particularly selected. Nutrition is a universal concern, affecting every individual regardless of background or profession. By anchoring the PBL experience in such a universally relevant issue, the study ensures immediate engagement and relevance for the students. The intricacies of nutrition, with its myriad of variables like calories, macronutrients, and micronutrients, provide a complex problem space ideal for computer science solutions. This complexity pushes students to think critically, design algorithms meticulously, and develop applications that are both functional and user-friendly. The immediate societal implications of their solutions—potentially aiding individuals in making healthier dietary choices—add an additional layer of motivation and responsibility, making the learning experience deeply personal and impactful.

The popularity of gluten-free and vegan diets has notably increased, with a 67% rise in gluten-free diets in the United States since 2013 [14], and a growing adoption of vegan diets, particularly in the Western world [15]. Table 1 summarizes the global prevalence of vegetarian, vegan, and gluten-free diets, highlighting the increasing trend and varying adoption across continents. The data indicates higher adherence to vegetarian diets in South America and Asia, a significant preference for vegan diets in South America, and a common observance of gluten-free diets in Asia, Oceania, and Europe. Overall, Table 1 illustrates the extensive scope of nutritional care challenges, suggesting that PBL can effectively address this widespread social issue by engaging students in real-world problem-solving. Thus, applications developed are envisioned to be of use for the vast area of nutritional information by making use of open access high-quality food databases. The challenge is designed to automate food selection based on individual dietary constraints, thereby empowering users to make informed and health-conscious decisions.

The significance of addressing this problem is multifold. It not only contributes to the advancement of educational methodologies in computer science but also has profound implications in the field of human nutrition and public health. By fostering a learning environment that encourages the development of practical and socially relevant applications, this study aims to cultivate a generation of researchers equipped with the skills and knowledge to address relevant social challenges. Adhering to a restricted diet is inherently challenging, necessitating careful planning to meet daily nutrient requirements [9]. Suboptimal diets can diminish disease protection and pose health risks, especially for those with mandatory restrictions due to allergies. Given the rise in dietary restrictions, providing efficient tools to navigate food choices is crucial, as many products lack detailed ingredient lists [13].

Table 1. Mean percentage population sticking to three well-known restricted diets (vegetarian, vegan, and gluten-free) by continent.

Continent	Vegetarian Mean %	Vegan Mean %	Gluten-Free Mean %	Sources
Africa	NA	NA	0.5	[16]
Asia	11.4	3.85	0.8	[16,17]
Europe	5.9	1.9	0.8	[16,18,19]
North America	8.7	2.65	0.5	[16,20,21]
Oceania	4	2	0.8	[16,22,23]
South America	14.9	9	0.6	[16,24,25]

Although the nutritional challenge offers a unique blend of complexity and societal relevance, the underlying principles of this PBL approach are highly generalizable to other areas within computer science. The essence of PBL is to immerse students in real-world problems, pushing them to apply, adapt, and extend their theoretical knowledge. Whether it is developing AI algorithms for traffic management, creating cybersecurity solutions for emerging threats, or designing user interfaces for e-commerce platforms, the core tenets remain the same: identify a genuine problem, understand its intricacies, and devise a solution using computer science principles. The nutritional challenge serves as a testament to the adaptability of PBL, demonstrating that with the right problem selection, students can be engaged, motivated, and equipped with skills that transcend the classroom, preparing them for diverse challenges in the ever-evolving landscape of computer science.

Research Questions (RQ)

This investigation seeks to explore the intersection of innovative educational methodologies and practical application development, focusing on the domain of Android programming and its implications in human nutrition. The research is guided by the following refined questions:

(RQ1) *Innovative Learning Impact*: How does the integration of Problem-Based Learning (PBL) within Android programming lectures enhance the learning experiences and outcomes of computer science students, compared to traditional instructional methods?

(RQ2) *Application Development Engagement:* To what extent does the development of Android applications addressing real-world nutritional challenges engage students and foster a deeper understanding of advanced programming concepts?

(RQ3) *Practical Implications and Accessibility:* How do the developed applications improve access to reliable and personalized nutritional information, and what are the implications of such improvements on individuals with specific dietary needs?

(RQ4) *Educational Significance:* How does the incorporation of real-world challenges in teaching methodologies contribute to the advancement of educational practices in computer science, and what is its broader impact on cultivating future researchers?

(RQ5) *Comparative Analysis*: How do the learning outcomes and student engagement levels compare between the courses implementing the PBL methodology and those following classical approaches in teaching Android programming?

Each of these questions is designed to delve into different facets of the research, exploring the impact of the innovative methodology on learning experiences, the engagement and understanding fostered by application development, the practical implications of the applications developed, and the broader significance of integrating real-world challenges in educational methodologies. By addressing these questions, this study aims to shed light on the transformative potential of integrating innovative educational approaches with practical application development in enhancing learning and addressing societal challenges.

The intended principal outcome is to show evidence of the application of PBL within lectures on computer programming and how it can be combined with application development in order to increase motivation in the classroom. PBL has the students learn, organize, and solve challenges while students themselves remain responsible for their own investigation and process of work. We propose to follow a series of milestones that incorporate agile development during the semester. Through this work, we aim to show that the use of PBL combined with application construction provides reliable evidence that a much deeper understanding of computer programming is attained by students participating in the challenge. The investigation also intends to evaluate if application development in Android poses sufficient engagement for students. In terms of technology and accessibility, the Google Android and Apple iOS markets have exponentially grown, reaching nearly 98% of the consumer market. As the relevance people currently put on healthy nutrition and the expansion of mobile applications increases, it is one of our aims to determine to what extent nutrition applications can be employed to set up challenging learning contexts.

3. Description of the PBL Method

To immerse students in a realistic software development project and to address the outlined research questions, this study adopts the method delineated by Rohde et al. [6], focusing on key performance indicators that assess the usability of food tracking applications from a user-centric perspective. This method is pivotal in evaluating the developed applications' efficacy in providing reliable and user-friendly nutritional information.

The cited study considers many of the popular food-tracking applications based on traditional behavior theory components. We also take into account [26,27] for our internal evaluation, which identified several aspects that should be offered by a food tracking application in order to be useful: (i) whether the application offers general knowledge and detailed information, (ii) whether the application implements cognitive strategies (perceived benefits, perceived barriers, perceived risks and efficacy), (iii) whether the application implements behavior strategies (monitoring capacity, realistic goal setting, time management, stimulus control, self-reward, social support, modeling or vicarious learning, relapse prevention, emotion-focused strategies, stress management, and negative affect management), and (iv), whether the application offers therapeutic interventions (skill-building, increasing knowledge, and motivational readiness). The list of relevant items identified in the mentioned categories is extensive, and so we summarize it in the following comprehensible table (Table 2). The table enumerates the most relevant aspects from the previously cited categories, which will be used to evaluate the applications developed by student teams. At the end of the semester, the applications developed by students are meticulously evaluated based on this comprehensive list of relevant items identified in the aforementioned categories. These items serve as the benchmark to assess whether the applications developed by student teams meet the desired outcomes in terms of usability, reliability, and user engagement.

Table 2. Main characteristics for nutritional application evaluation considering behavioral strategies.

Level	Category of Interaction	Description
1	Information or guidelines	Application provides primarily general information or data that are not individualized.
2	Assessment	Application asks the user for current behavioral practices or use of strategies.
3	Feedback	Application comments on the user's current behavioral practices or strategies.
4	General assistance	Application offers non individualized suggestions about how to change or apply a strategy that are not responses to any assessment (Item 2) and do not require feedback (Item 3)
5	Individually tailored assistance	Application has suggestions about how to change or apply a strategy specifically tailored to the user

The proposed method also integrates traditional behavior theory components, emphasizing cognitive and behavioral strategies in order to to develop applications that are not only informative but also conducive to promoting healthy dietary habits [26,27]. The applications are designed to offer general knowledge and detailed information and implement various strategies such as monitoring capacity, realistic goal setting, time management, stimulus control, self-reward, social support, modeling or vicarious learning, relapse prevention, emotion-focused strategies, stress management, and negative affect management.

4. Learning Materials

Student teams were tasked with developing applications that consult multiple food databases to retrieve detailed nutrient lists from food products, introducing the primary innovation of the challenge. This involves integrating various micro-services of open-access food databases, accessible via barcode scanning, a feature prevalent in health-related applications [26]. This interface facilitates instant access to extensive food product data and is a compelling functionality for students. Post-search applications are designed to display detailed information or filter items based on user preferences, alerting users to items matching their indicated preferences.

The investigation utilized several nutrient databases, including Open Food Facts, a collaborative project providing comprehensive information on global food products, updated daily under the Open Database License. FoodData Central, USDA's integrated system, offers extensive nutrient and food component data accessible via API or local download, allowing third-party applications to analyze multiple food items. EDAMAN provides distinct API functionalities, including the Nutrition Analysis API and the Food and Grocery Database API, offering complete nutritional analysis and detailed nutrition facts for products. Lastly,

EuroFIR collects detailed food product information for multiple countries, offering access to a wide range of item descriptions through its Food Explorer API.

Application Use Cases

Applications developed by teams were required to offer a set of diverse functionalities, including food product searches and detailed listing of nutrients. We also made an attempt to have students focus development on usability by implementing an engaging user interface based on a simple, ready-to-use experience. Some applications developed by students require users to log in by creating a personalized profile (see Figure 1 (left)) in which to define their specific conditions or restrictions (see Figure 1 (right)); this is how the application is aware of not allowed nutrients and based on these personal preferences the application sets its alarms when food searches are performed (see Figure 2 (left)).

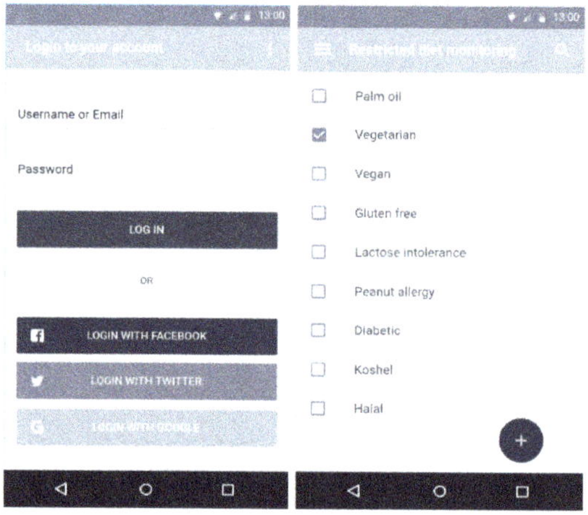

Figure 1. Login screen (**left**) and restricted diet monitoring screen (**right**).

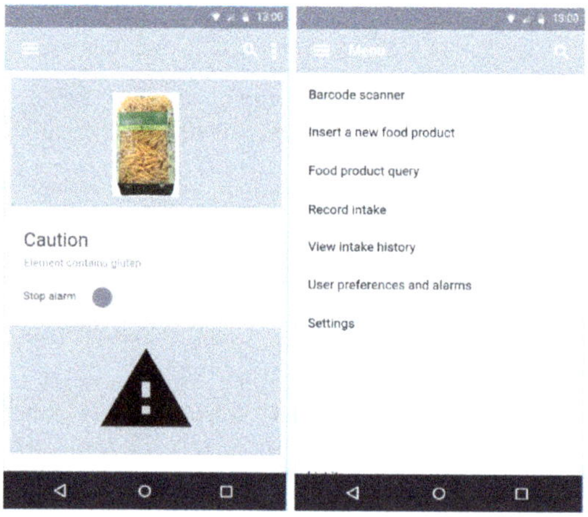

Figure 2. Alarm functionality (**left**) and main menu of the application (**right**).

Teams also implemented key functional aspects such as product analysis and detailed search (application main menu can be seen in Figure 2 (right)). Search is performed through queries, and queries contain some data that uniquely identifies an existing food product. Once the query is done and a product is found, the application shows a detailed list of nutrients for the given item (see Figure 3 (left)). The detailed list of the nutrients is expected to be sufficient in order to identify if a product is suitable or not for consumption. In case the product is identified as unsuitable for consumption, the application shows the reason why it has been discarded.

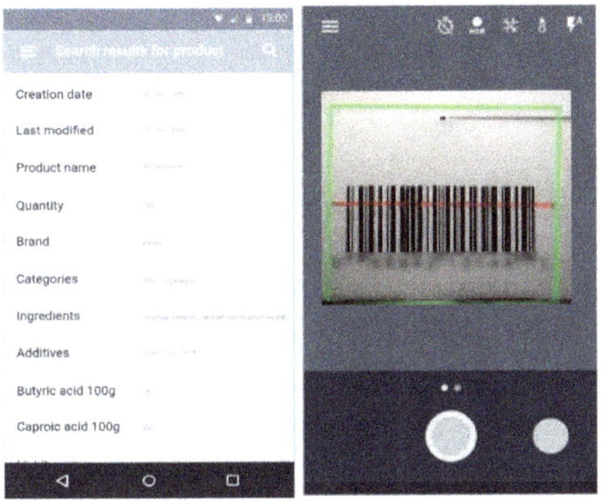

Figure 3. Food product search result (**left**) and barcode scanning functionality (**right**).

The majority of the students conducted the search process combining two different approaches: on the one hand, through the scanning of barcodes (see Figure 3 (right)). This process is performed by making use of the smartphone's camera service. In this case, the user is asked to point the camera to the food packaging label where the barcode is usually placed, and the application automatically detects the label, launches a query to the database systems, and displays its nutrients. On the other hand, students also implemented product searches by matching names. Finally, student teams were also requested to consider saving a logging history of consumed food products; this functionality can be used to keep track of nutritional factors, such as consumed energy, fat, saturated fat, carbohydrates, sugars, proteins, and salt (see Figure 4 (left)), and is also able to produce simple non-personalized feedback according to predefined health statistics (see Figure 4 (right)).

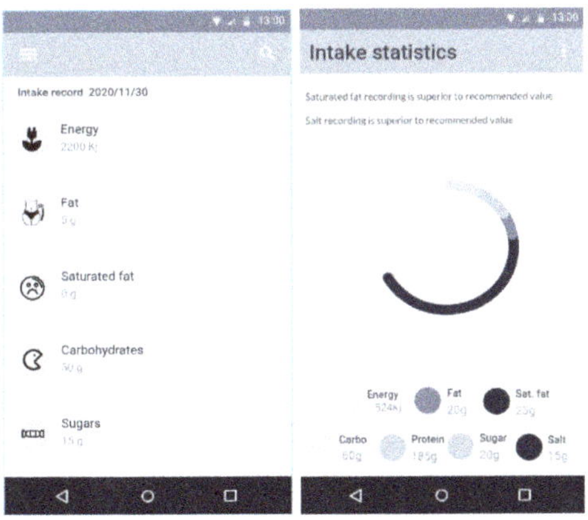

Figure 4. Food product search result (**left**) and barcode scanning functionality (**right**).

5. Participants and Workflow

Programming is a third-year first semester course in the Department of Informatic, Electronic, and Communication Technologies at the University of Deusto (San Sebastian faculty, Spain). The course introduces advanced elements of Java and Android programming to students, such as memory usage, inheritance, polymorphism, lambda expression, advanced data structures, thread management, and code optimization. The course provides a deep understanding of what actually advanced programming is, and it is based on a classical chalk-and-talk-style.

The course comprises four contact hours per week and an additional tutoring hour. It has traditionally been delivered in a face-to-face descriptive format using a chalk-and-talk style, aided by some laboratory programming assignments. The learning outcomes of the course are that upon successful completion of the course, students should be able to (i) identify, analyze, and define the significant elements of a computer program; (ii) use one's own experience and criteria in the analysis of requisites and design and build up a more effective and efficient solution; (iii) understand the advanced principles of inheritance and use it to design more solid and reusable architectures; (iv) formulate and describe application requisites using Unified Modelling Language diagrams and identify and apply an appropriate solving technique; and (v) define and apply good design patterns to solve different problems considered difficult. Thus, individuals who graduate in computer engineering are able to apply their knowledge to solve application development problems in different areas related to information technologies, providing the most appropriate solutions in each case. The main contribution of the subject of Computer Programming to the degree in computer engineering is the resolution of application development problems and the analysis and design of requisites based on existing requirements and applying the precise criteria of effectiveness, efficiency, costs, and benefits involved.

The topic of computer programming is an important field within computer science engineering. It is of great importance that computer engineers understand how applications are developed and how such processes are carried out in development teams. Students in computer science can deal with moderately complex design architectures; nevertheless, measuring real assessment of developed applications through questionnaires is not currently performed.

Regarding the workflow, we describe the working timelines of student teams to illustrate the main steps adopted and how these integrate within the semester course. Within the agile development framework, each student team commits to delivering incremental value to the end-product. Initially, student teams create the *Product Backlog*, a prioritized list of features, enhancements, and fixes that form the product's roadmap. After discussing the roadmap with the lecturer, the cycle begins with Sprint, Planning, a brainstorming session where teams select items from the Product Backlog to address in the next sprint. A sprint is a designated time period during which students' development progress is evaluated. In this period, they collaboratively set the scope, breaking down backlog items into manageable tasks. Throughout the sprint, teams engage in periodic meetings or stand-ups with both group members and the lecturer. In these concise, time-boxed meetings, members update on their current status, future plans, and any challenges, ensuring transparency and rapid problem-solving. The practice comprised three sprints or evaluation periods, each ending with a Sprint Review where teams present their completed work to the lecturer. This is an opportunity to assess achievements, obtain feedback, and plan for the next stages. For ongoing enhancement, teams participate in the Sprint Retrospective meetings, a session to reflect on successes, challenges, and areas for improvement in upcoming sprints. Figure 5 summarizes the described workflow.

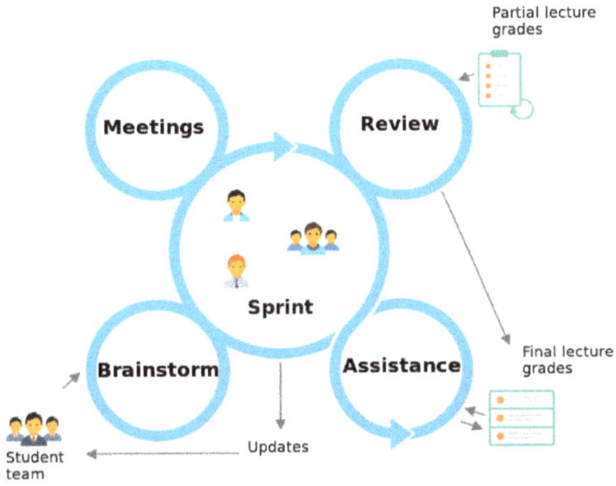

Figure 5. Student team workflow diagram. Student teams realized a total of three sprints in which they developed functionalities for their applications. Every sprint begins with a brainstorming session and ends with a review meeting in which the work is evaluated. During the working timeline, there were several scheduled meetings accompanied by the assistance of the lecturer.

6. Research Tools

The research tools employed in this study are meticulously selected to ensure the robustness and reliability of the research outcomes. These tools are pivotal in evaluating the developed applications and assessing the impact of the innovative teaching methodology on student engagement and learning outcomes. In order to measure the students' learning achievements, we employ a variety of resources that are directly mapped to the original research questions, which are: (i) the internal conclusions of the student teams, which correspond to the intra-evaluation reports of the students extracted from assignments (RQ1, RQ2, and RQ4), (ii) impressions of the lecturers throughout the semester (RQ1, RQ2, RQ4, and RQ5), (iii) assessment of developed applications (RQ3), (iv) final lecture grades (RQ1 and RQ5), and (v) student engagement evaluation reports collected using questionnaires by the University of Deusto (RQ1, RQ4, and RQ5).

6.1. Learning Achievements within Groups

The aim of the proposed problem has been non-trivial as it involved a full front-end and back-end implementation of a nutritional Android application. On the one hand, working in front-end development, students are able to focus on creating the user interface and experience. Some positive aspects noted by students involving front-end development include being able to see the resulting product immediately. Front-end developers can see the changes they make to an application in real-time, which can be rewarding and motivating. Front-end development also implies working with the latest technologies, which requires keeping up-to-date with the latest technologies and trends. On the other hand, working in back-end development means that students are able to focus on the server-side of an application. Some positive aspects noted by students involve creating robust and scalable applications, which requires a deep understanding of architecture and design patterns. Students also remarked that working in the back-end of a nutritional application implied working closely with data, which is actually one of the principal learning materials of the investigation. Overall, the results obtained from internal student reports revealed that the PBL remained as challenging as rewarding.

6.2. Impressions of the Lecturer throughout the Semester

The development of the project has been positively evaluated by the authors because of the following principal outcomes: (i) it generates a high interest as students face a social challenge involving nutrition; (ii) it is useful to tackle different specific, generic, and transversal competences from the computer science degree; (iii) students practice Android theory lectures observed in class, and act as facilitators of the knowledge to other students and, as a consequence, teams construct knowledge as the team evolves; and, (iv) students simulate an agile development unit that must apply according to some software development methodology. This adds extra motivation to the work as teams follow the very same rules they will eventually have in industry. It is noteworthy to mention that discussions within the development teams also favor communication between students and the lecturer.

6.3. Assessment of Developed Applications

In order to evaluate the usefulness of the applications developed, we conducted a user case study with 18 volunteers from superior courses from the Computer Science degree and let them experiment with the applications for one month. After this time, volunteers were asked to fill in a form regarding the characteristics addressed in Table 2. For each aspect under evaluation, we asked volunteers to rate characteristics on a scale between 1 and 10. Figure 6 shows the results of the user study.

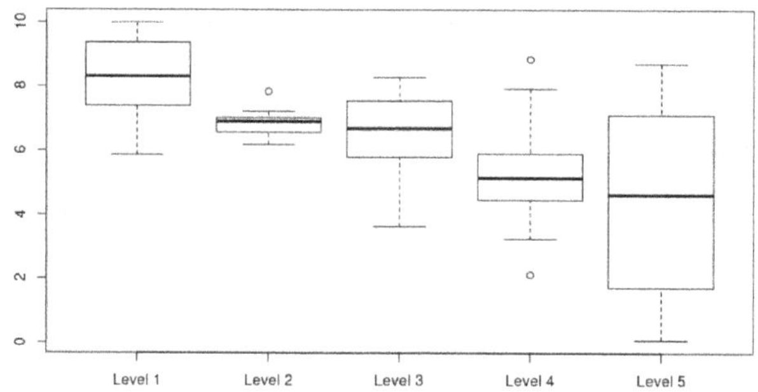

Figure 6. Box-plot results of the user study concerning the five levels of evaluation analyzed in Table 2.

According to the results, the best-valued features are related to level one, level two, and level three. It seems that by accessing open access databases, the applications are able to provide general information so as to satisfy the needs of users in a great manner. In the same way, the user preference-based information extraction form is also well-reviewed and is able to handle behavioral practices for users. Nutritional information graphics and simple visualizations are also valued, even though this feature has been evaluated to a lower extent. On the contrary, levels four and five are the worst-valued characteristics of the applications. As expected, even though the application handles alarms when restricted food products are found on searches, the capacity of the application as regards general or individually tailored assistance is limited.

6.4. Final Lecture Grades

Measuring student engagement through the analysis of final grades is a common practice in the state of the art within educational research [1]. In order to assert that the instructional strategy involving PBL is an effective approach to help students learn subjects, we compare distinct student performances across two consecutive academic courses in which the programming lecture has been taught following the same schedule and evaluation criteria but different learning processes. This way, we show results for one of the courses that has been taught involving traditional Android practices (2020/2021), while the second course has been taught with the PBL methodology (2021/2022).

The distribution of students alongside obtained statistics for grades is shown in Table 3 for the academic courses concerning 2020/2021 and 2021/2022. Assuming an underlying normal distribution on the grades indicated by a Shapiro–Wilk test of normality, we conducted a one-sample Wilcoxon signed-rank non-parametric test to check whether the performance mean values were significantly different. Test results indicate that student average performance has been higher when PBL activities have been carried out with regard to classical approaches ($V = 26$, p-value < 0.05). Significantly better student performance suggests that a higher level of engagement has been attained in the academic course 2021/2022, in which students were challenged with the development of a nutritional application.

Table 3. Distribution of students and statistics for grades attained by students.

Course	Method	Count	Mean	Std	Min	Max	25%	Median	75%
2020/2021	Classic	24	6.65	1.55	2	10	5.40	6.50	8.15
2021/2022	PBL	27	7.75	0.85	3	10	6.25	7.75	8.8

In addition to the final grades obtained by students, we also include the Student Engagement Evaluation Reports (SEER) that the University of Deusto collects every academic year with regard to all subjects collected by means of questionnaires designed and offered to students by third-party professionals. SEER questionnaires include a total of 30 items of evaluation regarding the impressions of students with regard to engagement intervention. SEER questionnaires are completely anonymous to lecturers, for which they can only access the final mean results. The items under evaluation fold into one of the following categories: (i) design and planning of the resource materials, (ii) learning management and capabilities of the activities, (iii) tutoring and evaluation capabilities, (iv) evaluation of the lecture, (v) review and improvement, (vi) collegiality and (vii) competence of the lecturer. Figure 7 shows the comparative results for the questionnaires in the 2020/2021 and 2021/2022 academic courses for the mentioned set of evaluation categories. As shown in the figure, almost all evaluation items are superior in the academic year 2021/2022, in which the student grades are also statistically higher.

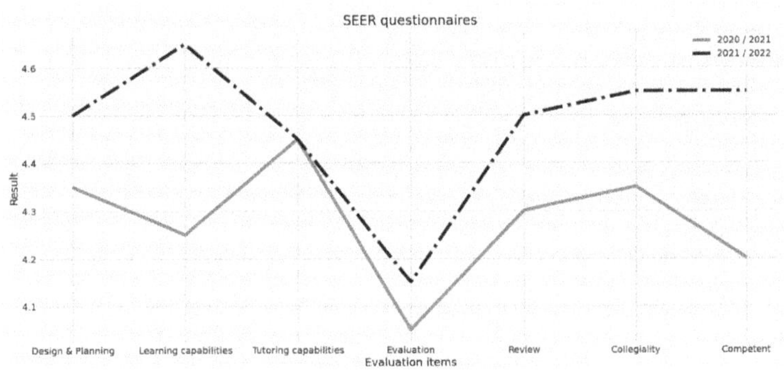

Figure 7. Student Engagement Evaluation Reports (SEER).

7. Conclusions

Leveraging the unprecedented growth in mobile applications due to rapid advancements in smartphone capabilities, this study explores the transformative potential of integrating innovative educational methodologies with practical application development. It unfolds within the programming lectures at the University of Deusto, involving students in the third academic course of the Computer Science degree, and employs Problem-Based

Learning (PBL) as a pivotal educational methodology to enhance the learning experience in programming. The focus is on developing socially innovative smartphone applications, with students tasked with creating applications aimed at improving access to knowledge in human nutrition. The nutritional challenge serves as a dynamic context for the learning process, leading students through the development process to harness detailed nutrient information from open-access food databases. The applications developed are meticulously designed to automate food selection for diets with constraints, presenting non-trivial solutions that assist individuals in adhering to restricted diets.

We now summarize the main contributions of the present work according to the initial research questions addressed.

(RQ1) **Innovative Learning Impact:** The core of our investigation revolves around the development of socially innovative smartphone applications. Students were entrusted with the task of creating applications to bolster access to knowledge in human nutrition. This nutritional challenge, far from being a mere academic exercise, provided a dynamic context for learning, guiding students to extract detailed nutrient information from open-access food databases. These applications, meticulously crafted, offer automated solutions for diet constraints, aiding individuals with restricted dietary needs. Internal conclusions of the students' teams, impressions of the lecturers throughout the semester, final lecture grades, and student engagement evaluation reports not only expose that innovative outcomes have been significant but also the practice served to enhance the learning experience.

(RQ2) **Application Development Engagement**: The rising interest in nutritional applications was leveraged to boost student engagement and instill a sense of responsibility. This strategy not only simplified access to esteemed nutritional databases but also spurred introspective thinking about the societal ramifications of the applications they developed. Internal conclusions of the students' teams, impressions of the lecturers throughout the semester, and student engagement evaluation reports confirm that addressing a real-world nutritional challenge highly engaged student performance.

(RQ3) **Practical Implications and Accessibility**: The applications, while technically sound, were also designed with a keen eye on usability and societal impact. They serve as tools that not only provide information but also influence dietary choices, especially for those with specific dietary restrictions. An in-depth state-of-the-art analysis was carried out to curate a list of different levels of evaluation as regards applications with behavioral strategies. The assessment through usability questionnaires curated from relevant evaluation items revealed that developed applications improved access to knowledge in reliable and personalized nutritional information.

(RQ4) **Educational Significance**: Our approach, which marries real-world challenges with academic learning, has manifested positive outcomes in terms of student engagement throughout the semester. It presents a holistic platform where theoretical constructs are tested against real-world developer challenges, enriching the educational journey by weaving in societal challenges. Internal conclusions of the students' teams, impressions of the lecturers throughout the semester, and student engagement evaluation reports revealed that the incorporation of real-world challenges in teaching methodologies contributes to the advancement of educational practices in computer science.

(RQ5) **Comparative Analysis**: Final evaluation results confirmed the significance of the PBL approach. There was a noticeable uptick in student outcomes and a richer learning experience compared to preceding courses.

All in all, this innovative approach of intertwining real-world problems with learning has shown positive evidence of more active student implication on the semester, offering a multifaceted platform where theoretical knowledge meets real-world developer challenges. It also enriches the educational experience by integrating societal challenges, molding students into mindful developers who are cognizant of the broader impacts of their applications. The methodology has not only sparked high interest and engagement but has also highlighted the importance of fostering a balanced learning environment that aligns technical proficiency with societal awareness.

8. Discussion

In the continually advancing field of computer science education, pedagogical strategies must evolve to accommodate the dynamic nature of technology and the distinct challenges it presents. The existing literature, while vast, often casts a wide net—endeavoring to tackle the overarching principles of teaching methodologies without necessarily zoning in on niche areas of concern. This investigation has tried to shed light on a specialized foray into areas such as the realm of Android programming education and its associated pedagogical nuances.

Positioning itself at the intersection of computer science education and Android development, our study addresses a crucial gap in the state of the art. As computer science educators often grapple with specific instructional challenges—ranging from students' varying prior knowledge to the ever-changing development environments—our research provides invaluable insights into one of the contemporary scenarios: fostering engagement in Android programming. By systematically exploring the unique hurdles and motivators in this domain, this investigation serves as a beacon for educators confronted with particular pedagogical situations. In a time when generic solutions often fall short, our study carves a niche by offering tailored strategies and considerations specifically for the Android development educational space.

Funding: This research received no external funding.

Institutional Review Board Statement: Not applicable.

Informed Consent Statement: Not applicable.

Data Availability Statement: Restrictions apply to the availability of these data. Data was obtained from student gradings and can not be publicly shared.

Acknowledgments: We thank the participants taking part on the use-case study that have volunteered to evaluate the developed application.

Conflicts of Interest: The author declare no conflict of interest.

References

1. Ozdem-Yilmaz, Y.; Bilican, K. Discovery Learning—Jerome Bruner. In *Science Education in Theory and Practice: An Introductory Guide to Learning Theory*; Springer: Berlin/Heidelberg, Germany, 2020; pp. 177–190.
2. Liu, W.; Lee, K.P.; Gray, C.M.; Toombs, A.L.; Chen, K.H.; Leifer, L. Transdisciplinary teaching and learning in UX design: A program review and AR case studies. *Appl. Sci.* **2021**, *11*, 10648. [CrossRef]
3. Almulla, M.A. The effectiveness of the project-based learning (PBL) approach as a way to engage students in learning. *Sage Open* **2020**, *10*, 2158244020938702. [CrossRef]
4. Guo, P.; Saab, N.; Post, L.S.; Admiraal, W. A review of project-based learning in higher education: Student outcomes and measures. *Int. J. Educ. Res.* **2020**, *102*, 101586. [CrossRef]
5. Sattarov, A.; Khaitova, N. Mobile learning as new forms and methods of increasing the effectiveness of education. *Eur. J. Res. Reflect. Educ. Sci.* **2019**, *7*, 1169–1175.
6. Rohde, A.; Lorkowski, S.; Dawczynski, C.; Brombach, C. Dietary mobile apps: Acceptance among young adults: A qualitative study. *Ernahrungs Umsch.* **2017**, *64*, 36–43.
7. Picard, R.W.; Papert, S.; Bender, W.; Blumberg, B.; Breazeal, C.; Cavallo, D.; Machover, T.; Resnick, M.; Roy, D.; Strohecker, C. Affective learning—A manifesto. *BT Technol. J.* **2004**, *22*, 253–269. [CrossRef]
8. Singh, A.; Rocke, S.; Pooransingh, A.; Ramlal, C.J. Improving student engagement in teaching electric machines through blended learning. *IEEE Trans. Educ.* **2019**, *62*, 297–304. [CrossRef]
9. Willett, W.C. Diet and health: What should we eat? *Science* **1994**, *264*, 532–537. [CrossRef]
10. Erdem, E. Examination of the effects of project based learning approach on students' attitudes towards chemistry and test anxiety. *World Appl. Sci. J.* **2012**, *17*, 764–769.
11. Larraza-Mendiluze, E.; Arbelaitz, O.; Arruarte, A.; Lukas, J.F.; Garay-Vitoria, N. JolasMATIKA: An experience for teaching and learning computing topics from university to primary education. *IEEE Trans. Educ.* **2019**, *63*, 136–143. [CrossRef]

12. Gallagher, S.A. Problem-based learning. In *Systems and Models for Developing Programs for the Gifted and Talented*; Routledge: London, UK, 2023; pp. 193–210.
13. Martin, C.K.; Han, H.; Coulon, S.M.; Allen, H.R.; Champagne, C.M.; Anton, S.D. A novel method to remotely measure food intake of free-living individuals in real time: The remote food photography method. *Br. J. Nutr.* **2008**, *101*, 446–456. [CrossRef] [PubMed]
14. Bulka, C.M.; Davis, M.A.; Karagas, M.R.; Ahsan, H.; Argos, M. The unintended consequences of a gluten-free diet. *Epidemiology* **2017**, *28*, e24. [CrossRef] [PubMed]
15. Richter, M.; Boeing, H.; Grünewald-Funk, D.; Heseker, H.; Kroke, A.; Leschik-Bonnet, E.; Oberritter, H.; Strohm, D.; Watzl, B. Vegan diet. Position of the German nutrition society (DGE). *Ernahrungs Umsch.* **2016**, *63*, 92–102.
16. Singh, P.; Arora, A.; Strand, T.A.; Leffler, D.A.; Catassi, C.; Green, P.H.; Kelly, C.P.; Ahuja, V.; Makharia, G.K. Global prevalence of celiac disease: Systematic review and meta-analysis. *Clin. Gastroenterol. Hepatol.* **2018**, *16*, 823–836. [CrossRef] [PubMed]
17. Al-Khusaibi, M. Arab traditional foods: Preparation, processing and nutrition. In *Traditional Foods: History, Preparation, Processing and Safety*; Springer: Berlin/Heidelberg, Germany, 2019; pp. 9–35.
18. Wrenn, C.L. The Vegan Society and social movement professionalization, 1944–2017. *Food Foodways* **2019**, *27*, 190–210. [CrossRef]
19. Koch, V.; Blenkuš, M.G.; Gregorič, M.; Kostanjevec, S. Risk factors as a result of unhealthy nutrition in the adult population in Slovenia with regard to sociodemographic variables. *Slov. J. Public Health* **2014**, *53*, 144–155. [CrossRef]
20. Reinhart, R. Snapshot: Few Americans vegetarian or vegan. Gallup Poll Social Series. *Gallup*, 1 August 2018.
21. Charlebois, S.; McCormick, M.; Juhasz, M. Meat consumption and higher prices: Discrete determinants affecting meat reduction or avoidance amidst retail price volatility. *Br. Food J.* **2016**, *118*, 2251–2270. [CrossRef]
22. Curtain, F.; Grafenauer, S. Plant-based meat substitutes in the flexitarian age: An audit of products on supermarket shelves. *Nutrients* **2019**, *11*, 2603. [CrossRef]
23. Banks, N.; Liddy, M.; van der Linden, C. *Australia Talks National Survey [Data File and Codebook]*; Vox Pop Labs Inc. [producer]: Toronto, ON, Canada; Australian Broadcasting Corporation [Distributor]: Ultimo, NSW, Australia, 2019.
24. Giacoman, C.; Joustra, C.; Del Río, F.; Aguilera Bornand, I.M. Reflexivity in Vegan Eating Practices: A Qualitative Study in Santiago, Chile. *Sustainability* **2023**, *15*, 2074. [CrossRef]
25. Costello Barroso, M.A. Alimentación basada en plantas en la Provincia de Buenos Aires: ¿ cómo llegar a una alimentación completa? Ph.D. Thesis, Universidad de Belgrano-Facultad de Ciencias de la Salud-Licenciatura, Zabala, Argentina, 2021.
26. Azar, K.M.; Lesser, L.I.; Laing, B.Y.; Stephens, J.; Aurora, M.S.; Burke, L.E.; Palaniappan, L.P. Mobile applications for weight management: Theory-based content analysis. *Am. J. Prev. Med.* **2013**, *45*, 583–589. [CrossRef]
27. Backinger, C.L.; Augustson, E.M. Where there's an app, there's a way? *Am. J. Prev. Med.* **2011**, *40*, 390. [CrossRef] [PubMed]

applied sciences

MDPI

Article

Dynamic and Energy Efficient Cache Scheduling Framework for IoMT over ICN

Abdullah Alourani [1], Muhammad Sardaraz [2], Muhammad Tahir [2,*] and Muhammad Saud Khan [3]

1 Department of Management Information Systems and Production Management, College of Business and Economics, Qassim University, P.O. Box 6640, Buraidah 51452, Saudi Arabia; ab.alourani@qu.edu.sa
2 Department of Computer Science, COMSATS University Islamabad, Attock Campus, Attock 43600, Pakistan
3 Department of Computer Science, Air University Aerospace and Aviation Campus, Kamra 43570, Pakistan
* Correspondence: m_tahir@cuiatk.edu.pk

Abstract: The Internet of Medical Things (IoMT) is the network of medical devices, hardware infrastructure, and software applications used to connect the healthcare information technology. Massive traffic growth and user expectations cause challenges in the current exhausting models of IoMT data. To reduce the IoMT traffic, Information Centric Network (ICN) is a suitable technique. ICN uses persistent naming multicast communication that reduces the response time. ICN in IoMT provides a promising feature to reduce the overhead due to the distribution of commonly accessed contents. Some parameters such as energy consumption, communication cost, etc., influence the performance of sensors in the IoMT network. Excessive and unbalanced energy consumption degrades the network performance and lifetime. This article presents a framework called Dynamic Cache Scheme (DCS) that implements energy-efficient cache scheduling in IoMT over ICN to reduce network traffic. The proposed framework establishes a balance between the multi-hop traffic and data item freshness. The technique improves the freshness of data; thus, updated data are provided to the end-users via the effective utilization of caching in IoMT. The proposed framework is tested on important parameters, i.e., cache-hit-ratio, stretch, and content retrieval latency. The results obtained are compared with the state-of-the-art models. Results' analysis shows that the proposed framework outperforms the compared models in terms of cache-hit-ratio, stretch, and content retrieval latency by 59.42%, 32.66%, and 18.8%, respectively. In the future, it is intended to explore the applicability of DCS in more scenarios and optimize further.

Keywords: ICN; cache scheduling; wireless network; energy efficiency; IoT; big data; algorithm

Citation: Alourani, A.; Sardaraz, M.; Tahir, M.; Khan, M.S. Dynamic and Energy Efficient Cache Scheduling Framework for IoMT over ICN. *Appl. Sci.* **2023**, *13*, 11840. https://doi.org/10.3390/app132111840

Academic Editors: Stefano Silvestri and Francesco Gargiulo

Received: 12 October 2023
Revised: 25 October 2023
Accepted: 27 October 2023
Published: 29 October 2023

1. Introduction

The Internet of Things (IoT) represents a network comprising interconnected devices, namely actuators and sensors, designed to measure various environmental variables and execute actions as per predefined directives [1]. Currently, there are billions of interconnected IoT devices generating an extensive volume of data, which has a significant impact on conventional Internet traffic patterns. The characteristics of IoT depict that anyone can be connected to the network at any time through any path from anywhere [2]. The IoT sector is presently experiencing remarkable growth and is capturing the attention of researchers due to its rapid expansion into diverse domains, including smart retail, smart agriculture, smart homes, smart health, and many others [3]. IoT devices collect and process data to understand the environment and make efficient and accurate decisions to improve daily life activities in different aspects [4]. IoT devices are considered resource-constrained in terms of memory, computing, and battery power [5].

Information Centric Network (ICN) is an effective technique for IoT networks and provides independent location content names in-network caching, which gives ICN valuable contribution to data dissemination [6]. ICN not only reduces the load on data producers but also overcomes delays via the concept of unique location [7]. ICN provides persistent naming multicast communication which reduces the response time and provides the concept of cache to minimize the network traffic [8]. Massive traffic growth and user expectations cause challenges in the current exhausting scheme of IoT data networks [9]. Millions of IoT devices are connected over the Internet which poses challenges for researchers. Sometimes many IoT devices request the same data item concurrently. It is necessary to minimize redundancy over the network and fetch fresh data items [10].

The number of IoT devices has increased significantly and a huge increase is expected in the future. IoT needs certain parameters for better performance and efficient resource utilization over the Internet [11]. One of the primary requirements of IoT is addressing the content over the Internet via unique content name rather than by IP address [12]. The content consumers and devices search for the content name instead of the IP address. If data are cached between the content producer and the content consumer, then instead of retrieving data items from the content producer (source node), data might be available in intermediate nodes. Hence, overall load on the source nodes is minimized and the content consumer can retrieve the data item directly from the caching node instead of the content producer. In this way, content consumers can obtain the data without activating the source node. If the IoT data item is cached properly between the intermediate nodes, the IoT network can achieve the advantage in terms of energy efficiency and source node load, and consumers will obtain fresh data quickly [13]. Connected devices often retrieve identical content, such as health reports, while running various applications. This redundancy contributes to network congestion and affects data freshness.

This article presents a framework for energy-efficient cache scheduling in the IoMT network. The proposed framework uses a multi-hop traffic load and freshness of the data items to achieve the desired goals. The key finding of this research is the Integration of IoMT with ICN, which enhances energy-efficient cache scheduling, balanced data traffic load, and data freshness. The proposed framework addresses the challenges associated with growing IoMT traffic and outperforms existing models in key performance aspects. The results obtained are compared with Tag-Based Caching Strategy (TCS) and Client-cache (CC) strategy. Results' analysis shows that the proposed framework outperforms the other methods on selected parameters. This research has the potential to significantly impact the efficiency and sustainability of IoMT in the healthcare sector and offers a promising avenue for future advancements and applications by a further exploration of DCS's applicability in diverse scenarios and its ongoing optimization. The rest of the paper is organized as follows. Section 2 presents the related work followed by materials and methods in Section 3. Section 4 presents an experimental evaluation with detailed results and discussion. Finally, Section 5 concludes the article.

2. Related Work

IoMT comprises intelligent devices, including wearables and medical monitors that are utilized in healthcare monitoring spanning personal use, homes, communities, clinics, and hospitals. These devices enable real-time location tracking, telehealth services, and various other functionalities. IoMT facilitates secure wireless communication among remote devices via the Internet, enabling swift and adaptable medical data analysis. Its impact on the healthcare industry is multifaceted, with significant benefits observed when deploying IoMT in various contexts, whether in a home setting, on an individual's body, within communities, or even within hospital facilities to obtain the most current data [14,15]. IoMT consumers consistently seek the latest published data due to its frequent updates, where IoT data are cached away from the network edge [16]. IoT devices are small and the data collected from billions of devices is so large that it can disrupt regular network traffic. Therefore, ICN can be used to enhance the network scalability of IoMT [17]. The integration of ICN with IoT is more suitable as it results in reliable data transmission and consumes less bandwidth as compared to IP-based network communication [18]. ICN plays a vital role in ensuring content availability over the network and facilitating rapid content access [2]. Several techniques have been proposed to address cache scheduling including the implementation of caching mechanisms with different objectives, such as data size, data lifetime, sensing cache, time-based cache, and collaborative caching. Some models utilize cloud computing to store medical data in cloud storage, where additional operations like scheduling and resource utilization prediction are performed [19–22].

Tag-based Caching Strategy (TCS) uses tag filters for the matching and lookup of the requested contents for dissemination to the target node [23]. In TCS, all network nodes are linked with specific lists of tags to identify highly requested content. Tag filters are generated from the tag list through a hash function to enhance content distribution. As the network node receives a request from a user, the corresponding tag filter decides whether to transmit the content cache to the intermediate location or not. In this caching strategy, the tags linked with the required contents are checked by the tag filters inside the CS, and all the tags are hashed and mapped in a counter to find the most requested content. If a tag counter for specific content crosses the threshold, then the content is considered popular. As a result, all the nodes check the tags to identify the content location and decide whether the content that needs to be cached reaches the preferred location or not. TCS appears to be a promising approach for improving content distribution efficiency in networks. However, its complexity and resource requirements, as well as the need for careful parameter tuning, are potential drawbacks that need to be carefully considered. Another article [24] presents the Client Cache (CC) strategy in which the cached contents inside the network nodes are observed and considered valid. The on-path caching approach is selected to cache transmitted contents which eliminates the requirements to inform the client which node is appropriate to cache the preferred content. Moreover, the number of nodes is reduced to be aware of the most essential nodes in terms of content quality and cache size. The main objective of CC is to extend the content validity, which is examined as the requested content is found inside the cache. The content material is considered valid if the lifetime within the publisher is higher than the lifetime of the version within the cache. While selecting the requested content, a validity test is performed to check the content inside the content publisher whenever a content material request arrives at the neighborhood-caching node. They show that the combination of the two proposed schemes results in a notable improvement in content validity at the expense of a certain degradation in both server-hit and hop reduction ratios. However, it requires a more extensive and in-depth analysis of the trade-offs and challenges associated with the proposed solutions. Authors in [25] presented a secure and energy-efficient framework using IoMT for E-healthcare (SEF-IoMT) and explored the growing popularity of IoT in the healthcare sector. The proposed framework explored the need for an improved framework to address issues related to energy consumption, communication costs, and data security. The proposed framework reduces energy consumption and communication overhead in IoMT. Comparative experimental results show the effectiveness of the proposed method in comparison to existing methods. However, it lacks a transparent evaluation of metrics and an in-depth analysis of its findings to validate its scientific contribution.

Another article [26] presents a secure and energy-efficient IoT model for e-health, focusing on the secure transmission and retrieval of biomedical images over IoT networks. The authors utilize compressive sensing and a five-dimensional hyper-chaotic map (FDHC) for image encryption, addressing the challenge of hyper-parameter tuning in FDHC. The encryption technique is image-sensitive, depending on the initial scrambled row and column for permutation and diffusion operations. Experimental results indicate that the proposed method outperforms existing image encryption techniques. Consequently, it is considered suitable for securing communication in energy-efficient IoT networks. However, a clear discussion of the hyper-parameter tuning problem, sensitivity to input images, and the practicality of the proposed method is missing. The study presented in [27] addresses a crucial issue in the field of healthcare IoT by emphasizing the need for data security and energy efficiency. This study addresses the critical challenges of storing sensitive medical data securely and preventing cyber threats in the rapidly growing IoMT network.

The integration of homomorphic secret sharing and artificial intelligence to enhance the maintainability of disease diagnosis systems and reinforce secure communication is highly important. However, the analysis of the results shows the proposed model suffers from an increased packet drop ratio and imbalanced energy consumption in the presence of high network load among IoT nodes. Age-based cooperative caching is presented in [28] for the efficient utilization of cache and routing in ICN. This framework is designed to minimize heavy computation and communication between routers. The algorithm dynamically updates the freshness of data in routers by pushing popular data over the network edges, while less popular data reside away from the edges. The method can be considered efficient for ICN, but these schemes work with special-purpose applications, i.e., P2P systems that mostly benefit web applications like web caching and distributed file systems. However, the evolving nature of ICN and how this approach might adapt to changing network conditions and requirements has not been considered for the evaluation and validation of the proposed model.

In another article, the authors [29] present a model that aims to balance between multi-hop communication costs and the freshness of transient data items. IoT devices create extra traffic load, and it is necessary to make caching decisions to minimize the traffic. The short lifetime of IoT data items leads to extra complexity in handling caching decisions. The cost function is used for data items generated at the source node to address the issue. The results analysis shows that this model effectively describes the effect of data transiency and accurately represents the benefits of a caching system, particularly in terms of reducing network load, and especially for substantially requested data items. However, practical implementation and scalability considerations, as well as addressing security and privacy concerns, are essential for the successful deployment of in-network caching solutions in IoT ecosystems, which has been not considered in this study. The article [30] discusses the role of TCP/IP in the Internet of Vehicles (IoV) and its limitations, such as weak scalability, low efficiency in dense environments, and unreliable addressing in high mobility situations. It highlights the potential of NDN technology in addressing these issues through content caching. It proposes a data caching scheme that considers the spatial-temporal characteristics of different message categories in VNDN, including emergency safety, traffic efficiency, and service messages. Experimental results show that this scheme outperforms existing data caching protocols, improving the average hit rate, hop count, and cache replacement times by approximately 50%. However, unreliable addressing in high mobility circumstances, especially considering vehicular networks, is challenging and involves vehicles moving at high speeds, which can lead to frequent changes in network topology. Moreover, Content-centric networking can raise concerns about data privacy and security. An analytical model is presented in [31] to balance the trade-off between multi-hop communication costs and data item freshness. Transient data caching decisions are used to ensure data freshness. This model is known as a pull-based caching scheme, as the scheme considers the rate of incoming requests from the content consumers and data item lifetime to cache data items. However, the paper does not delve into the technical challenges and complexities of implementing caching mechanisms for transient data. Practical issues related to cache management, cache replacement policies, and the scalability of such systems are not sufficiently discussed. Push-based caching is proposed in [32] to minimize the traffic load and explores the potential of named data networking (NDN) as a framework for facilitating IoT applications, particularly those requiring push-based communication. In the push-based caching scheme, data servers push the data items towards consumers with static networks. This scheme splits the IoT data traffic into four main parts, i.e., periodic data, event trigged data, command base, and data query supported by the NDN structure. However, reliability is still the issue in push models and, for instance, more comprehensive evaluation of the proposed model in practical IoT use cases is required, and lacks the consideration of potential challenges and drawbacks.

A caching scheme for the ICN-IoT data network is presented in [33]. The authors proposed a novel caching scheme based on the IoT data lifetime and user request rate, leveraging information ICN principles. This approach aims to reduce the energy consumption of IoT devices by intelligently caching data at various network nodes. The approach considers the incoming request rate of users to efficiently utilize the energy of IoT devices. The main idea is to keep the source node in sleep mode to save energy for the network. With the help of a cooperative caching scheme, the method also minimizes the traffic load and provides fresh data to the users. Data items are cached at intermediate nodes, i.e., between the content producers and content consumers, which leads to energy saving. The paper provides a valuable contribution to the field of IoT by addressing the crucial issue of energy efficiency through the innovative use of caching based on data lifetime and request rate. However, addressing scalability and security considerations is essential for the practical implementation of the proposed scheme in IoT networks. The paper [34] introduces the concept of a sensing cache, strategically positioned at a wireless gateway of IoT sensors to minimize energy consumption. A dynamic threshold adaptation algorithm allows the sensing cache to adjust its parameters in real time, maximizing the combined hit rate of the sensing service from multiple sensors. The sensor devices harvest energy from the environment to save energy for sending or receiving information. However, sensing errors may occur that can create problems with data freshness. The smart caching scheme for the IoT platform presented in [35] creates and maintains the balance between the freshness of data and energy of nodes. Freshness and energy consumption are the main parameters considered. When IoT data are combined over the Internet, issues like freshness loss, energy consumption, and increase in traffic load are raised. The freshness of data items and energy are considered parameters of the cache to provide fresh data to users while the energy of the sensors remains balanced. Data redundancy is also minimized in the smart cache scheme by dropping the data item from the cache nodes that are no longer needed. This leads to data freshness and less energy consumption. However, there are no details provided about the experiment, the methodology, or the results and it lacks critical analysis and empirical evidence. Freshness Aware Reverse Proxy (FARP) caching scheme is presented in [36]. The scheme is based on data item freshness and access performance. The caching scheme brings the advantage of access performance but when the data in the cache is not fresh and expires at the source node, the method creates additional burden. The cost function is used to balance the switching between used and unused data items present at the cache nodes. The method also adjusts the two parameters for the cache node to provide fresh data to the user. However, when the data expires, it may overlap with the latest published data at the source node. A probabilistic caching scheme for IoT networks is presented in [37]. This model considers the freshness of IoT data, energy, and storage as measurement parameters to optimize the retrieval of data. ICN content is fetched through unique name and location tags to ensure the freshness of data, data retrieval, ease of transmission cost, and sharing of data. In-network caching also helps to optimize data retrieval and manage network load. The proposed caching scheme also considers resource constraints, i.e., energy and space to provide fresh data to users. However, it does not provide a direct comparison with the state-of-the-art models. A coherent caching freshness scheme for IoT is proposed in [38]. The method increases the speed of data retrieval while minimizing the network load. The aim is to increase the cache hit rate and reduce network delays. The authors worked on on-path caching scheme to improve the energy of caching nodes. In this caching technique, the intermediate nodes not only resolve the problem of energy but also resolve the problems of data freshness and redundancy. The method uses the cost function for the energy-efficient utilization of caching nodes. However, several critical aspects have not been considered in this study including scalability, security, and interoperability.

All the cache frameworks discussed above have their advantages. Millions of IoT devices are connected to the Internet which causes huge traffic load and poses several challenges. The need for the efficient utilization of available resources to benefit from the

IoMT network is still challenging. The performance and lifetime of the sensors in IoMT are concerned with energy consumption, computation, and other parameters. The solutions designed for this purpose should consider the relation between related parameters to ensure that improving one parameter does not affect other parameters. Therefore, more research and robust cache frameworks are needed to achieve the maximum advantages of IoMT over ICN networks.

3. Materials and Methods

This section provides an overview of the proposed framework. Section 3.1 introduces the system model employed for experimental purposes. Section 3.2 elaborates on the Cache Routing and Replacement Policy utilized for the evaluation and analysis of this research study, and, finally, Section 3.3 outlines the operational aspects of the proposed framework.

3.1. System Model

The network system model comprises of N routers, i.e., set r_n is the number of each router, where $n = 1, 2, 3, \ldots, N$ as shown in Figure 1. The r router is the nearest to the content consumer, while router r_N is the nearest to the content generator. The term c is used to represent the size of the cache on the router r_k. The Poisson distribution is used to follow the average number of requests of content service with the request rate l for class k using the Zipf–Mandelbrot distribution with type factor λ_k for class k. Network contents are partitioned into three different classes, i.e., class a, b, and c, based on characteristics as discussed in [39]. The content classification depends on the jitter, delay, content utilization, and the pattern of request rate. Class a requires low jitter and delay integrated with repeatedly requested contents. Class b is user-generated content with less jitter and a medium required delay. This class includes the content that has been generated and distributed by volunteer subscribers, like sites, web-based social media content, etc. Class c comprises video-on-demand content which is not the target of this research study. This research follows Poisson distribution to make several requests for content service classes. Due to content popularity, the Zipf–Mandelbrot distribution is used for request modeling, which comprises a flattened factor [40–42]. The content on top rankings has more chance of being requested as compared with lower rankings content.

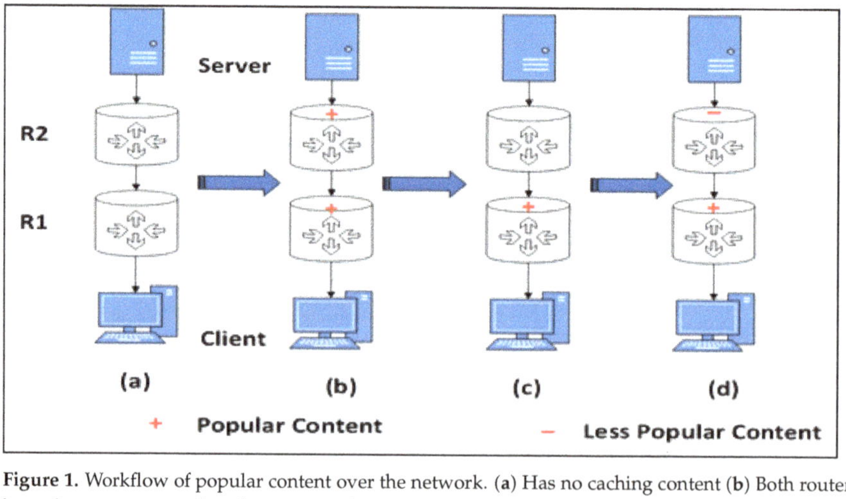

Figure 1. Workflow of popular content over the network. (**a**) Has no caching content (**b**) Both routers have the same content but the content of $R1$ is older than the content of $R2$. (**c**) After some time, the content of $R2$ expires. (**d**) Client needs less popular content, which is cached at $R2$. The age of the content is determined by the distance from the server or source node.

The cache receives request rate β, which is contingent upon the condition $\beta \geq 0$, denoting the request intensity. Let $P(i)$ be the probability of content requests; N is the total number of requests, q is the vector, and α is the exponential factor for content popularity. In this context, we can express the probability of accessing content i using Equation (1).

$$P(i) = \frac{(i+q)^{-\alpha}}{\sum_{i=1}^{N}(i+q)^{-\alpha}} \tag{1}$$

Each content may receive updates to replace the previous data item. It is assumed that the content n receives updates as per the Poisson distribution request model bounded with the refresh rate of $\lambda_n \geq 0$. As all the content of the data is subject to updates, then the same content item that resides in the local cache can be considered as an older version of the content. To measure the freshness of the content, the age Δ_n with respect to time t can be bounded as $\Delta_n(t) \in \{0, 1, 2, \ldots n\}$, where n represents the number of updates. The cost of the fetching content is subject to the condition, i.e., $c_f \geq 0$, in case of operations. For performance, the cost metric can be integrated with time as $c_a = \Delta_n(t)$ subject to $c_a \geq 0$, and linear growth rate.

3.2. Cache Routing and Replacement Policy

The caching technique characterizes the replication technique used to spread duplicates of the content in the cache. Replication techniques have two measurements. Content-based replication, which depends on attributes of the content and settles on caching choices, e.g., pick popular content to store and ignore others. Node-based replication depends on the qualities of the topology, e.g., picking more important nodes for storing the content. Both content-based and node-based replication are resource optimization approaches. Both techniques attempt to designate storage space to attain maximum advantage, e.g., increased cache-hit-ratio. The replication techniques explored in the context of ICN are all node-based since the content-based technique can work on a large Internet scale. There exists several caching approaches, i.e., Leave Copy Everywhere (LCE), Leave Copy Down (LCD), Bernoulli random caching, random choice caching, Probabilistic Caching (ProbCache), centrality-based caching, and hash-routing [40–43]. In the IoT over ICN network, caching nodes can be configured using one of the state-of-the-art cache eviction policies, i.e., Least Recently Used (LRU), Least Frequently Used (LFU), First in First Out (FIFO), and random. This research utilizes the LRU cache eviction policy because it is the most widely used cache replacement strategy. At an instance when new content is required to be pushed into the cache, it eliminates the least recently asserted content request. This replacement strategy is proficient for line speedup activities because both search and substitution replacement can be performed in consistent time, i.e., $O(1)$. Nonetheless, its efficiency degrades under the Independent Reference Model (IRM) supposition because of the likelihood that the current requested content does not rely upon previous content requests.

3.3. Proposed Framework

This article presents a Dynamic Caching Scheme (DCS) to improve the freshness of the cache contents and network performance. The proposed technique neither needs extensive computations nor tags, filters, metadata, and additional network communication that create extra overhead in IoT networks. Moreover, if the source node and user are at longer distances, it may extend the retrieval delay because of the smaller size of the cache nodes. In the IoMT network, each content has a lifetime and is expected to expire in some instance of time. The proposed framework is designed to dynamically push popular content towards edge nodes over the network by changing the data ages. Data ages are used to handle the lifetime of content over the network while removing the contents that are no longer needed. Each content in the cache has an age that decides the lifetime of the cached content. Popular content over the network has a longer age. First, at the router node, the content age is estimated in correlation with the freshness of the data item. If the age of the data item is not matched with the source node, it is removed from the cache. In the proposed framework, an Interest Record Table (IRT) integrated with cache control is added at the router to improve the working of CS while avoiding traffic load at the source node. Figure 1 illustrates the workflow of popular content across the network. This network consists of a client and server, each connected to their respective routers, $R1$ and $R2$. The server is responsible for generating two types of content: popular and less popular. Notably, both routers can store at least one content item at a time. In deciding whether to cache data or not, especially for transient small-sized data, a "period" field is introduced within the packet. This field supplies updated data directly from the source node. To accomplish this, the system incorporates the content's age with the data item, with the first router node establishing the initial age baseline. The quantitative findings indicate that when data items are not cached at the nodes, this incurs a higher cost in the IoT network. Caching policies are typically implemented in intermediate nodes. Each node possesses specific cache threshold requirements and can dynamically adjust these thresholds based on the request rate. To minimize retrieval delays, edge nodes employ smaller caching thresholds, allowing them to cache more data items. In contrast, the root node has a larger caching threshold, enabling it to cache data items for a longer duration. The system carefully considers both data lifetime and request rates to reduce energy consumption, data retrieval delays, and the overall network traffic load. When the request rate reaches the specified threshold, it is recommended to cache the requested data in the edge node.

Figure 2 illustrates the architecture of the proposed model, showing the frequently requested content cached at the edge nodes, i.e., $R6$ and $R9$. When the cache capacity of an edge node reduces, and the validity of the content persists, it is stored in the cache of an intermediate node. This strategy prevents excessive network load by accommodating incoming requests at intermediate nodes, avoiding the need to route them back to the source node. The Pending Interest Table (PIT) is involved in tracking unhandled interest packets and recording relevant data names, along with their incoming and outgoing edges. The Forwarding Information Base (FIB) aids in network bridging and routing by determining the appropriate output network edge controller. Content replacement across the network follows an LRU cache policy, primarily targeting content flows. Retrieving content directly from the source node can lead to delays in terms of cache hit ratios for IoT networks. The proposed framework utilizes diverse data types to optimize the bandwidth utilization and alleviate network congestion. When users $S1$ and $S2$ send interest packets for content $C1$, which is a popularly cached item at the edge node, the concept of content popularity becomes evident. If another request arises for content $C3$ to be cached at the edge node, but the cache is full, $C3$ is directed to an intermediate caching node. This approach minimizes content replication within the network, ensuring efficient memory utilization and a reduction in bandwidth consumption. The proposed framework enhances three key caching parameters: cache hit ratio, network stretch, and latency. Edge nodes copy content from the publisher, with content lifetime specified upon publishing data. IoT data adheres to specific lifetimes, and require termination at some point in the network. Consequently, the implementation of DCS enhances network performance and reduces the network traffic load on the source node. Algorithm 1 is used to deploy the routing policy for checking the age of the content at the cache of the edge node. If the content is expired and removed from the cache, then new content is added to the cache, and age is defined for this content. Upon receiving the age of the caching node, a message is sent to the router for an update, i.e., if it is replaced by the replica, then add a new age to the incoming contents until it expires and is removed from the cache node. If space is not available at the cache of the edge node, then the content is passed to the higher threshold value towards the central position. The workflow of the popular content over the network shows that it is periodic, as when users request come for content that is popular over the network, CS is first checked. If the requested content is available locally, then the same is provided. Otherwise, the procedure checks the cached content at CS, a call to IRT is performed, and the content is provided to the user. If the content is not available, then it is shifted to PIT to check whether it is the same content requested by any other node. In case of the same content, the request with respect is removed. Another entry is made with respect to the current request, and data are provided to the desired request. In contrast, the FIB broadcasts the request for popular content.

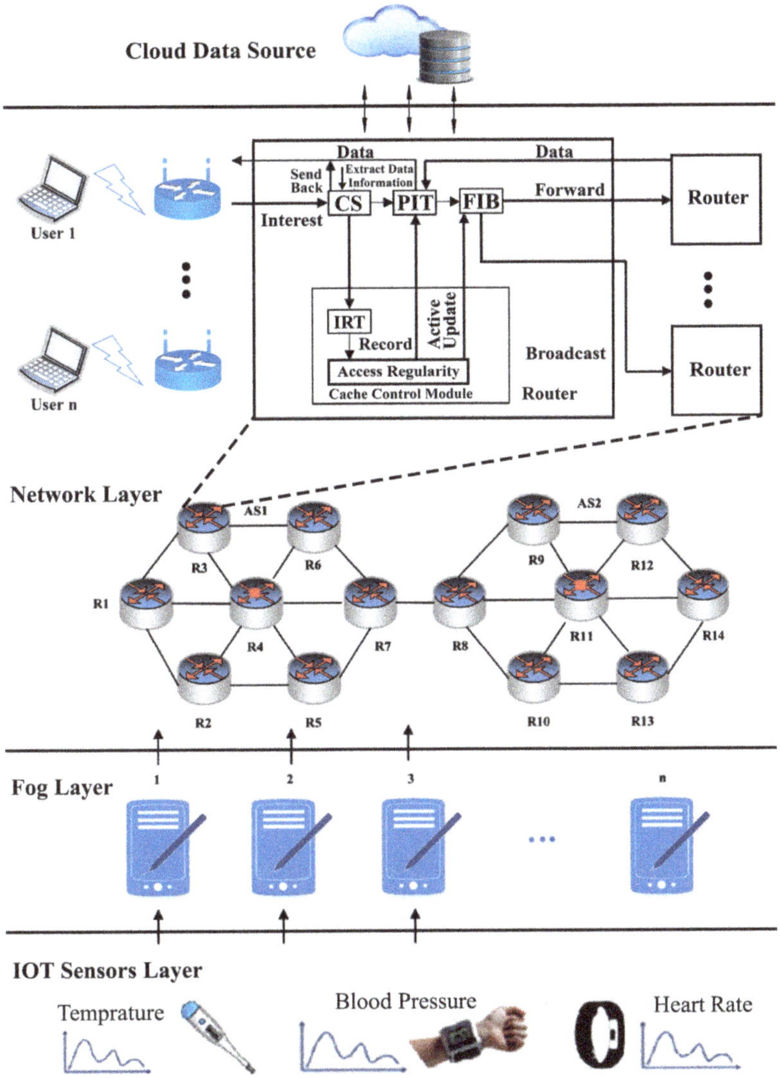

Figure 2. The architecture of the proposed system. The architecture presents the workflow of interest packets sent from biomedical sensor devices toward the cloud data source. Content producers and content consumers have caching nodes that cache the popular data for short lifetime. If the ordinary request comes over the network, it is forwarded to CS to check; if found, then it is sent to the consumer, or otherwise forwarded to PIT to check for any other entry in PIT. If it exists, then we discard the existing entry and add updated entry against this request; if data are not present, it is further sent to FIB to broadcast.

Algorithm 1: Receiving age of the IoMT data items at the caching nodes.

```
Input  : Interest data item arrives at cache
Output : Age of cache content
Remove expired content from the cache of node.
data_item arrives at intermediate node i
if (data_item is in cache) then
    if (freshness_of_data_item<freshness_of_cached_data_item) then
        refresh (cache)
        add to cache_edge_node (data_item)
        data_item_age = new_age (data_item)
        forward_the_data_item to the next_hop's_node
        else
            data_item_age = new_age (data_item)
            forward_the_data_item to the next_hop's_node
        end
else if (node_cache has more space) then
    cache (data_item)
    new_age(data_item)
    forward_the_data_item to the next_hop's_node
else if (lifetime_data_item≥ caching threshold) then
    while (node_cache_has_no_space) do
        call LRU replacement policy
    end
    cache (data_item)
    forward_the_data_item to the next_hop's_node
else
    forward_the_data_item to the next_hop's_node
end
```

4. Experimental Evaluation

This section presents an experimental evaluation of the proposed framework. First, the experimental setup is presented, including details of the parameters, the dataset used, the simulation environment, and the tools used for simulation. The experimental setup is followed by Section 4.2 that covers the detailed results with relevant discussion.

4.1. Experimental Setup

To assess the performance of the proposed model, a distributed network of virtual IoT devices is configured using open-source Icarus interlinked with the web-based Bevywise IoT simulator [44,45]. The WUSTL-EHMS-2020 dataset is used for simulation [46]. This dataset comprises 44 attributes, with 35 of them being network flow metrics, eight representing patients' biometric features, and one dedicated to the label. The configuration of essential parameters is presented in Table 1. Data freshness can be defined as the time elapsed between the creation of the IoT object and the retrieval of this object from the cache store [47]. The data age is the age of the data item, which is the time between the arrival at the router and the generation at the source node, while the period field is used to keep count of the age [48]. Three network topologies, namely Tree, Abilene, and GEANT, have been chosen for the comparative evaluation. To ensure a fair comparison, all algorithms were executed within the same environment. To demonstrate the validity and accuracy of the results, each experiment was repeated 100 times, and the average value of each parameter was employed for a comparative analysis. The parameter used to measure network performance utilization is the cache hit ratio CH_{ratio}, calculated with Equation (2) [49].

$$CH_{ratio} = \frac{\sum_{k=1}^{k} Hit_k}{\sum_{k=1}^{k} (Hit + Miss)'} \tag{2}$$

The content retrieval latency $Content_{Rlatency}$ parameter is used to monitor the traffic load over the network, i.e., the time taken by the interest packet to obtain content from the source node and send it back to the user. Let $|R|$ be the total number of requests sent by the user; then, the cache retrieval latency can be computed, as shown in Equation (3) [49].

$$Content_{Rlatency} = \frac{\sum_{i=1}^{|R|} latency\ R_i}{|R|} \tag{3}$$

The stretch shows the measurement of the distance from the content used to the content publisher. The stretch can be computed as shown in Equation (4) [49].

$$Stretch = \frac{\sum_{i=1}^{R} Hop - Traveled}{\sum_{i=1}^{R} Total - Hop'} \tag{4}$$

The nominator in Equation (4) shows the number of hops between the content user and the content publisher in terms of the cache hit occurrence. The denominator shows the total number of hops, i.e., hops between the content user and the source.

Memory consumption shows the measurement of the transmitted content that can be cached while downloading the data path for a time interval. Consumers can download the content from multiple routers. In ICN, memory consumption means the capacity that shows the volume utilized by interest and data contents, as shown in Equation (5).

$$memory_{consumption} = \frac{U_m}{T_m} \times 100 \tag{5}$$

where U_m shows the memory utilized by the cached content and T_m shows the cache storage (total memory) of the router and the data delivery path.

Table 1. Experimental setup simulation parameters.

Parameter Description	Parameter Value
Simulation time	48 h
Cache Size (elements)	500, 1000
Content size	10 MB
Catalog Size (elements)	10^6
Content Categories	File
Topology	Tree, Abilene, & GEANT
Zipf distribution (content popularity)	0.8 & 1.2
Replacement Policy	LRU

4.2. Results and Discussion

The proposed framework significantly improves network performance while reducing the traffic load directed at the source node. In contrast to DCS, the TCS employs tags that require separate computations and fail to accommodate popular content when it regains its popularity. Although the central caching node (CC) excels due to its strategic location, the limited number of such nodes results in inadequate content availability, characterized by a diminished cache-hit ratio, increased network stretch, and extended retrieval latency.

The proposed framework effectively leverages caching nodes to enhance the cache-hit ratio and minimize the network stretch. In the case of DCS, each node is equipped with a table that calculates interests to identify the most frequently requested data across the network, taking into account data names, access frequency, and a specified threshold value. This threshold value helps us to recognize the most frequently requested content that needs to be cached at the edge node, considering the cache's service to multiple devices. The results from these devices are consolidated by a central caching node.

The main challenge lies in selecting an optimal threshold to maximize the cache-hit rate. The threshold adaptation algorithm outlined in [37] is utilized to enable the caching node to learn and implement an optimal threshold strategy. Figures 3–5 depict graphical comparisons of cache-hit ratios, latency, and stretch for CC, TCS, and the proposed framework across various network topologies, including Tree, Abilene, and GEANT. The proposed model is rigorously tested and validated under different cache size and content popularity configurations, specifically, 500 and 0.8, 1000 and 0.8, 500 and 1.2, 1000 and 1.2. In DCS, the selection of optimal caching nodes, along with the essential role played by edge nodes in maintaining data freshness, works to minimize the distance between the source node and the end nodes. Figure 3 shows the results of the cache hit ratio for different numbers of cache sizes and popularity. Results' analysis of Figure 3a shows that the proposed framework gained 105.5%, 109%, and 21.42% improvement in terms of cache-hit ratio over CC executed on Tree, Abilene, and GEANT network topology, respectively, for cache size of 500 and popularity of 0.8. The improvement of DCS over TCS with the same parameters and configuration is 72%, 76%, and 11.47%, executed on Tree, Abilene, and GEANT network topologies, respectively. Figure 3b shows that the proposed framework achieved 132.4%, 122.8%, and 55.3% improvement in terms of the cache-hit ratio over CC executed on Tree, Abilene, and GEANT network topology, respectively, on the cache size of 1000 and popularity of 0.8. The improvement of the proposed model over TCS with the same parameters and configuration is 59.2%, 65.9%, and 17.7% in the case of Tree, Abilene, and GEANT network topologies, respectively.

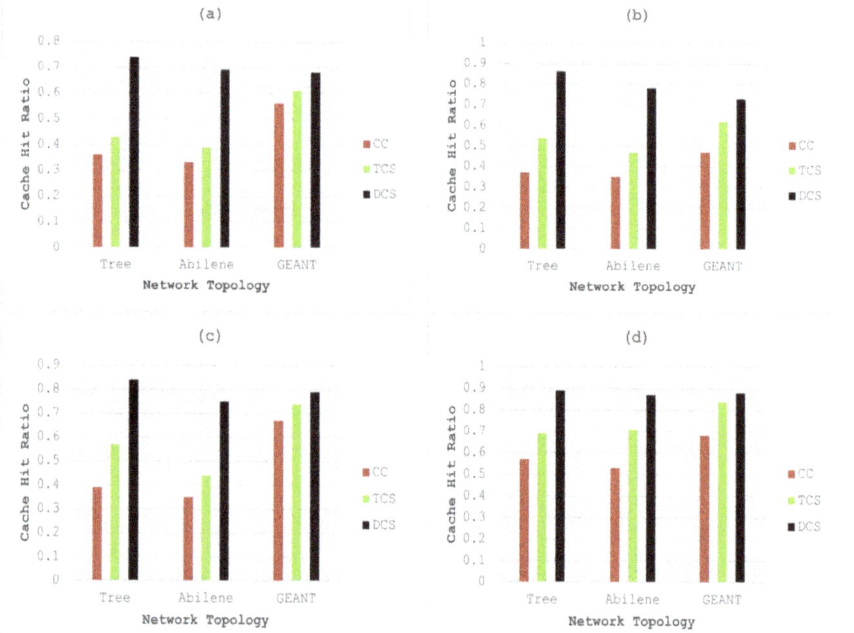

Figure 3. Comparative analysis of cache-hit ratio with cache sizes and popularity of (**a**) 500 and 0.8, (**b**) 1000 and 0.8, (**c**) 500 and 1.2, and (**d**) 1000 and 1.2.

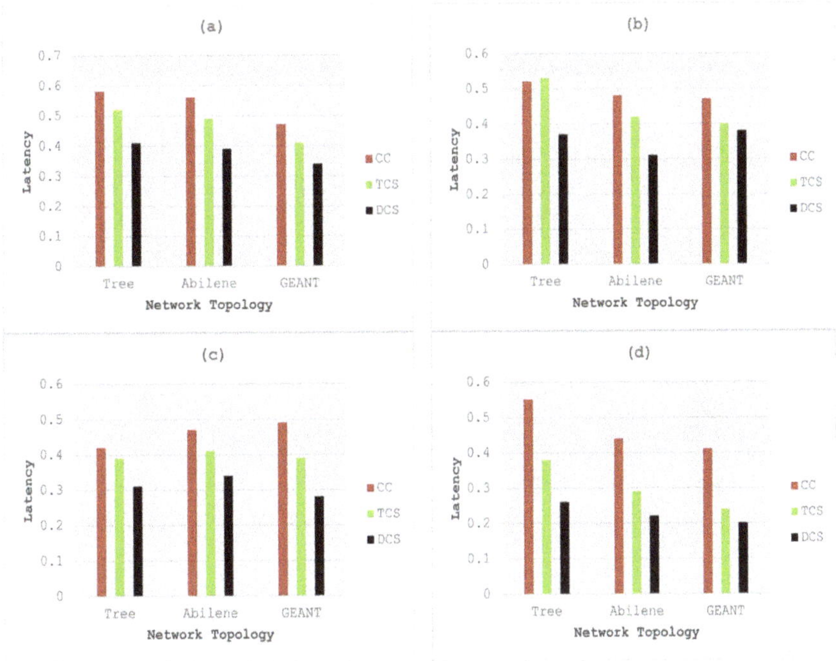

Figure 4. Comparative analysis of latency with cache sizes and popularity of (**a**) 500 and 0.8, (**b**) 1000 and 0.8, (**c**) 500 and 1.2, and (**d**) 1000 and 1.2.

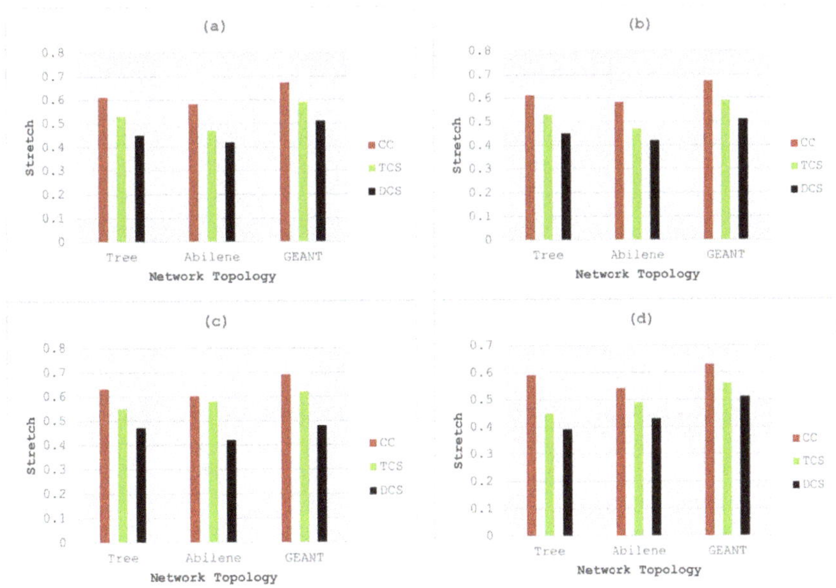

Figure 5. Comparative analysis of stretch with cache sizes and popularity of (**a**) 500 and 0.8, (**b**) 1000 and 0.8, (**c**) 500 and 1.2, and (**d**) 1000 and 1.2.

Figure 3c shows the comparative results of the cache-hit ratio of DCS with CC and TCS on the cache size of 500 and content popularity of 1.2. The results analysis shows that the proposed model is 115.3%, 114.2%, and 17.9% better than CC executed on Tree, Abilene, and GEANT network topology, respectively. The improvement of the proposed model over TCS with the same parameters and configuration is 47.3%, 70.4%, and 6.75% tested on Tree, Abilene, and GEANT network topologies, respectively. Figure 3d presents the comparison of the cache-hit ratio of DCS with CC and TCS for a cache size of 1000 and popularity of 1.2. The results analysis shows 56.14%, 64.15%, and 29.4% improvement over CC in the case of Tree, Abilene, and GEANT network topology, respectively. The improvement of the proposed model over TCS with the same parameters and configuration is 28.98%, 22.5%, and 4.76% executed on Tree, Abilene, and GEANT network topologies, respectively.

Figure 4 shows the comparative results in terms of the latency of DCS with CC and TCS for different cache sizes and content popularity. Figure 4a shows the results of models with 500 elements for cache size, and the content popularity was set to 0.8. Three different network topologies, i.e., Tree, Abilene, and GEANT were used in experiments for testing and validation. The results analysis shows that the proposed model consumes less time, i.e., a 29.31%, 30.35%, and 27.65% decrease in cache latency as compared to CC on Tree, Abilene, and GEANT topologies, respectively. Meanwhile, DCS is 21.15%, 20.4%, and 17.07% more efficient than TCS executed with the same configuration of parameters and topologies, respectively.

Figure 4b shows the comparative results of DCS with CC, and TCS in terms of cache latency. For these experiments, 1000 elements of cache size and a 0.8 value of content popularity are considered and executed on Tree, Abilene, and GEANT network topologies. The results analysis shows that the proposed model is 28.8%, 35.41%, and 19.1% more efficient than CC in the case of Tree, Abilene, and GEANT topologies, respectively. DCS is 30.1%, 26.19%, and 5.0% efficient in cache latency, as compared to TCS executed on the same configuration of parameters and topologies. Figure 4c shows comparative results of DCS with CC, and TCS in terms of cache latency for the cache size of 500 and content popularity of 1.2. An analysis of the results shows that the proposed model is 26.1%, 27.6%, and 42.8% more efficient than CC in the case of Tree, Abilene, and GEANT topologies, respectively. DCS is 20.5%, 17.0%, and 28.2% efficient in cache latency as compared to TCS executed on the same configuration of parameters and topologies. Figure 4d shows the comparative results of DCS with CC, and TCS in terms of cache latency. For these experiments, 1000 elements of cache size and a 1.2 value of content popularity are considered and executed on Tree, Abilene, and GEANT network topologies. The analysis shows that the cache latency of the proposed model is 52.7%, 50.0%, and 51.2% better than CC and executed in Tree, Abilene, and GEANT topologies, respectively. DCS is 30.5%, 24.1%, and 16.6% more efficient than TCS executed on the same configuration of parameters and topologies. CC showed a higher latency rate because of the long distance between the source and the central position of the caching nodes. TCS increases the amount of similar content over the network with the help of tags and filters near the source location, due to which it does not select the central node for the caching; thus, latency increases, as shown in the results. The proposed model retrieves a copy of the popular data item first in the edge node, then increases the number of interest and sends it to the central position, which decreases the distance that leads to a decrease in the latency.

Figure 5 depicts the comparative results of DCS with CC, as well as TCS in terms of stretch. Figure 5a shows the results of 500 elements of cache size and a 0.8 content popularity. The analysis shows that the stretch of the proposed model is 26.2%, 27.5%, and 23.8% better than CC executed on Tree, Abilene, and GEANT topologies, respectively. DCS is 15.0%, 10.6%, and 13.5% more efficient than TCS executed on the same configuration of parameters and network topologies.

Figure 5b shows the comparative results of DCS with CC, as well as TCS in terms of stretch. For experiments, 1000 elements of cache size and a 0.8 value of content popularity are considered and executed on Tree, Abilene, and GEANT network topologies. Results analysis shows that the stretch of DCS is 26.22%, 27.5%, and 23.8% more efficient than CC executed on Tree, Abilene, and GEANT topology, respectively. The proposed model achieved a percent improvement gain of 15.09%, 10.6%, and 13.5% as compared to TCS executed on the cache size of 1000 and content popularity rate of 0.8 on different network topologies. Figure 5c shows the comparative results of DCS with CC, as well as TCS in terms of stretch for the cache size of 500 with content popularity of 1.2 on Tree, Abilene, and GEANT network topologies. The analysis shows that the proposed model achieved a percent improvement gain of 25.3%, 30.0%, and 30.4% as compared to CC executed on Tree, Abilene, and GEANT topology, respectively. DCS is 14.5%, 27.5%, and 22.5% more efficient than TCS when executed on the same configuration of parameters and network topologies. Figure 5d shows the comparative results of DCS with CC, as well as TCS in terms of stretch. For these experiments, 1000 elements of cache size and a 1.2 value of content popularity are considered and executed on Tree, Abilene, and GEANT network topologies. The analysis shows that the stretch of the proposed model DCS is 33.9%, 20.3%, and 19.0% more efficient than CC executed on Tree, Abilene, and GEANT topology, respectively. DCS is 13.3%, 12.2%, and 8.9% more efficient than TCS when executed on the same configuration of parameters and network topologies. DCS moves the popular content near the user while the central position caching node is facilitated to provide the data item earlier than the source node because of the smaller stretch. Results clearly show that when the data item is placed near the user, it results in a decrease of the stretch.

5. Conclusions

IoMT is a significant and promising technology and provides an ease of access to real-world health data instantly. Currently, the number of IoMT devices is increasing exponentially, which intensifies the requirements. In the IoMT environment, the study of ICN caching policies is involved in terms of content placement strategies. IoMT contents are distributed in terms of scalability and cost-effectiveness. With the rapid growth of the IoMT network traffic, it is preemptory to be a suitable framework to address the challenges. This article introduces a dynamic caching strategy designed for the IoMT. By integrating IoMT with ICN, we propose a dynamic caching scheme aimed at reducing energy consumption within information-centric IoMT networks. This study considers key caching policy parameters, such as cache-hit ratio, stretch, and latency, to enhance the IoMT network performance. The proposed framework is evaluated on selected parameters through simulations while exploring various configurations involving network topology, cache size, and content popularity. An analysis of the results demonstrates the superior performance of the proposed caching framework, known as DCS, compared to others. The dynamic nature of the DCS approach yields significant results as compared to existing methods. In the future, it is intended to explore the pertinence of DCS in more scenarios and further optimize the data exchange processes. The proposed policy can be improved by including other related parameters including memory management of sensor nodes, security, etc.

Author Contributions: Conceptualization, M.S., A.A. and M.T.; methodology, M.S. and A.A.; software, M.T.; validation, M.T., M.S.K. and M.S.; formal analysis, M.S. and M.S.K.; investigation, M.T.; resources, A.A. and M.T.; data curation, M.S.K., M.T. and M.S.; writing—original draft preparation, M.T.; writing—review and editing, M.S., M.S.K. and A.A.; visualization, M.S.; supervision, M.T.; project administration, A.A. and M.S.; funding acquisition, A.A. All authors have read and agreed to the published version of the manuscript.

Funding: This work was supported by the Deanship of Scientific Research, Qassim University under project (2023-FFT-2-HSRC-37648).

Data Availability Statement: The datasets used are available publicly.

Acknowledgments: Researchers would like to thank the Deanship of Scientific Research, Qassim University for funding publication of this project.

Conflicts of Interest: There is no conflict of interest to report.

References

1. Amadeo, M.; Campolo, C.; Quevedo, J.; Corujo, D.; Molinaro, A.; Iera, A.; Aguiar, R.L.; Vasilakos, A.V. Information-centric networking for the internet of things: Challenges and opportunities. *IEEE Netw.* **2016**, *30*, 92–100. [CrossRef]
2. Nour, B.; Sharif, K.; Li, F.; Biswas, S.; Moungla, H.; Guizani, M.; Wang, Y. A survey of Internet of Things communication using ICN: A use case perspective. *Comput. Commun.* **2019**, *142*, 95–123. [CrossRef]
3. Quevedo, J.; Corujo, D.; Aguiar, R. Consumer driven information freshness approach for content centric networking. In Proceedings of the 2014 IEEE Conference on Computer Communications Workshops (INFOCOM WKSHPS), Toronto, ON, Canada, 27 April–2 May 2014; IEEE: Piscataway, NJ, USA, 2014; pp. 482–487.
4. Shajaiah, H.; Sengupta, A.; Abdelhadi, A.; Clancy, C. Performance Trade-offs in IoT Uplink Networks under Secrecy Constraints. In Proceedings of the 2019 IEEE 30th International Symposium on Personal, Indoor and Mobile Radio Communications (PIMRC Workshops), Istanbul, Turkey, 8 September 2019; IEEE: Piscataway, NJ, USA, 2019; pp. 1–6.
5. Abdullahi, I.; Arif, S.; Hassan, S. Survey on caching approaches in information centric networking. *J. Netw. Comput. Appl.* **2015**, *56*, 48–59. [CrossRef]
6. Din, I.U.; Hassan, S.; Khan, M.K.; Guizani, M.; Ghazali, O.; Habbal, A. Caching in information-centric networking: Strategies, challenges, and future research directions. *IEEE Commun. Surv. Tutor.* **2017**, *20*, 1443–1474. [CrossRef]
7. Alkhazaleh, M.; Aljunid, S.; Sabri, N. A review of caching strategies and its categorizations in information centric network. *J. Theor. Appl. Inf. Technol.* **2019**, *97*, 19.
8. Ascigil, O.; Reñé, S.; Xylomenos, G.; Psaras, I.; Pavlou, G. A keyword-based ICN-IoT platform. In Proceedings of the 4th ACM Conference on Information-Centric Networking, Berlin, Germany, 26–28 September 2017; pp. 22–28.
9. Tarnoi, S.; Suksomboon, K.; Kumwilaisak, W.; Ji, Y. Performance of probabilistic caching and cache replacement policies for content-centric networks. In Proceedings of the 39th Annual IEEE Conference on Local Computer Networks, Edmonton, AB, Canada, 8–11 September 2014; IEEE: Piscataway, NJ, USA, 2014; pp. 99–106.
10. Bedi, G.; Venayagamoorthy, G.K.; Singh, R.; Brooks, R.R.; Wang, K.C. Review of Internet of Things (IoT) in electric power and energy systems. *IEEE Internet Things J.* **2018**, *5*, 847–870. [CrossRef]
11. Wortmann, F.; Flüchter, K. Internet of things. *Bus. Inf. Syst. Eng.* **2015**, *57*, 221–224. [CrossRef]
12. Bosunia, M.R.; Hasan, K.; Nasir, N.A.; Kwon, S.; Jeong, S.H. Efficient data delivery based on content-centric networking for Internet of Things applications. *Int. J. Distrib. Sens. Netw.* **2016**, *12*, 1550147716665518. [CrossRef]
13. Liu, X.; Ravindran, R.; Wang, G.Q. Information Centric Networking Based Service Centric Networking, 2019. U.S. Patent 10,194,414, 19 January, 2019.
14. Palattella, M.R.; Dohler, M.; Grieco, A.; Rizzo, G.; Torsner, J.; Engel, T.; Ladid, L. Internet of things in the 5G era: Enablers, architecture, and business models. *IEEE J. Sel. Areas Commun.* **2016**, *34*, 510–527. [CrossRef]
15. Lindgren, A.; Abdesslem, F.B.; Ahlgren, B.; Schelén, O.; Malik, A.M. Design choices for the IoT in information-centric networks. In Proceedings of the 2016 13th IEEE Annual Consumer Communications & Networking Conference (CCNC), Vegas, NV, USA, 9–12 January 2016; IEEE: Piscataway, NJ, USA, 2016; pp. 882–888.
16. Xu, C.; Wang, X. Transient content caching and updating with modified harmony search for Internet of Things. *Digit. Commun. Netw.* **2019**, *5*, 24–33. [CrossRef]
17. Arshad, S.; Azam, M.A.; Rehmani, M.H.; Loo, J. Recent advances in information-centric networking-based Internet of Things (ICN-IoT). *IEEE Internet Things J.* **2018**, *6*, 2128–2158. [CrossRef]
18. Siris, V.A.; Thomas, Y.; Polyzos, G.C. Supporting the IoT over integrated satellite-terrestrial networks using information-centric networking. In Proceedings of the 2016 8th IFIP International Conference on New Technologies, Mobility and Security (NTMS), Larnaca, Cyprus, 21–23 November 2016; IEEE: Piscataway, NJ, USA, 2016; pp. 1–5.
19. Malik, N.; Sardaraz, M.; Tahir, M.; Shah, B.; Ali, G.; Moreira, F. Energy-efficient load balancing algorithm for workflow scheduling in cloud data centers using queuing and thresholds. *Appl. Sci.* **2021**, *11*, 5849. [CrossRef]
20. Malik, S.; Tahir, M.; Sardaraz, M.; Alourani, A. A resource utilization prediction model for cloud data centers using evolutionary algorithms and machine learning techniques. *Appl. Sci.* **2022**, *12*, 2160. [CrossRef]
21. Mohiyuddin, A.; Javed, A.R.; Chakraborty, C.; Rizwan, M.; Shabbir, M.; Nebhen, J. Secure cloud storage for medical IoT data using adaptive neuro-fuzzy inference system. *Int. J. Fuzzy Syst.* **2022**, *24*, 1203–1215. [CrossRef]
22. Ahad, A.; Tahir, M.; Aman Sheikh, M.; Ahmed, K.I.; Mughees, A.; Numani, A. Technologies trend towards 5G network for smart health-care using IoT: A review. *Sensors* **2020**, *20*, 4047. [CrossRef]
23. Song, Y.; Ma, H.; Liu, L. TCCN: Tag-assisted content centric networking for Internet of Things. In Proceedings of the 2015 IEEE 16th International Symposium on A World of Wireless, Mobile and Multimedia Networks (WoWMoM), Boston, MA, USA, 14–17 June 2015; IEEE: Piscataway, NJ, USA, 2015; pp. 1–9.
24. Meddeb, M.; Dhraief, A.; Belghith, A.; Monteil, T.; Drira, K. Cache coherence in machine-to-machine information centric networks. In Proceedings of the 2015 IEEE 40th Conference on Local Computer Networks (LCN), Clearwater Beach, FL, USA, 26–29 October 2015; IEEE: Piscataway, NJ, USA, 2015; pp. 430–433.
25. Saba, T.; Haseeb, K.; Ahmed, I.; Rehman, A. Secure and energy-efficient framework using Internet of Medical Things for e-healthcare. *J. Infect. Public Health* **2020**, *13*, 1567–1575. [CrossRef]
26. Kaur, M.; Singh, D.; Kumar, V.; Gupta, B.B.; Abd El-Latif, A.A. Secure and energy efficient-based E-health care framework for green internet of things. *IEEE Trans. Green Commun. Netw.* **2021**, *5*, 1223–1231. [CrossRef]

27. Rehman, A.; Saba, T.; Haseeb, K.; Larabi Marie-Sainte, S.; Lloret, J. Energy-efficient IoT e-health using artificial intelligence model with homomorphic secret sharing. *Energies* **2021**, *14*, 6414. [CrossRef]
28. Ming, Z.; Xu, M.; Wang, D. Age-based cooperative caching in information-centric networking. In Proceedings of the 2014 23rd International Conference on Computer Communication and Networks (ICCCN), Shanghai, China, 4–7 August 2014; IEEE: Piscataway, NJ, USA, 2014; pp. 1–8.
29. Vural, S.; Navaratnam, P.; Wang, N.; Wang, C.; Dong, L.; Tafazolli, R. In-network caching of Internet-of-Things data. In Proceedings of the 2014 IEEE International Conference on Communications (ICC), Sydney, Australia, 10–14 June 2014; IEEE: Piscataway, NJ, USA, 2014; pp. 3185–3190.
30. Chen, C.; Jiang, J.; Fu, R.; Chen, L.; Li, C.; Wan, S. An intelligent caching strategy considering time-space characteristics in vehicular named data networks. *IEEE Trans. Intell. Transp. Syst.* **2021**, *23*, 19655–19667. [CrossRef]
31. Vural, S.; Wang, N.; Navaratnam, P.; Tafazolli, R. Caching transient data in internet content routers. *IEEE/ACM Trans. Netw.* **2016**, *25*, 1048–1061. [CrossRef]
32. Amadeo, M.; Campolo, C.; Molinaro, A. Internet of things via named data networking: The support of push traffic. In Proceedings of the 2014 International Conference and Workshop on the Network of the Future (NOF), Paris, France, 3–5 December 2014; IEEE: Piscataway, NJ, USA, 2014; pp. 1–5.
33. Zhang, Z.; Lung, C.H.; Lambadaris, I.; St-Hilaire, M. IoT data lifetime-based cooperative caching scheme for ICN-IoT networks. In Proceedings of the 2018 IEEE International Conference on Communications (ICC), Kansas City, MO, USA, 20–24 May 2018; IEEE: Piscataway, NJ, USA, 2018; pp. 1–7.
34. Niyato, D.; Kim, D.I.; Wang, P.; Song, L. A novel caching mechanism for Internet of Things (IoT) sensing service with energy harvesting. In Proceedings of the 2016 IEEE International Conference on Communications (ICC), Kuala Lumpur, Malaysia, 23–27 May 2016; IEEE: Piscataway, NJ, USA, 2016; pp. 1–6.
35. Shrimali, R.; Shah, H.; Chauhan, R. Proposed caching scheme for optimizing trade-off between freshness and energy consumption in name data networking based IoT. *Adv. Internet Things* **2017**, *7*, 11. [CrossRef]
36. Takatsuka, Y.; Nagao, H.; Yaguchi, T.; Hanai, M.; Shudo, K. A caching mechanism based on data freshness. In Proceedings of the 2016 International Conference on Big Data and Smart Computing (BigComp), Hong Kong, China, 18–20 January 2016; IEEE: Piscataway, NJ, USA, 2016; pp. 329–332.
37. Hail, M.A.; Amadeo, M.; Molinaro, A.; Fischer, S. Caching in named data networking for the wireless internet of things. In Proceedings of the 2015 International Conference on Recent Advances in Internet of Things (RIoT), Singapore, 7–9 April 2015; IEEE: Piscataway, NJ, USA, 2015; pp. 1–6.
38. Meddeb, M.; Dhraief, A.; Belghith, A.; Monteil, T.; Drira, K.; AlAhmadi, S. Cache freshness in named data networking for the internet of things. *Comput. J.* **2018**, *61*, 1496–1511. [CrossRef]
39. Sandvine Intelligent Broadband Networks. Identifying and Measuring Internet Traffic: Techniques and Considerations. An Industry. Whitepaper, Version 2.20. 2015. Available online: https://www.sandvine.com/resources?filter=.whitepapers (accessed on 26 October 2023).
40. Che, H.; Wang, Z.; Tung, Y. Analysis and design of hierarchical web caching systems. In Proceedings of the IEEE INFOCOM 2001, Conference on Computer Communications, Twentieth Annual Joint Conference of the IEEE Computer and Communications Society (Cat. No. 01CH37213), Anchorage, AK, USA, 22–26 April 2001; IEEE: Piscataway, NJ, USA, 2001; Volume 3, pp. 1416–1424.
41. Hefeeda, M.; Saleh, O. Traffic modeling and proportional partial caching for peer-to-peer systems. *Ieee/Acm Trans. Netw.* **2008**, *16*, 1447–1460. [CrossRef]
42. Koplenig, A. Using the parameters of the Zipf–Mandelbrot law to measure diachronic lexical, syntactical and stylistic changes—A large-scale corpus analysis. *Corpus Linguist. Linguist. Theory* **2018**, *14*, 1–34. [CrossRef]
43. Jacobson, V.; Smetters, D.K.; Thornton, J.D.; Plass, M.F.; Briggs, N.H.; Braynard, R.L. Networking named content. In Proceedings of the 5th International Conference on Emerging Networking Experiments and Technologies, Rome, Italy, 1–4 December 2009; pp. 1–12.
44. Saino, L.; Psaras, I.; Pavlou, G. Icarus: A caching simulator for information centric networking (ICN). In Proceedings of the SIMUTools 2014: 7th International ICST Conference on Simulation Tools and Techniques , Lisbon, Portugal, 17–19 March 2014; ICST: Lisbon, Portugal, 2014; Volume 7, pp. 66–75.
45. Bevywise IoT Simulator, 2021. Available online: https://www.bevywise.com/iot-simulator/help-document.html (accessed on 19 July 2021).
46. Hady, A.A.; Ghubaish, A.; Salman, T.; Unal, D.; Jain, R. Intrusion detection system for healthcare systems using medical and network data: A comparison study. *IEEE Access* **2020**, *8*, 106576–106584. [CrossRef]
47. Duan, P.; Jia, Y.; Liang, L.; Rodriguez, J.; Huq, K.M.S.; Li, G. Space-reserved cooperative caching in 5G heterogeneous networks for industrial IoT. *IEEE Trans. Ind. Inform.* **2018**, *14*, 2715–2724. [CrossRef]

48. Jin, H.; Xu, D.; Zhao, C.; Liang, D. Information-centric mobile caching network frameworks and caching optimization: A survey. *Eurasip J. Wirel. Commun. Netw.* **2017**, *2017*, 1–32. [CrossRef]
49. Naeem, M.A.; Ali, R.; Kim, B.S.; Nor, S.A.; Hassan, S. A periodic caching strategy solution for the smart city in information-centric Internet of Things. *Sustainability* **2018**, *10*, 2576. [CrossRef]

applied sciences

MDPI

Article

Machine Learning for COVID-19 and Influenza Classification during Coexisting Outbreaks

Iris Viana dos Santos Santana [1,†], Álvaro Sobrinho [2,*,†], Leandro Dias da Silva [1,†] and Angelo Perkusich [3,†]

1 Computing Institute, Federal University of Alagoas, Maceió 57072-260, Brazil; ivss@ic.ufal.br (I.V.d.S.S.); leandrodias@ic.ufal.br (L.D.d.S.)
2 Center for Technological Innovation and Entrepreneurship, Federal University of the Agreste of Pernambuco, Garanhuns 55292-270, Brazil
3 Virtus Research, Development and Innovation Center, Federal University of Campina Grande, Campina Grande 58429-000, Brazil; perkusic@virtus.ufcg.edu.br
* Correspondence: alvaro.alvares@ufape.edu.br; Tel.: +55-87-9-8149-3955
† These authors contributed equally to this work.

Abstract: This study compares the performance of machine learning models for selecting COVID-19 and influenza tests during coexisting outbreaks in Brazil, avoiding the waste of resources in healthcare units. We used COVID-19 and influenza datasets from Brazil to train the Decision Tree (DT), Multilayer Perceptron (MLP), Gradient Boosting Machine (GBM), Random Forest (RF), eXtreme Gradient Boosting (XGBoost), K-Nearest Neighbors, Support Vector Machine (SVM), and Logistic Regression algorithms. Moreover, we tested the models using the 10-fold cross-validation method to increase confidence in the results. During the experiments, the GBM, DT, RF, XGBoost, and SVM models showed the best performances, with similar results. The high performance of tree-based models is relevant for the classification of COVID-19 and influenza because they are usually easier to interpret, positively impacting the decision-making of health professionals.

Keywords: COVID-19; influenza; machine learning

Citation: Viana dos Santos Santana, I.; Sobrinho, Á.; Silva, L.D.d.; Perkusich, A. Machine Learning for COVID-19 and Influenza Classification during Coexisting Outbreaks. *Appl. Sci.* **2023**, *13*, 11518. https://doi.org/10.3390/app132011518

Academic Editor: Stefano Silvestri and Francesco Gargiulo

Received: 22 August 2023
Revised: 16 October 2023
Accepted: 18 October 2023
Published: 20 October 2023

1. Introduction

The control of outbreaks of viral infectious diseases in Brazil presents a pertinent challenge, given the size of the population, population density, social habits, and constrained testing strategies with limited test availability [1]. This challenge is further amplified when simultaneous outbreaks of diseases occur, such as COVID-19 and influenza [2]. Therefore, studies are needed to assist in mitigating issues associated with concurrent outbreaks of such diseases. Due to their constrained testing resources, test prioritization is a pertinent public health strategy for low- and middle-income countries.

Machine Learning (ML) models can be a foundation for developing eHealth and mHealth systems [3–5]. These systems can support healthcare professionals and policymakers in test prioritization. To facilitate real-world clinical application and integration into the current clinical workflow, classification models can be made accessible, and attribute relevance information can be leveraged through web services for consumption by a healthcare system. These eHealth and mHealth systems should provide classification results to healthcare professionals through clear and concise graphical user interfaces. Thus, the direct interpretability of the ML models is crucial to enhance the confidence of healthcare professionals in the classification results [6]. For instance, healthcare systems of Brazilian public healthcare units can reuse models deployed by web services to prioritize scarce testing resources.

Amidst the COVID-19 pandemic, the challenge of testing resource scarcity became evident in numerous countries, such as Brazil [7]. Brazil's first COVID-19 case occurred in March 2020, and over an extended period, the Ministry of Health reported a consistent increase in confirmed cases and fatalities. The Brazilian government reported over 30 million COVID-19 cases and over 664,000 fatalities. Considering Brazil's most recent data from the Ministry of Health, from January to September 2023, the unfortunate toll of COVID-19 resulted in over 12,000 individuals (https://covid.saude.gov.br/, accessed on 10 October 2023).

The limited number of tests becomes even more critical when concurrent outbreaks of viral infectious diseases (concomitant outbreaks) occur. During the most challenging pandemic phases, the Brazilian population faced at least two coexisting outbreaks of viral infectious diseases: COVID-19 and influenza. Therefore, it is pertinent to assist policymakers in formulating solutions to address concurrent outbreaks of viral infectious diseases (present and future).

This article extends our previous research [8] by presenting ML models to assist in test prioritization based on symptoms during concurrent outbreaks of COVID-19 and influenza in Brazil. To our knowledge, no prior studies are experimenting with Brazilian datasets for COVID-19 and influenza classification in this context. In the clinical scenario we envision, symptomatic patients present themselves at the hospital's testing site during a coexisting outbreak of COVID-19 and influenza. Before conducting tests for COVID-19 or influenza, which can be limited resources in certain countries, healthcare professionals can gather patient information as input data for an ML model. This approach can empower healthcare providers to make more informed decisions about which test to administer to specific patients, optimizing resource allocation and patient care.

We implemented ML models that rely on supervised learning, employing the following algorithms: Decision Tree (DT), Multilayer Perceptron (MLP), Gradient Boosting Machine (GBM), Random Forest (RF), eXtreme Gradient Boosting (XGBoost), K-Nearest Neighbors (KNN), Support Vector Machine (SVM), and Logistic Regression (LR). To address our multi-class problem, which involves distinguishing between COVID-19, non-COVID-19, influenza, and non-influenza cases, we conducted training and testing of algorithms using datasets containing demographic attributes and symptom information. This approach reduces the necessity for expensive exams (e.g., computed tomography scans).

The remainder of this article is structured as follows. Section 2 discusses the materials and methods, encompassing data collection, preprocessing, attribute selection, validation procedures, and details about the algorithms employed. Section 3 presents and discusses our results. Section 4 concludes from our findings and presents future research directions.

2. Related Works

Studies on viral infection outbreaks are relevant for public administration (for instance, in the context of surveillance systems) from a diagnostic standpoint. For instance, Son et al. [9] used a South Korean time series of influenza incidence to detect initial outbreaks, aiming to assist in policy formulation for control. Indeed, a pandemic presents a challenging scenario. In another study, Kumar [10] analyzed and enhanced the monitoring of COVID-19 in India by cluster analysis, offering insights into how the disease affected Indian states. The authors considered a total of twenty-eight states and eight Indian territories.

The existing literature also offers studies that explore the concurrent outbreaks of COVID-19 and influenza. For instance, Aftab et al. [11] experimented with deep-learning models for COVID-19 and influenza classification during coexisting outbreaks based on chest X-ray images. Li et al. [12] applied an XGBoost model to detect patients with both COVID-19 and influenza. The authors used clinical data, including laboratory test results, to train the XGBoost and baseline algorithms.

In another study, Zhou et al. [13] used data from patients at Zhongnan Hospital of Wuhan University to implement an XGBoost model. The authors also considered symptoms and laboratory test results when training the algorithm.

Furthermore, Elbasi et al. [14] addressed the classification of influenza and COVID-19 by employing the Bayes network, naive Bayes, locally weighted learning, MLP, and RF algorithms. Like the studies above, the authors used demographic data, symptoms, risk factors, and laboratory test results for training the ML models.

Phu et al. [15] compared the XGBoost and RF algorithms for classifying influenza and COVID-19, considering symptoms and laboratory test results. Their findings indicated that the XGBoost model outperformed RF.

Nevertheless, the need for expensive laboratory test results could limit the practical application of the previously proposed models, particularly when considering low- and middle-income populations. Thus, using Brazilian datasets, our study investigates the performance of ML models with different characteristics (e.g., tree-based and distance-based approaches) by only considering demographic data and reported symptoms.

3. Materials and Methods

This study considers data preprocessing, creation of new datasets, attribute selection, 10-fold cross-validation, statistical comparisons, and attribute importance. The following sections present an overview of these steps.

3.1. Data Collection and Preprocessing

Data collection is not considered a contribution of this study. The raw data used in this study was collected by the public health agency of Campina Grande, located in the Paraíba State of Northeast Brazil. This public agency receives information from all COVID-19 tests conducted in Campina Grande [8]. To ensure patient privacy, the agency's staff removed patient identification details, and the de-identified data were then made available for reuse in this study. The raw dataset contains various categorical features, including information about health professionals, security professionals, ethnicity, test types, symptoms (e.g., fever, sore throat, dyspnea, olfactory disorders, cough, coryza, taste disorders, and headache), additional symptoms, test results, comorbidities, test status, and symptom descriptions. Therefore, raw data from 55,676 Brazilian individuals were preprocessed to establish new datasets containing information on symptomatic patients tested for COVID-19.

Additionally, we gathered data from a sample of 14,570 Brazilian individuals, which included information about symptomatic patients who underwent testing for influenza. As for COVID-19, the tests encompassed Reverse Transcription Polymerase Chain Reaction (RT-PCR) and rapid tests (antibody and antigen). We sourced information from the OpenDatasus platform (https://opendatasus.saude.gov.br/dataset/srag-2021-a-2023, accessed on 10 October 2023) the Brazilian Ministry of Health provided for this dataset.

We performed data preprocessing using the Python programming language. During this preprocessing stage, we applied string-matching algorithms to address inconsistencies in the raw dataset. One notable inconsistency we addressed was the presence of empty columns related to symptoms, as the same symptoms were available within a column designated for general symptom descriptions. We also excluded certain instances from the initial samples based on our predefined exclusion criteria.

For the COVID-19 dataset, these criteria encompassed patients with incomplete tests or undefined final classifications (12,929 instances), duplicated instances (12,929 instances), outliers resulting from input errors (10,408 instances), test types that were not RT-PCR or rapid (771 instances), individuals with undefined gender (27 instances), and asymptomatic patients (11,269 instances). The exclusion of asymptomatic patients was necessary because the algorithms relied on demographic characteristics and symptom data for accurate processing. We applied the same criteria to the influenza dataset. For example, the raw dataset, which was unbalanced, contained 5954 instances. After filtering and removal, the dataset was reduced to 4212 instances.

We filtered the data to generate new datasets, including patients tested for COVID-19 and influenza. This process ensures that a patient tested positive for COVID-19 also tested negative for influenza. However, we acknowledge that a patient can be infected with both diseases simultaneously, even though this scenario is more uncommon. We did not consider this scenario in our study. The following attributes were considered: respiratory distress, vomiting, saturation, fatigue, diarrhea, abdominal pain, gender, healthcare professional status, fever, sore throat, dyspnea, olfactory disorder, cough, runny nose, taste disorder, and headache.

We formulated six preprocessed datasets by combining COVID-19 and influenza data: unbalanced RT-PCR, balanced RT-PCR, unbalanced rapid, balanced rapid, both unbalanced, and both balanced. Thus, during the preprocessing, we oversampled the data by applying the near-miss technique [16]. In the datasets, the numbers 0 and 1 denote positive and negative results for COVID-19, while 2 and 3 represent positive and negative outcomes for influenza. In the balanced RT-PCR datasets, each class contains 916 samples, the rapid test datasets have 646 samples for each class, and the combined datasets of both tests contain 1564 samples. For the unbalanced sets, the RT-PCR dataset consists of 0 (916 samples), 1 (1863 samples), 2 (1502 samples), and 3 (1423 samples). The rapid test dataset includes class 0 (648 samples), 1 (16,594 samples), 2 (691 samples), and 3 (646 samples). In the combined dataset of both tests, class 0 has 1564 samples, class 1 has 18,457 samples, class 2 has 2106 samples, and class 3 has 2148 samples.

3.2. Attribute Selection

We applied the chi-squared test to the new datasets to assist in attribute selection with a $p < 0.01$ threshold, examining attribute relevance for classification tasks through dependence and independence relationships [17]. The chi-squared test for independence was employed to compare four variables within a contingency table, determining whether they are related.

3.3. Validation Method and Algorithms

We used the 10-fold cross-validation method with five repetitions to validate the ML models MLP, GBM, DT, RF, XGBoost, KNN, SVM, and LR (weak/strong regularization). An MLP is a feedforward neural network, meaning data travels in a single direction [18]. This model comprises one (or more) hidden neurons between the layers related to inputs and outputs.

In contrast, the GBM is a decision tree with a fixed size that uses a boosting strategy [19]. This algorithm features integrated attribute selection, producing an estimation, approximation, or the function denoted as $F^*(x)$, which maps the input x to the output y while minimizing the expected value by using a loss function $L(y, F(x))$ across the joint distribution [20].

A DT algorithm commonly applies a divide-and-conquer strategy to construct a directed acyclic graph, where rule splitting is determined by maximizing information gain [21]. DT algorithms such as C4.5 include internal attribute selection, and the information gain is influenced by the concept of entropy, which quantifies the uncertainty or randomness associated with a discrete random variable. DT offers the advantage of straightforward result interpretation by following the decision rules of a single tree [22–24].

Similarly, the RF relies on classification and regression tree principles while following specific guidelines for tree growth, combination, self-testing, and post-processing [25]. The algorithm includes an embedded attribute selection mechanism, evaluated using the Gini impurity criterion index. RF also facilitates a straightforward interpretation of results from the individual trees within the ensemble.

Relying on a different approach, KNN is a distance-based algorithm that classifies new instances using the distance from neighbor instances [26]. Given an instance as a point in space, KNN computes the distance between two points.

SVM is an algorithm designed to handle binary data using a linear separator to maximize the distance between data points. The algorithm considers concepts such as the separation hyperplane, maximum margin hyperplane, and soft margin [18].

Lastly, LR extends linear regression, assessing the connections between variables in probabilistic classifications. The algorithm employs a sigmoid function to model these relationships and predict the probability of class membership [27]. Regularization can also be employed to prevent overfitting. We used the LR algorithm as a baseline to compare the linear model with the above ML approaches.

Moreover, we calculated the mean results for classification metrics, including precision, accuracy, recall, Brier score, Receiver Operating Characteristic Curve (ROC), and Area Under the Precision-Recall (PR) curve. We used the random search method to fine-tune the hyperparameters of the algorithms, aiming to enhance their performance. Furthermore, we analyzed recall-related outcomes using the Friedman and Nemenyi statistical tests to improve the comparisons among the ML models [28]. The Friedman test is a valuable statistical method for identifying differences between models. The Nemenyi test is pertinent for grouping classification models based on assessing differences through many comparisons. We determined the Critical Difference (CD) between the ML models by employing the Nemenyi test, with a significance level set at $\alpha = 0.1$. If the performance differences among models are within an interval more minor than the CD, it suggests that the models are indistinguishable from each other [8].

3.4. Attribute Importance

Finally, we performed attribute ranking for each ML model with the best performance through the permutation-based attribute importance method, which provided mean importance and Standard Deviation (SD) as the evaluation criteria. The attribute ranking relied on the permutation feature importance method to gauge the importance of an attribute by evaluating the decrease in the model's score, thereby assessing the degree of reliance of the model on that particular attribute [29]. Our discussions center around the top five attributes with the highest importance.

4. Results and Discussion

The COVID-19 and influenza datasets were merged to form a unified dataset for implementing the models. As mentioned in Section 2, the numbers 0 and 1 indicated positive and negative cases of COVID-19, while 2 and 3 indicated positive and negative cases of influenza. The balanced RT-PCR datasets contained 916 instances for each class, the rapid test datasets contained 646 instances for each class, and both tests combined included 1564 instances for each class. The unbalanced RT-PCR datasets contained class 1 (1863), 2 (1502), 3 (1423), and 0 (916); the rapid test datasets contained class 1 (16,594), 2 (691), 0 (648), and 3 (646); and both tests combined included class 1 (18,457), 3 (2148), 2 (2106), and 0 (1564).

The tree-based models, considering the combination of COVID-19 and influenza, are among those that exhibited superior outcomes. Table 1 presents the results of the 10-fold cross-validation. We computed precision, recall, accuracy, and Brier score. LR and LRR denote weak and strong regularization models, respectively.

Tables 2 and 3 present the mean importance and SD for attributes considering the tree-based models and MLP and SVM, respectively. Table 4 displays the top five most significant attributes for test prioritization. Such analyses consider the imbalanced datasets.

Throughout the experiments, attributes were not removed based on the chi-squared test results, as all attributes exhibited dependence. To provide a more detailed illustration of the outcomes, for instance, in Figures 1 and 2, the average results for the ROC and PR curves using cross-validation for the decision tree model are depicted, employing both the balanced and unbalanced datasets of both tests, respectively. As mentioned, we conducted a 10-fold cross-validation five times to enhance our confidence in the results. We presented the results for each of the four classes of our multi-class problem.

Table 1. Performance of the classification models.

Database	Model	Precision	Recall	Accuracy	Brier Score
PCR Imbalanced (Balanced)	MLP	82.44 (82.72)	82.72 (82.26)	82.37 (82.25)	0.088 (0.088)
	GBM	82.59 (82.48)	82.92 (82.14)	82.54 (82.14)	0.08 (0.089)
	RF	83.04 (82.96)	83.12 (82.47)	82.84 (82.47)	0.085 (0.087)
	DT	82.46 (82.37)	82.60 (81.76)	82.27 (81.76)	0.088 (0.091)
	XGBoost	82.73 (82.67)	82.99 (82.27)	82.65 (82.27)	0.086 (0.088)
	KNN	82.16 (82.35)	82.22 (81.51)	82.07 (81.61)	0.089 (0.092)
	SVM	82.23 (81.93)	82.55 (81.57)	82.27 (81.57)	0.088 (0.092)
	LRR	71.76 (71.65)	70.13 (70.78)	71.37 (70.78)	0.143 (0.145)
	LR	72.29 (72.29)	70.85 (71.38)	72.02 (71.38)	0.139 (0.143)
Rapid Imbalanced (Balanced)	MLP	85.30 (81.40)	79.41 (81.40)	96.44 (81.40)	0.171 (0.092)
	GBM	85.61 (81.14)	79.40 (81.15)	96.46 (81.15)	0.017 (0.094)
	RF	86.38 (81.50)	79.25 (81.56)	96.53 (81.56)	0.017 (0.092)
	DT	85.42 (80.99)	79.61 (80.93)	96.53 (80.93)	0.017 (0.095)
	XGBoost	85.76 (80.89)	79.32 (80.96)	96.47 (80.96)	0.017 (0.095)
	KNN	87.81 (80.52)	78.93 (79.90)	96.56 (79.90)	0.017 (0.100)
	SVM	86.12 (80.97)	79.11 (81.11)	96.49 (81.11)	0.017 (0.094)
	LRR	73.32 (68.78)	55.60 (68.98)	93.24 (68.98)	0.033 (0.155)
	LR	72.42 (70.70)	58.37 (70.24)	93.50 (70.24)	0.032 (0.148)
Both imbalanced (Balanced)	MLP	85.93 (80.95)	71.11 (80.47)	90.73 (80.95)	0.046 (0.097)
	GBM	85.89 (81.14)	71.16 (80.64)	90.70 (80.64)	0.046 (0.096)
	RF	86.85 (81.50)	71.63 (80.95)	90.96 (80.95)	0.045 (0.095)
	DT	85.60 (80.74)	71.66 (80.13)	90.76 (80.13)	0.046 (0.099)
	XGBoost	86.07 (81.28)	71.39 (80.77)	90.79 (80.77)	0.046 (0.096)
	KNN	82.23 (80.33)	66.15 (79.58)	88.98 (79.58)	0.055 (0.102)
	SVM	86.43 (80.54)	70.95 (80.11)	90.77 (80.11)	0.046 (0.099)
	LRR	68.87 (70.16)	52.82 (70.10)	85.54 (70.10)	0.072 (0.149)
	LR	71.16 (71.24)	55.39 (71.22)	86.29 (71.22)	0.068 (0.143)

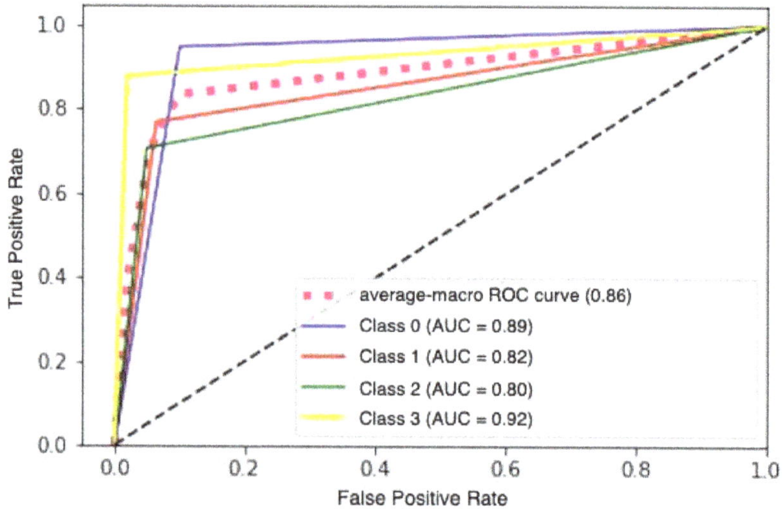

Figure 1. Average ROC curve for each class of the DT model using both balanced tests.

Table 2. Mean importance and SD for attributes in tree-based classification models using the imbalanced datasets.

Dataset	Feature	GBM	DT	RF	XGBoost
PCR	Respiratory distress	0.141 (0.008)	0.155 (0.008)	0.156 (0.008)	0.144 (0.008)
	Vomit	0.037 (0.004)	0.036 (0.004)	0.035 (0.004)	0.037 (0.004)
	Saturation	0.149 (0.007)	0.166 (0.008)	0.161 (0.007)	0.154 (0.008)
	Fatigue	0.055 (0.006)	0.047 (0.005)	0.057 (0.006)	0.058 (0.006)
	Diarrhea	0.028 (0.003)	0.024 (0.003)	0.027 (0.003)	0.028 (0.003)
	Abdominal pain	0.013 (0.003)	0.006 (0.002)	0.011 (0.002)	0.013 (0.002)
	Gender	0.138 (0.007)	0.133 (0.007)	0.137 (0.007)	0.137 (0.007)
	Health professional	0.029 (0.003)	0.026 (0.002)	0.029 (0.003)	0.031 (0.003)
	Fever	0.235 (0.009)	0.230 (0.008)	0.234 (0.008)	0.230 (0.008)
	Sore throat	0.077 (0.006)	0.073 (0.005)	0.075 (0.005)	0.079 (0.005)
	Dyspnoea	0.098 (0.007)	0.095 (0.006)	0.093 (0.007)	0.092 (0.007)
	Smell disorder	0.009 (0.002)	0.017 (0.002)	0.004 (0.002)	0.010 (0.002)
	Cough	0.105 (0.007)	0.101 (0.007)	0.102 (0.007)	0.102 (0.007)
	Runny nose	0.007 (0.002)	0.006 (0.002)	0.007 (0.002)	0.005 (0.002)
	Taste disorder	0.019 (0.002)	0.014 (0.002)	0.009 (0.002)	0.010 (0.002)
	Headache	0.012 (0.002)	0.012 (0.002)	0.013 (0.002)	0.008 (0.002)
Rapid	Respiratory distress	0.109 (0.007)	0.113 (0.007)	0.156 (0.008)	0.121 (0.008)
	Vomit	0.019 (0.004)	0.017 (0.003)	0.015 (0.004)	0.020 (0.004)
	Saturation	0.140 (0.008)	0.194 (0.008)	0.165 (0.008)	0.154 (0.007)
	Fatigue	0.056 (0.005)	0.072 (0.006)	0.055 (0.005)	0.055 (0.005)
	Diarrhea	0.013 (0.003)	0.012 (0.003)	0.009 (0.002)	0.015 (0.004)
	Abdominal pain	0.004 (0.002)	0.008 (0.002)	0.003 (0.001)	0.007 (0.002)
	Gender	0.096 (0.009)	0.096 (0.010)	0.100 (0.009)	0.095 (0.008)
	Health professional	0.013 (0.003)	0.014 (0.002)	0.015 (0.002)	0.018 (0.003)
	Fever	0.148 (0.008)	0.158 (0.009)	0.148 (0.007)	0.152 (0.007)
	Sore throat	0.080 (0.006)	0.073 (0.006)	0.072 (0.006)	0.075 (0.006)
	Dyspnoea	0.130 (0.008)	0.144 (0.009)	0.136 (0.008)	0.136 (0.008)
	Smell disorder	0.083 (0.005)	0.096 (0.006)	0.087 (0.006)	0.084 (0.005)
	Cough	0.075 (0.007)	0.086 (0.008)	0.072 (0.007)	0.067 (0.008)
	Runny nose	0.054 (0.004)	0.046 (0.003)	0.039 (0.003)	0.048 (0.003)
	Taste disorder	0.042 (0.004)	0.036 (0.004)	0.023 (0.004)	0.039 (0.004)
	Headache	0.047 (0.004)	0.053 (0.004)	0.045 (0.004)	0.055 (0.004)
Both	Respiratory distress	0.140 (0.004)	0.148 (0.004)	0.147 (0.004)	0.143 (0.005)
	Vomit	0.035 (0.003)	0.041 (0.004)	0.039 (0.004)	0.038 (0.003)
	Saturation	0.171 (0.006)	0.191 (0.005)	0.190 (0.006)	0.184 (0.006)
	Fatigue	0.053 (0.003)	0.062 (0.003)	0.057 (0.003)	0.055 (0.003)
	Diarrhea	0.017 (0.002)	0.017 (0.002)	0.015 (0.002)	0.018 (0.002)
	Abdominal pain	0.018 (0.002)	0.010 (0.002)	0.010 (0.002)	0.018 (0.002)
	Gender	0.123 (0.005)	0.126 (0.006)	0.121 (0.005)	0.119 (0.005)
	Health professional	0.020 (0.002)	0.016 (0.002)	0.019 (0.002)	0.020 (0.002)
	Fever	0.182 (0.006)	0.187 (0.006)	0.183 (0.007)	0.179 (0.007)
	Sore throat	0.084 (0.004)	0.087 (0.004)	0.082 (0.004)	0.083 (0.004)
	Dyspnoea	0.103 (0.005)	0.108 (0.005)	0.103 (0.005)	0.107 (0.005)
	Smell disorder	0.047 (0.003)	0.053 (0.003)	0.039 (0.003)	0.048 (0.003)
	Cough	0.086 (0.004)	0.088 (0.004)	0.087 (0.005)	0.084 (0.004)
	Runny nose	0.017 (0.001)	0.016 (0.001)	0.017 (0.002)	0.016 (0.001)
	Taste disorder	0.024 (0.003)	0.027 (0.003)	0.019 (0.003)	0.024 (0.003)
	Headache	0.035 (0.003)	0.033 (0.002)	0.028 (0.003)	0.031 (0.003)

Table 3. Mean importance and SD for attributes in MLP and SVM models using the imbalanced datasets.

Dataset	Feature	MLP	SVM
RT-PCR	Respiratory distress	0.139 (0.009)	0.135 (0.008)
	Vomit	0.041 (0.005)	0.039 (0.004)
	Saturation	0.146 (0.008)	0.152 (0.007)
	Fatigue	0.056 (0.005)	0.059 (0.005)
	Diarrhea	0.025 (0.003)	0.028 (0.003)
	Abdominal pain	0.015 (0.003)	0.015 (0.003)
	Gender	0.137 (0.007)	0.125 (0.006)
	Health professional	0.043 (0.003)	0.021 (0.002)
	Fever	0.230 (0.008)	0.219 (0.008)
	Sore throat	0.081 (0.007)	0.069 (0.006)
	Dyspnoea	0.100 (0.006)	0.080 (0.006)
	Smell disorder	0.013 (0.003)	0.010 (0.002)
	Cough	0.105 (0.007)	0.098 (0.007)
	Runny nose	0.010 (0.002)	0.003 (0.002)
	Taste disorder	0.018 (0.002)	0.014 (0.002)
	Headache	0.020 (0.002)	0.007 (0.002)
Rapid	Respiratory distress	0.090 (0.007)	0.092 (0.007)
	Vomit	0.019 (0.004)	0.019 (0.004)
	Saturation	0.132 (0.007)	0.125 (0.007)
	Fatigue	0.067 (0.005)	0.061 (0.006)
	Diarrhea	0.018 (0.003)	0.017 (0.004)
	Abdominal pain	0.011 (0.003)	0.007 (0.002)
	Gender	0.090 (0.009)	0.076 (0.007)
	Health professional	0.017 (0.003)	0.016 (0.003)
	Fever	0.141 (0.007)	0.143 (0.007)
	Sore throat	0.064 (0.006)	0.062 (0.006)
	Dyspnoea	0.129 (0.008)	0.118 (0.007)
	Smell disorder	0.074 (0.005)	0.075 (0.005)
	Cough	0.071 (0.007)	0.068 (0.008)
	Runny nose	0.041 (0.003)	0.047 (0.003)
	Taste disorder	0.032 (0.004)	0.034 (0.003)
	Headache	0.049 (0.005)	0.044 (0.004)
Both	Respiratory distress	0.123 (0.005)	0.123 (0.005)
	Vomit	0.038 (0.003)	0.035 (0.004)
	Saturation	0.146 (0.005)	0.157 (0.006)
	Fatigue	0.052 (0.003)	0.047 (0.003)
	Diarrhea	0.017 (0.002)	0.016 (0.002)
	Abdominal pain	0.020 (0.002)	0.018 (0.002)
	Gender	0.122 (0.005)	0.109 (0.005)
	Health professional	0.025 (0.002)	0.018 (0.002)
	Fever	0.180 (0.006)	0.173 (0.006)
	Sore throat	0.083 (0.004)	0.083 (0.004)
	Dyspnoea	0.108 (0.005)	0.092 (0.005)
	Smell disorder	0.058 (0.003)	0.040 (0.002)
	Cough	0.089 (0.005)	0.079 (0.005)
	Runny nose	0.023 (0.02)	0.017 (0.001)
	Taste disorder	0.030 (0.003)	0.022 (0.003)
	Headache	0.048 (0.003)	0.028 (0.003)

Table 4. The five most relevant attributes for test prioritization when dealing with imbalanced datasets.

Dataset	Model	Top 1	Top 2	Top 3	Top 4	Top 5
PCR	MLP	Fever	Saturation	Respiratory distress	Gender	Cough
	GBM	Fever	Saturation	Respiratory distress	Gender	Cough
	RF	Fever	Saturation	Gender	Respiratory distress	Cough
	DT	Saturation	Fever	Gender	Cough	Respiratory distress
	XGBoost	Saturation	Health professional	Respiratory distress	Fever	Fatigue
	SVM	Fever	Saturation	Respiratory distress	Gender	Cough
Rapid	MLP	Fever	Saturation	Dyspnoea	Respiratory distress	Gender
	GBM	Saturation	Dyspnoea	Fever	Smell disorder	Respiratory distress
	RF	Saturation	Fever	Dyspnoea	Fatigue	Gender
	DT	Fever	Saturation	Gender	Respiratory distress	Smell disorder
	XGBoost	Saturation	Smell disorder	Runny nose	Headache	Respiratory distress
	SVM	Fever	Saturation	Dyspnoea	Respiratory distress	Gender
Both	MLP	Fever	Saturation	Respiratory distress	Gender	Dyspnoea
	GBM	Diarrhea	Abdominal pain	Taste disorder	Headache	Runny nose
	RF	Abdominal pain	Diarrhea	Runny nose	Headache	Health professional
	DT	Health professional	Abdominal pain	Headache	Taste disorder	Runny nose
	XGBoost	Taste disorder	Cough	Gender	Dyspnoea	Sore throat
	SVM	Fever	Saturation	Respiratory distress	Gender	Dyspnoea

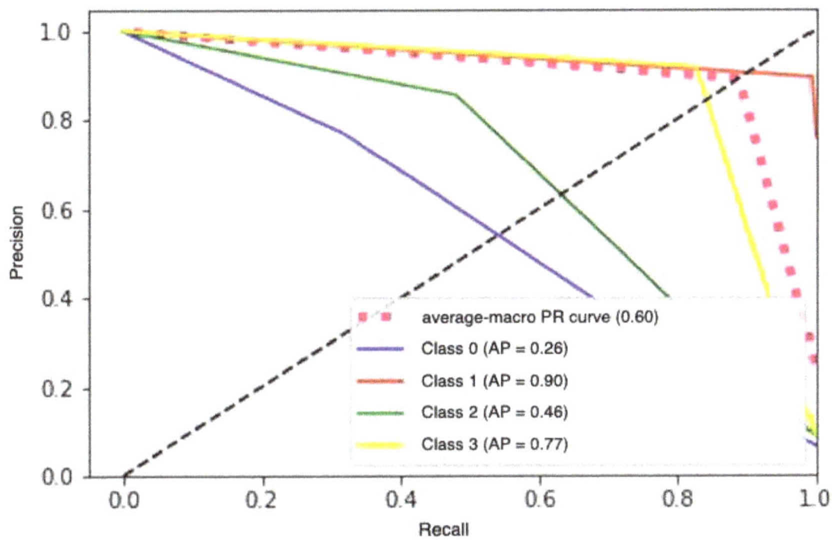

Figure 2. Average precision-recall curve for each class of the DT model using both unbalanced tests.

The ROC and PR curves were computed using five random folds for each class. The tree-based models exhibited the highest Average Precision (AP) values, ranging from 58% to 86%, using the balanced dataset with both tests. Additionally, AP values ranged from 30% to 92% using the unbalanced dataset with both types of tests.

Afterward, using the Friedman and Nemenyi tests increased confidence in validating the ML models. They were compared using the six COVID-19 and influenza datasets. The comparison predominantly concentrates on recall outcomes due to the significant adverse effects of false negatives in COVID-19 and influenza applications. Figure 3 depicts the recall results for the employed datasets.

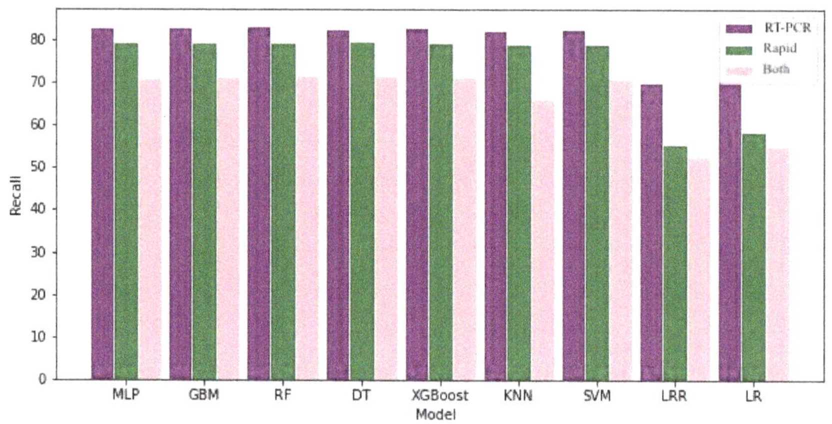

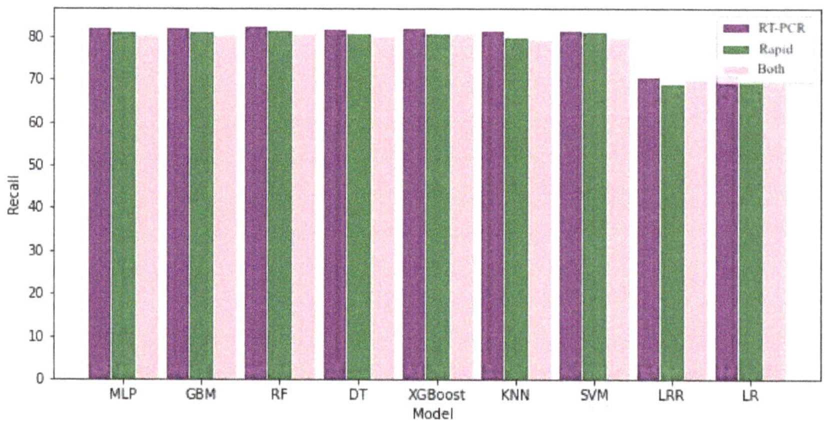

Figure 3. (**A**) Mean recall for the models using unbalanced datasets for RT-PCR, rapid, and both types. (**B**) Mean recall for the models using balanced datasets for RT-PCR, rapid, and both types.

The null hypothesis and the results were as follows: for unbalanced RT-PCR (t = 217.363), balanced RT-PCR (t = 231.788), unbalanced rapid (t = 234.098), balanced rapid (t = 188.243), unbalanced both datasets (t = 221.810), and balanced both datasets (t = 253.074). The results suggest that the difference in mean recall was likely statistically significant ($p < 0.05$). Additionally, depending on the dataset, MLP and GBM appeared to be statistically indistinguishable, as were DT, RF, XGBoost, KNN, and SVM.

Using the permutation-based attribute importance method across the six datasets, we ranked the most significant five attributes for the ML models, demonstrating the highest performance. Fever and oxygen saturation symptoms displayed higher mean importance values in the case of the balanced datasets for RT-PCR and rapid tests. However, the symptoms with mean importance values appeared more diverse when both tests were balanced.

As a result, the preprocessing of raw datasets facilitated the implementation, validation, and comparison of classification models with diverse characteristics, including using neural layers, tree ensembles, and data distance computation. This preprocessing also led to the public availability of patient data, including individuals tested as symptomatic using RT-PCR and rapid tests, as referenced in [8].

We conducted training and testing of the algorithms using both unbalanced and balanced datasets to improve data representativeness. When considering test-type grouping, the best classification metric results were achieved in both unbalanced and balanced scenarios for RT-PCR and rapid tests. While the classification model performances were similar for RT-PCR and rapid test scenarios, the RT-PCR testing scenario holds greater clinical relevance due to the high confidence associated with RT-PCR testing. The accuracy of RT-PCR testing enhances diagnostic confidence even if the patient has been tested in the early days after the onset of symptoms.

The recall metric is relevant in our context because of the adverse consequences of false negatives in clinical practice. We improved the quality of comparisons between ML models using the Friedman and Nemenyi tests, which relied on the recall performance across the six datasets.

The tree-based classification models examined in this study demonstrated superior performance and were grouped based on their classification metric outcomes and statistical test results. This observation is of particular importance because tree-based models are highly interpretable, which can positively influence the decision-making process of healthcare professionals. In clinical practice, the acceptance of ML-based systems increases when healthcare practitioners can easily comprehend and interpret the outputs of classification models to understand the decision-making logic, as referenced in [30].

Additionally, it is important to acknowledge that in a real-world scenario, the presence of asymptomatic patients may be seen as a limitation in the applicability of ML models [31]. However, in the context of this study, its relevance persists due to the presence of symptomatic cases that demand the attention of healthcare professionals and government authorities. Evaluating symptomatic patients remains crucial to avoid the inadvertent overuse of testing resources, especially in the face of concurrent disease outbreaks in Brazil caused by other viral infections (e.g., COVID-19 and influenza). Certain viral infections can present with similar symptoms, making it challenging for healthcare professionals to decide the appropriate type of testing needed.

A symptomatic patient with limited symptoms can pose challenges for ML models. However, attribute ranking and additional information, such as whether the patient has had contact with infected individuals, are valuable factors to supplement ML models. They provide additional context and data that can aid healthcare professionals and policymakers in making informed decisions.

Another limitation of this study is the number of ML models experimented with. However, we addressed this limitation by considering a set of well-established algorithms that cover various approaches, including tree-based models, linear regression, statistical learning, distance-based methods, and neural concepts.

5. Conclusions

The results emphasize the importance of employing ML models for test prioritization in Brazil during coexisting COVID-19 and influenza outbreaks, mainly focusing on non-expensive input data. The elevated performance of tree-based ML models holds significance for the healthcare domain due to their high interpretability reported in recent literature, which positively influences the final decision-making process of healthcare professionals.

Therefore, tree-based models have been identified as the most suitable ML models when considering the ease of interpretation and performance criterion. They can effectively aid in prioritizing the testing of symptomatic patients. The relevance of utilizing symptoms that do not require costly tests is evident, for instance, in underserved and hard-to-reach communities. These communities usually depend on public services to conduct expensive exams, which may only sometimes be promptly available.

Our experiments have demonstrated the viability of employing ML models to aid in prioritizing testing when concurrent outbreaks of COVID-19 and influenza occur. These

ML models can be seamlessly integrated into the clinical practice workflow at testing sites, enhancing the efficiency and effectiveness of the testing process. However, it is important to note that one limitation of our model is that it does not account for the scenario where a patient could be simultaneously infected with both COVID-19 and influenza. We recognize this as a significant aspect for future research and further development of our model.

Moreover, the solution proposed in this study holds the potential for scalability to decision support systems, considering the high number of existing viral infectious diseases. As a future endeavor, the intention is to develop a clinical decision support system based on the proposed approach, utilizing web technologies. Additionally, usability tests are planned, adhering to established standards in the literature, for the developed system to assess user-friendliness and perception, considering the potential diverse target audience for this type of system.

Author Contributions: Conceptualization, I.V.d.S.S., Á.S., L.D.d.S. and A.P.; Methodology, I.V.d.S.S.; Validation, I.V.d.S.S.; Investigation, I.V.d.S.S.; Writing—original draft, I.V.d.S.S., Á.S., L.D.d.S. and A.P.; Writing—review & editing, Á.S., L.D.d.S. and A.P. All authors have read and agreed to the published version of the manuscript.

Funding: The APC was funded by the VIRTUS Research, Development & Innovation Center, Federal University of Campina Grande (Paraíba/Brazil).

Institutional Review Board Statement: Not applicable.

Informed Consent Statement: Not applicable.

Data Availability Statement: The data presented in this study are openly available in OpenDatasus at [https://opendatasus.saude.gov.br/dataset/srag-2021-a-2023] and Mendeley Data at [https://doi.org/10.17632/b7zcgmmwx4.3].

Acknowledgments: We would like to thank VIRTUS Research, Development & Innovation Center, Federal University of Campina Grande (Paraíba/Brazil) and Alagoas Research Foundation for supporting this research.

Conflicts of Interest: The authors declare no conflict of interest.

References

1. Monteiro de Oliveira, M.; Fuller, T.L.; Brasil, P.; Gabaglia, C.R.; Nielsen-Saines, K. Controlling the COVID-19 pandemic in Brazil: A challenge of continental proportions. *Nat. Med.* **2020**, *26*, 1505–1506. [CrossRef] [PubMed]
2. Konala, V.M.; Adapa, S.; Gayam, V.; Naramala, S.; Daggubati, S.R.; Kammari, C.B.; Chenna, A. Co-infection with Influenza A and COVID-19. *Eur. J. Case Rep. Intern. Med.* **2020**, *7*, 001656. [CrossRef] [PubMed]
3. Istepanian, R.S.H.; Al-Anzi, T. m-Health 2.0: New perspectives on mobile health, machine learning and big data analytics. *Methods* **2018**, *151*, 34–40. [CrossRef] [PubMed]
4. da Silveira, A.C.M.; Sobrinho, Á.; Dias da Silva, L.; de Barros Costa, E.; Pinheiro, M.E.; Perkusich, A. Exploring Early Prediction of Chronic Kidney Disease Using Machine Learning Algorithms for Small and Imbalanced Datasets. *Appl. Sci.* **2022**, *12*, 3673. [CrossRef]
5. Sobrinho, A.; Queiroz, A.C.M.D.S.; Silva, L.D.D.; Costa, E.D.B.; Pinheiro, M.E.; Perkusich, A. Computer-Aided Diagnosis of Chronic Kidney Disease in Developing Countries: A Comparative Analysis of Machine Learning Techniques. *IEEE Access* **2020**, *8*, 25407–25419. [CrossRef]
6. Kar, K.; Kornblith, S.; Fedorenko, E. Interpretability of artificial neural network models in artificial intelligence versus neuroscience. *Nat. Mach. Intell.* **2022**, *4*, 1065–1067. [CrossRef]
7. Belard, A.; Buchman, T.; Forsberg, J.; Potter, B.K.; Dente, C.J.; Kirk, A.; Elster, E. Precision diagnosis: A view of the clinical decision support systems (CDSS) landscape through the lens of critical care. *J. Clin. Monit. Comput.* **2017**, *31*, 261–271. [CrossRef]
8. Viana Dos Santos Santana, Í.; Cm da Silveira, A.; Sobrinho, Á.; Chaves E Silva, L.; Dias da Silva, L.; Santos, D.F.S.; Gurjão, E.C.; Perkusich, A. Classification Models for COVID-19 Test Prioritization in Brazil: Machine Learning Approach. *J. Med. Internet Res.* **2021**, *8*, e27293. [CrossRef]
9. Son, W.S.; Park, J.E.; Kwon, O. Early detection of influenza outbreak using time derivative of incidence. *EPJ Data Sci.* **2020**, *9*, 28. [CrossRef]
10. Kumar, S. Monitoring Novel Corona Virus (COVID-19) Infections in India by Cluster Analysis. *Ann. Data Sci.* **2020**, *7*, 417–425. [CrossRef]
11. Aftab, M.; Amin, R.; Koundal, D.; Aldabbas, H.; Alouffi, B.; Iqbal, Z. Classification of COVID-19 and Influenza Patients Using Deep Learning. *Contrast Media Mol. Imaging* **2022**, *2022*, 8549707. [CrossRef] [PubMed]

12. Li, W.; Ma, J.; Shende, N.; Castaneda, G.; Chakladar, J.; Tsai, J.C.; Apostol, L.; Honda, C.O.; Xu, J.; Wong, L.M.; et al. Using machine learning of clinical data to diagnose COVID-19: A systematic review and meta-analysis. *BMC Med. Inform. Decis. Mak.* **2020** *20*, 247. [CrossRef]
13. Zhou, X.; Wang, Z.; Li, S.; Liu, T.; Wang, X.; Xia, J.; Zhao, Y. Machine Learning-Based Decision Model to Distinguish Between COVID-19 and Influenza: A Retrospective, Two-Centered, Diagnostic Study. *Risk Manag. Healthc. Policy* **2021**, *14*, 595–604 [CrossRef]
14. Elbasi, E.; Zreikat, A.; Mathew, S.; Topcu, A.E. Classification of influenza H1N1 and COVID-19 patient data using machine learning. In Proceedings of the 44th International Conference on Telecommunications and Signal Processing (TSP), Brno, Czech Republic, 26–28 July 2021; pp. 278–282.
15. Phu, D.N.; Vinh, P.C.; Quoc, N.K. Enhanced Diagnosis of Influenza and COVID-19 Using Machine Learning. *EAI Endorsed Trans. Context Aware Syst. App. [Internet]* **2023**, *9*, 1–6 [CrossRef]
16. Shilaskar, S.; Ghatol, A. Diagnosis system for imbalanced multi-minority medical dataset. *Soft Comput.* **2018**, *23*, 4789–4799. [CrossRef]
17. Chatterjee, A.; Gerdes, M.W.; Martinez, S.G. Identification of Risk Factors Associated with Obesity and Overweight—A Machine Learning Overview. *Sensors* **2020**, *20*, 2734. [CrossRef]
18. Almansour, N.A.; Syed, H.F.; Khayat, N.R.; Altheeb, R.K.; Juri, R.E.; Alhiyafi, J.; Alrashed, S.; Olatunji, S.O. Neural network and support vector machine for the prediction of chronic kidney disease: A comparative study. *Comput. Biol. Med.* **2019**, *109*, 101–111. [CrossRef]
19. Biau, G.; Cadre, B.; Rouvière, L. Accelerated gradient boosting. *Mach. Learn.* **2019**, *108*, 971–992. [CrossRef]
20. Friedman, J.H. Greedy function approximation: A gradient boosting machine. *Ann. Stat.* **2001**, *5*, 1189–1232. [CrossRef]
21. Xing, W.; Bei, Y. Medical Health Big Data Classification Based on KNN Classification Algorithm. *IEEE Access* **2020**, *8*, 28808–28819. [CrossRef]
22. Valdes, G.; Luna, J.; Eaton, E.; Simone, C.B., II; Ungar, L.H.; Solberg, T.D. MediBoost: A Patient Stratification Tool for Interpretable Decision Making in the Era of Precision Medicine. *Sci. Rep.* **2016**, *6*, 37854. [CrossRef] [PubMed]
23. Gao, X.; Alam, S.; Shi, P.; Dexter, F.; Kong, N. Interpretable machine learning models for hospital readmission prediction: A two-step extracted regression tree approach. *BMC Med. Inform. Decis. Mak.* **2023**, *23*, 104. [CrossRef] [PubMed]
24. Joyce, D.W.; Kormilitzin, A.; Smith, K.A.; Cipriani, A. Explainable artificial intelligence for mental health through transparency and interpretability for understandability. *NPJ Digit. Med.* **2023**, *6*, 6. [CrossRef]
25. Ahamad, M.M.; Aktar, S.; Rashed-Al-Mahfuz, M.; Uddin, S.; Liò, P.; Xu, H.; Summers, M.A.; Quinn, J.M.W.; Moni, M.A. A machine learning model to identify early stage symptoms of SARS-Cov-2 infected patients. *Expert Syst. Appl.* **2020**, *160*, 113661. [CrossRef] [PubMed]
26. Sarica, A.; Cerasa, A.; Quattrone, A. Random Forest Algorithm for the Classification of Neuroimaging Data in Alzheimer's Disease: A Systematic Review. *Front. Aging Neurosci.* **2017**, *9*, 329. [CrossRef] [PubMed]
27. Schober, P.; Vetter, T.R. Logistic Regression in Medical Research. *Anesth. Analg.* **2021**, *132*, 365–366. [CrossRef]
28. Demsar, J. Statistical comparisons of classifiers over multiple data sets. *J. Mach. Learn. Res.* **2006**, *7*, 1–30.
29. Choi, S.; Park, J.; Park, S.; Byon, I.; Choi, H.Y. Establishment of a prediction tool for ocular trauma patients with machine learning algorithm. *Int. J. Ophthalmol.* **2021**, *14*, 1941–1949. [CrossRef]
30. The Lancet Respiratory Medicine. Opening the black box of machine learning. *Lancet Respir. Med.* **2018**, *6*, 801. [CrossRef]
31. Boyton, R.J.; Altmann, D.M. The immunology of asymptomatic SARS-CoV-2 infection: What are the key questions? *Nat. Rev. Immunol.* **2021**, *21*, 762–768. [CrossRef]

applied sciences

MDPI

Article

Cybersecurity and Medical Imaging: A Simulation-Based Approach to DICOM Communication

Stylianos Karagiannis [1,2,*,†], Emmanouil Magkos [2,†], Christoforos Ntantogian [2], Ricardo Cabecinha [3] and Theofanis Fotis [4]

1 PDMFC, R. Fradesso da Silveira, 4-1B, 1300-609 Lisboa, Portugal
2 Department of Informatics, Ionian University, Plateia Tsirigoti 7, 49100 Corfu, Greece; emagos@ionio.gr (E.M.); dadoyan@ionio.gr (C.N.)
3 Hospital do Espírito Santo de Évora, EPE, Largo Senhor da Pobreza, 7000-811 Évora, Portugal; rjcabecinha@hevora.min-saude.pt
4 Centre for Secure, Intelligent and Usable Systems (CSIUS), School of Sport & Health Sciences, University of Brighton, Brighton BN2 4AT, UK; t.fotis@brighton.ac.uk
* Correspondence: stylianos.karagiannis@pdmfc.com or skaragiannis@ionio.gr
† These authors contributed equally to this work.

Abstract: Medical imaging plays a crucial role in modern healthcare, providing essential information for accurate diagnosis and treatment planning. The Digital Imaging and Communications in Medicine (DICOM) standard has revolutionized the storage, transmission, and sharing of medical images and related data. Despite its advantages, implementation and deployment of the DICOM protocol often suffers from incomplete understanding, leading to vulnerabilities within the healthcare ecosystem. This research paper presents an implementation of DICOM communication and the development of a practical demonstration for simulation purposes The simulation can be used for conducting cybersecurity tests in the context of DICOM communication. Overall, the simulation provides a digital environment that can help in retrieving valuable insights into the practical aspects of DICOM communication and PACS integration, serving as a valuable resource for medical imaging professionals, researchers, and developers. These research results provide practical insights, and the DICOM simulation can be used in realistic contexts to showcase a variety of security scenarios.

Keywords: medical imaging; DICOM; PACS; eHealth; simulation

Citation: Karagiannis, S.; Magkos, E.; Ntantogian, C.; Cabecinha, R.; Fotis, T. Cybersecurity and Medical Imaging: A Simulation-Based Approach to DICOM Communication. *Appl. Sci.* **2023**, *13*, 10072. https://doi.org/10.3390/app131810072

Academic Editor: Christos Bouras

Received: 26 July 2023
Revised: 31 August 2023
Accepted: 4 September 2023
Published: 6 September 2023

1. Introduction

Medical imaging is of the utmost importance in modern healthcare for accurate diagnosis and treatment planning [1–7]. DICOM, a widely used standard, has revolutionized the storage, transmission, and sharing of medical images and associated data [8–11]. DICOM stands for "Digital Imaging and Communications in Medicine". It is a widely used standard for the communication, storage, and management of medical images [12]. DICOM enables interoperability among various medical imaging devices and systems, ensuring that medical images and associated data can be easily exchanged and interpreted across different vendors and institutions. As part of the DICOM infrastructure, the Picture Archiving and Communication System (PACS) plays a key role in enabling the storage, retrieval, and distribution of medical images and associated information [13,14].

Past attacks targeting DICOM systems have exposed vulnerabilities in the security infrastructure of medical imaging technology [15]. These attacks highlight the need for heightened security measures around the safeguarding of sensitive patient data to maintain the integrity of medical images. For example, in 2017 researchers from Massachusetts General Hospital identified thousands of unprotected DICOM servers globally and hundreds in the United States, potentially revealing patient information [16]. Similarly, in 2018 a security researcher employed an internet scanning tool to access unprotected DICOM servers, and even produced a 3D model of a single individual's anatomy [17]. These incidents underscore the urgency of implementing robust security protocols, including encryption, authentication, network segmentation, and regular security audits, to mitigate risks and protect patient privacy within the DICOM ecosystem.

Despite the indispensability of DICOM and PACS, there is often a lack of comprehensive understanding and implementation in healthcare organizations [18,19]. This lack of comprehension and implementation can lead to various security challenges and vulnerabilities [20,21]. The existing literature highlights the security vulnerabilities in these systems, such as unencrypted communications, weak authentication mechanisms, and inadequate access controls [15,22–24]. Nevertheless, healthcare organizations often fail to implement robust security measures or conduct comprehensive security testing, leaving them vulnerable to cyberattacks [25,26].

This research paper proposes a DICOM simulation with the aim of improving understanding of the DICOM network protocol. The simulation serves as a practical demonstration that can enhance comprehension and implementation. By simulating data transfer using the DICOM protocol from a healthcare modality, the practical aspects of DICOM communication and PACS integration can be further investigated. The simulation involves the replication of the network layer for DICOM transfers and establishing the necessary connections to a PACS server.

1.1. Contribution

This research paper makes significant contributions to the field of medical imaging by providing a practical demonstration of DICOM data transfer in a medical imaging environment. The code has been uploaded to GitHub [27]. The key contributions of this research paper are as follows:

- We present a practical demonstration of data transfer in a medical imaging environment by simulating DICOM data transfer in a virtual environment. This demonstration provides an environment that can facilitate better understanding of DICOM communication and the integration of PACS in a realistic setting.
- We provide a step-by-step implementation and code snippets that serve as a valuable resource for education and learning in order to confer a better understanding of DICOM communication and PACS integration.
- The presented simulation offers a digital environment that enables hands-on experience of a realistic implementation for DICOM communication and PACS integration and allows interaction with the simulated environment.
- The simulated environment can be utilized as a valuable asset for security and privacy tests. By simulating DICOM transfers and PACS integration, common and critical vulnerabilities can be uncovered and comprehensive security testing conducted to address cybersecurity concerns in medical imaging systems.

1.2. Related Works

Several works have contributed to understanding DICOM communications and PACS integration in medical imaging. Zhou et al. [28] identified a lack of tools for PACS training and developed a Radiology Information System (RIS) simulator. However, advancements in medical imaging, DICOM communication, PACS integration, and cybersecurity have occurred subsequently. Coutinho et al. [21] introduced a cybersecurity methodology and tools for healthcare operational information systems with a focus on cybersecurity, for which they used Orthanc [29] and ONIS [30]. Other researchers have provided extensively details on the advantages of the Fast Healthcare Interoperability Resources (FHIR) protocol while outlining a user-friendly approach for individuals who are new to these concepts [31].

In the present research, a DICOM simulator was developed in a virtual lab context for use in conducting security tests. This study emphasizes in-depth analysis and learning aspects related to the fundamental attributes of the DICOM protocol, and the approach remains flexible for subsequent extensions, providing openings for further utilization by researchers according to their particular requirements.

Potter et al. [32] discussed the significance of the DICOM Validation Toolkit (DVTk) [33], which offers potential for individuals working with the DICOM standard. Other researchers [34] have utilized DVTk and highlighted the benefits of HIS, RIS, and PACS systems in healthcare management. Additionally, Oemig et al. [35] presented a collection of tools, including DVTk [33] and HAPI [36], to explore their development and integration with PACS. Mantri et al. [37] conducted a comparative study of DICOM API libraries, while NIST [38] identified software and managed risks within the PACS ecosystem. Mileva et al. [39] introduced covert channels for DICOM transport mechanisms, offering possibilities for covert communications, data exfiltration, and privacy leaking attacks.

Table 1 showcases the comprehensive differentiations and additions from the existing pertinent research. Within this study, a DICOM simulation and a topology are introduced to showcase the interaction between DICOM and PACS. This research is valuable to a broader audience interested in DICOM communication and for the practical application of DICOM simulations in real-world scenarios for learning and testing purposes.

Table 1. Comparison between related works and presented DICOM simulation.

Paper	Main Focus	Contribution of DICOM Simulation
[28]	Lack of tools for practical PACS training.	Comprehensive demonstration of DICOM data transfer within a medical imaging environment. It offers step-by-step implementation guidance and code snippets, enabling a better understanding of DICOM communication and integration with PACS systems.
[21]	Focus primarily on cybersecurity methodology.	The simulation serves as a controlled environment for conducting security assessments related to DICOM data transfer, offering a unique contribution by merging simulation with cybersecurity considerations.
[32]	Emphasis on the DICOM Validation Toolkit (DVTk).	Offers detailed Python library implementations that focus on fundamental DICOM communication concepts. Notably, it provides adaptable code that can be tailored to specific use-case requirements.
[35]	Exploration of DICOM software development and integration.	Enhances the practicality of training for medical imaging professionals, offering a contribution that bridges the gap between software development and medical imaging.
[37]	Comparative study of DICOM API libraries.	Practical understanding of data exchange, adding value by examining and by using DICOM APIs in a simulated environment.
[38]	Identification of risks within the PACS ecosystem.	Establish a practical baseline environment for comprehending and addressing security concerns in DICOM systems, offering valuable insights into risk identification.
[39]	Introduction of covert channels for DICOM transport mechanisms.	Extends the understanding of potential vulnerabilities and hidden pathways within DICOM communication.

1.3. Paper Structure

The rest of this paper is structured as follows. Section 3 presents the methodology employed to develop the DICOM simulation software. Section 4 provides details on the implementation and explanation of the Python code. Simulation results, validation, and analysis reports are provided in Section 5, along with a further explanation of the DICOM protocol. Finally, the paper concludes in Section 6 with a discussion of potential future research avenues.

2. Background

DICOM defines a set of entities representing different aspects of medical imaging and patient information [40]:

- Patients (P) encapsulates individual patient data, including attributes such as name, ID, and birthdate. A patient p can be associated with one or more studies ($P \rightarrow [S_1, S_2, \ldots]$).
- Study and Study Series (S and Se) includes related medical images and metadata, while Series groups images within a study based on common characteristics. A study s can include one or more series ($Se = [S_1, S_2, \ldots]$).
- Image (I) refers to a set of DICOM images I; Series Se groups related images ($Se \rightarrow [I_1, I_2, \ldots]$).
- Physician (Ph) represents healthcare professionals; images I are interpreted by a physician Ph ($Ph \rightarrow [I_1, I_2, \ldots]$).
- Modalities (M) refers to imaging-related equipment or healthcare modalities, including imaging devices, specifying manufacturer details and software version. Images I are generated by a specific modality M ($M \rightarrow [I_1, I_2, \ldots]$).

DICOM is designed for the management of medical images and associated data within a healthcare environment.

2.1. Picture Archiving and Communication System (PACS)

PACS is a crucial system utilized in the medical field for the storage, management, and distribution of medical images and associated patient information. It replaces traditional film-based systems by enabling healthcare providers to capture, store, retrieve, and view medical images electronically. With PACS, the cumbersome task of managing physical film records is replaced by a digital infrastructure that facilitates easy image access and promotes efficient collaboration among healthcare professionals. Orthanc [29,41], on the other hand, is an open-source implementation of a PACS server. It provides a lightweight, vendor-neutral, and standards-compliant solution for managing medical images and associated data. Orthanc serves as a software platform that can be utilized to establish a PACS server infrastructure. Its open-source nature offers flexibility and customization options, making it an appealing choice for institutions and developers seeking to create their own PACS environment.

2.2. Encoding and Compression Techniques in DICOM

The Transfer Syntax [42] in DICOM refers to the encoding and compression techniques used to represent and transmit DICOM data. It determines how DICOM objects, including images, are serialized into a byte stream that can be transmitted or stored. DICOM supports multiple Transfer Syntaxes to provide flexibility, interoperability, and efficient handling of various data formats. Commonly used Transfer Syntaxes in DICOM include the following [42]:

- **Implicit VR Little Endian:** a Transfer Syntax that uses a combination of implicit value representation encoding and little-endian byte ordering. It is widely used for uncompressed DICOM images, and supports a variety of data types. This is the default Transfer Syntax for most DICOM files.
- **Explicit VR Little Endian:** a Transfer Syntax that uses explicit VR encoding and little-endian byte ordering. Commonly used for uncompressed DICOM images, it provides explicit VR tags, which make it easier to parse and understand the data.
- **JPEG Lossless:** a Transfer Syntax that employs the Joint Photographic Experts Group (JPEG) Baseline algorithm for lossless compression of DICOM images, JPEG Lossless [12,42] is utilized when a balance between compression and preservation of image quality is required. It achieves significant compression ratios while maintaining the integrity of the image data. JPEG Lossless is particularly useful for storing or transmitting DICOM images where lossy compression is not acceptable.

- **JPEG Baseline:** a specific Transfer Syntax that utilizes the JPEG Baseline algorithm for compressing DICOM images, JPEG Baseline [42,43] is a lossy compression technique that achieves significant compression ratios while maintaining acceptable image quality for many medical imaging applications. JPEG Baseline is often used for transmitting DICOM images over networks with limited bandwidth or storage capacity, as it helps reduce the size of image data.

By supporting various Transfer Syntaxes, DICOM enables interoperability between different systems, ensuring that medical imaging data can be exchanged and interpreted correctly across diverse platforms and applications.

2.3. Service–Object Pair (SOP) Class and Transfer Syntax

SOP Classes [42] are service objects that encapsulate DICOM image files. An SOP Class defines a specific type of medical imaging or non-imaging service that can be performed on a DICOM object. It represents a combination of a service and an object on which the service can be performed. Popular SOP Classes include, among others [42]:

- **CT Image Storage (1.2.840.10008.5.1.4.1.1.2):** stores Computed Tomography (CT) images, which are used for diagnostic purposes and provide detailed cross-sectional views of the body.
- **MR Image Storage (1.2.840.10008.5.1.4.1.1.4):** stores Magnetic Resonance Imaging (MRI) images, which are used to visualize internal structures of the body using magnetic fields and radio waves, providing detailed anatomical information.
- **Ultrasound Image Storage (1.2.840.10008.5.1.4.1.1.6.1):** stores ultrasound images; ultrasound imaging uses high-frequency sound waves to generate images of organs and tissues in real-time, and is often used in obstetrics, cardiology, and other medical applications.
- **X-ray Radiography Image Storage (1.2.840.10008.5.1.4.1.1.1):** stores X-ray images; widely used for various medical purposes, X-rays provide two-dimensional images that can help diagnose bone fractures, detect abnormalities, and visualize internal structures.

The above SOP Classes define the necessary metadata, attributes, and operations required to handle and interpret images of their respective modalities.

2.4. Presentation Contexts

Presentation Contexts in DICOM define the combination of a specific SOP Class and one or more supported Transfer Syntaxes that an AE can handle for communication purposes. When two DICOM devices establish a connection or association, they negotiate the set of services and data formats that they can support. This negotiation is accomplished using Presentation Contexts. A Presentation Context consists of the following components [42]:

- **Abstract Syntax:** this identifies the class or type of DICOM object being transmitted or requested, and represents a specific SOP Class, such as CT Image Storage or MR Image Storage.
- **Transfer Syntaxes:** these define the encoding and compression techniques used to represent and transmit the DICOM data, and specify how the DICOM object is serialized into a byte stream. Multiple Transfer Syntaxes can be associated with a single Abstract Syntax, allowing for flexibility in data formats and compression options.

The process of association negotiation in the context of medical imaging involves the exchange of information between two devices. During this negotiation, both devices share a list of supported Presentation Contexts. Each Presentation Context is composed of an Abstract Syntax along with one or more Transfer Syntaxes that the device is capable of supporting for that specific Abstract Syntax.

The two devices then compare the lists of Presentation Contexts they have shared and work towards finding a mutually supported Presentation Context. When this mutual agreement is reached, it signifies that the devices can effectively communicate and conduct operations involving DICOM objects. This is done using the designated Abstract Syntax, while the agreed-upon Transfer Syntax is employed for the communication.

For instance, consider a scenario in which two devices establish a Presentation Context with an Abstract Syntax. This agreement indicates that the devices are now equipped to exchange and manipulate magnetic resonance image data using the JPEG Baseline compression algorithm. This enables seamless and efficient communication between the devices while ensuring compatibility in handling medical image information.

2.5. *Application Entities (AEs)*

The AE concept [42] is fundamental to Digital Imaging and DICOM standards. It represents a node or device in a network that communicates using DICOM protocols. An AE can be a piece of medical imaging equipment, such as a CT scanner, MRI machine, or PACS server. In the context of DICOM, an AE is identified by a unique AE title, which serves as its network address. The AE title is used to establish connections and enable communication between different entities in a DICOM network. Each AE is responsible for sending and receiving DICOM objects, including medical images, patient information, and related metadata.

AEs provide services such as querying/retrieval, storage, and printing of DICOM objects. They can act as a Service Class Provider (SCP), which receives requests for services, or a Service Class User (SCU) [42], which initiates requests and interacts with other endpoints. The roles of SCPs and SCUs can be performed by the same AE or by different endpoints depending on the system architecture and requirements. An Application Entity represents a DICOM node or device in the network. In the DICOM simulator, an AE is created using the AE class from *Pynetdicom*. The AE title is set to *"MODALITY"*, which identifies the simulated modality in the network.

3. Methodology

This section provides an in-depth explanation of the methodology used to implement the DICOM simulator in Python. It outlines the key steps involved in establishing communication with the PACS server, configuring the necessary libraries, and sending DICOM images. To understand the interactions between DICOM modalities and PACS servers, a mathematical model can be formulated to describe the association between DICOM modalities and PACS servers.

The association between a DICOM modality and a PACS server involves several parameters that define the communication and data exchange. Let us consider a DICOM modality M and a $PACS$ server. The relationship between M and $PACS$ can be represented using Equation (1):

$$A(M, S) = \{AE_M, AE_{PACS}, SOP_{\text{class}}, TS\} \quad (1)$$

where $A(M, S)$ represents the association between the modality M and PACS server $PACS$, AE_M is the Application Entity representing the DICOM modality in the network, AE_S is the Application Entity representing the PACS server in the network, SOP_{class} denotes the SOP Class specifying the type of medical image or information being exchanged, and TS is the transfer syntax that defines how the data are encoded and decoded during transmission.

Application Entities (AE) can be represented as nodes in a network graph. Each node corresponds to an AE, which can be either the DICOM modality or the PACS server. The communication between these nodes is facilitated by the DICOM protocol, as presented in Equation (2). Equation (2) describes nodes and edges as the elements of a graph, where AE_M and AE_S are nodes representing entities within the network and edges (AE_M, AE_S) signify a connection or relationship between these nodes:

$$\text{Nodes: } N = \{AE_M, AE_S\} \text{ and Edges: } E = \{(AE_M, AE_S)\} \quad (2)$$

where N is the set of nodes representing the DICOM modality and PACS server and E is the set of edges indicating the communication links between the modality and the server.

SOP classes define the type of medical image or object being exchanged, while the Transfer Syntax specifies how the data are encoded and compressed for transmission. The association of SOP classes and transfer syntax is presented in Equation (3):

$$A(SOP_{\text{class}}, TS) = \{SOP_{\text{class}}, TS\} \tag{3}$$

where A is a function that takes two parameters, namely, SOP_{class} and TS, while SOP_{class} represents a parameter related to the class of SOP in the context of DICOM, TS similarly represents the Transfer Syntax in DICOM, SOP_{class} represents the specific type of medical image or information, TS denotes the transfer syntax used for encoding and decoding, and the function A in Equation (3) takes two DICOM-related parameters and constructs a set containing their values.

DICOM communication often involves sensitive patient data, necessitating secure protocols [44]. Transport Layer Security (TLS) and Secure Sockets Layer (SSL) ensure encrypted data transmission and authentication, while Internet Protocol Security (IPsec) offers secure network-layer communication. DICOM Secure Communication Profiles define secure communication guidelines for enhanced data privacy and integrity in medical imaging networks. The choice of protocol depends on security needs, regulatory compliance, and infrastructure compatibility. The dependency graph (Figure 1) depicts the DICOM architecture followed in this research. These concepts, although only briefly summarized in this section, are explored in greater depth later on, shedding light on their profound influence within the field of medical imaging.

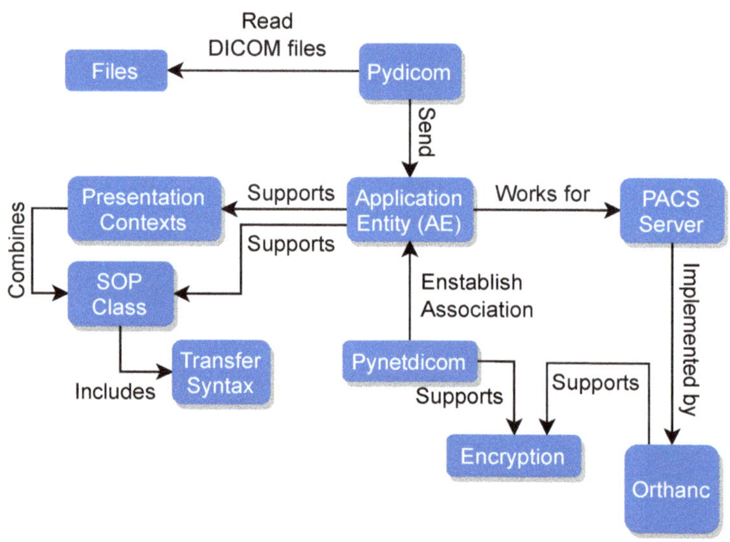

Figure 1. Dependency graph for DICOM/PACS communication.

At the core of DICOM is the AE, which designates network-connected devices such as imaging systems, workstations (Figure 1), or healthcare modalities. Playing a crucial role in simplifying accessibility for healthcare professionals, PACS servers are responsible for the storage, retrieval, and orchestration of medical images and their associated data.

The SOP Classes play a categorical role in delineating various types of medical studies or objects, each tailored to a specific imaging modality such as CT scanners or MRI machines. They detail the required attributes and structural elements crucial for accurate representation of data. Intimately connected to this are the concepts around Transfer Syntaxes, which encompass the encoding principles governing the compression and formatting of DICOM data. These principles ensure seamless interoperability across a diverse array of devices.

During communication, Presentation Contexts come into play by establishing agreements between devices regarding the supported SOP Classes and Transfer Syntaxes for the duration of the communication session. These fundamental concepts, intricate in their complexity and significant in their role, are poised for a more profound exploration later in this section.

As presented in Figure 1, to establish the association between the AE and the PACS, in this research we employed *Pynetdicom* [45]. *Pynetdicom* is a Python implementation of the DICOM networking protocol that enables communication between different DICOM entities. It provides the necessary functionalities to establish association, transfer DICOM data, and manage network connections. In terms of data security during transmission, both Orthanc and *Pynetdicom* support encryption. Encryption is a crucial aspect of securing sensitive medical data during transmission to ensure privacy and prevent unauthorized access. The use of encryption adds an extra layer of protection to the data being transferred between the AE and the PACS, reducing the risk of potential security breaches.

3.1. *Pydicom: Modify and Write DICOM Files with Python*

In this research, *Pydicom* [46] was used as a tool to read DICOM files and send them to the Application Entity (AE). The AE supports Presentation Contexts, which consist of SOP Classes and Transfer Syntaxes [39,42,46]. The integration as presented in Figure 1 focuses on the integration between the AE and the PACS server.

Pydicom is a widely-used Python library that offers a range of functionalities for working with DICOM files. It is specifically designed to handle DICOM data, allowing users to read, manipulate, and write DICOM files effectively. In the context of our presented DICOM simulator, *Pydicom* is utilized to read the DICOM files from the local folder and prepare them for transmission to the PACS server. The library provides the necessary tools and functions to parse the DICOM files, extracting relevant information and organizing it into a structured format.

One of the key functions provided by the *Pydicom* library is *dcmread()*. This function is used to read and parse DICOM files in Python. It accepts the path or a file-like object of the DICOM file as input and returns a Dataset object. The Dataset object represents the parsed data and contains various attributes and methods to access and manipulate the DICOM information. By utilizing the *dcmread()* function, the DICOM simulator can read the DICOM files and extract the required information, such as patient data, imaging parameters, and study details. This information can then be utilized to simulate the transmission of DICOM data to the PACS server.

3.2. *Pynetdicom: A Python Implementation of the DICOM Networking Protocol*

Pynetdicom is a Python library that implements the DICOM network protocol and enables communication between DICOM applications. It provides functionalities to establish associations between DICOM nodes, and facilitates the sending and receiving of DICOM data. In the context of the DICOM simulator, *Pynetdicom* is utilized to establish a connection with the PACS server and transmit DICOM images. The library offers an AE class, which is employed to create an Application Entity representing the local node or device in the simulator. To define the supported presentation contexts, which determine the combination of SOP Classes and Transfer Syntaxes that the AE can handle, the *supported_contexts* attribute of the AE class is set. This attribute specifies the supported DICOM services and protocols.

The *add_requested_context()* method is used to specify additional requested contexts, allowing the AE to indicate the SOP Classes and Transfer Syntaxes that it wants to use for communication with the remote DICOM entity. The *associate()* method establishes an association with the PACS server, enabling subsequent data exchange. This method initiates the DICOM association negotiation process, which involves negotiating supported presentation contexts, transferring the DICOM application context, and verifying the compatibility between the local and remote DICOM entities.

To transmit DICOM datasets to the connected PACS server, the *send_c_store()* method is utilized. This method ensures proper encoding and delivery of the DICOM data. It handles the DICOM C-STORE service, which is responsible for storing DICOM datasets on the PACS server. The *send_c_store()* method provides status codes to indicate the success or failure of the storage request. Finally, the *release()* method is used to terminate the association between DICOM entities. This method initiates a graceful closure of the communication session by sending release request messages to both the local and remote entities.

3.3. Association Establishment between AE and PACS

In the diagram provided in Figure 2, the deployment of a simulation on Host 1 is illustrated. The main process, labeled *"Association"*, is associated with the AE within the simulation. The AE serves as a representation of a device or node within the network, denoted as AE. Similarly, the Orthanc PACS server is represented as $PACS$. The initiation of communication between these entities is facilitated by the following method, establishing a connection for seamless data exchange, as defined in Equation (4).

$$association\_successful = associate(AE, PACS) \quad (4)$$

The success of this initiation is captured by the variable association_successful, indicating whether or not the association process was successful. Data transmission, which involves the exchange of medical images and related information, can be visually represented as a flow using directional arrows. This abstraction aids in understanding the dynamic exchange between different components of the system. The connectivity and integrity of the communication link are monitored using the function presented in Equation (5), allowing the verification outcome to be defined as Equation (6).

$$status = check\_status(modality, PACS) \quad (5)$$

$$association\_successful = associate(AE, PACS) \quad (6)$$

Data processing and release encompasses a sequence of operations applied to DICOM data, and fulfills specific tasks within the system. The established communication link between the AE and PACS is vital for seamless data exchange and successful execution of communication operations. Figure 2 visualizes the connection between the simulation and the PACS server, showcasing the flow of DICOM data and communication within the simulated environment. This connection enables the transmission of DICOM images and associated information from the simulation to the PACS server, mimicking real-world scenarios and facilitating the exploration and understanding of DICOM communication and PACS integration.

The simulation involves processing a dataset and initiating a request. The Association process reads the dataset and performs various operations. A status check is applied to verify the connection of the DICOM modality to the PACS server hosted on Host 2. If the connectivity is confirmed, the Association process sends the processed data to the PACS server. After the data transmission is successful, the Association process releases the connection. Overall, the diagram showcases the flow of data processing and communication between Host 1, the Association process, and the PACS server on Host 2.

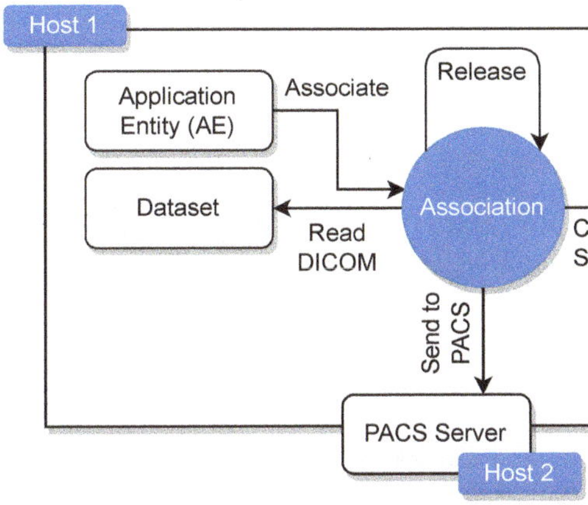

Figure 2. Establishment of the association between the AE and the PACS server.

To establish a connection with the PACS server, the AE utilizes the *associate()* method from the *Pynetdicom* library. This method serves as a way for the AE to initiate an association with the PACS server, enabling communication between them.

The *associate()* method requires several input parameters, including the IP address and port number of the PACS server, as well as the AE title associated with the PACS server. When this method is invoked, the AE triggers the association process. If the process is successful, it results in the creation of a communication link between the AE and the PACS server. When this association has been successfully established, the AE gains the ability to effectively interact with the PACS server.

This interaction encompasses various tasks, such as sending and retrieving medical images and the associated data. By leveraging the established connection, the AE can transmit DICOM data objects to the PACS server.

3.4. Encryption

The DICOM simulator provides an option to add a TLS layer for encryption, which is supported by Orthanc as well. Enabling TLS support in the DICOM simulator ensures that the transmission of DICOM data between the simulator and PACS server is encrypted, thereby enhancing data security. To enable TLS support in ORTHANC, the following steps should be completed:

- **Building a TLS Context.** A TLS context needs to be created within ORTHANC. The TLS context defines the configuration and settings for the TLS encryption.
- **Loading the Necessary Certificate and Private Key.** To establish secure communication, a valid TLS certificate, and its corresponding private key need to be provided. The TLS certificate is obtained from a trusted Certificate Authority (CA) and serves as proof of identity for the server.
- **Adding the Supported Context with the TLS Context to the AE.** In Orthanc, an AE represents a network entity that can communicate using the DICOM protocol. The TLS context is then added to the AE configuration in order to associate the TLS encryption capabilities with the AE.

By completing these steps and configuring the TLS settings correctly, the DICOM simulator with TLS support ensures that DICOM data transmitted between the simulator and the PACS server is encrypted. This encryption helps to protect the confidentiality and integrity of the data during transmission, mitigating the risk of unauthorized access or tampering.

4. Implementation

This section provides detailed insights into the implementation of the DICOM simulator, with a focus on the necessary configurations, setup of the environment, and the steps involved in establishing communication with the PACS server and sending DICOM images.

4.1. Setting Up the Python Libraries

Before implementing the DICOM simulator, it is essential to set up and install the required *Pydicom* and *Pynetdicom* libraries. The provided code is written in Python and demonstrates a function for sending DICOM files to a PACS server. Providing a pip requirements file or setting up an isolated environment can be streamlined using services such as Docker [47], which simplifies the environment setup process and ensures enhanced portability [27]. An extended explanation of the code follows in the code listing below.

In Listing 1, the necessary modules and classes required for the code are imported. *os* is imported to perform file operations, *dcmread* is imported from the *Pydicom* library for reading DICOM files, *JPEG Baseline* is imported from *pydicom.uid* for specifying the Transfer Syntax and AE, *StoragePresentationContexts* is imported from *Pynetdicom* for managing the application entity and storage presentation contexts, and *CTImageStorage* is imported from *pynetdicom.sop_class* for specifying the DICOM storage context.

Listing 1: Importing the libraries.

```
import os
from pydicom import dcmread
from pydicom.uid import JPEG Baseline
from pynetdicom import AE, StoragePresentationContexts
from pynetdicom.sop_class import CTImageStorage
```

The main function *send_dicom_to_pacs()* (Listing 2) receives as input four arguments: *dicom_folder* (the path to the folder containing DICOM files), *pacs_ip* (the IP address of the PACS server), *pacs_port* (the port number of the PACS server), and *pacs_ae_title* (the AE title of the PACS server). Inside the function, an instance of AE is created, with the AE title set to *"MODALITY"*. The supported storage presentation contexts are set to *StoragePresentationContexts*, and a requested context for X-ray Angiographic Image Storage is added with the UID *"1.2.840.10008.5.1.4.1.1.12.1"* and the transfer syntax *[JPEGBaseline]*.

Listing 2: The main function.

```
def send_dicom_to_pacs(dicom_folder,pacs_ip,pacs_port,pacs_ae_title):
    # Create an Application Entity
    ae = AE(ae_title='MODALITY')
    ae.supported_contexts = StoragePresentationContexts

    # Add the requested transfer syntax for the X-ray Angiographic Image Storage contextae.add_requested_context('1.2.840.10008.5.1.4.1.1.12.1', [JPEGBaseline])
```

An association is established (Listing 3) with the PACS server using the associate method of the AE instance, binding the IP address of the PACS server, port number, and defined the AE title as arguments. Then, a message is printed indicating the successful connection.

Listing 3: Connecting to the PACS server.

```
    assoc = ae.associate(pacs_ip, pacs_port, ae_title=pacs_ae_title)
    if assoc.is_established:
        print('Connected to the PACS server.')
```

Inside the established association, the function, as presented in Listing 4, iterates over the files in the specified *dicom_folder*. If a file has the extension *.DCM*, then its full path is obtained using *os.path.join*. The DICOM file is read using *dcmread* and stored in the dataset variable. The *send_c_store* method of the association is called to send the DICOM dataset to the PACS server. The status of the storage request is checked, and appropriate messages are printed based on the success or failure of the operation.

Listing 4: Iterating over DICOM files in the folder.

```
        for filename in os.listdir(dicom_folder):
            if filename.endswith('.DCM'):
                dicom_file = os.path.join(dicom_folder, filename)
                # Read the DICOM file
                dataset = dcmread(dicom_file)
                # Send the DICOM image to the PACS server
                status = assoc.send_c_store(dataset)
                # Check the status of the storage request
                if status:
                    print(f'Successfully sent {dicom_file} to the PACS server.')
                else:
                    print(f'Failed to send {dicom_file} to the PACS server.')
```

After processing all the DICOM files, the association is released (Listing 5) using the release method and a message is printed indicating the disconnection from the PACS server. If the initial association could not be established, a message is printed indicating the failure to connect to the PACS server.

Listing 5: Releasing the association.

```
        # if assoc.is_established=true then Release the association
        assoc.release()
        print('Disconnected from the PACS server.')
    else:
        print('Failed to connect to the PACS server.')
# The send_dicom_to_pacs main function finishes
```

Listing 6 demonstrates how to use the *send_dicom_to_pacs* function. The *dicom_folder*, *pacs_ip*, *pacs_port*, and *pacs_ae_title* variables are defined with sample values. These should be replaced with the actual values corresponding to the specific setup instance. The function is then called with these arguments to initiate the DICOM transfer process. The commented-out lines related to the TLS layer and certificate paths, indicating that while TLS encryption is not currently being used in this code, it can be implemented by uncommenting and modifying these lines.

Listing 6: Usage Example.

```
dicom_folder = r'C:\Users\bloodraven\Desktop\02_Projects\DT\dicom'
pacs_ip = '192.168.0.162'  # Replace with the actual IP address
pacs_port = 4242  # Replace with the actual port number
pacs_ae_title = 'ORTHANC'  # Replace with the actual AE name/title

# Call the main function send_dicom_to_pacs
send_dicom_to_pacs(dicom_folder, pacs_ip, pacs_port, pacs_ae_title)
```

5. Simulation Results and Analysis

The diagram in Figure 3 represents the simulated environment and the integration between the DICOM simulation and the PACS server. It comprises three key components: a Windows 10 machine on which the DICOM simulation is executed, an Ubuntu Virtual Machine (VM) with a Docker container as a deployment for Orthanc, and a dedicated KALI Linux machine to enable packet sniffing. The simulation and the deployed topology can be used as a sandbox for DICOM communication security scenarios.

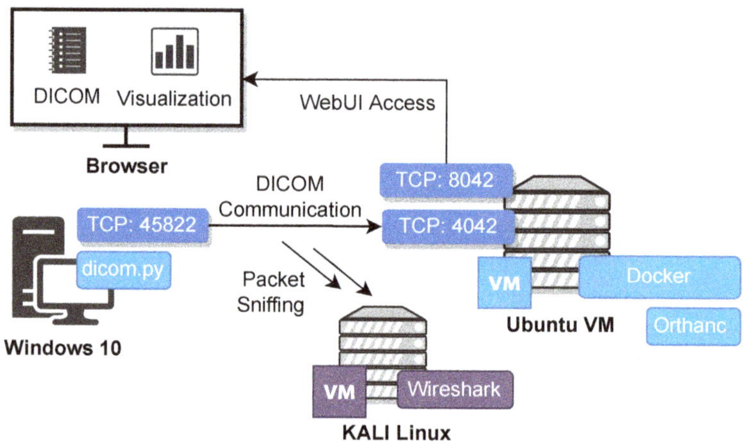

Figure 3. The DICOM/PACS simulated environment.

To ensure device identification within the local network (Figure 3), specific IP addresses are assigned for the VMs of Windows 10, Ubuntu VM, and KALI Linux. The reserved IP addresses facilitate communication and data exchange among the different components of the simulated environment.

5.1. Setting Up Orthanc to Accept Data from the Modality Simulator

Within the configuration of Orthanc (*/etc/orthahnc/orthanc.json*), the *"DicomModalities"* section should be changed to accept data from the specific modality. The example contains three parameters [41]:

- Application Entity Title (AET): this parameter represents the unique identifier of the remote modality. It cannot exceed 16 characters in length. In the example, *"MODALITY"* is used as the AET.
- Remote Network Address: this parameter specifies the IP address or hostname of the remote modality. In the example, *"192.168.0.105"* (Windows 10) is used as the address.
- TCP port number: this parameter defines the port number on which the DICOM protocol is running on the remote modality. The default port for DICOM is 104.

The configuration (Listing 7) suggests that multiple DICOM modalities can be listed under the *"DicomModalities"* section [41], each one identified by a unique AET and associated with a specific network address and port number for communication.

Listing 7: Configuration options for Orthanc: adding the DICOM modalities.

```
``DicomModalities'' : {
  /**
   * The first parameter is the
   * AET of the remote modality (cannot be longer than 16
   * characters), the second one is the remote network address,
   * and the third one is the TCP port number corresponding
   * to the DICOM protocol on the remote modality (usually 104).
   **/
  // ``sample'' : [ ``STORESCP'', ``127.0.0.1'', 2000 ]
  ``modality'' : [ ``MODALITY'', ``192.168.0.105'', 104 ]
}
```

5.2. Enabling SSL/TLS

Enabling TLS in Orthanc (Listing 8) involves several steps, as outlined below [41]:

1. SSL enabled: the *"SslEnabled"* option in the configuration file should be set to true. By default, this option is initially set to false; changing it to true is necessary to enable SSL/TLS encryption.
2. Specify the path to the SSL certificate: the value of *"SslCertificate"* needs to be updated with the file path of the SSL certificate. It is important that the certificate file is in the PEM format and contains both the certificate and the private key.
3. Set the minimum accepted SSL protocol version (optional): the introduction of the *"ssl_protocol_version"* option in Orthanc 1.8.2 allows for the specification of the minimum accepted SSL protocol version. This option can be added if desired, with the default requirement being for SSL 1.2. The available protocol versions and their corresponding values can be found in the documentation or configuration file.

Listing 8: SSL/TLS options for Orthanc.

```
/**
   * Security-related options for the HTTP server
   **/
  // Whether remote hosts can connect to the HTTP server
  ``RemoteAccessAllowed'' : true,
  // Whether or not SSL is enabled
  ``SslEnabled'' : false,
  // Path to the SSL certificate used by the HTTP server. The file
  // must be stored in the PEM format, and must contain both the
  // certificate and the private key. This option is only ↩
     meaningful
  // if ``SslEnabled'' is true.
  ``SslCertificate'' : ``certificate.pem'',
  // Sets the minimum accepted SSL protocol version
  // (cf. ``ssl_protocol_version'' option of civetweb). By default,
  // require SSL 1.2. This option is only meaningful if ``↩
     SslEnabled''
  // is true. (new in Orthanc 1.8.2)
**/
```

When these changes have been made, the configuration file must be saved and the Orthanc server restarted to implement the modifications. As a result, the HTTP server of Orthanc becomes accessible over a secure TLS connection.

5.3. Validation Tests: Scenario Test Execution

Two distinct scenarios are illustrated in Listing 9 from the script outputs. The scenarios depict different outcomes related to the transfer of data to a PACS server for validation purposes related to the present research.

Listing 9: Validation testing.

```
# Scenario 1: Successful transfer - Output of the successful connection
C:\Users\bloodraven\Desktop\02_Projects\DT>python dicom.py
Connected to the PACS server.
Successfully sent C:\Users\bloodraven\Desktop\02_Projects\DT\dicom\0002.DCM to the PACS server.
Disconnected from the PACS server.

# Scenario 2: Incorrect IP or Port Number - Output of failed connection
C:\Users\bloodraven\Desktop\02_Projects\DT>python dicom.py
Failed to connect to the PACS server.
```

Upon initiating the script execution (Listing 9), the command prompt confirms a successful connection establishment with the PACS server. This connection allows subsequent data transmission. Specifically, the output specifies that the file *"0002.DCM"* is located at the specified path. Similarly, in Scenario 2 the output reveals that there is an inability to establish the intended connection, indicating that an erroneous IP address or port number was specified in the script or that other network-related complications impeded the connection process.

5.4. Network Traffic Analysis: TCP/DICOM Communication Flow

This section provides the mathematical model that describes the progression of the TCP/DICOM communication flow of the DICOM Communication. Moreover, Listings 10–13 show the progression of the TCP/DICOM communication flow between the DICOM modality and the PACS server.

Listing 10: Network flow: association initialization.

```
# Time|Message Type|Information|(Port Numbers)
T_{1} 7.633204882|A-ASSOCIATE request|DICOM: A-ASSOCIATE request MODALITY --> ORTHANC|(55822) --> (4242)
T_{2} 7.633597464|A-ASSOCIATE accept|DICOM: A-ASSOCIATE accept MODALITY <-- ORTHANC|(55822) <-- (4242)
```

Listing 11: TCP segments in between the DICOM communication: data transmission.

```
# Time|Message Type|Information|(Port Numbers)
T_{3,4,...} **Multiple TCP flows [TCP segment of a reassembled PDU]
```

Listing 12: Data reassembly, storage, and command execution.

```
# Time|Message Type|Information|(Port Numbers)
**Multiple TCP flows [TCP segment of a reassembled PDU]

T_{6} 7.671284786|P-DATA, C-STORE-RQ I|DICOM: P-DATA, C-STORE-RQ ID=1|(55822) --> (4242)
T_{7} 7.671830832|P-DATA, X-ray Angiog|DICOM: P-DATA, X-ray Angiographic Image Storage Fragment (reassembled in #1394)|(55822) --> (4242)
T_{8} 7.684974645|P-DATA, X-ray Angiog|DICOM: P-DATA, X-ray Angiographic Image Storage|(55822) --> (4242)
T_{9} 7.750206628|P-DATA, Command ID=1|DICOM: P-DATA, Command ID=1 (Success)|(55822) <-- (4242)
```

Listing 13: Association termination.

```
# Time|Message Type|Information|(Port Numbers)
T_{10} 7.755639129|A-RELEASE request|DICOM: A-RELEASE request|(55822) --> (4242)
T_{11} 7.755860145|A-RELEASE response|DICOM: A-RELEASE response|(55822) <-- (4242)
```

5.4.1. Association Initialization

At the start of the communication, the `MODALITY` entity initiates the process by sending an `A-ASSOCIATE request` to `Orthanc` indicating its intention to establish a DICOM association. This request occurs at time T_1, and is represented as Equation (7).

$$MODALITY \xrightarrow{\text{A-ASSOCIATE request}} PACS \quad \text{at time } T_1 \tag{7}$$

In response to the request, `Orthanc` acknowledges the establishment of the association by sending an `A-ASSOCIATE accept` message back to `MODALITY`. This acceptance message occurs at time T_2, and is defined by Equation (8).

$$MODALITY \xleftarrow{\text{A-ASSOCIATE accept}} PACS \quad \text{at time } T_2 \tag{8}$$

This includes the establishment of the association, data transmission, successful command execution, and the termination of the connection (Listing 10).

A-ASSOCIATE request. The A-ASSOCIATE request is the initial step in establishing a DICOM association between the MODALITY entity and the Orthanc entity. It is sent by the MODALITY device/system to the Orthanc device/system. The request contains information about the supported DICOM services, transfer syntaxes, and other negotiation parameters.

A-ASSOCIATE accept. The A-ASSOCIATE accept message is sent by Orthanc in response to the A-ASSOCIATE request from MODALITY. It indicates that Orthanc accepts the association. This message contains negotiated parameters, such as the agreed-upon DICOM services, transfer syntaxes, and other configuration details.

5.4.2. Data Transmission

Throughout the communication session, `MODALITY` sends multiple TCP segments, which are acknowledgments (ACKs), to `PACS`. These segments are transmitted at different times, denoted as T_3, T_4, etc., representing a series of communication events. as presented in Equation (9):

$$MODALITY \xrightarrow{\text{TCP segments}} PACS \quad \text{at times } T_3, T_4, \ldots, \tag{9}$$

where each T_i corresponds to a specific ACK transmitted by `MODALITY`. A sample of the data transmission in TCP segments is presented in Listing 11.

Multiple TCP flows in between (TCP segment of a reassembled PDU). The TCP segments (Listing 11) are acknowledgments (ACK) sent from the AE, namely, MODALITY to Orthanc acknowledging the successful reception of a previous PDU fragment. The *"S"* indicates a TCP segment of a reassembled PDU, suggesting that this is part of the reassembly process involving the fragmented data mentioned previously.

5.4.3. Data Reassembly and Storage

As the data transmission continues, `MODALITY` sends `P-DATA` messages, specifically, `C-STORE-RQ` (C-STORE request) messages, to `Orthanc` for the purpose of storing DICOM objects. `Orthanc` receives and reassembles the data fragments. The reassembly events occur at times T_6, T_7, T_8, etc., forming the sequence of reception events expressed in Equation (10):

$$PACS \xrightarrow{\text{Reassembled fragments}} MODALITY \quad \text{at times } T_6, T_7, T_8, \ldots, \tag{10}$$

where each T_i indicates the reception and reassembly of data fragments by `Orthanc`. Then, `MODALITY` notifies the successful execution of a command by transmitting a `P-DATA` message containing the relevant information, including `Command ID=1 (Success)`, to `PACS`. This message is received by `PACS` at time T_9, as presented in Equation (11).

$$MODALITY \xleftarrow{\text{P-DATA, Command ID=1 (Success)}} PACS \quad \text{at time } T_9 \tag{11}$$

P-DATA, C-STORE-RQ I. The P-DATA message is used to transfer DICOM data between the MODALITY and Orthanc entities; in this case, it is a C-STORE request (C-STORE-RQ) sent by MODALITY to Orthanc. Here, *"ID=1"* indicates that this is the first C-STORE request in the communication session. This request (Listing 12) includes information about the data to be stored, such as the DICOM object or image. A C-STORE request (C-STORE-RQ) is a DICOM message used to request the storage of DICOM objects, such as medical images, in a destination device or system. It contains information about the object to be stored, including its unique identifier and transfer syntax; C-STORE-RQ enables the standardized and reliable transfer of DICOM objects in healthcare environments.

P-DATA, X-ray Angiog (reassembled fragment). This message (Listing 12) represents a fragment of the X-ray Angiographic Image Storage data. The message continues as long as the transmission of the X-ray Angiographic Image Storage data continues, and is reassembled in a final P-DATA network packet. This signifies that the data transmission is ongoing and more fragments are being sent to complete the image or object.

PDATA, Command ID=1 (Success). This message (Listing 12) represents a complete DICOM P-DATA message containing the entire X-ray Angiographic Image Storage. It indicates that the data transmission for this particular object or image is complete.

5.4.4. Association Termination

To conclude the communication, `MODALITY` initiates the termination process by sending an `A-RELEASE request` to `Orthanc` at time T_{10}, as expressed in Equation (12).

$$MODALITY \xrightarrow{\text{A-RELEASE request}} PACS \quad \text{at time } T_{10} \tag{12}$$

`PACS` responds by acknowledging the request with an `A-RELEASE response`, which is received by `MODALITY` at time T_{11}, as presented in Equation (13).

$$MODALITY \xleftarrow{\text{A-RELEASE response}} PACS \quad \text{at time } T_{11} \tag{13}$$

A-RELEASE Request. The A-RELEASE request is sent by MODALITY to initiate the termination (Listing 13) of the DICOM association between MODALITY and Orthanc. This indicates the intention to close the connection gracefully. A-RELEASE is a message used in the DICOM protocol to initiate the termination of a DICOM association between two devices or systems. The A-RELEASE message is sent by one entity to the other to indicate an intention to gracefully close the connection. Upon receiving the A-RELEASE message, the recipient entity acknowledges the request by sending an A-RELEASE response. The A-RELEASE process allows for the orderly termination of the DICOM association, ensuring the proper release of resources and connections associated with the session. This is an essential step in maintaining the integrity and efficiency of DICOM communication between devices or systems in healthcare environments.

A-RELEASE Response. The A-RELEASE response is sent by Orthanc in response to the A-RELEASE request from MODALITY. It acknowledges the termination request and signifies the successful termination of the DICOM association.

5.5. Discussion

The simulated environment for DICOM communication serves as a platform for testing and addressing essential aspects of network security and related cybersecurity issues. The environment is designed to replicate DICOM communication scenarios, and facilitates a comprehensive understanding of potential threats as well as the actions needed to mitigate them. DICOM communication is susceptible to several cyberthreats, and the presented simulation can assist in conducting security assessments as well as in implementation and testing of mitigation actions in an isolated and realistic environment. Cyberthreats selected as important can be replicated within the simulation, including the following:

1. Insecure communication: without encryption, sensitive DICOM data transmitted over the network are vulnerable to eavesdropping and unauthorized access.
2. Weak authentication: insufficient user authentication mechanisms can lead to unauthorized users gaining access to DICOM systems, resulting in compromised data integrity.
3. Outdated software: running outdated DICOM software components can expose vulnerabilities that malicious actors can exploit for unauthorized access or data manipulation.
4. Insufficient training: lack of user awareness and training can result in successful social engineering attacks, leading to unauthorized data access.
5. Unprotected networks: failure to segment and secure the network exposes DICOM systems to potential breaches from unauthorized network traffic.
6. Data manipulation: without proper integrity checks, attackers might manipulate DICOM data during transmission, leading to compromised diagnoses or treatments.
7. Unauthorized access: poorly managed access control can result in unauthorized users gaining entry to DICOM resources.
8. Lack of intrusion detection: absence of intrusion detection mechanisms makes it challenging to detect and respond to unauthorized network activities.
9. Auditing and weakness identification (M1047): it is crucial to perform regular audits and scans on DICOM systems in order to identify weaknesses that could compromise communication security.

Similarly, OWASP has published a comprehensive guide to the secure deployment of medical devices [48]. Furthermore, a CSRF vulnerability for ORTHANC was presented in [49]. Similarly, Nmap Scripting Engine (NSE) scripts have been published related to DICOM [50,51]. These scripts aim to perform brute force attacks on the AET of a DICOM server.

Table 2 outlines a set of MITRE mitigation actions along with their relevance to DICOM communication security. Each MITRE ID corresponds to a specific mitigation action designed to address a particular security concern in the context of DICOM communication.

In regard to the OWASP guide and the vulnerabilities and threats mentioned above, Table 2 lists MITRE mitigation actions that correspond to the above-mentioned security issues. According to MITRE [52], mitigations embody security principles and categories of technologies that can be employed to thwart the successful execution of a technique or subtechnique. As such, the information in Table 2 can be used to identify other potential cyberthreats by looking to the relevant MITRE ATT&CK Navigator Layer according to the particular mitigation measures.

The DICOM simulation featured in this research provides valuable insights into addressing potential cybersecurity vulnerabilities and implementing corresponding mitigation strategies. However, it is crucial to acknowledge certain inherent limitations and constraints associated with the simulation's findings. The simulation's results are contingent upon a series of assumptions and simplifications made during the modeling phase. These assumptions might not always align with the intricacies of real-world scenarios, introducing the potential for variations that could impact the accuracy of the conclusions derived from the simulation.

Table 2. MITRE Mitigation Actions and Relevance to DICOM.

MITRE ID	Mitigation Action	Realization and Relevance to DICOM
M1047	Perform audits or scans to identify weaknesses.	Regularly audit DICOM systems, configurations, and permissions to identify potential vulnerabilities that could impact DICOM communication.
M0804	Require user authentication.	Implement strong user authentication mechanisms before granting access to DICOM data or devices to prevent unauthorized access or data manipulation.
M1041	Encrypt Sensitive Information.	Apply strong encryption to sensitive DICOM data to ensure its confidentiality during transmission and storage.
M1051	Update Software.	Regularly update DICOM software components to patch vulnerabilities and reduce the risk of exploitation during communication.
M1017	User Training.	Train users involved in DICOM communication to recognize and respond to potential access or manipulation attempts, such as spearphishing or social engineering attacks.
M0930	Network Segmentation.	Segment the network to isolate critical DICOM systems from other network segments, preventing unauthorized access and protecting DICOM communication from potential threats.
M0931	Network Intrusion Prevention.	Use intrusion detection techniques that don't disrupt real-time DICOM communication protocols to identify and block unauthorized or malicious network traffic.
M1037	Limit Access to Resources Over Network.	Restrict network access to DICOM file shares and remote access points, reducing exposure to potential attackers and ensuring secure communication.
M1035	Filter Network Traffic.	Utilize network appliances and endpoint software to filter incoming and outgoing DICOM network traffic, blocking potentially harmful or unauthorized data flows.

Furthermore, the simulation did not involve the actual execution of cyberattacks or vulnerability assessments. This omission is attributed to the reliance on specific deployment parameters, making it difficult to accurately replicate authentic cyberattack scenarios. Consequently, the simulation's representations of real-world cyberattacks may lack full complexity and nuanced intricacies, potentially influencing the realism of its findings.

Moreover, the simulation's scope might not encompass the entirety of potential cyberthreats. The rapidly evolving landscape of cybersecurity introduces the possibility of emerging and sophisticated threats that were not explicitly accounted for in the simulation. This limitation is a result of the inherent challenge of predicting and accommodating the myriad attack vectors that can emerge over time.

6. Conclusions

In this research, a DICOM simulator incorporating advanced features of virtualized environments and cloud computing was developed within a virtual lab context. The focus of this study was on conducting in-depth analyses and facilitating learning related to the fundamental attributes of the DICOM protocol. The DICOM simulator provides a flexible approach that can be further developed and customized to meet the specific needs of researchers. By utilizing cloud computing capabilities, the simulator can emulate complex scenarios and facilitate interoperability between different systems and devices. This enables researchers to explore and experiment with various aspects of DICOM communication and PACS integration. Moreover, the simulation has the capability to produce network traffic through the utilization of the DICOM protocol. This traffic generation results in the creation of authentic datasets, which can be effectively employed for the advancement of machine learning, deep learning technologies, and anomaly detection techniques.

The presented topology and deployment can serve as a platform for conducting security control testing, allowing researchers to evaluate the robustness of security measures, identify vulnerabilities, and test different security configurations in a controlled and safe environment. In this way, it provides researchers with an opportunity to gain a comprehensive understanding of DICOM communication and its practical implementation.

Future Work

A significant future milestone involves fostering enhanced interoperability between PACS while encompassing other medical imaging devices or formats. This expanded interoperability can facilitate seamless communication and data exchange across various SOP classes, extending the simulation support to encompass a wider range of scenarios and medical imaging modalities. Moreover, an area of promising exploration is the extension of research in the development and utilization of digital twins for medical imaging modalities. The development and utilization of digital twins for replicating healthcare or medical modalities can unlock a multitude of possibilities.

Finally, an important focus of future research involves addressing cyberthreats, conducting security assessments, creating a readily deployable topology (cyber range), and developing adversary emulation strategies aligned with the threats mentioned in this research.

Author Contributions: Conceptualisation, S.K. and R.C.; methodology, S.K.; software, S.K.; validation, S.K. and R.C.; formal analysis, E.M. and T.F.; writing—original draft preparation, S.K.; writing—review and editing E.M., C.N. and R.C.; supervision, E.M. and T.F. All authors have read and agreed to the published version of the manuscript.

Funding: This work was funded by the European Union's Horizon 2020 Research and Innovation Programme under Grant Agreements No. 883273 (AI4HEALTHSEC) and No. 101070450 (AI4CYBER).

Institutional Review Board Statement: Not applicable.

Informed Consent Statement: Not applicable.

Data Availability Statement: Sample logs can be obtained by contacting the authors.

Acknowledgments: The authors would like to acknowledge support and funding provided by the projects AI4HEALTHSEC and AI4CYBER.

Conflicts of Interest: The authors declare no conflict of interest.

References

1. Bercovich, E.; Javitt, M.C. Medical imaging: From roentgen to the digital revolution, and beyond. *Rambam Maimonides Med. J.* **2018**, *9*, e0034. [CrossRef] [PubMed]
2. Dash, S.; Shakyawar, S.K.; Sharma, M.; Kaushik, S. Big data in healthcare: Management, analysis and future prospects. *J. Big Data* **2019**, *6*, 54. [CrossRef]
3. Osteaux, M.; Van den Broeck, R.; Verhelle, F.; de Mey, J. Picture archiving and communication system (PACS): Medical perspectives. *J. Belg. Radiol.* **1997**, *80*, 128–132. [PubMed]

4. Nichols, J.A.; Herbert Chan, H.W.; Baker, M.A. Machine learning: Applications of artificial intelligence to imaging and diagnosis. *Biophys. Rev.* **2019**, *11*, 111–118. [CrossRef] [PubMed]
5. Latreche, A.; Kelaiaia, R.; Chemori, A.; Kerboua, A. Reliability and validity analysis of MediaPipe-based measurement system for some human rehabilitation motions. *Measurement* **2023**, *214*, 112826. [CrossRef]
6. Latreche, A.; Kelaiaia, R.; Chemori, A.; Kerboua, A. A New Home-Based Upper-and Lower-Limb Telerehabilitation Platform with Experimental Validation. *Arab. J. Sci. Eng.* **2023**, *48*, 10825–10840. [CrossRef] [PubMed]
7. Hussain, T.; Nguyen, Q.T. Molecular imaging for cancer diagnosis and surgery. *Adv. Drug Deliv. Rev.* **2014**, *66*, 90–100. [CrossRef] [PubMed]
8. Bidgood, W.D., Jr.; Horii, S.C.; Prior, F.W.; Van Syckle, D.E. Understanding and using DICOM, the data interchange standard for biomedical imaging. *J. Am. Med. Inform. Assoc.* **1997**, *4*, 199–212. [CrossRef] [PubMed]
9. Lebre, R.; Costa, C. An Efficient and Reliable Architecture for Distributing Medical Imaging Data. In Proceedings of the 2021 International Conference on e-Health and Bioengineering (EHB), Iasi, Romania, 18–19 November 2021; pp. 1–4. [CrossRef]
10. Supriya, S.; Padaki, S. Data security and privacy challenges in adopting solutions for IOT. In Proceedings of the 2016 IEEE International Conference on Internet of Things (iThings) and IEEE Green Computing and Communications (GreenCom) and IEEE Cyber, Physical and Social Computing (CPSCom) and IEEE Smart Data (SmartData), Chengdu, China, 15–18 December 2016; pp. 410–415. [CrossRef]
11. Jeyakumar, V.; Abirami, K.R.; Saraswathi, S.; Kumaran, R.S.; Marthi, G. Secure medical image storage and retrieval for Internet of Medical Imaging Things using blockchain-enabled edge computing. In *Intelligent Edge Computing for Cyber Physical Applications*; Elsevier: Amsterdam, The Netherlands, 2023; pp. 85–110. [CrossRef]
12. Mustra, M.; Delac, K.; Grgic, M. Overview of the DICOM standard. In Proceedings of the 2008 50th International Symposium ELMAR, Zadar, Croatia, 10–12 September 2008; Volume 1, pp. 39–44.
13. Fennell, N.; Ralston, M.D.; Coleman, R.M. PACS and Other Image Management Systems. In *Practical Imaging Informatics: Foundations and Applications for Medical Imaging*; Springer: Berlin/Heidelberg, Germany, 2021; pp. 131–142. [CrossRef]
14. Cooke, R.E., Jr.; Gaeta, M.G.; Kaufman, D.M.; Henrici, J.G. Picture Archiving and Communication System. U.S. Patent 6,574,629, 3 June 2003.
15. Desjardins, B.; Mirsky, Y.; Ortiz, M.P.; Glozman, Z.; Tarbox, L.; Horn, R.; Horii, S.C. DICOM images have been hacked! Now what? *Am. J. Roentgenol.* **2020**, *214*, 727–735. [CrossRef] [PubMed]
16. Stites, M.; Pianykh, O.S. How secure is your radiology department? Mapping digital radiology adoption and security worldwide. *AJR Am. J. Roentgenol.* **2016**, *206*, 797–804. [CrossRef] [PubMed]
17. Beek, C. Mcafee Researchers Find Poor Security Exposes Medical Data to Cybercriminals. McAfee Blogs. 2018. Available online: https://www.mcafee.com/blogs/other-blogs/mcafee-labs/mcafee-researchers-find-poor-security-exposes-medical-data-to-cybercriminals/ (accessed on 5 September 2023).
18. Oliveira, P.A.M.; Junior, E.C.; Andrade, R.M.; Santos, I.S.; Neto, P.A.S. Ten Years of eHealth Discussions on Stack Overflow. 2022.
19. Cronin, S.; Kane, B.; Doherty, G. A qualitative analysis of the needs and experiences of hospital-based clinicians when accessing medical imaging. *J. Digit. Imaging* **2021**, *34*, 385–396. [CrossRef] [PubMed]
20. Eichelberg, M.; Kleber, K.; Kämmerer, M. Cybersecurity in PACS and medical imaging: An overview. *J. Digit. Imaging* **2020**, *33*, 1527–1542. [CrossRef] [PubMed]
21. Coutinho, B.; Ferreira, J.; Yevseyeva, I.; Basto-Fernandes, V. Integrated cybersecurity methodology and supporting tools for healthcare operational information systems. *Comput. Secur.* **2023**, *129*, 103189. [CrossRef]
22. Kumar, P.; Singh, A.; Sengupta, A. Securing Cyber-Resilience in Healthcare Sector. In *Cyber Security in Intelligent Computing and Communications*; Springer: Berlin/Heidelberg, Germany, 2022; pp. 211–226. [CrossRef]
23. Wang, Z.; Li, Q.; Wang, Y.; Liu, B.; Zhang, J.; Liu, Q. Medical protocol security: DICOM vulnerability mining based on fuzzing technology. In Proceedings of the 2019 ACM SIGSAC Conference on Computer and Communications Security, London, UK, 11–15 November 2019; pp. 2549–2551. [CrossRef]
24. Wang, Z.; Li, Q.; Liu, Q.; Liu, B.; Zhang, J.; Yang, T.; Liu, Q. DICOM-Fuzzer: Research on DICOM vulnerability mining based on Fuzzing technology. In Proceedings of the Communications and Networking: 14th EAI International Conference, ChinaCom 2019, Shanghai, China, 29 November–1 December 2019; Springer: Berlin/Heidelberg, Germany, 2020; pp. 509–524. [CrossRef]
25. Paul, M.; Maglaras, L.; Ferrag, M.A.; AlMomani, I. Digitization of healthcare sector: A study on privacy and security concerns. *ICT Express* **2023**, *9*, 571–588. [CrossRef]
26. Abouelmehdi, K.; Beni-Hssane, A.; Khaloufi, H.; Saadi, M. Big data security and privacy in healthcare: A Review. *Procedia Comput. Sci.* **2017**, *113*, 73–80. [CrossRef]
27. GitHub-ionianCTF/dicom_simulation: A DICOM Simulator in Python Sending ".dcm" Files from a Local Folder to a PACS server Using Pynetdicom and Pydicom.—Github.com. Available online: https://github.com/ionianCTF/dicom_simulation (accessed on 8 July 2023).
28. Zhou, Z.; Law, M.Y.; Huang, H.; Cao, F.; Liu, B.J.; Zhang, J.; Mogel, G.T.; Zhuang, J. Educational RIS/PACS simulator. In Proceedings of the Medical Imaging 2003: PACS and Integrated Medical Information Systems: Design and Evaluation. *SPIE* **2003**, *5033*, 139–147. [CrossRef]
29. Orthanc—DICOM Server—Orthanc-Server.com. Available online: https://www.orthanc-server.com/ (accessed on 8 July 2023).
30. Onis Viewer—Dicom Viewer and PACS—Onis-Viewer.com. Available online: https://onis-viewer.com (accessed on 8 July 2023).

31. Hussain, M.A.; Langer, S.G.; Kohli, M. Learning HL7 FHIR using the HAPI FHIR server and its use in medical imaging with the SIIM dataset. *J. Digit. Imaging* **2018**, *31*, 334–340. [CrossRef] [PubMed]
32. Potter, G.; Busbridge, R.; Toland, M.; Nagy, P. Mastering DICOM with DVTk. *J. Digit. Imaging* **2007**, *20*, 47–62. [CrossRef] [PubMed]
33. DVTK/RIS_Emulator at Master·151706061/DVTK—Github.com. Available online: https://github.com/151706061/DVTK/tree/master/RIS_Emulator (accessed on 8 July 2023).
34. Piraino, D. Radiology information system and picture archiving and communication system: Interfacing and integration. In *Digital(r) Evolution in Radiology*; Springer: Berlin/Heidelberg, Germany, 2001; pp. 47–55. [CrossRef]
35. Oemig, F.; Snelick, R.; Oemig, F.; Snelick, R. Testing Tools. *Healthcare Interoperability Standards Compliance Handbook: Conformance and Testing of Healthcare Data Exchange Standards*; Springer: Berlin/Heidelberg, Germany, 2016; pp. 525–558. [CrossRef]
36. GitHub—Hapifhir/hapi-hl7v2—Github.com. Available online: https://github.com/hapifhir/hapi-hl7v2 (accessed on 8 July 2023).
37. Mantri, M.; Taran, S.; Sunder, G. DICOM integration libraries for medical image interoperability: A technical review. *IEEE Rev. Biomed. Eng.* **2020**, *15*, 247–259. [CrossRef] [PubMed]
38. Cawthra, J.; Hodges, B.; Kuruvilla, J.; Littlefield, K.; Niemeyer, B.; Peloquin, C.; Wang, S.; Williams, R.; Zheng, K. *Securing Picture Archiving and Communication System (PACS) Cybersecurity for the Healthcare Sector*; Nist Special Publication: Gaithersburg, MD, USA, 2019.
39. Mileva, A.; Velinov, A.; Dimitrova, V.; Caviglione, L.; Wendzel, S. Information hiding in the dicom message service and upper layer service with entropy-based detection. *Entropy* **2022**, *24*, 176. [CrossRef] [PubMed]
40. Fritz, S.L.; Roys, S.R.; Munjal, S. Design requirements for DICOM patient, study, and results management. In Proceedings of the Medical Imaging 1996: PACS Design and Evaluation: Engineering and Clinical Issues, Newport Beach, CA, USA, 13–15 February 1996; Volume 2711, pp. 98–108.
41. Welcome to the Orthanc Book 2014; Orthanc Book Documentation—Book.Orthanc-Server.com. Available online: https://book.orthanc-server.com/index.html (accessed on 8 July 2023).
42. Association, N.E.M. Digital Imaging and Communication in Medicine (DICOM). NEMA PS 3 Supplement 23 Structured Reporting. 1997. Available online: https://www.dicomstandard.org/current (accessed on 5 September 2023).
43. Hamamoto, K. Standardization of JPEG quantization table for medical ultrasonic echo images. In Proceedings of the ICECS'99. Proceedings of ICECS'99. 6th IEEE International Conference on Electronics, Circuits and Systems (Cat. No. 99EX357), Paphos, Cyprus, 5–8 September 1999; Volume 2, pp. 683–686. [CrossRef]
44. Security—Dicomstandard.org. Available online: https://www.dicomstandard.org/using/security (accessed on 24 August 2023).
45. GitHub—Pydicom/Pynetdicom: A Python Implementation of the DICOM Networking Protocol—Github.com. Available online: https://github.com/pydicom/pynetdicom (accessed on 8 July 2023).
46. GitHub—Pydicom/Pydicom: Read, Modify and Write DICOM files with Python Code—Github.com. Available online: https://github.com/pydicom/pydicom (accessed on 8 July 2023).
47. Docker—Github.com. Available online: https://github.com/docker (accessed on 22 August 2023).
48. Frenz, C. OWASP Secure Medical Device Deployment Standard Version 2.0. Available online: https://owasp.org/www-pdf-archive/OWASP_Secure_Medical_Devices_Deployment_Standard_7.18.18.pdf (accessed on 8 July 2023).
49. DICOM Security—Sdnewhop/Dicom:—Github.com. Available online: https://github.com/sdnewhop/dicom (accessed on 22 August 2023).
50. Dicom-Brute NSE Script 2014; Nmap Scripting Engine Documentation—Nmap.org. Available online: https://nmap.org/nsedoc/scripts/dicom-brute.html (accessed on 22 August 2023).
51. Dicom-Ping NSE Script 2014; Nmap Scripting Engine Documentation—Nmap.org. Available online: https://nmap.org/nsedoc/scripts/dicom-ping.html (accessed on 22 August 2023).
52. Mitigations—Enterprise | MITRE ATT&CK—Attack.mitre.org. Available online: https://attack.mitre.org/mitigations/enterprise/ (accessed on 22 August 2023).

applied sciences

MDPI

Article

Leveraging Language Models for Inpatient Diagnosis Coding

Kerdkiat Suvirat [1,†], Detphop Tanasanchonnakul [2,†], Sawrawit Chairat [1] and Sitthichok Chaichulee [1,*]

[1] Department of Biomedical Sciences and Biomedical Engineering, Faculty of Medicine, Prince of Songkla University, Songkhla 90110, Thailand
[2] Faculty of Medicine, Prince of Songkla University, Songkhla 90110, Thailand
* Correspondence: sitthichok.c@psu.ac.th
† These authors contributed equally to this work.

Abstract: Medical coding plays an essential role in medical billing, health resource planning, clinical research and quality assessment. Automated coding systems offer promising solutions to streamline the coding process, improve accuracy and reduce the burden on medical coders. To date, there has been limited research focusing on inpatient diagnosis coding using an extensive comprehensive dataset and encompassing the full ICD-10 code sets. In this study, we investigate the use of language models for coding inpatient diagnoses and examine their performance using an institutional dataset comprising 230,645 inpatient admissions and 8677 diagnosis codes spanning over a six-year period. A total of three language models, including two general-purpose models and a domain-specific model, were evaluated and compared. The results show competitive performance among the models, with the domain-specific model achieving the highest micro-averaged F1 score of 0.7821 and the highest mean average precision of 0.8097. Model performance varied by disease and condition, with diagnosis codes with larger sample sizes producing better results. The rarity of certain diseases and conditions posed challenges to accurate coding. The results also indicated the potential difficulties of the model with long clinical documents. Our models demonstrated the ability to capture relevant associations between diagnoses. This study advances the understanding of language models for inpatient diagnosis coding and provides insights into the extent to which the models can be used.

Keywords: electronic health records; healthcare informatics; natural language processing; text classification; diagnosis code; inpatient care

Citation: Suvirat, K.; Tanasanchonnakul, D.; Chairat, S.; Chaichulee, S. Leveraging Language Models for Inpatient Diagnosis Coding. *Appl. Sci.* **2023**, *13*, 9450. https://doi.org/10.3390/app13169450

Academic Editors: Stefano Silvestri and Francesco Gargiulo

Received: 20 July 2023
Revised: 14 August 2023
Accepted: 16 August 2023
Published: 21 August 2023

1. Introduction

Medical coding is the process of assigning standardised codes to diagnoses, procedures, treatments, tests and other services [1,2]. It involves converting extensive clinical information into alphanumeric codes that represent specific medical conditions, interventions and related data [2]. This task is complicated and time-consuming, requiring expertise and attention to detail [3]. These codes are essential for various purposes, including reimbursement, clinical research, service analysis and quality assessment [2].

The main system for coding diagnoses in health care is the International Classification of Diseases (ICD) [4–6], which provides codes for diagnosing diseases and other health conditions. Medical coders play a crucial role in the coding process. They review patient records, including doctor's notes, laboratory test results, radiology reports and other relevant documentation, to extract the necessary information for assigning the appropriate codes [1–3]. Medical coders must have a thorough understanding of medical terminology, anatomy, physiology and coding guidelines to ensure accurate and consistent coding [3].

The ICD is a comprehensive system maintained by the World Health Organization (WHO) [4–6]. Over time, the ICD has been revised periodically to ensure accuracy and relevance in recording medical conditions and procedures. The current version is ICD-11 [6], published on 1 January 2022, and its widespread adoption is a gradual process. Most countries currently use ICD-10 [5] and some countries still use ICD-9 or even ICD-8 [4].

Each subsequent revision of ICD brings expanded code sets that capture a broader range of diagnoses and procedures. ICD-10 includes an extensive range of codes organised into 22 chapters with subclassifications that allow additional details such as cause, manifestation, severity, anatomical site and type of disease to be specified [5]. Some countries have implemented modifications to accommodate their specific needs and healthcare practices, such as the ICD-10-AM (Australian Modification) and the ICD-10-TM (Thai Modification).

The structure of ICD-10 is designed to provide a systematic approach to coding (see Figure 1) [5]. It utilizes a seven-character format, with the first three characters referred to as "blocks" and providing a general classification of the type of disease. The following four characters represent sub-classifications allowing for more precise identification and categorisation.

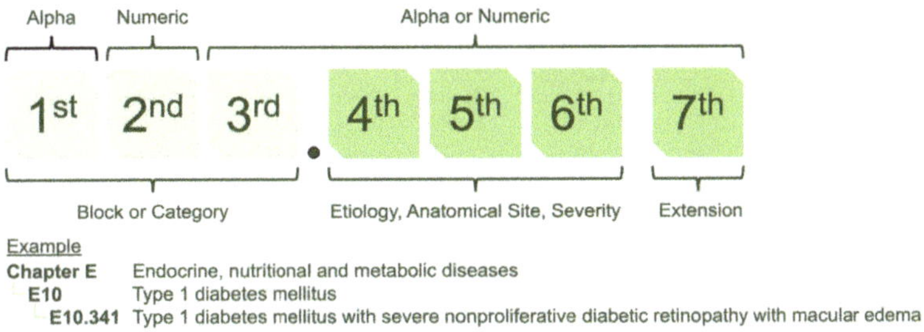

Figure 1. The ICD-10 coding structure is a hierarchical system with alphanumeric codes. The first three characters represent the general classification of the type of disease, while additional characters indicate more specific details such as location and severity.

Accurate medical coding is essential for reimbursement and contributes to data analysis, resource allocation, clinical research and data sharing between healthcare providers [2]. The increasing workload due to the growing number of patient records makes medical coding an intensive task [3]. Advanced technologies such as artificial intelligence (AI) and natural language processing (NLP) can automate or semi-automate coding, reducing the burden on human coders and improving efficiency [7,8]. For example, AI-powered systems can analyse clinical records such as doctor's notes and medical records, as well as historical coding data, to suggest appropriate codes based on the documented information [8]. They can also compare coded information with clinical documentation to identify discrepancies or potential errors, ensuring coding integrity and compliance with coding guidelines.

The application of NLP in medical coding has attracted much attention in recent years [7–16]. In 2001, Chapman et al. [9] introduced a rule-based algorithm that uses regular expressions to identify diseases in discharge summaries. In 2007, Crammer et al. [10] proposed a combined learning system from three different learning techniques for ICD-9-CM code assignment. More recently, the field has shifted from rule-based techniques to machine learning methods. Hasan et al. [11] compared Convolutional Neural Networks (CNN) and Support Vector Machine (SVM) models for ICD classification. The authors suggested that CNN performed well on diagnosis codes with many training examples, while SVM performed better than CNN on diagnosis codes with few training examples. Moons et al. [12] used a multiple-view CNN with regularised label-dependent attention. Xu et al. [13] used a multimodal model integrating data from multiple modalities to predict ICD-10 codes. In a non-English context, Boytcheva [14] used SVM for ICD classification of Bulgarian medical records. Yu et al. [15] used a multilayer bidirectional recurrent neural network (RNN) for ICD classification in a Chinese dataset. Almago et al. [16] used an ensemble multi-label text classification algorithm for Spanish hospital summaries. They suggested that when the class distribution is extreme, using an ensemble approach that takes coding frequency into account may lead to better results.

A language model is an AI model that learns the statistical patterns, relationships and structures of language. It is typically pre-trained using large amounts of textual data so that it can develop a deep understanding of language structures and semantics. During pre-training, the language model is exposed to unlabelled text and learns to predict masked words, next words, or sequences of words in sentences. This process enables the model to grasp grammar, syntax and semantic relationships between words. The pre-trained language model can then be fine-tuned using labelled data for specific language comprehension tasks, such as text generation, completion, translation, sentiment analysis and question answering.

BERT (Bidirectional Encoder Representations from Transformers) [17] is a language model that has revolutionised NLP through its ability to understand and capture the semantic meaning and context of words and sentences. BERT has shown remarkable performance on various NLP tasks. BERT was originally trained on 3.3 billion English words from Wikipedia and has been extended to multilingual domains such as mBERT [17] and XLM [18], as well as domain-specific languages, such as BioBERT [19] and ClinicalBERT [20], which were pre-trained on biomedical data. Recently, Amin et al. [21] and Biseda et al. used BioBERT and ClinicalBERT, respectively, for ICD-10 classification using the MIMIC dataset [22]. ClinicalBERT outperformed BioBERT in terms of performance. Silvestri et al. [23] used XLM for ICD-10 classification, focusing on the Italian context. Lopez-Garcia et al. [24] used mBERT for automatic clinical coding in the Spanish context. In addition, Remmer et al. [25] used KB-BERT for ICD classification in the Swedish context. However, these studies cannot be directly compared because of the different methods and datasets. Each study used a different approach. Some studies specifically analysed the block level of the ICD code or focused only on some of the most common codes from the extensive range of over ten thousand ICD-10 codes. To date, due to the public availability of clinical data, there have been relatively few studies that have harnessed the power of large institutional datasets that include the full ICD-10 code sets. In this context, the full performance potential of language models for automatic ICD-10 coding remains largely untapped.

This study aimed to explore the potential of using language models to support coding of inpatient diagnoses. We investigated how language models can be used to analyse clinical records and extract relevant diagnosis codes. For our study, we used our extensive clinical data, which spans 6 years and includes 230,645 inpatient admissions and 8677 diagnosis codes. Our goal was to address two important questions: (1) How accurate can a language model-based algorithm for ICD-10 classification be when clinical data of one institution are utilized? and (2) To what extent can the algorithm be used? We investigated the performance of the algorithm on different types of diagnoses, including common diseases and rare and complex cases. We explored the scope of the algorithm and identified specific areas where it might excel or encounter challenges. This can provide valuable insights into whether automatic or semi-automatic coding of diagnoses is ready for application in hospital information systems (HIS).

This study makes notable contributions to inpatient diagnosis coding by investigating the effectiveness of language models on a comprehensive dataset spanning a six-year period with the full ICD-10 code sets. We examined both general-purpose language models and a domain-specific language model. Our results illustrate the competitive performance of the language models and highlight their potential to improve coding accuracy. We analysed the performance of the models on different diagnostic codes, providing insights into the impact of sample size on coding accuracy. We used co-occurrence analysis to ensure that the models were able to capture relevant associations between diagnoses. We also identified factors that influence performance, including disease rarity and document length. This work highlights the need for larger datasets, class imbalance strategies, multi-hospital collaboration and integration of multidimensional data to improve automatic coding systems.

2. Materials and Methods

2.1. Dataset

Our study used discharge summaries and corresponding ICD-10 assignments of patients admitted and discharged from Songklanagrind Hospital, Thailand, between 1 January 2017 and 31 December 2022 (6 years). We included inpatient admissions with a length of stay of more than one day. It is worth noting that the full implementation of ICD-10 coding standard at the institution started in mid 2016. Ethical approval for our study was obtained from the Office of Human Research Ethics Committee, Faculty of Medicine, Prince of Songkla University (REC.65-120-38-2). All ICD-10 codes were assigned by physicians and professional clinical coders according to the Thailand's ICD-10-TM coding standard. Figure 2 shows an example of a discharge summary.

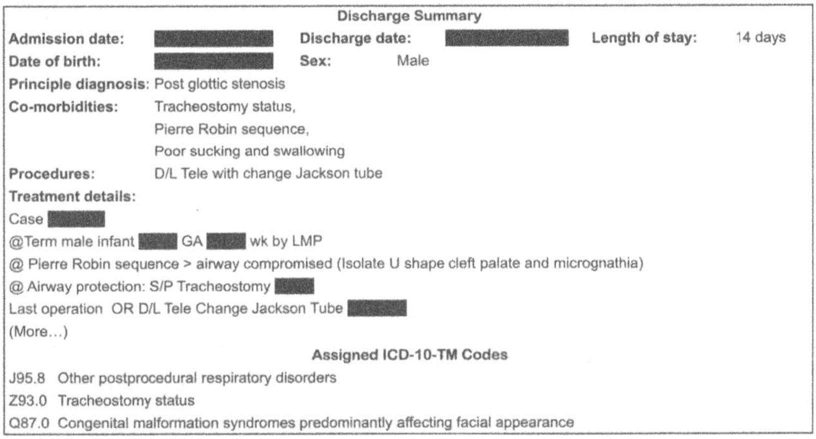

Discharge Summary

Admission date: [redacted] **Discharge date:** [redacted] **Length of stay:** 14 days
Date of birth: [redacted] **Sex:** Male
Principle diagnosis: Post glottic stenosis
Co-morbidities: Tracheostomy status,
Pierre Robin sequence,
Poor sucking and swallowing
Procedures: D/L Tele with change Jackson tube
Treatment details:
Case [redacted]
@Term male infant [redacted] GA [redacted] wk by LMP
@ Pierre Robin sequence > airway compromised (Isolate U shape cleft palate and micrognathia)
@ Airway protection: S/P Tracheostomy [redacted]
Last operation OR D/L Tele Change Jackson Tube [redacted]
(More...)

Assigned ICD-10-TM Codes

J95.8 Other postprocedural respiratory disorders
Z93.0 Tracheostomy status
Q87.0 Congenital malformation syndromes predominantly affecting facial appearance

Figure 2. Example of a discharge summary.

2.2. Data Exploration

Our dataset contains 230,645 inpatient admissions and 8677 diagnosis codes. The average number of codes assigned per discharge summary is 4.1. Figure 3a illustrates the distribution of discharge summaries over time. On average, there are approximately 3200 inpatient admissions per month. The number of admissions fluctuates during the period when the COVID-19 lockdown policies were introduced. This was as a result of reduced elective procedures and delayed non-urgent admissions. Figure 3b presents the distribution of the 50 most frequently coded ICD-10 codes. The distribution shows a considerable degree of skewness and dispersion, which is due to the varying prevalence of diseases and the fine-grained nature of ICD-10 codes.

Figure 3c shows the rank size distribution of the ICD-10 codes. Some codes were less frequently utilised due to the rarity of the corresponding diagnoses. This highlights the heterogeneity of disease prevalence and the complex coding landscape in which certain conditions are more prevalent and consequently more frequently coded. This dispersion in the use of codes also reflects the diverse range of conditions found in the study population.

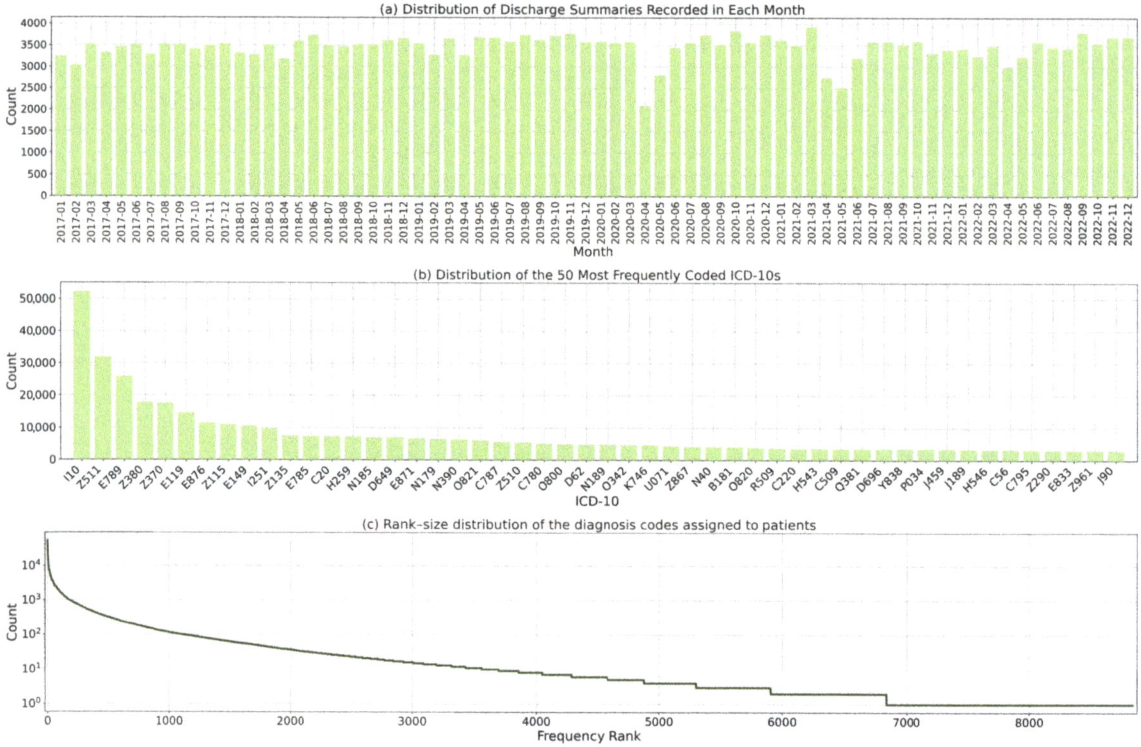

Figure 3. Dataset statistics: (**a**) Distribution of discharge summaries by month; (**b**) Distribution of the 50 most commonly coded diagnosis codes; and (**c**) Rank-size distribution of the diagnosis codes.

2.3. Data Preparation

For each inpatient discharge summary, we used four main fields: principle diagnosis, co-morbidities, procedures and treatment details. We concatenated all fields to create a single document (see Figure 1). The average number of characters per document is 1669. For each document, we removed newline characters. We kept punctuation characters and symbols because they often contain important meanings, such as measurement values. As our institution is based in Thailand, the clinical text used in this study is a mixture of English and Thai words. English terminology is used for diseases, procedures and medicines, while Thai is used for surrounding clinical context. Thai texts are usually written without spaces between words. Word segmentation allows us to separate the text into individual word units. We segmented the Thai text into individual word units using the dictionary-based maximal matching algorithm in the PyThaiNLP library [26]. The same strategy was used the pre-training of the language models used in the study [17,27].

Consequently, we divided our dataset into two parts. The first part includes clinical records of patients admitted and discharged between 2017 and 2021, which were further randomly split into a training and validation set in a 90:10 ratio (172,437 and 19,160 admissions, respectively). The second part comprises clinical records of patients admitted and discharged in 2022, which was then served as a test set (39,048 admissions). This results in the walk-forward test set to ensure that the algorithms were validated in the same way as when they were deployed in HIS.

2.4. Language Model Finetuning

We formulated our problem as a multi-label classification task, where each instance can be assigned multiple labels simultaneously. In our case, the labels represent different ICD-10 codes that we aim to predict for a given document. We evaluated three pre-trained language models:

- **Multilingual BERT** [17] or mBERT is a variant of the BERT model pre-trained on a multilingual corpus. It captures contextual information from words and sentences using a transformer architecture. Through training with different languages, the model learns to understand and generate representations for multiple languages. Multilingual BERT has been used in various NLP applications due to its ability to process multiple languages with a single model.
- **Multilingual E5** [27] is a version of the E5 model that supports multiple languages. It was trained using a simple contrastive training approach. The training data for this model were collected from various sources on the Internet, resulting in an extensive text dataset. Multilingual E5 is a versatile embedding model that can be easily used for various tasks where a representation of text data is required.
- **MEDPSU-RoBERTa** is our institutional language model with the RoBERTa architecture that was pre-trained on a comprehensive dataset of over 80 million clinical documents from Songklanagarind Hospital, Thailand. We adhered to pre-training guidelines, following the standard approach detailed in the original RoBERTa paper [28] with the transformer library [29]. In this way, MEDPSU-RoBERTa has been tailored to captures the nuances of clinical language allowing it can understand and analyse medical texts with a high degree of accuracy and precision.

For each pre-trained language model, we removed the layers corresponding to the language model head, which are originally responsible for text generation. We then extended the pre-trained language models by using the output of the last hidden states for the [CLS] classification token and passing it through a classification head consisting of two dense layers (see Figure 4).

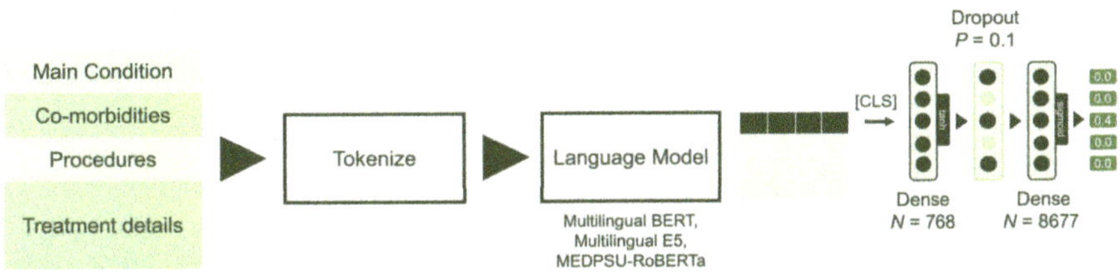

Figure 4. Model architecture: The model utilizes data from four main fields: principal diagnosis, co-morbidities, procedures and treatment details. The language models were fine-tuned with two dense layers, each with output sizes of 768 and 8677, respectively. Sigmoid activation was employed to obtain the multilabel probabilities.

Given that $\mathrm{LM}_{\mathrm{last}}$ represents the output of the last hidden state for the [CLS] classification token as a 768-dimensional vector, the output of the classification head can be calculated as:

$$\hat{y} = L_2(D(\tanh(L_1(\mathrm{LM}_{\mathrm{last}})))) \quad (1)$$

where L_1 is the first dense layer with 768 hideen units, tanh is a hyperbolic tangent activation function, D is a dropout layer with a probability of 0.1 and L_2 is the final dense layer with 8677 outputs, representing the output of the model $\hat{y}$ containing raw prediction values. The sigmoid function is then applied to these raw prediction values to obtain probabilities, $\hat{p}$, in the range of 0 and 1.

Focal loss was used during the fine-tuning process to address the issue of imbalanced data. It addresses the problem of negative samples dominating the training process by assigning higher weights to difficult or misclassified samples. This weighting scheme thus emphasises the learning of hard-to-classify samples and reduces the influence of easy samples, resulting in better handling of class imbalances during training.

Given $y \in \{0, 1\}$ is the binary ground truth and $\hat{p} \in [0, 1]$ is the predicted probability of the true class. The individual focal loss is define as

$$\text{Focal Loss} = \begin{cases} -\alpha(1-\hat{p})^{\gamma}\log(\hat{p}) & \text{if } y = 1 \\ -(1-\alpha)\hat{p}^{\gamma}\log(1-\hat{p}) & \text{if } y = 0 \end{cases} \quad (2)$$

where α is the class weight assigned to each class label in order to balance their contribution to the loss calculation and γ the focusing parameter that controls the degree of emphasis on hard-to-classify samples.

In the case of training over multiple samples with multiple labels, the focal loss can therefore be formulated as:

$$\text{Focal Loss} = -\frac{1}{N}\sum_{i=1}^{N}\sum_{j=1}^{C}[\alpha_j(1-\hat{p}_{ij})^{\gamma}\log(\hat{p}_{ij}) + (1-\alpha_j)(\hat{p}_{ij})^{\gamma}\log(1-\hat{p}_{ij})] \quad (3)$$

where N is the number of samples, C is the number of classes, $\hat{p}_{ij}$ is the predicted probability of class j for sample i and α_j represents the class weight for class j. In our implementation, we calculated the class weights based on the class distribution within each mini-batch during training. This allows us to dynamically adjust the class weights based on the current mini-batch, which can be beneficial if the class distribution varies greatly across different mini-batches. We used $\gamma = 2.0$ to place strong emphasis on hard-to-classify samples.

Our models were fine-tuned using the AdamW optimiser with a learning rate of 5×10^{-5}, a weight decay of 10^{-4} and a batch size of 24 samples for 200,000 iterations (27.9 epochs). The optimiser iteratively updates the model parameters based on the gradients calculated from the loss function, which measures the discrepancy between the predictions and the ground truth. Throughout the training process, we closely monitored the loss value and the micro F1 score to ensure that the loss was decreasing and to prevent overfitting.

For the baseline approach, we employed TF-IDF (Term Frequency-Inverse Document Frequency), which is a widely used technique for text representation and analysis.

This study was performed on a 32-core workstation with 128 gigabytes of memory and an NVIDIA GeForce RTX 4090 24GB graphics card. We used Python v3.10, CUDA v11.7, PyTorch v2.0.1, PyThaiNLP v.4.0.2, pandas v.2.0.1, swifter v1.3.5, scikit-learn v1.2.2 and transformers v4.29.2.

2.5. Evaluation Metric

To evaluate the performance of the models, we used several evaluation schemes. First, we used common metrics for binary classification, including precision, which measures the proportion of correctly predicted positive instances out of all instances predicted as positive; recall, which measures the proportion of correctly predicted positive instances out of all true positive instances; and F1 score, which is the harmonic mean of precision and recall. To account for imbalanced datasets, we used micro-average scores so that equal weight is assigned to each instance to ensure a fair score for all classes.

Second, to specifically address multi-label classification, two additional metrics are commonly used: exact match ratio, which measures the proportion of instances where all predicted labels exactly match the true labels, and mean average precision, which calculates the average precision across all instances and labels, taking into account the order of the predicted labels. These metrics provide valuable insights into the accuracy and quality of multi-label predictions. To assess whether the differences in performance between the methods were statistically significant, we used bootstrapping and the Friedman test [30], a non-parametric test used to compare multiple methods across multiple dependent variables. If the differences between the methods were statistically significant, the next step was to use the post hoc Nemenyi test [31] to identify the methods that showed notable differences in performance. The significance level was set at 0.05.

Finally, to evaluate the models in providing recommendations, the other two metrics are used: recall@5 and precision@5. Recall@5 calculates the proportion of classes that are successfully predicted among the top 5 predicted classes, thus measuring the model's ability to capture relevant recommendations. Precision@5, on the other hand, measures the proportion of correctly predicted classes among the top 5 recommendations, thus focusing on the accuracy of the suggestions. These metrics are valuable when the user is presented with a limited number of recommendations and the goal is to maximise both the relevance and accuracy of the suggestions.

3. Results

All models were trained and validated using the training and validation data spanning the years 2016 to 2021. All performance measures presented in the table were calculated based on the predictions made by the models using the test data collected in the year 2022. This approach ensures an unbiased evaluation of the models' performance on unseen data and provides a realistic assessment of their generalisation capabilities.

Table 1 shows a comparison of the performance metrics of the different models. The model finetuned from MEDPSU-RoBERTa, our institutional pre-trained language model, achieved the highest precision, highest recall, highest F1 score, highest exact match ratio, highest mean average precision, highest recall@5 and highest precision@5 compared to the other models. However, there is a slight difference in performance between the MEDPSU-RoBERTa, Multilingual BERT and Multilingual E5 models on various metrics. The running time for each model is impressively low. The basic model TF-IDF takes 17.29 ms to process one document, and the more advanced models such as Multilingual BERT, Multilingual E5 and MEDPSU-RoBERTA achieve even faster processing times of 4.66 ms, 4.76 ms and 4.81 ms, respectively.

Table 1. Performance scores of all models calculated from the test set.

Model/Architecture	Run Time	Precision	Recall	F1 Score	Exact Match	Mean AP	Recall@5	Precision@5
TF-IDF (baseline)	17.29 ms [1]	**0.8456**	0.5400	0.6590	0.2062	0.6928	0.5545	0.7085
Multilingual BERT	4.66 ms [2]	0.8439	0.7149	0.7735	0.3411	0.7975	0.6126	0.7826
Multilingual E5	4.76 ms [2]	0.8426	0.7155	0.7738	0.3380	0.8071	0.6155	0.7863
MEDPSU-RoBERTa	4.81 ms [2]	0.8423	**0.7299**	**0.7821**	**0.3470**	**0.8097**	**0.6181**	**0.7885**

Exact Match: Exact Match Ratio; Mean AP: Mean Average Precision; Bold values indicate the highest score for each metric; Run time measured under parallel computation in milliseconds (ms); [1] Inference performed in CPU; [2] Inference performed in GPU.

Looking at precision, recall and F1 score, the three models show relatively similar performance. The values for precision range from 0.8423 to 0.8439, for recall from 0.7149 to 0.7299 and for F1 score from 0.7735 to 0.7821. These results show that all three models have comparable abilities in detecting positive cases and minimising false positives and false negatives. For metrics such as exact match ratio, mean average precision, recall@5 and precision@5, the differences among the models are relatively small.

The Friedman test revealed significant differences among the models ($p < 0.05$) for recall, exact match ratio, F1 score, and mean AP (see Figure 5). Specifically, for recall, TF-IDF differs significantly from Multilingual E5 and MEDPSU-RoBERTa ($p < 0.05$), while Multilingual BERT differs significantly from MEDPSU-RoBERTa ($p < 0.05$). For the exact match ratio, TF-IDF differs significantly from Multilingual BERT and MEDPSU-RoBERTa ($p < 0.05$), and Multilingual E5 differs significantly from MEDPSU-RoBERTa. In terms of the F1 score, all methods differ significantly from each other ($p < 0.05$), except for Multilingual BERT and Multilingual E5, which do not exhibit a significant difference. Regarding mean AP, TF-IDF differs significantly from Multilingual E5 and MEDPSU-RoBERTa ($p < 0.05$), while Multilingual BERT differs significantly from MEDPSU-RoBERTa ($p < 0.05$).

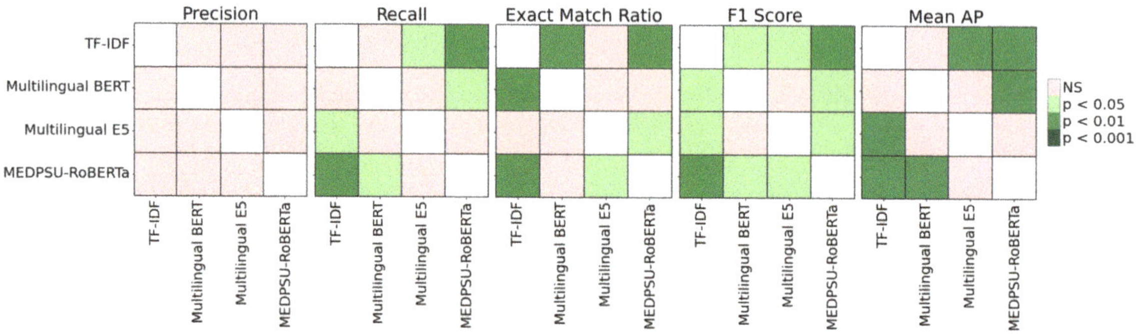

Figure 5. Significance plots of p values calculated using Nemenyi post hoc test.

Figure 6 shows a precision-recall curve illustrating the trade-off between precision and recall for all models. It shows how the performance of the model performance varies as the classification threshold changes. In our multi-label setting, we calculated the micro-averaged precision-recall curve from all labels for each model. The precision-recall curve for the MEDPSU-RoBERTa model showed a better trade-off between precision and recall at most thresholds compared to the other models.

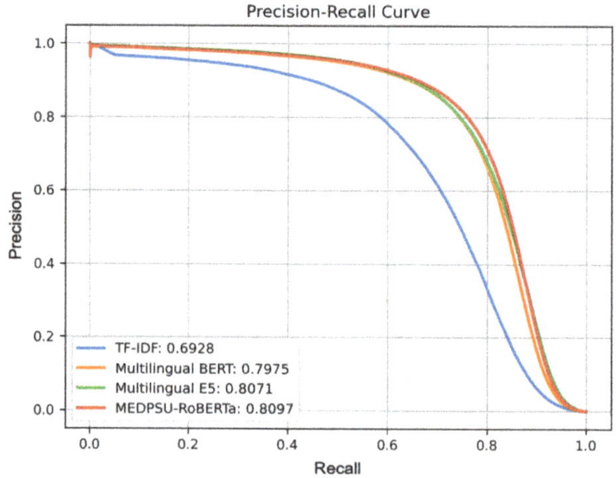

Figure 6. Precision-recall curves of all models calculated from the test set.

4. Discussion

In our study, we investigated different language models for the task of automated coding of inpatient diagnoses. We used a separate test set from a different time period to evaluate the models' ability to generalise to new and unseen data, and to assess their performance in real-world scenarios beyond the training period. Our results show that all our models generalised well towards unseen data.

4.1. Comparison of Different Pre-Trained Language Models

As expected, the model fine-tuned from MEDPSU-RoBERTa scored highest among the other language models. It is important to note that MEDPSU-RoBERTa was trained with data from our institution's HIS since its implementation until 31 December 2021. This time frame was different from the data used for the test set, which was collected in 2022. This presents further evidence of the generalisability of the model.

However, we had originally expected that the results of the model fine-tuned from MEDPSU-RoBERTa would significantly outperform the results of general-purpose language models such as Multilingual BERT or Multilingual E5. Surprisingly, the observed differences were only marginal, ranging between 1% and 2% in terms of performance metrics. The general-purpose models showed competitive performance that was not inferior. These results show that general-purpose language models are capable of handling the complex tasks of coding diagnoses. Although these models were not specifically tailored to our institutional data or fine-tuned with domain-specific knowledge, they demonstrated a remarkable ability to capture relevant information. This suggests that the general language models can still provide reliable results for specific applications or scenarios where fine-tuning to institution-specific data is not possible or necessary.

MEDPSU-RoBERTa consistently outperformed the other models across different thresholds (see Figure 6). Although the differences in performance are only 1% to 2%, even a small reduction in the error rate can have significant practical implications, especially in healthcare where the stakes are high. The reduction in false positives and false negatives can potentially decrease the need for case reviews and the likelihood of misdetections, resulting in a reduced workload.

In practise, clinical coders rely on various sources of information, including doctor notes, nurse progress notes, laboratory results, and medical procedures, in addition to the discharge report, to identify the appropriate diagnosis codes. However, these additional documents were not used in training the algorithm. Therefore, the algorithm may encounter difficulties in accurately assigning diagnosis codes due to the lack of these additional details. The lack of this contextual information could potentially lead to errors in assigning diagnosis codes in our models.

4.2. Model Performance across Different Labels

Further analysis was carried out for MEDPSU-RoBERTa, the highest-scoring model. Figure 7 shows the individual F1 score of the model across different diagnosis codes. These results provide valuable insights when considered alongside Figure 3b. The model consistently achieved an F1 score above 0.80 for the top 250 diagnosis codes or labels with more than 1000 samples. The model performs less well on class labels with a small sample size. This suggests that the performance of the model is affected by the availability of training samples for each class label, especially for the frequency rank above 1251 or the class label with less than 100 samples, the F1 score tends to be below 0.5.

4.3. Model Performance across Different Document Lengths

Figure 8 shows the performance of the model at different document lengths. Contrary to our initial assumption that longer clinical details would lead to better performance, our results showed a slight drop in performance for long documents. The F1 score decreases with increasing document length. This observation could be due to the limited comprehension capabilities of the BERT-based models when processing long documents, or to the potential confusion caused by very detailed or elaborate clinical descriptions. We suspect that the model better excels at processing short and concise clinical notes.

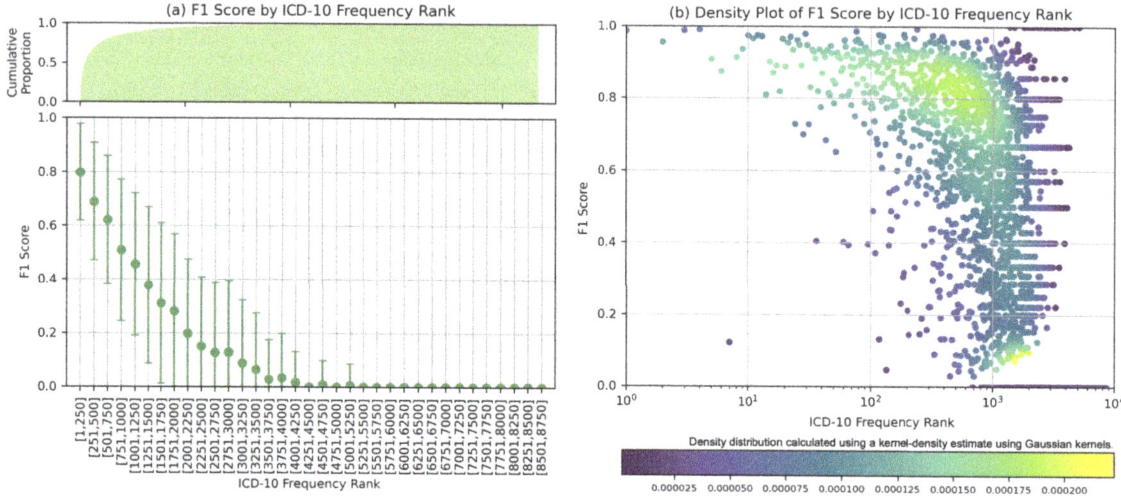

Figure 7. F1 score by ICD frequency rank: (**a**) Mean F1 scores based on frequency rank with cumulative count on the top. (**b**) Density plot displayed on logarithmic scales, highlighting the distribution of F1 scores in class labels with large number of samples.

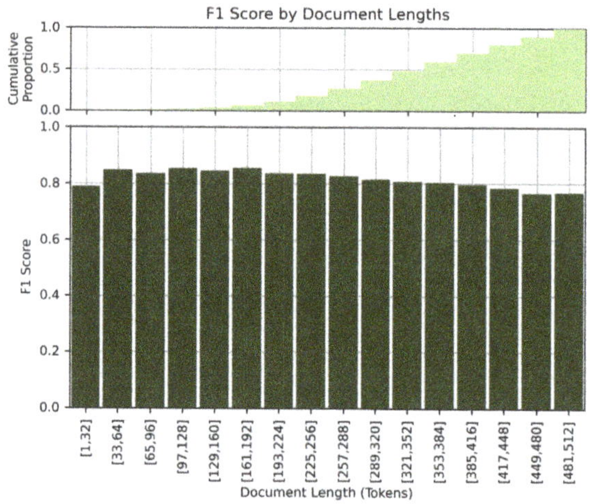

Figure 8. F1 score by document lengths.

4.4. Co-Occurrence Analysis

Co-occurrence analysis examines the relationships and patterns of co-occurrence between different diagnostic codes. In the context of automated inpatient coding, co-occurrence analysis could help identify which diagnosis codes frequently occur together in patient records. This can provide insights into the relationships between medical conditions and help improve the accuracy of automated coding systems. For example, suppose that in a dataset of patient records, the diagnosis codes for "diabetes" and "hypertension" frequently occur together. This co-occurrence indicates that these two diseases are often diagnosed in the same patients. By identifying such co-occurring diagnostic codes, an automated coding system could be designed to recognise the likelihood of co-occurrence of these conditions and apply or suggest both relevant codes simultaneously, thereby improving the coding process. We assume that the model can capture the co-occurrence and associations between certain diagnoses in the same patterns as they occur in ground truth. Figure 9 shows the diagrams of the co-occurrence matrix of both ground truth and prediction. In the predictions, we found that the classifier performed poorly on class labels with small sample sizes, so that some associations became unclear. However, we were able to identify similar patterns of association in both diagrams, confirming the model's ability to capture relevant co-occurrence relationships.

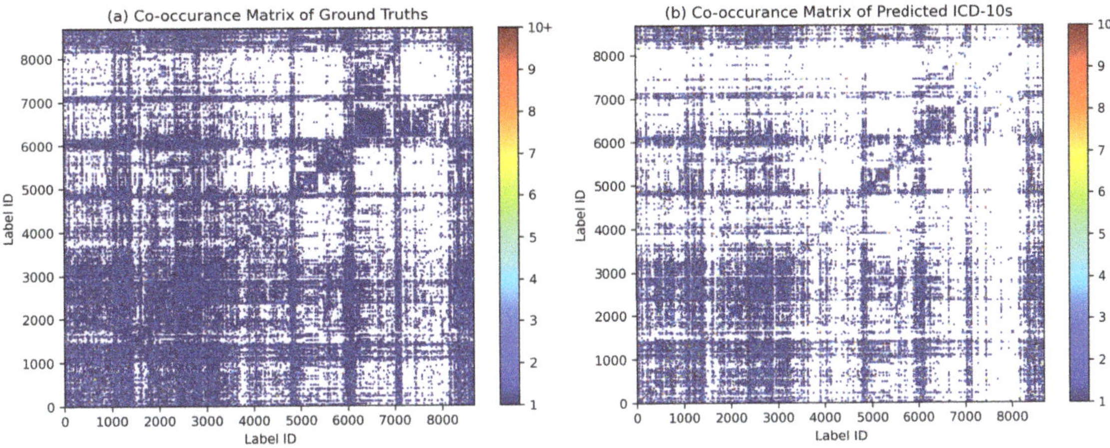

Figure 9. Diagrams of the co-occurrence matrix for (**a**) ground truth and (**b**) predictions reveal similar patterns of associations between diagnosis codes.

Figure 10 shows the diagrams of the co-occurrence network in the top 200 diagnosis codes in both ground truth and prediction. A highly similar pattern of associations between the two was observed, reinforcing the model's ability to capture meaningful associations between diagnoses.

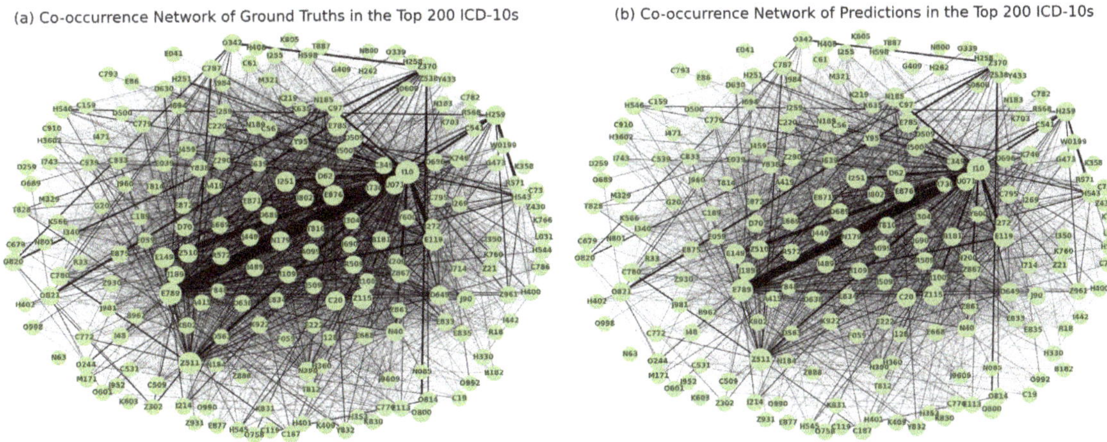

Figure 10. Diagrams of the co-occurrence network for the 200 most frequently coded diagnosis codes in the (**a**) ground truth and (**b**) predictions show patterns of co-occurrence that are consistent with actual coding practise.

4.5. Training and Validation Loss

Figure 11 shows the training and validation loss as well as the validation F1 score during model training for all models. No overfitting was observed. Training was stable and the validation F1 score was increased until convergence.

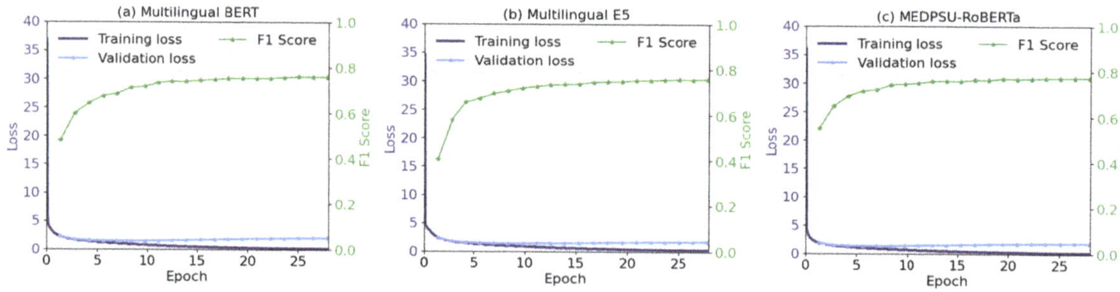

Figure 11. The training and validation loss, along with the F1 score, indicate the convergence of the model.

4.6. Comparison to Other Studies

Compared to previous studies [15,21,23,25,32] that employed BERT-based models, our study addresses the problem using a significantly larger dataset of clinical documents and diagnosis codes. Amin et al. [21] employed BioBERT and achieved an F1-score of 0.73. Biseda et al. [32] utilized ClinicalBERT and obtained an F1-score of 0.75. Silvestri et al. [23] applied XLM to Italian clinical documents and reported an exact match ratio of 0.77 using 2172 clinical notes and 24 unique ICD codes. Remmer et al. [25] employed Swedish KB-BERT and achieved an F1-score of 0.58 on a dataset of 6062 records with 10 unique ICD-10 blocks. Yu et al. [15] developed Chinese ICD-10 classification algorithms using RNN to support 488 different ICD blocks and achieved a micro-averaged F1-score of 0.77. The better performance of our results can be attributed to several factors, the inclusion of a more extensive institutional dataset as well as and the comprehensive nature of our discharge reports and clinical coding criteria.

4.7. Study Limitations

The results of our study are subject to several limitations. First, although the dataset used for training and evaluation was relatively large, there are few examples of some class labels. This may have limited the model's ability to generalise and capture the full complexity of the coding task for inpatient diagnoses. Second, although we used dynamic class weights, dealing with class imbalance is still poses a challenge as certain diagnosis codes have limited representation in the dataset, which affects the performance of the model for these specific diagnosis codes. Thirdly, the lack of use of historical data prevents the model from incorporating temporal trends and longitudinal information from patients that could provide valuable context for accurate diagnosis coding. Next, our models have shown strong performance with ICD-10-TM in Thai context and mixed English–Thai clinical notes, however its applicability in different settings remains uncertain due to language differences. Our models can certainly useful in different hospitals and regions of Thailand, but their effectiveness in other countries needs to be further evaluated through extensive testing. Finally, the lack of qualitative assessments to evaluate the performance of the model when used by clinicians or professional coders. This may hinder understanding of usability and user experience in real-world scenarios.

4.8. Practical Implications

The practical implications of our study are twofold. First, the rarity of diseases may pose a challenge in implementing the system [33,34]. To overcome this problem, one possible solution is to pool data from the HIS of multiple hospitals to create a more comprehensive training dataset. By pooling data from different sources, an algorithm can learn from a wider range of cases, including rare diseases, increasing the number of training samples and improving its ability to accurately code and diagnose such conditions. Secondly, the system could be transformed into a recommendation system offering suggestions and guidance to medical professionals [7]. However, it is important to ensure that the system effectively communicates the presence and importance of rare diseases to users. Clear and concise messages can ensure that rare diseases also receive appropriate attention and consideration, ultimately leading to increased diagnostic accuracy and better workflows [8].

4.9. Future Directions

Future research directions offer several possibilities. First, addressing the problem of rare diseases, which may lead to underdiagnosis, requires innovative approaches. Exploring methods to improve rare disease detection and classification could help increase the accuracy and completeness of the automated coding system. Second, more effective integration of historical data into the modelling process could provide valuable context and improve the predictive capabilities of the model. The use of longitudinal data on patients, treatment histories and outcomes can provide the model with a more comprehensive understanding of diagnoses. In addition, integrating the automated coding system with other sources of health data such as laboratory results, radiology reports and genetic information can provide a more holistic approach to diagnosis coding. Finally, future work should also focus on how the automated coding system can be implemented into the infrastructure of HIS, taking into account factors such as data privacy, interoperability and user acceptance.

Apart from inpatient diagnosis coding, NLP offers promising perspectives in various other domains. For example, the development of recommendation systems based on relevant clinical documentation could support healthcare workflows by suggesting relevant terms or concepts related to patients, such as recommendation systems for drugs and treatments. In this way, clinical decision-making processes could be streamlined and the workflow of HIS improved.

5. Conclusions

This study investigated the use of language models for inpatient diagnosis coding. Using our institutional dataset of over 230,645 admissions, our study highlighted the competitive performance of general-purpose language models, Multilingual BERT and Multilingual E5, and a domain-specific language model, MEDPSU-RoBERTa. Model performance also varied across diseases, with larger sample sizes leading to better results. The rarity of certain diseases poses a challenge for accurate coding, with more than 100 samples per diagnosis label suggested. We also analysed the impact of document length on performance and found that longer documents could pose a challenge to the model. Co-occurrence analysis demonstrated the model's ability to capture relevant associations. The results highlight the need for larger datasets, strategies to deal with class imbalance, and integration of historical data to improve performance. Future research directions include improving the handling of rare diseases, improving the integration of historical data, integrating additional healthcare data sources and focusing on the implementation of coding systems in hospital information systems. These results contribute to the further development of diagnosis coding systems, highlighting their potential to facilitate accurate and efficient workflows.

Author Contributions: Conceptualization, K.S. and D.T.; methodology, K.S. and D.T.; software, K.S. and D.T.; validation, K.S., D.T., S.C. (Sawrawit Chairat) and S.C. (Sitthichok Chaichulee); formal analysis, K.S. and D.T.; investigation, K.S. and D.T.; resources, S.C. (Sitthichok Chaichulee); data curation, S.C. (Sitthichok Chaichulee) and D.T.; writing—original draft preparation, K.S., S.C. (Sawrawit Chairat) and S.C. (Sitthichok Chaichulee); writing—review and editing, K.S., S.C. (Sawrawit Chairat) and S.C. (Sitthichok Chaichulee); visualization, K.S. and S.C. (Sitthichok Chaichulee); supervision, S.C. (Sitthichok Chaichulee); project administration, S.C. (Sitthichok Chaichulee); funding acquisition, S.C. (Sitthichok Chaichulee). All authors have read and agreed to the published version of the manuscript.

Funding: This work was supported by the National Science, Research and Innovation Fund (NSRF) and Prince of Songkla University (Grant No. MED6601201S). Kerdkiat Suvirat and Sawrawit Chairat received graduate scholarships from the Faculty of Medicine of Prince of Songkla University.

Institutional Review Board Statement: The study was approved by the Human Research Ethics Committee, Faculty of Medicine, Prince of Songkla University (REC.65-120-38-2) and was conducted in accordance with the principles of the Declaration of Helsinki and the International Conference on Harmonization in Good Clinical Practice.

Informed Consent Statement: Informed consent was waived due to the retrospective nature of the study.

Data Availability Statement: Due to privacy concerns and the inclusion of sensitive patient information, the dataset used in this study was not published. MEDPSU-RoBERTa is a private clinical language model pre-trained on clinical documents from Songklanagarind Hospital. Due to the risk of data leakage during language generation, this model is not publicly available.

Conflicts of Interest: The authors declare no conflict of interest.

Abbreviations

The following abbreviations are used in this manuscript:

AI	Artificial Intelligence
BERT	Bidirectional Encoder Representations from Transformers
CNN	Convolutional Neural Network
HIS	Hospital Information System
ICD	International Classification of Diseases
ICD-10-AM	International Classification of Diseases, Tenth Revision, Australian Modification
ICD-10-TM	International Classification of Diseases, Tenth Revision, Thai Modification
NLP	Natural Language Processing
RNN	Recurrent Neural Network
SVM	Support Vector Machine
TF-IDF	Term Frequency-Inverse Document Frequency
WHO	World Health Organization
XLM	Cross-lingual Language Model

References

1. Manchikanti, L.; Falco, F.J.E.; Hirsch, J.A. Ready or not! Here comes ICD-10. *J. Neurointerv. Surg.* **2011**, *5*, 86–91. [CrossRef] [PubMed]
2. Khera, R.; Dorsey, K.B.; Krumholz, H.M. Transition to the ICD-10 in the United States. *JAMA* **2018**, *320*, 133–134. [CrossRef] [PubMed]
3. Alonso, V.; Santos, J.V.; Pinto, M.; Ferreira, J.; Lema, I.; Lopes, F.; Freitas, A. Health records as the basis of clinical coding: Is the quality adequate? A qualitative study of medical coders' perceptions. *Health Inf. Manag. J.* **2019**, *49*, 28–37. [CrossRef] [PubMed]
4. World Health Organization. *ICD-9: International Classification of Diseases 9th Revision*; World Health Organization: Geneva, Switzerland, 1978.
5. World Health Organization. *ICD-10: International Statistical Classification of Diseases and Related Health Problems 10th Revision*, 2nd ed.; World Health Organization: Geneva, Switzerland, 2004.
6. World Health Organization. *ICD-11: International Statistical Classification of Diseases and Related Health Problems 11th Revision*; World Health Organization: Geneva, Switzerland, 2022.
7. Dong, H.; Falis, M.; Whiteley, W.; Alex, B.; Matterson, J.; Ji, S.; Chen, J.; Wu, H. Automated clinical coding: What, why, and where we are? *NPJ Digit. Med.* **2022**, *5*, 159. [CrossRef]
8. Venkatesh, K.P.; Raza, M.M.; Kvedar, J.C. Automating the overburdened clinical coding system: Challenges and next steps. *NPJ Digit. Med.* **2023**, *6*, 16. [CrossRef]
9. Chapman, W.W.; Bridewell, W.; Hanbury, P.; Cooper, G.F.; Buchanan, B.G. A simple algorithm for identifying negated findings and diseases in discharge summaries. *J. Biomed. Inf.* **2001**, *34*, 301–310. [CrossRef]
10. Crammer, K.; Dredze, M.; Ganchev, K.; Talukdar, P.P.; Carroll, S. Automatic Code Assignment to Medical Text. In Proceedings of the Workshop on BioNLP 2007, Prague, Czech Republic, 29 June 2007; Association for Computational Linguistics: Stroudsburg, PA, USA, 2007; pp. 129–136.

11. Hasan, M.; Kotov, A.; Carcone, A.; Dong, M.; Naar, S.; Hartlieb, K.B. A study of the effectiveness of machine learning methods for classification of clinical interview fragments into a large number of categories. *J. Biomed. Inf.* **2016**, *62*, 21–31. [CrossRef]
12. Moons, E.; Khanna, A.; Akkasi, A.; Moens, M.F. A Comparison of Deep Learning Methods for ICD Coding of Clinical Records. *Appl. Sci.* **2020**, *10*, 5262. [CrossRef]
13. Xu, K.; Lam, M.; Pang, J.; Gao, X.; Band, C.; Mathur, P.; Papay, F.; Khanna, A.K.; Cywinski, J.B.; Maheshwari, K.; et al. Multimodal Machine Learning for Automated ICD Coding. In Proceedings of the 4th Machine Learning for Healthcare Conference, Ann Arbor, MI, USA, 9–10 August 2019; pp. 197–215.
14. Boytcheva, S. Automatic Matching of ICD-10 codes to Diagnoses in Discharge Letters. In Proceedings of the Second Workshop on Biomedical Natural Language Processing, Hissar, Bulgaria, September 2011; Association for Computational Linguistics: Stroudsburg, PA, USA, 2011, pp. 11–18.
15. Yu, Y.; Li, M.; Liu, L.; Fei, Z.; Wu, F.X.; Wang, J. Automatic ICD code assignment of Chinese clinical notes based on multilayer attention BiRNN. *J. Biomed. Inf.* **2019**, *91*, 103114. [CrossRef]
16. Almagro, M.; Unanue, R.M.; Fresno, V.; Montalvo, S. ICD-10 Coding of Spanish Electronic Discharge Summaries: An Extreme Classification Problem. *IEEE Access* **2020**, *8*, 100073–100083. [CrossRef]
17. Devlin, J.; Chang, M.W.; Lee, K.; Toutanova, K. BERT: Pre-training of Deep Bidirectional Transformers for Language Understanding. *arXiv* **2019**, arXiv:1810.04805.
18. Lample, G.; Conneau, A. Cross-lingual Language Model Pretraining. *arXiv* **2019**, arXiv:1901.07291.
19. Lee, J.; Yoon, W.; Kim, S.; Kim, D.; Kim, S.; So, C.H.; Kang, J. BioBERT: A pre-trained biomedical language representation model for biomedical text mining. *Bioinformatics* **2019**, *36*, 1234–1240. [CrossRef] [PubMed]
20. Huang, K.; Altosaar, J.; Ranganath, R. ClinicalBERT: Modeling Clinical Notes and Predicting Hospital Readmission. *arXiv* **2020**, arXiv:1904.05342.
21. Amin, S.; Neumann, G.; Dunfield, K.; Vechkaeva, A.; Chapman, K.; Wixted, M. MLT-DFKI at CLEF eHealth 2019: Multi-label Classification of ICD-10 Codes with BERT. In Proceedings of the 10th Conference and Labs of the Evaluation Forum, Lugano, Switzerland, 9–12 September 2019.
22. Johnson, A.E.; Pollard, T.J.; Shen, L.; Lehman, L.W.H.; Feng, M.; Ghassemi, M.; Moody, B.; Szolovits, P.; Anthony Celi, L.; Mark, R.G. MIMIC-III, a freely accessible critical care database. *Sci. Data* **2016**, *3*, 160035. [CrossRef]
23. Silvestri, S.; Gargiulo, F.; Ciampi, M.; De Pietro, G. Exploit Multilingual Language Model at Scale for ICD-10 Clinical Text Classification. In Proceedings of the IEEE Symposium on Computers and Communications (ISCC), Rennes, France, 7–10 July 2020; pp. 1–7. [CrossRef]
24. López-García, G.; Jerez, J.M.; Ribelles, N.; Alba, E.; Veredas, F.J. Transformers for Clinical Coding in Spanish. *IEEE Access* **2021**, *9*, 72387–72397. [CrossRef]
25. Remmer, S.; Lamproudis, A.; Dalianis, H. Multi-label Diagnosis Classification of Swedish Discharge Summaries—ICD-10 Code Assignment Using KB-BERT. In Proceedings of the Conference Recent Advances in Natural Language Processing, Varna, Bulgaria, 1–3 September 2021; pp. 1158–1166.
26. Phatthiyaphaibun, W.; Chaovavanich, K.; Polpanumas, C.; Suriyawongkul, A.; Lowphansirikul, L.; Chormai, P. PyThaiNLP: Thai Natural Language Processing in Python. 2023. Available online: https://github.com/PyThaiNLP/pythainlp (accessed on 15 August 2023).
27. Wang, L.; Yang, N.; Huang, X.; Jiao, B.; Yang, L.; Jiang, D.; Majumder, R.; Wei, F. Text Embeddings by Weakly-Supervised Contrastive Pre-training. *arXiv* **2022**, arXiv:2212.03533.
28. Liu, Y.; Ott, M.; Goyal, N.; Du, J.; Joshi, M.; Chen, D.; Levy, O.; Lewis, M.; Zettlemoyer, L.; Stoyanov, V. RoBERTa: A Robustly Optimized BERT Pretraining Approach. *arXiv* **2019**, arXiv:1907.11692. [CrossRef]
29. Wolf, T.; Debut, L.; Sanh, V.; Chaumond, J.; Delangue, C.; Moi, A.; Cistac, P.; Rault, T.; Louf, R.; Funtowicz, M.; et al. Transformers: State-of-the-Art Natural Language Processing. In Proceedings of the 2020 Conference on Empirical Methods in Natural Language Processing: System Demonstrations, Online, 16–20 November 2020; Association for Computational Linguistics: Stroudsburg, PA, USA, 2020; pp. 38–45.
30. Friedman, M. A comparison of alternative tests of significance for the problem of m rankings. *Ann. Math. Stat.* **1940**, *11*, 86–92. [CrossRef]
31. Nemenyi, P.B. Distribution-Free Multiple Comparisons. Ph.D. Thesis, Princeton University, Princeton, NJ, USA, 1963.
32. Biseda, B.; Desai, G.; Lin, H.; Philip, A. Prediction of ICD Codes with Clinical BERT Embeddings and Text Augmentation with Label Balancing using MIMIC-III. *arXiv* **2020**, arXiv:2008.10492.
33. Wu, H.; Toti, G.; Morley, K.I.; Ibrahim, Z.M.; Folarin, A.; Jackson, R.; Kartoglu, I.; Agrawal, A.; Stringer, C.; Gale, D.; et al. SemEHR: A general-purpose semantic search system to surface semantic data from clinical notes for tailored care, trial recruitment, and clinical research. *J. Am. Med. Inf. Assoc.* **2018**, *25*, 530–537. [CrossRef] [PubMed]
34. Dong, H.; Suárez-Paniagua, V.; Zhang, H.; Wang, M.; Casey, A.; Davidson, E.; Chen, J.; Alex, B.; Whiteley, W.; Wu, H. Ontology-driven and weakly supervised rare disease identification from clinical notes. *BMC Med. Inf. Decis. Mak.* **2023**, *23*, 86. [CrossRef] [PubMed]

applied sciences

MDPI

Article

Challenges and Opportunities for Conducting Dynamic Risk Assessments in Medical IoT

Ricardo M. Czekster [1,*], Paul Grace [1], César Marcon [2], Fabiano Hessel [2] and Silvio C. Cazella [3]

1 Department of Software Engineering and Cybersecurity, School of Computer Science and Digital Technologies, Aston University, Birmingham B4 7ET, UK; p.grace@aston.ac.uk
2 Graduate Program in Computer Science (PPGCC), Polytechnic School, Pontifical Catholic University of Rio Grande do Sul (PUCRS), Porto Alegre 90619-900, Brazil; cesar.marcon@pucrs.br (C.M.); fabiano.hessel@pucrs.br (F.H.)
3 Department of Exact and Applied Social Sciences, Federal University of Health Sciences of Porto Alegre (UFCSPA), Porto Alegre 90050-170, Brazil; silvioc@ufcspa.edu.br
* Correspondence: r.meloczekster@aston.ac.uk; Tel.: +44-(0)-121-204-4544

Abstract: Modern medical devices connected to public and private networks require additional layers of communication and management to effectively and securely treat remote patients. Wearable medical devices, for example, can detect position, movement, and vital signs; such data help improve the quality of care for patients, even when they are not close to a medical doctor or caregiver. In healthcare environments, these devices are called Medical Internet-of-Things (MIoT), which have security as a critical requirement. To protect users, traditional risk assessment (RA) methods can be periodically carried out to identify potential security risks. However, such methods are not suitable to manage sophisticated cyber-attacks happening in near real-time. That is the reason why dynamic RA (DRA) approaches are emerging to tackle the inherent risks to patients employing MIoT as wearable devices. This paper presents a systematic literature review of RA in MIoT that analyses the current trends and existing approaches in this field. From our review, we first observe the significant ways to mitigate the impact of unauthorised intrusions and protect end-users from the leakage of personal data and ensure uninterrupted device usage. Second, we identify the important research directions for DRA that must address the challenges posed by dynamic infrastructures and uncertain attack surfaces in order to better protect users and thwart cyber-attacks before they harm personal (e.g., patients' home) and institutional (e.g., hospital or health clinic) networks.

Keywords: dynamic risk assessment; cyber security; medical IoT; systematic literature review

Citation: Czekster, R.M.; Grace, P.; Marcon, C.; Hessel, F.; Cazella, S.C. Challenges and Opportunities for Conducting Dynamic Risk Assessments in Medical IoT. *Appl. Sci.* **2023**, *13*, 7406. https://doi.org/10.3390/app13137406

Academic Editors: Dimitris Mourtzis and Stefano Silvestri

Received: 1 June 2023
Revised: 16 June 2023
Accepted: 20 June 2023
Published: 22 June 2023

1. Introduction

The latest advances in remote asset management have significantly changed the healthcare industry. Due to low costs and widespread adoption of the Internet-of-Things (IoT), wearable computing has enabled organisations to track and sense patients over secure telecommunication [1]. It is possible to attach devices to vulnerable patients under treatment and monitor essential physiological signs, such as cardiac rates, temperature, movement, and sugar levels, in near real-time [2]. Leveraging these IoT technologies away from hospital premises helps medical doctors make better and more timely decisions. This is due to the availability of important additional data that can then be analysed by automated information systems. Wearable devices can also empower patients to better understand and control their personal data sharing, thus preserving privacy objectives. However, these devices do pose a number of threats and vulnerabilities requiring attention and mitigative actions, and others have dubbed it the Internet of Threats [3].

In the healthcare domain, devices must adhere to additional constraints to ensure the safety and security of stakeholders. They must be compliant with other specifications and not interfere with underlying technologies. These devices are equipment referred to as Medical Internet-of-Things (MIoT), a subclass of IoT. MIoT sits within a broader cyber-physical system (CPS) [4] adding remote management capabilities over distributed assets [5–8]. Modern infrastructure design has incorporated MIoT into healthcare settings [9], especially after the COVID-19 pandemic [10]. Employing IoT in the patient's environment is highly advantageous; this typically involves IoT sensors monitoring patients and promptly transmitting data to sinks or servers for analysis. Solutions vary and examples include health prescription assistants (HPA), healthcare status monitoring (heartbeat, temperature, CO_2 levels, sensing features), tracking patients' movements, and detecting whether someone has fallen. Since its inception, security has been a key concern [11–13] and significant research has sought to address the security challenges and develop and deploy hardened solutions. All these inter-connected devices extend the feature set available to end-users; however, this comes with trade-offs between privacy and cyber security objectives. Despite having to comply with regulations by vendors, they must be sufficiently equipped with mechanisms to cope with accidental and deliberate malfunctions. These failures could be caused by flawed designs, poor testing, or active cyber-attacks aiming to exfiltrate personal and identifiable information (PII) [14] from stakeholders. Governments and organisations are enforcing legislation to protect users and patients, for instance, the Health Insurance Portability and Accountability Act (HIPAA), in the US, and the General Data Protection Regulation (GDPR), in the UK and European Union (EU). These efforts signal the need to safeguard and protect data with clear repercussions for violations; this further highlights the importance of secure MIoT systems.

Stakeholders employing these technologies are under constant risk (for different meanings of 'risk', please refer to Appendix A.1) arising from different threat sources with varied impacts and occurrence likelihoods. Asset managers sitting on the edge of the infrastructure desire to offer end-users, customers or patients hardened MIoT equipment with protective assurances to ensure seamless interactions. They employ embedded software communicating status and health-related data that feed information systems (IS) so medical doctors can make timely choices to improve care delivery. These platforms, albeit tested widely by vendors before shipping, are not immune to the malicious advances of sophisticated threat actors. One remedy for establishing protections is to perform risk assessment (RA), choosing a methodology [15] with specific considerations for medical-based IoT [16]. Alternatives are the ISO 31000:2018 standard [17], NIST 800-30r1 [18], operationally critical threat, asset, and vulnerability evaluation (OCTAVE) and OCTAVE Allegro [19], as well as a plethora of RAs available for risk managers [20].

While RA is a proven method in identifying and mitigating security risks, it is traditionally only performed periodically. In highly dynamic systems, the important factor is change. This is especially true of IoT, where the system or the environment may change (changing the attack surface). For example, new sensors can be deployed, or devices may switch to a new network. Furthermore, new attacks will emerge. Periodic RA is unable to respond to these changes and ensure risk is managed in a timely fashion. Zio (2018) [21] has discussed the future of RA, establishing the most relevant aspects to incorporate dynamic elements directly into the analysis. This RA variant called dynamic risk assessment (DRA) targets continuous, near real-time, on-the-fly reassessments. Applying DRA in IoT is not new, as it has been addressed in many discussions [22,23] and case studies for threat-based RA in smart homes [24–27]. These studies highlight that DRA provides better observability (this term comes from control theory and distributed systems [28]; it is used nowadays as a means to understand a system's states by inspecting the data it generates in event logs, metrics, etc. to append protective features) features to systems when tackling unknowns situations [29], i.e., events that "we do not know we do not know" [30].

The driving motivation here is the fact that, where MIoT systems are deployed and utilised, there is a dynamic attack surface. While existing risk assessment methods have proven successful in traditional systems, the dynamic nature of this environment requires RA to be revisited and led to the consideration of dynamic RA. There have been few research/studies into this and, hence, this review and its observations are important, timely and novel. The motivation described has been explicitly introduced in the introduction.

Thus, this work discusses the inherent challenges of conducting DRA in MIoT to enumerate effective ways of tackling *emergent risks* to patients through wearable computing in healthcare. The paper makes three key contributions:

- A comprehensive systematic literature review (SLR) of risk analysis and its application to MIoT; this highlights the current trends and existing approaches in this domain.
- An exploration of effective strategies for mitigating the impact of unauthorised intrusions and safeguarding end-users against the leakage of PII or the disruption of equipment usage in dynamic MIoT systems.
- The identification of the key research directions for DRA that must address the challenges posed by dynamic MIoT infrastructures and uncertain attack surfaces in order to better protect users and thwart cyber-attacks.

We focus on malicious opportunities that sophisticated threat actors may explore in MIoT. Our investigation outlines the most common risk approaches in large attack surfaces and the issues behind using DRA when coping with service and system interruptions.

The paper is organised as follows: Section 2 outlines the context for MIoT and Section 3 explores related work and our SLR. This is continued in Section 4, which details the challenges and opportunities behind tackling RA and DRA in IoT. We end our contribution in Section 5 with conclusions and discussion of future work.

2. Contextualisation

2.1. Threat Modelling, Static and Dynamic Risk Analysis

Recent years have witnessed the ever-increasing adoption of IoT-based devices in a myriad of application contexts [31]. Examples are Industrial IoT (IIoT), smart manufacturing, smart cities [32,33], energy generation/storage, and healthcare domains [34]. Although these devices offer remote management capabilities and near real-time sensing, when considering cyber security and privacy, they have considerably enlarged the potential attack surface to protect [35]. Integrating RA and threat modelling (TM) is a traditional information security approach to protect such distributed assets. A noteworthy approach is the process for attack simulation and threat analysis (PASTA), a risk-oriented TM framework that assumes security practitioners are risk managers [36]. It is targeted at helping organisations tackle inherent risks in software to devise hardened products to sustain response to cyber-attacks. Wolf et al. (2021) [37] applied the approach to IoT ecosystems showcasing its use with DFDs to demonstrate trust boundaries, as well as presenting an abuse-case diagram for a light control system.

According to the ISO [17], tackling risk is about determining *uncertainty*, whereas for NIST/US [18], it is a holistic approach encompassing organisations, business processes and information systems. DRA is a relatively recent approach to handle change and assess risk continuously, i.e., to update the RA as new evidence (data) emerges in networks and feeds, proactively preparing for malicious incursions as they progress [23,38,39]. As previous work has discussed in detail in the recent literature [40,41], conducting such analysis in IoT is not trivial, a theme we shall cover in Section 4.

TM is an exercise in assessing opportunities for system abuse by threat actors and creating the means to cope, withstand or mitigate existing vulnerabilities [42–44]. Threat analysts could perform TM in the early stages and continuously as managers and system administrators incorporate new technologies and devices into the solution. TM has been successfully used in healthcare [45] to promote better countermeasures and mitigations to specific attacks inherent in IoT shortcomings [46]. Among many techniques available to analysts, we highlight attack trees/graphs and data-flow diagrams (DFD) [47] to depict such concerning situations and employ TM to understand how to address and mitigate governing issues, among other approaches.

Regarding specific RA frameworks tailored to MIoT, we highlight the IoMT security assessment framework (IoMT-SAF) [48]. It involves healthcare stakeholders in risk processes, allowing them to assess the level of security as observed in distributed MIoT devices across the attack surface. The framework identifies security issues, recommends responses and creates scenarios for stakeholders using an ontological approach. The IoMT-SAF's process encompasses identifying security properties, such as: (i) medical operation security; (ii) vulnerability type (user, system, hardware); (iii) attack origin (local, remote), attack type (passive, active), attack difficulty (theoretical, difficult, easy, tools available); (iv) security function (detection, prevention, incident response); and (v) medical data threat (interception, interruption, modification, fabrication, replication).

2.2. Medical IoT

Working with IoT technologies in healthcare, there are a myriad of similar notions and definitions that we differentiate next. For instance, we have encountered references to the Health Internet of Things (HIoT) [49], the Internet of Health Things (IoHT) [50,51], the IoT-Health [52], the Internet of Medical Things (IoMT) [53–55], and the Medical Internet of Things (MIoT) [1,2,56]. In this work, we shall refer to the latter (MIoT) as a base definition as we think it captures the fundamental differences between general IoT systems versus those applied to medical/healthcare contexts with its more specific subtleties. MIoT empowers patients and clinical staff (in general) to understand care paths and plan interventions. It allows tracking, sensing and near real-time screening of patients that alert responsible personnel in case they detect or observe any anomaly using tailored algorithms that are either running on devices or using auxiliary information systems.

Understanding risk in systems is typically founded upon understanding the system itself. Evaluating a system architecture is, therefore, a starting point. Within IoT systems, the architecture has most simply been considered as a basic three-layer approach, composed of the *perception layer*, the *network layer* and the *application layer* [57]. While it is beyond the scope of this work to assess what is the best architecture to underpin security and privacy risk assessment, we note that these basic models constrain the system viewpoints potentially missing key IoT vulnerabilities. Hence, architecture model extensions, such as a *middleware layer*, a *business layer*, an *end-user layer*, a *processing layer* and a *service management layer* [58–60] could offer a better perspective. Security analysts overseeing large dynamic attack surfaces may then consider threat actors attempting to circumvent controls and exploit vulnerabilities on each layer as they have specific protocols and inter-layer dynamics [61,62]. Farahani et al. (2018) [63] go beyond this notion and consider different scales of *IoT layers*, dividing these into three types—wearables, smart homes and smart cities—across four layers: interface, service, networking and sensing.

2.3. MIoT Security and Privacy

Recently, NIST/US published a draft version for Trusted IoT Device Network-Layer Onboarding and Lifecycle Management (NIST SP 1800-36) [64], showcasing how to tackle credentials to connect to networks securely (Link to NIST/US site: https://www.nccoe.nist.gov/projects/trusted-iot-device-network-layer-onboarding-and-lifecycle-management, accessed on 19 June 2023).

One assumes that this document would be used alongside NIST's cybersecurity framework (NIST SP 800-37) (NIST Cybersecurity Framework: https://www.nist.gov/cyberframework, accessed on 19 June 2023), a guide to help organisations seeking to improve cyber security risk management. In the same direction, the UK's National Cyber Security Centre (NCSC) publishes risk management guidance (NCSC Risk Management Guidance: https://www.ncsc.gov.uk/collection/risk-management-collection, accessed on 19 June 2023), and the European Union Agency for Cybersecurity (ENISA/EU) has tackled risk management and assessment, providing tools and interoperability discussions among the many frameworks available to organisations (ENISA Risk Management and RA Framework: https://www.enisa.europa.eu/topics/threat-risk-management/risk-management/current-risk/business-process-integration/the-enisa-rm-ra-framework, accessed on 19 June 2023).

Elhoseny et al. (2021) [57] suggested that MIoT has stricter security and privacy requirements in contrast to 'usual' IoT. The complex MIoT ecosystem presents a massive attack surface requiring constant monitoring, confidential communication among trusted parties, data integrity, resilience to attacks, auditing (for backtraces or forensics), access control, authentication, and privacy [16]. For healthcare settings located at home, these assurances must hold, preventing attacks, avoiding exposure, and thwarting attacks before they cascade to adjacent networks and systems. It is outside the scope of this work to list and comment on specific cyber-attacks on MIoT as there has been a host of research explaining these over the years [15,27,35,62].

Complementing the MIoT ecosystem with cyber security counterparts, one could add the usual protections, i.e., intrusion detection systems (IDS), firewalls (and filtering scripts), encryption and access control (and varieties such as rule-based and attribute-based) as well as privacy-enhancing technologies , such as private information retrieval (PIR), virtual private networks (VPNs), transport layer security (TLS), combined with domain name system (DNS) SECurity extensions (DNSSEC). Nowadays, in the areas of IoT and trust mechanisms, there have been discussions on incorporating distributed ledger technologies (DLT) [65] or *blockchains* to enact effective *chains of trust* among multiple counterparts, objects and services in a decentralised manner [66–68]. Yadav et al. (2023) [69] have employed blockchain-based technologies in IoT to enable secure and reliable communications in smart cities. There are efforts to improve the scalability, resilience and trust mechanisms offered by DLT through a technology called IoT application (IOTA) [70–73], a next-generation blockchain solution.

Other noteworthy concepts associated with healthcare, and which use technologies to sustain additional communication and remote management features, include employing patient health information (PHI) and storing it under electronic health records (EHR). Some authors have also included so-called healthcare systems, such as electronic medical recording (EMR), order communication systems (OCS), and picture archiving and communication systems (PACS) [41]. These systems must comply with underlying cyber security IS, such as IDS, firewall/filtering, security information and event management (SIEM), and continuous cyber security monitoring and logging practices [74].

IoT and MIoT are targets for a host of cyber-attacks [35,62,75]. As Alsubaei et al. (2019) [48] commented, approximately 45% of all ransomware attacks dating 2017 were directed at the healthcare sector. In 2018, cybercriminals deployed WannaCry ransomware and Zero-day attacks in healthcare facilities in the UK's National Health Service (NHS), encrypting all data in unpatched systems [76,77]. Stellios et al. (2018) [75] discussed IoT security and TM in detail, highlighting attack venues explored by threat actors. For instance, they highlighted issues such as DoS, physical threats, eavesdropping, node capture and compromisation. Their work focused on modelling IoT-enabled cyber-attacks by understanding: (i) adversaries (access, motivations, capabilities); (ii) IoT devices (embedded system vulnerabilities, network vulnerabilities); and (iii) actual targets connectivity (direct, indirect, no connection to critical infrastructure).

3. Systematic Literature Review

We conducted an SLR to better understand how researchers consider risk assessment in MIoT/IoT. It employed the Preferred Reporting Items for Systematic Reviews and Meta-Analyses (PRISMA) 2020 recommendations [78], following the 27-point checklist for deriving a substantial synthesis of research priorities, where we use the relevant items as dictated by the PRISMA process. We provide below a summary of the PRISMA 2020 Checklist (referring to items from the recommendations as #) with regard to the 'Introduction' and 'Methods':

- Rationale (#3)—the literature about risks in MIoT must be better understood. In past years there has been a proliferation of research that would profit from synthesis and discussion to organise knowledge and identify gaps.
- Objectives (#4)—the guiding question is *"What are the factors underpinning risk assessments in MIoT?"*.
- Eligibility criteria (#5)—as inclusion criteria, we are interested in the latest results (published in the last five years, i.e., May 2018 to May 2023) mentioning risk assessment (any type, i.e., normal, i.e., in this context, we refer to the *usual* way organisations

conduct RA, by following guidelines and deriving the most likely risk scenarios that could arise, vulnerabilities, impact and mitigation effort that follows—or dynamic, describing case studies in healthcare that used MIoT for data gathering and communication). Our exclusion criteria do not consider any poster not providing fundamental research outcomes, results not focused on cyber security or privacy, as well as RA that does not consider the use of IoT/MIoT.

- Information sources (#6)—Google Scholar, ACM Digital Library and IEEExplore (Respectively, https://scholar.google.com, accessed on 19 June 2023, https://dl.acm.org, accessed on 19 June 2023, and https://ieeexplore.ieee.org, accessed on 19 June 2023).
- Search strategy (#7)—our basic template for input was:
  - Query: `(dynamic risk assessment or risk assessment) and (''medical IoT'' or MIoT) and healthcare and (cybersecurity or ''cyber security'' or cyber-security).`

  We adapted it to match the particularities of the information source under scrutiny.
- Selection process (#8)—case studies employing risk assessment of MIoT/IoT in healthcare settings.
- Data collection process (#9)—we performed the search, analysed titles and abstracts and then retrieved the entire paper for in-depth inspection as to eligibility.
- Data items (#10)—for the selected papers that passed previous stages of scrutiny, we extracted RA methodology and relevant risk-related components, healthcare settings (if any), MIoT/IoT specification (if any), year and case study explanation. Depending on the selected research, we were interested in any cyber-attack or specific vulnerability comprising MIoT/IoT devices.

Our guiding search strategy was directed at RA approaches that were either static/periodic or dynamic. We also investigated the security issues that the technologies try to solve or tackle, i.e., blockchains used for trust parties, lightweight authentication, or fast encryption for confidential data manipulation. In addition, we addressed the most likely types of cyber-attacks that threat actors could attempt when abusing systems.

We tweaked the searching input query to match the specific requirements of the information sources—for instance, using parentheses is mandatory to convey precise relationships. For Google Scholar, we executed the template query explained above and then selected the "Custom Range" parameter to retrieve papers sorted by relevance from 2017 to 2022. As this platform does not only scan scientific venues per se, we were interested in all retrieved gray literature, such as dissertations, manuals, and white papers.

Specifically for ACM-DL, the mechanism required logical connectors all to be uppercase. The query was:

```
[[Full Text: dynamic risk assessment] OR [Full Text: risk assessment]] AND
[[Full Text: ''medical iot''] OR [Full Text: miot]] AND
[[Full Text: cybersecurity] OR [Full Text: ''cyber security''] OR
[Full Text: cyber-security]] AND
[E-Publication Date: (01/01/2017 TO 31/12/2022)]
```

For IEEExplore, the same query used in Scholar and ACM-DL yielded zero results, prompting us to edit the *Advanced Query* option to *build* the query as the platform expected. Then, for this source, we had to edit the query manually, so it applied the logical connectors with parentheses following this query filtered out by year (2017 to 2022):

```
((''All Metadata'': ''dynamic risk assessment''
OR ''risk assessment'') AND
(''All Metadata'': ''medical iot''
OR ''miot'' OR ''iot'') AND
(''All Metadata'': ''cybersecurity''
OR ''cyber security''
OR ''cyber-security''))
```

3.1. Related Work on RA/DRA in MIoT

We conducted the SLR between 2 May 2023 and 6 May 2023 for all the chosen information sources. Figure 1 shows the suggested PRISMA 2020 flow diagram for SLR, which includes searches of databases.

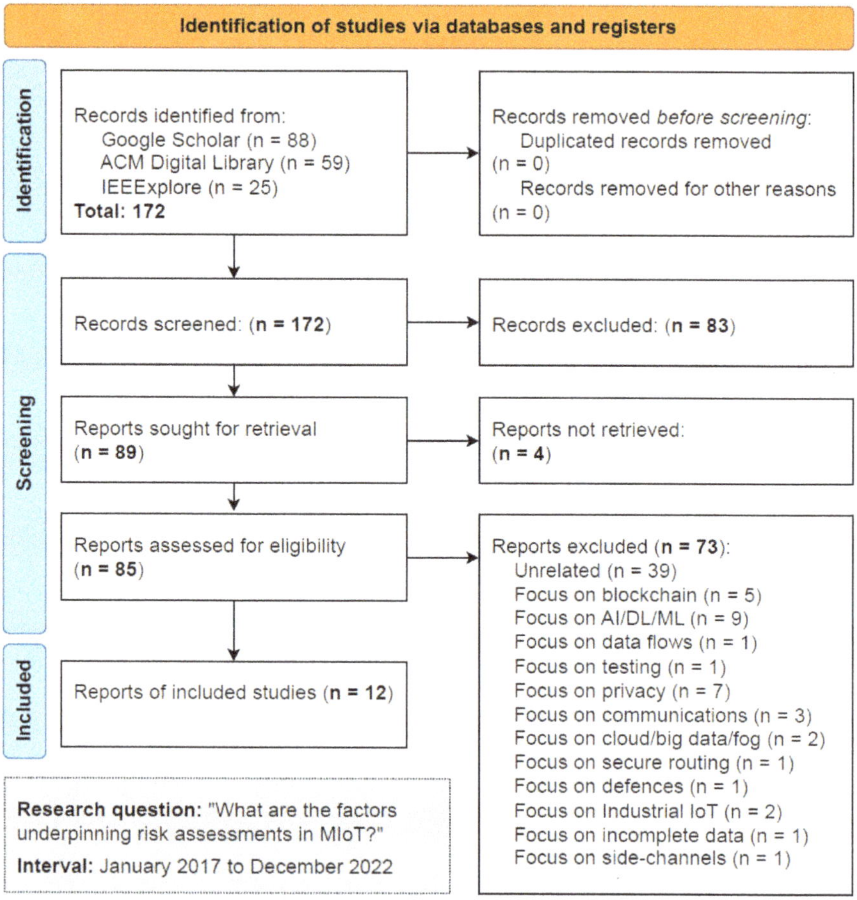

Figure 1. PRISMA 2020 identification of studies.

Regarding the process, the initial identification resulted in 172 records, with four removed for being duplicates or unavailable. The next phase screened these records and excluded 83 because the title or abstract was unrelated to our SLR proposition. We assessed 85 reports, reading all the work and excluding 73 for various reasons related to not meeting the previously identified eligibility criteria. The process finished with selecting 12 studies, where we extracted significant risk-associated elements, frameworks, standards, attacks, and methodologies to support our discussion. Table 1 summarises the main findings from the SLR, presenting an overview of selected work on RA/DRA. Note that some literature is specific to MIoT, and some discusses IoT in broader terms.

Le et al. (2018) [79] devised a DRA framework in the context of autonomous vehicles. This work did not make it into the SLR because it was not applied to healthcare; however, it includes important discussions and observations for proposing a dynamic framework for tackling risk. The authors comment on the requirements and challenges for developing a DRA framework in highly dynamic environments with frequent threats, vulnerabilities and technological changes. They justified the need for such an approach because systems should quickly adapt to unstable environments from various IoT sources. As stated, the risk framework should:

1. Deal with heterogeneous data.
2. Eliminate inconsistency and incompleteness, managing uncertainty errors and missing values, increasing data *reliability*.
3. Reduce the data scale for efficient processing.
4. Provide run-time risk analysis for effective and actionable decision making.

Table 1. Overview of selected literature on RA/DRA in IoT/MIoT.

#	Authors	Domain	Highlights
#01	Kandasamy et al. (2020) [80]	IoT, MIoT	Showcases RA frameworks in IoT, computes MIoT risk, IoT risk vectors and risk ranking
#02	Lee (2020) [58]	IoT	Proposition of a four-layer IoT cyber risk management framework, risk identification, quantification
#03	Ksibi et al. (2021) [81]	MIoT	Dynamic agent-based risk management, generic case studies in IoT/MIoT, enhance trustworthiness of MIoT
#04	Malamas et al. (2021) [16]	MIoT	SLR, discussing risk assessment frameworks in MIoT, comments on "medical risk" and risk methods
#05	Stellios et al. (2018) [75]	IoT, MIoT	Methodology uses attack model to output qualitative criticality level of IoT-enabled devices
#06	Elhoseny et al. (2021) [57]	MIoT	Focus on security and privacy of MIoT, CIA, resilience, access control, usability, data issues
#07	Kandasamy et al. (2022) [82]	IoT	Risk assessment focused on NIST Cyber Security Framework using self-assessment survey instruments
#08	Newaz et al. (2021) [83]	IoT	Discusses the benefits of fault-tolerant designs to improve security, a survey of known attacks in IoT
#09	Gressl et al. (2020) [84]	IoT	Use of known methods to address risk, e.g., design space exp. (DSE), Bayesian attack graphs, risk trees
#10	Datta (2020) [23]	IoT	Combination of risk assessment framework with security incident and event management altogether
#11	Nurse et al. (2017) [40]	IoT	Describes core RA concepts in IoT, Comments on deficiencies of RA approaches and their inadequacy
#12	Nurse et al. (2018) [41]	IoT	Discusses the need for automated and collaborative RA in IoT, with industrial comments and practices

3.2. Analysis of Selected Results

We next comment the selected papers and conduct an in-depth analysis outlining the major strengths and relevant considerations for tackling risks in IoT/MIoT ecosystems. The number of included studies is low because, after executing all of the PRISMA procedure, it favours quality over quantity, i.e., we will retrieve and scrutinise only the most relevant results aligned with the SLR's research question.

#01 by Kandasamy et al. (2020) [80] comments on IoT-based vulnerabilities, such as complex architecture, inappropriate security configuration, physical security, and insecure firmware or software; it discusses how to address computation of cyber-risk referring to risk ranking, risk vectors, and risk assessment frameworks. The work tackles known impact factors, likelihood, and risk levels in IoT and comments on the risk assessment process (RAP) of known standards, such as NIST, ISO/IEC, OCTAVE, GSMA (It is called the Self Assessment Risk Management Toolkit, link: https://www.gsma.com/mobilefordevelopment/resources/self-assessment-risk-management-toolkit-summary/, accessed on 19 June 2023) (based on OCTAVE), and threat assessment and remediation analysis (TARA). It compares various RA frameworks specifically for IoT, computing the MIoT risk for medical devices and discussing RA scales and rankings. It comments on known IoT risk vectors and risk rank calculation, devising numerical weights for computing risk likelihood parameters.

#02 by Lee (2020) [58] discusses qualitative, e.g., ISO, cyber kill chain (CKC), OCTAVE, capability maturity model integration (CMMI), and consensus audit guidelines (CAG), as well as quantitative approaches, namely, Bayesian decision network (BDN), AVARCIBER, an extension of ISO 27005, and NIST's approach geared towards cyber security risk management. The four-layer risk management framework comprises the following: (i) an IoT cyber ecosystem layer; (ii) an IoT cyber infrastructure layer; (iii) an IoT cyber risk assessment layer; and (iv) an IoT cyber performance layer. It identifies risk by inspecting IoT assets, vulnerabilities and cyber threats and quantifying risk by looking at each IoT asset's impact, frequency, and defence probability in terms of vulnerabilities and classifying it into different cyber threat groupings. It allocates IoT resources in a financial/budget scheme for cost-benefit analysis with mechanisms to break down IoT-based layers in a divide-and-conquer risk approach.

#03 by Ksibi et al. (2021) [81] proposes a risk management framework relying on an orchestrator and three agents for managing risks in the device, network and storage and processing areas. It focuses on RA, specifically e-health that employs haemodialysis and cardiac devices. The objective is to simplify the complexity of cyber-risk management efforts and to establish a fine-grained risk management process. The main idea is to evaluate the cumulative risk associated with global e-health service and to automate response for risk mitigation. It proposes dynamic agent-based risk management with risk identification, analysis/evaluation, and adaptation, followed by classification and risk evaluation, encompassing risk impact/cost, anomaly probability, global risk evaluation, and model evaluation. The framework is generic to IoT/MIoT, and it aims to study security challenges in e-health networks, enhancing trustworthiness in MIoT communicating nodes for decision-making on a layered risk management model.

#04 by Malamas et al. (2021) [16] provides a comprehensive comparison among RA methodologies and TM applied to MIoT, e.g., ISO, NIST, EU Regulation 2017/745 for Medical Devices, Open Worldwide Application Security Project (OWASP) IoT vulnerabilities, MAYO Clinic, ENISA, Association for the Advancement of Medical Instrumentation (AAMI), Australia's Therapeutic Goods Administration (TGA), and MITRE/US. For TM, they cover spoofing, tampering, repudiation, information disclosure, denial-of-service, elevation of privilege (STRIDE), damage, reproducibility, exploitability, affected users, discoverability (DREAD), attack trees, and multiple-valued logic (MVL). The authors propose a generic risk model for MIoT inspired by NIST's terminology (e.g., predisposing conditions and adverse impact). This generic model invites security analysts to conduct thorough security assessments for threat, vulnerability, and impact assessment, risk mitigation or risk treatment. The work suggests that traditional RA methodologies cannot be applied to MIoT contexts because they belong to untrustworthy environments where the designer favours end-customer usability over security.

#05 by Stellios et al. (2018) [75] focuses on 'verified attacks', i.e., real-world incidents or attacks published by researchers with applications on IIoT, e-health IoT and smart systems. The authors explain attacks in depth as applied to critical infrastructure, which encompasses smart infrastructure and healthcare, among others. The work details an e-health medical IoT system for two ecosystems, comprising *in-hospital* and *near-patient*. Consistent with the direction of our work, the authors suggest that security attacks targeted explicitly at CPS and IoT have been addressed throughout the years; however, they have only sometimes been fully assessed and understood.

#06 by Elhoseny et al. (2021) [57] compartmentalises IoT provisions and attacks perpetrated on each layer, detailing protections and protocols. The authors also comment on available countermeasures, e.g., access control, data encryption, data auditing, IoT healthcare policies, data search, data minimisation and anonymisation, inventory devices, network segmentation, following the security community's best practices, awareness, and continuous monitoring and reporting. There is a focus on the security and privacy requirements of MIoT, such as confidentiality, data integrity and availability, resilience to attacks, data usability, access control, data auditing/authentication, and privacy of patient information. The work details the MIoT infrastructure comprised of wireless body area networks (WBAN), sensing, cloud, and medical staff, all contributing towards effective patient care. They describe real-time location services (RTL) for IoT devices for tracking employees, patients, visitors, and assets. Finally, they comment on the need to perform regular RA to identify potential risks associated with MIoT. This should be set up and designed to understand vulnerabilities better before the environment becomes operational.

#07 by Kandasamy et al. (2022) [82] focuses on the NIST cyber security framework combined with self-assessment survey instruments for understanding vulnerability and risk. The work refers to vulnerability and threat pairs that produce two other risk indices, risk management culture (RMC) and risk process and technology (RPT), applied to Asia-based healthcare cyber-attacks. The objective was to understand cyber security maturity from a vulnerability and risk perspective in order to compute a so-called enriched vulnerability priority score (EVPS) to prioritise vulnerabilities for managers to consider for counteracting attacks.

#08 by Newaz et al. (2021) [83] considers medical standards for cyber security ((IEC 62304:2006, ISO/IEC 27032:2012, IEC 82304-1:2016, ISO/IEC 8001 (Risk Management of Medical Devices on a Network), IEC/TR 80002-1:2009, ISO/TR 800020-2:20017, IEC/TR 80002- 3:2014). The authors comment on fault-tolerant designs to harden the infrastructure. The work comprises a survey that provides good explanations and classification of medical concerns employing IoT/IoMT. For instance, the authors suggest the following classification: *non-invasive* devices, *invasive* devices (transient use, short-term, long-term and connected), and *active therapeutic* devices (e.g., muscle stimulators and hearing aids). They offer a classification of sensors in terms of *physiological* (measure ECG, electromyography), *biological* (glucose, alcohol), and *environmental* sensors (accelerometer and gyroscope in smartwatches). In terms of cyber security protections, the work suggests using intrusion detection mechanisms to infer and confirm attacks, fine-grained access controls, privacy-preserving healthcare systems, employing artificial intelligence and machine learning (AI/ML) and big data, and in-depth investigation of smart medical devices and existing threats.

#09 by Gressl et al. (2020) [84] presents and explains design space exploration (DSE), Bayesian attack graphs (BAG), and risk trees (RISKEE). The authors provide a design framework to study a system's attack susceptibility to model security constraints. They comment on the need to incorporate RA in early system design and the advantages of drawing upon these choices. The paper showcases examples of limited capacity infrastructure, where they compute attack probabilities and the mean risk value for the setting under study.

#10 by Datta (2020) [23] presents three critical elements for performing thorough RA: (i) cyber security risk assessment framework; (ii) security incident and event management; and (iii) resilience framework. It extends the European Telecommunications Standards Institute (ETSI) risk-based security assessment. It showcases the framework using the following steps: (i) understanding business cases and regulatory contexts; (ii) business processes identification and security requirements; (iii) risk identification, estimation, evaluation and security testing; (iv) assets—cloud web services, IoT devices and networks;

and (v) upgrading software modules of end-to-end IoT platforms. This work brings together a risk assessment framework and an SIEM system as a significant contribution.

#11 by Nurse et al. (2017) [40] describes *core RA concepts*, as generally understood, as the process of identifying, estimating and prioritising risks to comprise organisational assets and fulfil operations. It comments on the usual approaches for RA, namely, NIST SP 800-30, ISO/IEC 27001, OCTAVE, the Central Communication and Telecommunication Agency (CCTA) Risk Analysis and Management Method (CRAMM), and *Expression des Besoins et Identification des Objectifs de Sécurité* (EBIOS) (ENISA's link: https://www.enisa.europa.eu/topics/risk-management/current-risk/risk-management-inventory/rm-ra-methods/m_ebios.html, accessed on 19 June 2023). It discusses particularities related to IoT dynamics including: (i) variability of scale in devices and systems; (ii) dynamism and temporality of connections between devices; and (iii) heterogeneity of actors interacting with IoT ecosystems. The authors provide substantial discussions to consider *"where current risk assessment methods fail?"*. They argue that it is mainly a result of lack of periodic assessment triggered by unobserved changes in the system (attack surface), business processes, or new information arising from threat intelligence mechanisms in place. The authors outline why current RA approaches are inherently inadequate when tackling IoT, providing interesting discussions. As a remedy, they advocate automated and continuous RA and the development of supporting tools to assist in simulation and modelling to enhance prediction and enable better preparedness.

#12 by Nurse et al. (2018) [41] refers to the IoTRiskAnalyzer framework [85], probabilistic model checking, Bayesian techniques combined with attack graphs and inference networks, and SecKit as a valid approach to provide model-based security and to address IoT-related risks. The authors discuss the need for automated RA in the IoT and collaborative risk assessment practices to enhance timely analysis. In the discussions provided, they refer to the *"perceived infeasibility of fully automated risk assessment in the IoT, and a view towards inter-organisational assessment of risk given IoT's wide connectivity"*. This factor is based upon the opinions of cyber security professionals taking part in the user study, as opposed to any experimental work showing what is/is not technically possible. The work describes an exciting set of industrial practices, including with fruitful discussions relating to concerns and observations about the difficulties of tackling timely RA in IoT.

After closely inspecting these results, some themes emerged. For instance, authors often remarked on the need to engage in layered approaches when tackling risk in IoT/MIoT networks [58,81]. Understanding the types of devices (invasive, non-invasive), as well as the types of sensors (physiological, biological, environmental), could also help understand underlying protections to adopt [83]. There are also comments on risk quantification as referred to in a significant number of studies [80–82]. The need for understanding how organisational culture could address cyber security and withstand or mitigate cyber-attacks as they progress as well as maturity-related concerns was also highlighted [82]. There were also comments on the requirement for continuous RA and collaborative RA to enact timely protections for stakeholders [40,41] and relating to response automation [81].

Next, we provide an overview of interesting ideas and concepts extracted from our in-depth results analysis:

- Risk-related standards (for a list of standards, please refer to Appendix A.3)—ISO 27000, IEC 62304:2006, ISO/IEC 27032:2012, IEC 82304-1:2016, ISO/IEC 8001 (Risk Management of Medical Devices on a Network), IEC/TR 80002-1:2009, ISO/TR 800020-2:2017, IEC/TR 80002-3:2014, ETSI's risk-based security assessment, CCTA CRAMM, EBIOS.
- Organisations—MITRE/US, AAMI, TGA, EU regulations, ENISA, OWASP, ETSI.
- Other standards—CMMI, CAG.
- RA methodologies—ISO 27000, NIST 800-30, OCTAVE and OCTAVE Allegro.
- Other methodologies applied to risk—IoTRiskAnalyzer, SecKit, attack graphs.
- Threat modelling and techniques—STRIDE, DREAD, TARA, attack/risk trees, MVL, CKC, BDN, DSE.

- Catalogues of vulnerabilities—OWASP Top 10 IoT vulnerabilities.
- IoT services and features—security (CIA attributes, as explained in Section 4) and safety; device and system interoperability; resilience to attacks and fault-tolerant design; authorisation, authentication, access control; use of real-time location services (RTL) for tracking employees, patients, visitors, and assets; accounting for dynamism and temporality of devices in dynamic settings.
- Risk quantification—likelihood, impact, and vulnerability prioritisation.
- IoT ecosystems—in-hospital (within a hospital's premises) and near-patient (within patients, wherever they are located, e.g., at home or in other settings).
- IoT layers—basic representations encompass three layers, namely, perception, network, and application; however, as previously mentioned, the literature considers extensions such as middleware, business, end-user, processing, and service management, which can drive assessment efforts as each layer presents its own set of weaknesses that sophisticated threat actors can potentially exploit.

From a patient's perspective, their smart-based apparatuses may interfere with their medical equipment. For instance, Pal et al. (2018) [86] studied IoT in smart homes and the future prevalence of ambient assisted living (AAL) technologies to revolutionise remote care and treatments for the elderly. The benefits of such technologies should meet stringent security requirements, but offer a balance in terms of respecting privacy whilst monitoring patients. One cannot dismiss the fact that these novel smart home setups are not immune to cyber-attacks as sophisticated actors may deploy malware or eavesdrop on communications for financial gain or for other motives.

4. Challenges in Performing Risk Assessment in MIoT

Cyber security generally entails addressing attributes such as confidentiality, integrity, and availability, known as the CIA triad [87,88]. Over the years, some authors have started to define these attributes in terms of related characteristics, such as authorisation, authentication, non-repudiation, auditing and accountability; however, these are almost synonyms to the terms used by CIA. Any attack directed at a system attempts to disrupt one of these attributes, so security officers enact protections to assets by designing robust systems that may withstand malicious incursions and stop attack progression before affecting other systems. The methodology we follow next consists of identifying relevant literature on RA and DRA, mapping concerns and challenges, and discussing significant shortcomings and difficulties whilst addressing risks in IoT/MIoT.

Nowadays, organisations hire proficient cyber security personnel to guide protective actions and comply with regulations to protect customers. Failure to do so can be caused by poor preparedness, lack of specific training in cyber security (unskilled staff), situational awareness deficiencies in understanding and mapping the attack surface (poor asset visibility), and unfocused security monitoring, among other factors. Hiring proficient cyber security personnel with a background in mitigation, responses, and with pro-active cyber security skills certainly helps organisations cope with impending attacks and to thwart malicious occurrences, and to differentiate between localised anomalies caused by incompetent configurations or improper device use [89,90].

Other vital cyber security research [91] addresses the (i) sheer scale of cyberspace, where potentially billions of interconnected devices interact, and the (ii) asymmetry between attack and defence, where threat actors only need to identify a single point of attack, while defenders seek to prevent or block any vulnerabilities in their systems and services. Another recurrent issue is related to the poor design and implementation of software or firmware that permeates the industry and insufficient testing that allows vulnerable products and services to reach end-customers [11,92].

Risk in medical devices has been addressed in early literature dating back to 2007 [93] under the ANSI/AAMI/ISO 14971:2007 standard (please refer to Appendix A.2 for the definition), which suggests that risk has two components: (i) the probability of occurrence of harm; and (ii) how severe that harm might be. In recent years, both concepts have been integrated (for risk and medical devices). For instance, the ISO 31000:2018 publication suggests that risk is about 'uncertainty on objectives' [17], whereas the USA Food and Drug Administration (FDA) adopts the principle that a medical device is an instrument intended for use in the diagnosis, cure, mitigation, treatment, or prevention of disease (Federal Food, Drug, and Cosmetic Act (FD&C Act) (Link: https://www.fda.gov/regulatory-information/laws-enforced-fda/federal-food-drug-and-cosmetic-act-fdc-act, accessed on 19 June 2023) [16,83]).

4.1. Particularities of IoT Relevant to RA

One key issue in any RA concerns its *quantification*. NIST suggests using qualitative metrics (i.e., low, medium, high) when addressing likelihood and impacts in risk models [40], which risks multiple interpretations and abstractions and a lack of precision as managers might consider different aspects when determining perceived risks associated with threats. Current RA approaches might fail in IoT due to this dynamic nature, as prior assessments could quickly become obsolete when new devices emerge in networks with different requirements, technologies, objectives, and capabilities. As pointed out in a previous study [40], an effective RA requires predicting devices that could ingress into networks before the assessment, which is highly challenging.

A round of discussion with professionals in the industry on the benefits and shortcomings of RA in IoT unveiled interesting points [41], including the following:

- Incorporate security in early designs through effective shift-left approaches within DevOps [94], i.e., addressing security-related concerns since system specification.
- Quantification of risk is not trivial to accomplish, as the industry still favours qualitative measures (e.g., low, medium and high, as suggested by NIST).
- Careful thinking on how to balance dynamism, automation and human aspects when enacting effective RA in complex environments characterised by frequent connection requests and disconnections.
- Addressing new emerging risks in partially unknown systems; this occurs when potentially malicious devices participating in the network demand service or interactions to act as stepping stones to larger cyber-attacks.

The authors mention in their final remarks one critical point that remains neglected in RA frameworks and methodologies: the industry still believes in the *"perceived infeasibility of fully automated risk assessment in the IoT"*, mostly due to the issues raised throughout this paper, namely dynamism and temporality.

IoT is a technological solution to address many problems in communicating information across multiple CPS and IS, with applications ranging from industry, healthcare and smart infrastructure, to mention a few. The dynamics and temporality of connections among devices distinguish IoT from other systems and services [95]. Next, we comment on the challenges in highly interconnected networks in IoT/MIoT, including:

- Quantification of the communication of information to other devices that are aligned with the organisation's risk appetite and its scale when accommodating many interacting devices.
- Clear shortcomings of *periodic* RA that do not account for unknown system boundaries, latest vulnerabilities (as advertised by vendors and security-oriented organisations), and failure to recognise that IoT-based assets are sometimes the initiators or the promoters of larger attacks [41].
- Lack of rigorous *dynamic* risk approaches [40] that are instead substituted by *periodic* assessment approaches.
- Accounting devices with different capabilities and objectives, i.e., sets requiring connections to happen only once or twice, as well as persistent connections and unsigned devices seeking to connect with signed/authorised devices that represent increases in risk and likelihood of attacks.
- Consideration of the heterogeneity of devices interacting in healthcare-related IoT/MIoT ecosystems.

- The need for *automated, continuous and collaborative* RA coupled with supporting tools based on simulation and modelling to enhance the understanding of which new devices might emerge in networks, what they might request or perform, and communication patterns that could be developed through time.

The most commonly desired properties of systems deployed to end-users include robustness, resilience (ability to retain operation even in the presence of catastrophic events), performance, and usability. Regarding MIoT, security officers also consider safety, privacy, seamless system-wide integration, and interoperability with other systems. This is especially relevant when we consider healthcare settings where MIoT designers tailor their systems and interfaces to accommodate vulnerable patients, i.e., elderly, undergoing recovery (post-procedure or after surgery), pregnant women experiencing discomfort or undergoing following up, as well as non-human counterparts, e.g., hospital equipment, beds, and infrastructure to sustain IS and services.

Standard protections include encryption for communication and storage, security systems, such as IDS and firewalls, and raising awareness of cyber security and the most likely threats facing stakeholders. Under a comprehensive and scaled MIoT setting, we focus on sophisticated, hard-to-track or identify cyber-attacks posed by advanced threat actors. The plethora of healthcare devices and their inherent characteristics play an important role in detecting and thwarting cyber-attacks before they propagate over other systems and networks.

Figure 2 depicts a typical MIoT ecosystem illustrating how hospital healthcare management and cyber security systems may be integrated. It shows how a DRA proposition could work and the necessary underpinning features and considerations to be effective. It is worth noting that, throughout any MIoT/IoT life-cycle, there are interactions with third-party devices and a myriad of participants (both 'normal' and malicious users), where the communication patterns could symbolise cyber-attacks, but, in fact, represent incompetent use or accidental actions. It is the job of security officers to differentiate these behaviours and to confirm or refute cyber-attacks on-the-fly to protect end-users and offer valuable user experience whilst using the technologies.

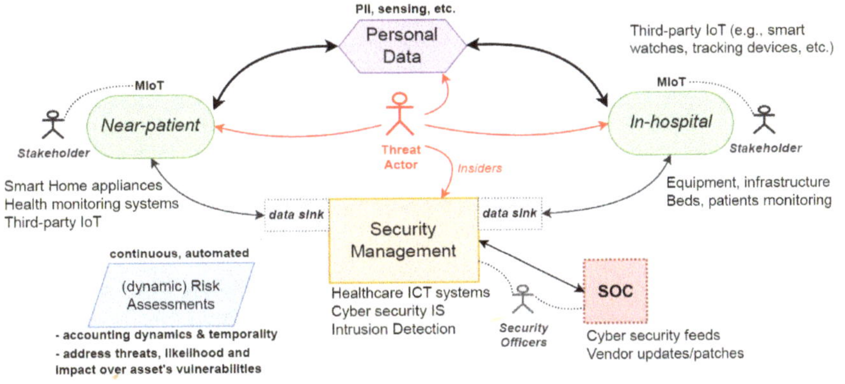

Figure 2. General MIoT ecosystem and the issues surrounding DRA propositions.

The figure also shows that the solution must work with existing cyber security and information and communications technology (ICT) systems in hospitals coupled with existing security operational centres (SOC) and then account for the myriad of potential MIoT that will participate in the network. The *data sinks* involve data gathering and may encompass other systems and technologies so that they can function seamlessly and securely, relaying data across public and private networks. SOC has access to all ICT-related systems that utilise dashboards extensively to observe the entire attack surface and continuously monitor the network's health to direct responses (mitigations in the case of attacks) and to perform remote management of distributed assets. Within this framework, sophisticated threat actors continuously inspect networks for vulnerabilities on any level, i.e., near-patient and in-hospital.

4.2. Similar RA Approaches Specific to IoT

Sicari et al. (2018) [96] proposed a risk analysis methodology tailored to end-to-end systems considering the whole data life-cycle of IoT. It accounts for both static and dynamic features of IoT-based systems to tackle risks throughout layers of data flow. The authors suggest five steps to follow: (i) Identify and model a threat as an attack tree, listing the possible attack vectors towards the threat realisation and identifying the principal vulnerabilities (as leaves); (ii) Map to each vulnerability a qualitative exploitability level translated to a quantitative numerical value within (0:10); (iii) Generate a graph highlighting all dependencies among the identified vulnerabilities; (iv) Compute an exploitability value for all the edges of the graph; (v) Account for dependencies by updating the model following iterative formulas. When considering a dynamic risk approach, however, the methodology lacks a support tool to devise the attack trees and graphs and all the required updates. The mechanism provided is interesting in mapping potential vulnerabilities over IoT assets and converting qualitative scales to quantitative values.

Abie and Balasingham (2012) [97] considered autonomous IoT that requires a risk-based adaptive assessment framework for risk analysis that can sustain predictions for impending issues regarding assets, impact prediction, implementing planned actions for mitigation and reducing risk exposure [41]. They proposed the adaptation of two models for predicting uncertainty, namely, Cyber Value at Risk (CVR) [98] and MicroMort [99], and a mechanism to compute the economic impact of IoT risks. The authors proposed quantifying uncertainties in IoT domains, identifying the most likely attack vectors and combining risk approaches. The manual alternative does not account for any dynamics and changes in attack surface as multiple IoT participate in networks.

Matheu-García et al. (2019) [100] suggest using a certification methodology that combines security risk assessment with security testing to certify devices across application contexts. The proposed approach is derived from ETSI (based on ISO 31000 and ISO 29119) and extended to include labelling activities to address certification and tackle security risks related to IoT domains. The work calculates base scores for each identified vulnerability employing a common vulnerability scoring system (CVSS) formula. It proposes an approach to quantifying risks in IoT environments by integrating different standards with known scoring systems; however, it does not address any system dynamics or changes in the attack surface over time, which represent fundamental characteristics of these systems.

Formal approaches for modelling and assessing IoT security have been proposed, for instance, by Ge et al. (2017) [101], who combined a hierarchical attack representation model (HARM) to evaluate it using the known symbolic hierarchical automated reliability and performance evaluator (SHARPE). In contrast, Mohsin et al. (2017) [85] devised IoTRiskAnalyzer to analyse risks using a quantitative probabilistic model-checking approach. These techniques, unfortunately, fall short of the required abstractions to represent complex MIoT, as they must analyse a massive state space when modelling. These shortcomings are alleviated by probabilistic model checking that sustains partial state space analysis; however, these problems will still be present in over-scaled MIoT/IoT networks.

Finally, we mention the work of Duan et al. (2021) [102] who implemented an end-to-end assessment framework for IoT, consisting of a vulnerability assessment model equipped with visualisation using AI/ML to process vulnerability descriptions and predict severity scores. The proposed framework has four phases: (i) generation of a system model comprising specifications of smart devices and connectivity information; (ii) data processing using AI/ML integrated with known vulnerability catalogues, namely, the National Vulnerability Database (NVD) maintained by NIST; (iii) adoption of a graphical security model based on a two-layer HARM methodology; and (iv) a visualisation interface to present the assessment results. A drawback is that the approach is static and requires frequent changes given the inherent dynamics of IoT networks.

4.3. Discussion

A substantial amount of research has addressed the difficulties posed by *quantifying risk*, a common theme with regard to risk in general. There are also attempts to integrate risk frameworks with cyber security catalogues, usually maintained by the community, that update discovered vulnerabilities, so that managers can take preventive actions to tackle cyber-attacks. We have summarised vital factors when tackling dynamic RA in MIoT ecosystems, as follows:

- Improvement in the identification of the potential attack surface posed by dynamic IoT-based assets in complex networks [35].
- Tackling the dynamics and temporality of transient and intermittent behaviours characteristic of MIoT environments. Account for the inherent complexities of performing these tasks in (near) real-time settings.
- Adherence to MIoT/IoT-specific guidance and regulations, aligning them to hospital technologies, equipment and communication protocols.
- Effective and seamless TM in early designs when considering MIoT as a technological solution to encompass other IS/ICT in place and aligned with SOC objectives.
    - One interesting approach supported by OWASP is to employ a tool called `pytm` (OWASP pytm, a Pythonic framework for TM: https://owasp.org/www-project-pytm/, accessed on 19 June 2023). It helps stakeholders to build a textual representation of a business setting or environment and to generate a DFD or a sequence diagram to highlight the most likely threats within the system.
- Account and adapt to dynamic attack surface and third-party equipment that is in contact with MIoT over its life-cycle.
- Employ and incorporate known and community-driven vulnerability catalogues and cyber intelligence feeds.
- Enhance cyber security awareness and personnel training with regards to the latest cyber-attacks and threats to improve preparedness, tackle mitigations and pro-actively protect MIoT/IoT-based services and systems.
- Better visualise attacks [101,103] to understand threat actor's progression over IoT-based assets.

Security is an all-encompassing problem faced by all organisations. With regard to managerial implications for the healthcare domain, we highlight the need for asset visibility, where SOC operators understand cyber-attack repercussions as they progress in the networks [90,104,105]. Zhang and Navimipour (2022) [106] discuss IoT-based medical management systems and inherent open issues. Modern SOC should take multiple data feeds to provide context and to undermine cyber-attacks as they happen. Standard services implemented by SOC include event and incident management and response, dispatching teams to solve issues, user behaviour analytics, cyber threat intelligence, vulnerability management, and risk assessment. Nowadays, the trend is towards automating the processes of triaging multiple data for effective and timely analysis, tool integration, and adherence to regulation and guidance by established cyber security institutions (e.g., the US' NIST, the EU's ENISA, or the UK's NCSC). Security officers must orchestrate these systems to work together by performing relevant and timely risk assessments.

There has been substantial research relating to DRA in isolation without considering its applicability to IoT.

For instance, Riesco and Villagrá (2019) [107] employed cyber threat intelligence (CTI) combined with DRA using so-called *semantic reasoners* to enact realistic RA and to support decision-making. The approach used standardised intelligence specifications so that a broader community could participate in the security effort. Another example is provided by Antonello et al. (2022) [108]. They suggested performing DRA using modelling and simulation combined with systems theory, providing a systematic analysis approach for studying dynamic scenarios.

An interesting study by Kavallieratos et al. (2019) [26] focused on TM applied to smart home ecosystems. The authors identified information (user credentials, data collection, status information, logs, media, location, and PII) and physical assets (IoT devices, hubs, gateways, sensors/actuators, cloud servers). Then they developed DFD models to represent interactions and analysed the system using STRIDE. The consideration of dynamic approaches is a multi-factor problem that involves multiple research areas. In order to work towards better usability and user experience for risk analysis, Collen et al. (2022) [109] employed a user-friendly interface to guide DRA, appending iterative feedback directed at non-technical users. The authors suggested ways to create decision-making trees to add transparency to decisions focusing on the smart home.

Figure 3 shows a comparative analysis between traditional RA and DRA. It showcases the main RA objectives in contrast with DRA, aiming to derive automated, continuous, and collaborative tasks throughout the IoT/MIoT ecosystem. For each aspect, it lists frameworks and cyber security concepts to factor in when incorporating DRA in solutions. Specifically, with respect to MIoT, DRA must seamlessly track activities and process data to determine 'under attack' situations or events that pose a substantial risk to patients. One significant idea is to not only deduplicate entries across multiple datasets, but to triage them in a way that helps the decision-making process enact timely protective measures for end-users by denying access momentarily or blocking devices until further notice.

As mentioned earlier, there are non-trivial challenges to address in such complex environments posed by the sheer scale of MIoT networks. Organisations need to acknowledge that current RA methodologies are often reviewed only periodically and at an undesirable pace. We envision opportunities in risk analysis to address these considerations and adapt current frameworks to withstand stricter security requirements as demanded by MIoT technologies. Researchers working with IoT/MIoT could seek to understand the techniques and methodologies employed by researchers working with DRA in other contexts and then adapt them to work with the observed healthcare requirements.

Finally, we highlight the use of *automation* to address cyber security tasks in the massive and dynamic settings presented by IoT/MIoT networks with multiple owners, vendors, and stakeholders. Given the massive amount of data that can potentially be produced hourly from sensors, IS, monitoring applications and tracking devices, compounded by the fact that sophisticated algorithms require quality data to make timely predictions and decisions, the level of automation for IoT-based solutions will dictate its effectiveness in combatting cybercrime-related risks to the infrastructure. Admittedly, automation comes with trade-offs and, if poorly executed, can pose negative impacts to organisations. For instance, automated systems may produce more data than they can handle (i.e., data deluge), or triage and remove more entries than required (e.g., whilst handling outliers), or sophisticated threat actors may influence the algorithms using advanced data poisoning techniques.

Figure 4 illustrates the risks and exposures that are potentially created for end-users or patients in IoT/MIoT settings. The figure indicates the usual attack vectors present in this kind of infrastructure and also highlights how dynamic behaviours triggered by sophisticated threat actors may impact the end-user of the technology and undermine trust in systems and services. It is worth mentioning that, as discussed throughout this work, other risks are not mapped due to lack of knowledge and uncertainty as to novel attack venues that can be employed by cyber-attackers. End-users and patients want to use MIoT devices due to the high service-level aggregated value that they offer; however, they also want to be safeguarded from unwanted intrusions and cyber-attacks directed at the equipment.

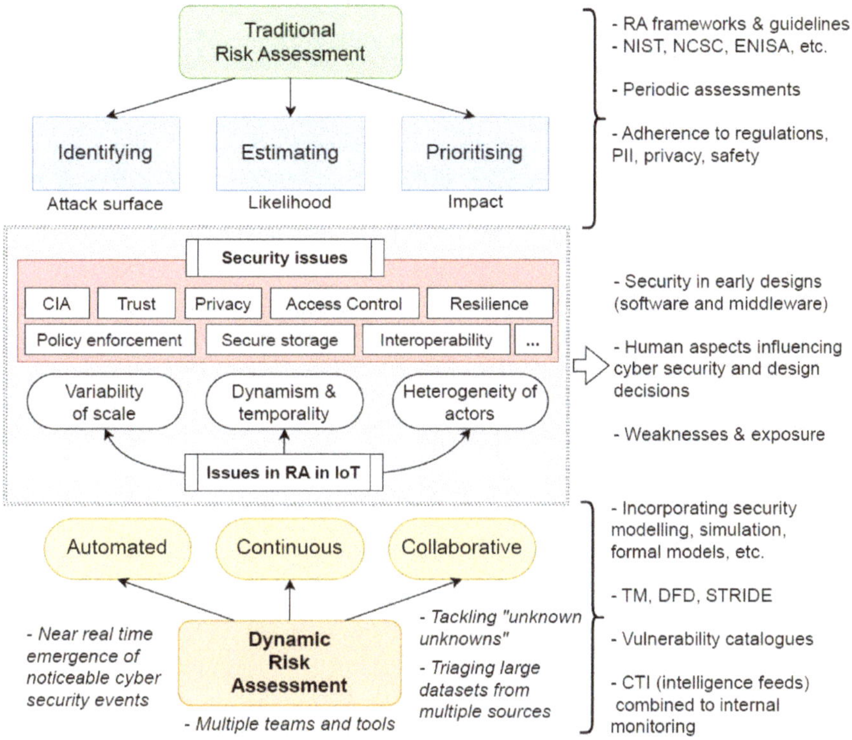

Figure 3. Comparative analysis contrasting traditional RA with DRA propositions.

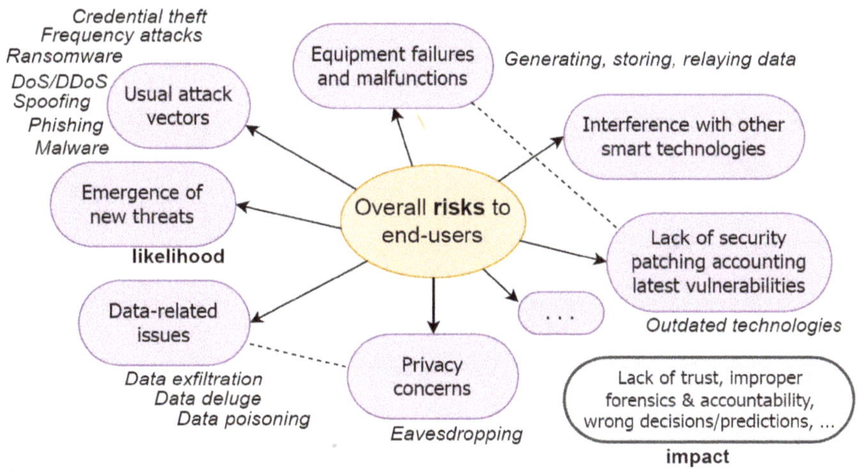

Figure 4. Overall risks to end-users posed by IoT/MIoT settings.

5. Conclusions

Our objective was to consider the foremost challenges with respect to DRA in MIoT and how managers and developers across the ecosystem can deal with emergent patient risks when employing wearable computing in healthcare settings. The contributions of the paper included presentation of an SLR outlining current trends and existing approaches, and provision of recommendations on how to address the impact of intrusions and mitigations to protect end-users. The work discussed risks associated with using MIoT and enumerated approaches to protection when working with these technologies. In the meta-analysis associated with the SLR, we sought to broaden understanding of how healthcare settings can tackle risks using MIoT/IoT. We were interested in detailing how these organisations have applied RA effectively and the operational issues associated with addressing emergent risks for improving patient care.

It is undoubtedly true that cyber security offers end-users a protective layer with controls that can prevent data leakage, protect PII, and ensure smooth use and data storage of confidential information. It may also efficiently thwart, prevent, or respond to cyber-attacks or malicious circumstances arising in MIoT networks, tackling threats and preventing them from cascading to other systems. The problem we have identified when employing MIoT devices to track patients' healthcare is how to differentiate local measurement deviations and anomalies from actual cyber-attacks. The healthcare architecture needs to be improved by developing a framework on top of the basic functionalities that prevent unwarranted cyber-attacks. The idea is to improve architecture resilience properties so that the limited hardware of a device can generate valuable data even under duress and with the overhead needed to support these capabilities.

Future Work and Research Directions

In this research area there are numerous opportunities for improvements with respect to privacy, safety, and cyber security. For instance, we envision the incorporation of CTI into the dynamic and automated RA effort in IoT, as discussed in previous work on applications in Industry 4.0 [110], and, more generically, to smart devices [111]. Moreover, we cannot dismiss the benefits and strengths of AI/ML (and related approaches, e.g., deep learning [112], and so on) in cyber security applied to RA in MIoT/IoT [113–116]. The combination of these approaches with security analysis allows risk analysts to enhance decision making and predictive capabilities, enabling them to anticipate and withstand cyber-attacks before they develop in systems and networks. These approaches, however, require further investigation to determine their usefulness in real-world settings and to understand the complex infrastructure, behaviours, and interactions.

As Nurse et al. (2017) [40] have outlined, future RA approaches must be coupled with simulation and modelling to enhance the predictive nature of massive IoT/MIoT dynamics (arrival/departure) and temporality. In this sense, a digital twins approach, where virtual and physical counterparts devise a model for thorough analysis, is one way to improve prediction. Our investigation has also identified how the use of modern approaches, such as cloud and fog computing [117–119], in healthcare can help patients receive better care whilst seamlessly protecting their data and equipment. We have argued that these approaches need more timely analysis features, as the abstraction demanded to compute numerical indices sometimes hinders decision-making capabilities due to the sheer complexity of the potential state space posed by MIoT/IoT. Despite these shortcomings, we believe that advancements in digital twins applied to healthcare [120,121], where physical and virtual counterparts interact, offers realistic opportunities to enhance the analysis and understanding of attack progression. These provisions, coupled with standards recognised by the industry [122], can help healthcare stakeholders offer better service levels to patients. The ability to integrate virtual and physical elements has huge potential for answering complex *'what if?'* questions in massive attack surfaces, such as those posed by MIoT/IoT.

Author Contributions: Conceptualisation, R.M.C., P.G., C.M., F.H. and S.C.C.; methodology, R.M.C., P.G., C.M., F.H. and S.C.C.; validation, R.M.C., P.G., C.M., F.H. and S.C.C.; formal analysis, R.M.C., P.G., C.M., F.H. and S.C.C.; investigation, R.M.C., P.G., C.M., F.H. and S.C.C.; resources, R.M.C., P.G., C.M., F.H. and S.C.C.; data curation, R.M.C., P.G., C.M., F.H. and S.C.C.; writing—original draft preparation, R.M.C.; writing—review and editing, R.M.C., P.G., C.M., F.H. and S.C.C.; visualisation, R.M.C., P.G., C.M., F.H. and S.C.C.; supervision, R.M.C., P.G., C.M., F.H. and S.C.C.; project administration, R.M.C., P.G., C.M., F.H. and S.C.C.; funding acquisition, R.M.C., P.G., C.M. and F.H. All authors have read and agreed to the published version of the manuscript.

Funding: This research was funded by FAPERGS/RS/Brazil under call CONFAP—UK ACADEMIES, grant reference: 22/2551-0001368-6.

Institutional Review Board Statement: Not applicable.

Informed Consent Statement: Not applicable.

Data Availability Statement: SLR analysis data: https://github.com/czekster/SLR-miot, accessed on 19 June 2023.

Acknowledgments: We thank our respective academic institutions for supporting this research.

Conflicts of Interest: The authors declare no conflict of interest.

Abbreviations

AAL	Ambient Assisted Living
AI/ML	Artificial Intelligence and Machine Learning
BAG	Bayesian Attack Graphs
CCTA	Central Communication and Telecommunication Agency
CIA	Confidentiality, Integrity, Availability
CKC	Cyber Kill Chain
CMMI	Capability Maturity Model Integration
CPS	Cyber-Physical System
CRAMM	CCTA Risk Analysis and Management Method
CTI	Cyber Threat Intelligence
CVR	Cyber Value at Risk
CVSS	Common Vulnerability Scoring System
DFD	Data Flow Diagram
DLT	Distributed Ledger Technologies
DNS	Domain Name System
DNSSEC	DNS SECurity extensions
DDoS/DoS	Distributed Denial-of-Service
DRA	Dynamic Risk Assessment
DREAD	Damage, Reproducibility, Exploitability, Affected Users, Discoverability
DSE	Design Space Exploration
EBIOS	*Expression des Besoins et Identification des Objectifs de Sécurité* (FR)
EHR	Electronic Health Records
EMR	Electronic Medical Recording
ENISA	European Union Agency for Cybersecurity (EU)
ETSI	European Telecommunications Standards Institute
EU	European Union
FDA	Food and Drug Administration (US)
GDPR	General Data Protection Regulation
HARM	Hierarchical Attack Representation Model
HIoT	Health Internet of Things
HIPAA	Health Insurance Portability and Accountability Act
HPA	Health Prescription Assistant
ICT	Information and Communications Technology
IDS	Intrusion Detection Systems
IEC	International Electrotechnical Commission
IIoT	Industrial IoT
IoHT	Internet of Health Things
IoMT	Internet of Medical Things
IoT	Internet-of-Things
IOTA	IoT Application
IS	Information Systems
ISO	International Organization for Standardization
MIoT	Medical Internet-of-Things
MVL	Multiple-Valued Logic
NCSC	National Cyber Security Centre (UK)

NHS	National Health Service
NIST	National Institute of Standards and Technology (US)
NVD	National Vulnerability Database (NIST/US)
OCS	Order Communication Systems
OCTAVE	Operationally Critical Threat, Asset, and Vulnerability Evaluation
OWASP	Open Worldwide Application Security Project
PACS	Picture Archiving and Communication Systems
PASTA	Process for Attack Simulation and Threat Analysis
PET	Privacy Enhancing Technologies
PHI	Patient Health Information
PII	Personally and Identifiable Information
PIR	Private Information Retrieval
PRISMA	Preferred Reporting Items for Systematic Reviews and Meta-Analyses
RA	Risk Assessment
RAP	Risk Assessment Process
RTL	Real-time Location Services
SHARPE	Symbolic Hierarchical Automated Reliability and Performance Evaluator
SIEM	Security Information and Event Management
SLR	Systematic Literature Review
SOC	Security Operational Centre
STRIDE	Spoofing, Tampering, Repudiation, Information Disclosure, DoS, Elevation of Privilege
TARA	Threat Assessment and Remediation Analysis
TLS	Transport Layer Security
TM	Threat Modelling
VPN	Virtual Private Networks
WBAN	Wireless Body Area Networks

Appendix A. Definitions

Appendix A.1. Risk

According to ISO 31000:2018 [17], risk is "uncertainty on objectives". NIST's glossary (NIST Computer Security Research Center Glossary (CSRC): https://csrc.nist.gov/glossary, accessed on 19 June 2023) and publication NIST SP 800-30 Rev-1 [18] states that *"Risk arises through the loss of confidentiality, integrity, or availability of information or information systems considering impacts on organizational operations and assets, individuals, other organizations, and the Nation"*.

Appendix A.2. Medical Device

ANSI/AAMI/ISO 14971:2007 standard [93] states that a medical device is *"any instrument, apparatus, implement, machine, appliance, implant, in vitro reagent or calibrator, software, material, or other similar or related article, intended by the manufacturer to be used, alone or in combination, for human beings for one or more of the specific purpose(s) of (i) diagnosis, prevention, monitoring, treatment or alleviation of disease, (ii) diagnosis, monitoring, treatment, alleviation of or compensation for an injury, (iii) investigation, replacement, modification, or support of the anatomy or of a physiological process, (iv) supporting or sustaining life, (v) control of conception, (vi) disinfection of medical devices, (vii) providing information for medical purposes by means of in vitro examination of specimens derived from the human body, and which does not achieve its primary intended action in or on the human body by pharmacological, immunological, or metabolic means, but which may be assisted in its function by such means"*.

Appendix A.3. Standards and guidance

These are relevant standards and guidance related to risk, medical devices and health software.

- **ISO/IEC 27000:2018**: Information technology—Security techniques—Information security management systems—Overview and vocabulary (https://www.iso.org/standard/73906.html, accessed on 19 June 2023)

- **IEC 62304:2006**: Medical device software—Software life cycle processes (https://www.iso.org/standard/38421.html, accessed on 19 June 2023)
- **ISO/IEC 27032:2012**: Information technology—Security techniques—Guidelines for cybersecurity (https://www.iso.org/standard/44375.html, accessed on 19 June 2023)
- **IEC 82304-1:2016**: Health software—Part 1: General requirements for product safety (https://www.iso.org/standard/59543.html, accessed on 19 June 2023)
- **IEC 80001-1:2021**: Application of risk management for IT-networks incorporating medical devices—Part 1: Safety, effectiveness and security in the implementation and use of connected medical devices or connected health software (https://www.iso.org/standard/72026.html, accessed on 19 June 2023)
- **IEC/TR 80001-2-2:2012**: Application of risk management for IT-networks incorporating medical devices—Part 2-2: Guidance for the communication of medical device security needs, risks and controls (https://www.iso.org/standard/57939.html, accessed on 19 June 2023)
- **IEC/TR 80002-1:2009**: Medical device software—Part 1: Guidance on the application of ISO 14971 to medical device software (https://www.iso.org/standard/54146.html, accessed on 19 June 2023)
- **ISO/TR 80002-2:2017**: Medical device software—Part 2: Validation of software for medical device quality systems (https://www.iso.org/standard/60044.html, accessed on 19 June 2023)
- **IEC/TR 80002-3:2014**: Medical device software—Part 3: Process reference model of medical device software life cycle processes (IEC 62304) (https://www.iso.org/standard/65624.html, accessed on 19 June 2023)
- **ISO/IEC 30141:2018**: Internet of Things (IoT)—Reference Architecture (https://www.iso.org/standard/65695.html, accessed on 19 June 2023)
- **ETSI TS 103 645 V2.1.2 (2020-06)**: CYBER; Cyber Security for Consumer Internet of Things: Baseline Requirements (https://www.etsi.org/deliver/etsi_ts/103600_103699/103645/02.01.02_60/ts_103645v020102p.pdf, accessed on 19 June 2023)
- **NIST SP 1800-36**: Trusted IoT Device Network-Layer Onboarding and Lifecycle Management (https://www.nccoe.nist.gov/projects/trusted-iot-device-network-layer-onboarding-and-lifecycle-management, accessed on 19 June 2023)

References

1. Dimitrov, D.V. Medical internet of things and big data in healthcare. *Healthc. Inform. Res.* **2016**, *22*, 156–163. [CrossRef] [PubMed]
2. Haghi, M.; Thurow, K.; Stoll, R. Wearable devices in medical internet of things: Scientific research and commercially available devices. *Healthc. Inform. Res.* **2017**, *23*, 4–15. [CrossRef] [PubMed]
3. Meneghello, F.; Calore, M.; Zucchetto, D.; Polese, M.; Zanella, A. IoT: Internet of threats? A survey of practical security vulnerabilities in real IoT devices. *IEEE Internet Things J.* **2019**, *6*, 8182–8201. [CrossRef]
4. Humayed, A.; Lin, J.; Li, F.; Luo, B. Cyber-physical systems security—A survey. *IEEE Internet Things J.* **2017**, *4*, 1802–1831. [CrossRef]
5. Mahmoud, R.; Yousuf, T.; Aloul, F.; Zualkernan, I. Internet of things (IoT) security: Current status, challenges and prospective measures. In Proceedings of the IEEE 10th International Conference for Internet Technology and Secured Transactions (ICITST), London, UK, 4–16 December 2015; pp. 336–341.
6. Lin, J.; Yu, W.; Zhang, N.; Yang, X.; Zhang, H.; Zhao, W. A survey on internet of things: Architecture, enabling technologies, security and privacy, and applications. *IEEE Internet Things J.* **2017**, *4*, 1125–1142. [CrossRef]
7. Sun, W.; Cai, Z.; Li, Y.; Liu, F.; Fang, S.; Wang, G. Security and privacy in the medical internet of things: A review. *Secur. Commun. Netw.* **2018**, *2018*, 1–9. [CrossRef]
8. Noor, M.b.M.; Hassan, W.H. Current research on Internet of Things (IoT) security: A survey. *Comput. Netw.* **2019**, *148*, 283–294. [CrossRef]
9. Pradhan, B.; Bhattacharyya, S.; Pal, K. IoT-based applications in healthcare devices. *J. Healthc. Eng.* **2021**, *2021*, 1–18. [CrossRef]
10. Javaid, M.; Khan, I.H. Internet of Things (IoT) enabled healthcare helps to take the challenges of COVID-19 Pandemic. *J. Oral Biol. Craniofac. Res.* **2021**, *11*, 209–214. [CrossRef]
11. Alaba, F.A.; Othman, M.; Hashem, I.A.T.; Alotaibi, F. Internet of Things security: A survey. *J. Netw. Comput. Appl.* **2017**, *88*, 10–28. [CrossRef]
12. Yang, Y.; Wu, L.; Yin, G.; Li, L.; Zhao, H. A survey on security and privacy issues in Internet-of-Things. *IEEE Internet Things J.* **2017**, *4*, 1250–1258. [CrossRef]

13. Ammar, M.; Russello, G.; Crispo, B. Internet of Things: A survey on the security of IoT frameworks. *J. Inf. Secur. Appl.* **2018**, *38*, 8–27. [CrossRef]
14. Schwartz, P.M.; Solove, D.J. The PII problem: Privacy and a new concept of personally identifiable information. *NYUL Rev.* **2011**, *86*, 1814.
15. Alsubaei, F.; Abuhussein, A.; Shiva, S. Security and privacy in the internet of medical things: Taxonomy and risk assessment. In Proceedings of the 2017 IEEE 42nd Conference on Local Computer Networks Workshops (LCN Workshops), Singapore, 9 October 2017; pp. 112–120.
16. Malamas, V.; Chantzis, F.; Dasaklis, T.K.; Stergiopoulos, G.; Kotzanikolaou, P.; Douligeris, C. Risk assessment methodologies for the internet of medical things: A survey and comparative appraisal. *IEEE Access* **2021**, *9*, 40049–40075. [CrossRef]
17. *ISO 31000:2018*; Risk Management—Guidelines. International Organization for Standardization: Geneva, Switzerland, 2018. Available online: https://www.iso.org/standard/65694.html (accessed on 19 June 2023).
18. *800-30 REV. 1*; Guide for Conducting Risk Assessments. NIST Joint Task Force Transformation Initiative: Washington, DC, USA, 2012. Available online: https://csrc.nist.gov/publications/detail/sp/800-30/rev-1/final (accessed on 19 June 2023).
19. Caralli, R.A.; Stevens, J.F.; Young, L.R.; Wilson, W.R. *Introducing OCTAVE Allegro: Improving the Information Security Risk Assessment Process*; Technical Report; Software Engineering Institute—Carnegie Mellon University: Pittsburgh, PA, USA, 2007.
20. Gritzalis, D.; Iseppi, G.; Mylonas, A.; Stavrou, V. Exiting the risk assessment maze: A meta-survey. *ACM Comput. Surv. CSUR* **2018**, *51*, 1–30. [CrossRef]
21. Zio, E. The future of risk assessment. *Reliab. Eng. Syst. Saf.* **2018**, *177*, 176–190. [CrossRef]
22. Collen, A.; Nijdam, N.A. Can I Sleep Safely in My Smarthome? A Novel Framework on Automating Dynamic Risk Assessment in IoT Environments. *Electronics* **2022**, *11*, 1123. [CrossRef]
23. Datta, S.K. DRAFT-A Cybersecurity Framework for IoT Platforms. In Proceedings of the IEEE 2020 Zooming Innovation in Consumer Technologies Conference (ZINC), Novi Sad, Serbia, 26–27 May 2020; pp. 77–81.
24. Nurse, J.R.; Atamli, A.; Martin, A. Towards a usable framework for modelling security and privacy risks in the smart home. In *Human Aspects of Information Security, Privacy, and Trust: 4th International Conference, HAS 2016, Held as Part of HCI International 2016, Toronto, ON, Canada, 17–22 July 2016*; Springer: Cham, Switzerland, 2016; pp. 255–267.
25. Pandey, P.; Collen, A.; Nijdam, N.; Anagnostopoulos, M.; Katsikas, S.; Konstantas, D. Towards automated threat-based risk assessment for cyber security in smarthomes. In Proceedings of the 18th European Conference on Cyber Warfare and Security (ECCWS 2019), Coimbra, Portugal, 4–5 July 2019; pp. 4–5.
26. Kavallieratos, G.; Gkioulos, V.; Katsikas, S.K. Threat analysis in dynamic environments: The case of the smart home. In Proceedings of the IEEE 2019 15th International Conference on Distributed Computing in Sensor Systems (DCOSS), Santorini, Greece, 29–31 May 2019; pp. 234–240.
27. HaddadPajouh, H.; Dehghantanha, A.; Parizi, R.M.; Aledhari, M.; Karimipour, H. A survey on internet of things security: Requirements, challenges, and solutions. *Internet Things J.* **2021**, *14*, 100129. [CrossRef]
28. Sridharan, C. *Distributed Systems Observability: A Guide to Building Robust Systems*; O'Reilly Media: Sebastopol, CA, USA, 2018.
29. Möller, D.P. Threats and Threat Intelligence. In *Guide to Cybersecurity in Digital Transformation: Trends, Methods, Technologies, Applications and Best Practices*; Springer: Cham, Switzerland, 2023; pp. 71–129.
30. Susskind, N.G. Cybersecurity compliance and risk management strategies: What directors, officers, and managers need to know. *N. Y. Univ. J. Law Bus.* **2014**, *11*, 573.
31. Bhuiyan, M.N.; Rahman, M.M.; Billah, M.M.; Saha, D. Internet of things (IoT): A review of its enabling technologies in healthcare applications, standards protocols, security, and market opportunities. *IEEE Internet Things J.* **2021**, *8*, 10474–10498. [CrossRef]
32. Arasteh, H.; Hosseinnezhad, V.; Loia, V.; Tommasetti, A.; Troisi, O.; Shafie-khah, M.; Siano, P. Iot-based smart cities: A survey. In Proceedings of the 2016 IEEE 16th International Conference on Environment and Electrical Engineering (EEEIC), Florence, Italy, 7–10 June 2016; pp. 1–6.
33. Zanella, A.; Bui, N.; Castellani, A.; Vangelista, L.; Zorzi, M. Internet of things for smart cities. *IEEE Internet Things J.* **2014**, *1*, 22–32. [CrossRef]
34. Islam, S.R.; Kwak, D.; Kabir, M.H.; Hossain, M.; Kwak, K.S. The internet of things for health care: A comprehensive survey. *IEEE Access* **2015**, *3*, 678–708. [CrossRef]
35. Rizvi, S.; Orr, R.; Cox, A.; Ashokkumar, P.; Rizvi, M.R. Identifying the attack surface for IoT network. *Internet Things J.* **2020**, *9*, 100162. [CrossRef]
36. UcedaVelez, T.; Morana, M.M. *Risk Centric Threat Modeling: Process for Attack Simulation and Threat Analysis*; John Wiley & Sons: Hoboken, NJ, USA, 2015.
37. Wolf, A.; Simopoulos, D.; D'Avino, L.; Schwaiger, P. The PASTA threat model implementation in the IoT development life cycle. *Informatik* **2021**, *2020* .
38. Kalinin, M.; Krundyshev, V.; Zegzhda, P. Cybersecurity risk assessment in smart city infrastructures. *Machines* **2021**, *9*, 78. [CrossRef]
39. Malik, A.A.; Tosh, D.K. Dynamic Risk Assessment and Analysis Framework for Large-Scale Cyber-Physical Systems. *EAI Endorsed Trans. Secur. Saf.* **2022**, *8*, 1. [CrossRef]
40. Nurse, J.R.; Creese, S.; De Roure, D. Security risk assessment in Internet of Things systems. *IT Prof.* **2017**, *19*, 20–26. [CrossRef]

41. Nurse, J.R.; Radanliev, P.; Creese, S.; De Roure, D. If you can't understand it, you can't properly assess it! The reality of assessing security risks in Internet of Things systems. In Proceedings of the Living in the Internet of Things: Cybersecurity of the IoT, London, UK, 28–29 March 2018.
42. Tarandach, I.; Coles, M.J. *Threat Modeling: A Practical Guide for Development Teams*, 1st ed.; O'Reilly Media: Sebastopol, CA, USA, 2020; ISBN-13: 978-1492056553.
43. Shevchenko, N.; Chick, T.A.; O'Riordan, P.; Scanlon, T.P.; Woody, C. *Threat Modeling: A Summary of Available Methods*; Technical Report; Software Engineering Institute—Carnegie Mellon University: Pittsburgh, PA, USA, 2018.
44. Yskout, K.; Heyman, T.; Van Landuyt, D.; Sion, L.; Wuyts, K.; Joosen, W. Threat modeling: From infancy to maturity. In Proceedings of the ACM/IEEE 42nd International Conference on Software Engineering: New Ideas and Emerging Results, Seoul, Republic of Korea, 27 June–19 July 2020; pp. 9–12.
45. Omotosho, A.; Ayemlo Haruna, B.; Mikail Olaniyi, O. Threat modeling of internet of things health devices. *J. Appl. Secur. Res.* **2019**, *14*, 106–121. [CrossRef]
46. Abbas, S.G.; Vaccari, I.; Hussain, F.; Zahid, S.; Fayyaz, U.U.; Shah, G.A.; Bakhshi, T.; Cambiaso, E. Identifying and mitigating phishing attack threats in IoT use cases using a threat modelling approach. *Sensors* **2021**, *21*, 4816. [CrossRef]
47. Faily, S.; Scandariato, R.; Shostack, A.; Sion, L.; Ki-Aries, D. Contextualisation of data flow diagrams for security analysis. In *Graphical Models for Security: 7th International Workshop, GraMSec 2020, Boston, MA, USA, 22 June 2020*; Springer: Cham, Switzerland, 2020; pp. 186–197.
48. Alsubaei, F.; Abuhussein, A.; Shandilya, V.; Shiva, S. IoMT-SAF: Internet of medical things security assessment framework. *Internet Things J.* **2019**, *8*, 100123. [CrossRef]
49. Alamri, B.; Crowley, K.; Richardson, I. Cybersecurity Risk Management Framework for Blockchain Identity Management Systems in Health IoT. *Sensors* **2022**, *23*, 218. [CrossRef] [PubMed]
50. Rodrigues, J.J.; Segundo, D.B.D.R.; Junqueira, H.A.; Sabino, M.H.; Prince, R.M.; Al-Muhtadi, J.; De Albuquerque, V.H.C. Enabling technologies for the internet of health things. *IEEE Access* **2018**, *6*, 13129–13141. [CrossRef]
51. Da Costa, C.A.; Pasluosta, C.F.; Eskofier, B.; Da Silva, D.B.; da Rosa Righi, R. Internet of health things: Toward intelligent vital signs monitoring in hospital wards. *Artif. Intell. Med.* **2018**, *89*, 61–69. [CrossRef] [PubMed]
52. Jaigirdar, F.T.; Rudolph, C.; Bain, C. Can I trust the data I see? A Physician's concern on medical data in IoT health architectures. In Proceedings of the Australasian Computer Science Week Multiconference, Sydney, Australia, 29–31 January 2019; pp. 1–10.
53. Vishnu, S.; Ramson, S.J.; Jegan, R. Internet of medical things (IoMT)-An overview. In Proceedings of the IEEE 5th International Conference on Devices, Circuits and Systems (ICDCS), Coimbatore, India, 5-6 March 2020; pp. 101–104.
54. Ghubaish, A.; Salman, T.; Zolanvari, M.; Unal, D.; Al-Ali, A.; Jain, R. Recent advances in the internet-of-medical-things (IoMT) systems security. *IEEE Internet Things J.* **2020**, *8*, 8707–8718. [CrossRef]
55. Joyia, G.J.; Liaqat, R.M.; Farooq, A.; Rehman, S. Internet of medical things (IoMT): Applications, benefits and future challenges in healthcare domain. *J. Commun.* **2017**, *12*, 240–247. [CrossRef]
56. Gaurav, A.; Psannis, K.; Peraković, D. Security of cloud-based medical internet of things (miots): A survey. *Int. J. Softw. Sci. Comput. Intell.* **2022**, *14*, 1–16. [CrossRef]
57. Elhoseny, M.; Thilakarathne, N.N.; Alghamdi, M.I.; Mahendran, R.K.; Gardezi, A.A.; Weerasinghe, H.; Welhenge, A. Security and privacy issues in medical internet of things: Overview, countermeasures, challenges and future directions. *Sustainability* **2021**, *13*, 11645. [CrossRef]
58. Lee, I. Internet of Things (IoT) cybersecurity: Literature review and IoT cyber risk management. *Future Internet* **2020**, *12*, 157. [CrossRef]
59. Rajawat, A.S.; Goyal, S.; Bedi, P.; Shrivastava, A.; Constantin, N.B.; Raboaca, M.S.; Verma, C. Security Analysis for Threats to Patient Data in the Medical Internet of Things. In Proceedings of the IEEE 2022 11th International Conference on System Modeling & Advancement in Research Trends (SMART), Moradabad, India, 16–17 December 2022; pp. 248–253.
60. Nagajayanthi, B. Decades of Internet of Things towards twenty-first century: A research-based introspective. *Wirel. Pers. Commun.* **2022**, *123*, 3661–3697. [CrossRef]
61. Touqeer, H.; Zaman, S.; Amin, R.; Hussain, M.; Al-Turjman, F.; Bilal, M. Smart home security: Challenges, issues and solutions at different IoT layers. *J. Supercomput.* **2021**, *77*, 14053–14089. [CrossRef]
62. Deogirikar, J.; Vidhate, A. Security attacks in IoT: A survey. In Proceedings of the IEEE 2017 International Conference on I-SMAC (IoT in Social, Mobile, Analytics and Cloud) (I-SMAC), Tamil Nadu, India, 10–11 February 2017; pp. 32–37.
63. Farahani, B.; Firouzi, F.; Chang, V.; Badaroglu, M.; Constant, N.; Mankodiya, K. Towards fog-driven IoT eHealth: Promises and challenges of IoT in medicine and healthcare. *Future Gener. Comput. Syst.* **2018**, *78*, 659–676. [CrossRef]
64. Fagan, M.; Marron, J.; Watrobski, P.; Souppaya, M.; Mulugeta, B.; Symington, S.; Harkins, D.; Barker, W.; Richardson, M. *Trusted Internet of Things (IoT) Device Network-Layer Onboarding and Lifecycle Management: Enhancing Internet Protocol-Based IoT Device and Network Security (Preliminary Draft)*; Technical Report; National Institute of Standards and Technology: Gaithersburg, MD, USA, 2022.
65. Farahani, B.; Firouzi, F.; Luecking, M. The convergence of IoT and distributed ledger technologies (DLT): Opportunities, challenges, and solutions. *J. Netw. Comput. Appl.* **2021**, *177*, 102936. [CrossRef]
66. Panarello, A.; Tapas, N.; Merlino, G.; Longo, F.; Puliafito, A. Blockchain and iot integration: A systematic survey. *Sensors* **2018**, *18*, 2575. [CrossRef]

67. Uddin, M.A.; Stranieri, A.; Gondal, I.; Balasubramanian, V. A survey on the adoption of blockchain in iot: Challenges and solutions. *Blockchain Res. Appl.* **2021**, *2*, 100006. [CrossRef]
68. Novo, O. Blockchain meets IoT: An architecture for scalable access management in IoT. *IEEE Internet Things J.* **2018**, *5*, 1184–1195. [CrossRef]
69. Yadav, L.; Mitra, M.; Kumar, A.; Bhushan, B.; Al-Asadi, M.A. Nullifying the Prevalent Threats in IoT Based Applications and Smart Cities Using Blockchain Technology. In *Low Power Architectures for IoT Applications*; Springer: Singapore, 2023; pp. 241–261.
70. Popov, S.; Lu, Q. IOTA: Feeless and free. In *IEEE Blockchain Technical Briefs*; Institute of Electrical and Electronics Engineers: Piscataway, NJ, USA, 2019.
71. Alshaikhli, M.; Elfouly, T.; Elharrouss, O.; Mohamed, A.; Ottakath, N. Evolution of Internet of Things from blockchain to IOTA: A survey. *IEEE Access* **2021**, *10*, 844–866. [CrossRef]
72. Conti, M.; Kumar, G.; Nerurkar, P.; Saha, R.; Vigneri, L. A survey on security challenges and solutions in the IOTA. *J. Netw. Comput. Appl.* **2022**, *203*, 103383. [CrossRef]
73. Ullah, I.; De Roode, G.; Meratnia, N.; Havinga, P. Threat modeling—How to visualize attacks on IoTA? *Sensors* **2021**, *21*, 1834. [CrossRef] [PubMed]
74. Argaw, S.T.; Troncoso-Pastoriza, J.R.; Lacey, D.; Florin, M.V.; Calcavecchia, F.; Anderson, D.; Burleson, W.; Vogel, J.M.; O'Leary, C.; Eshaya-Chauvin, B.; et al. Cybersecurity of Hospitals: Discussing the challenges and working towards mitigating the risks. *BMC Med. Inform. Decis. Mak.* **2020**, *20*, 146. [CrossRef] [PubMed]
75. Stellios, I.; Kotzanikolaou, P.; Psarakis, M.; Alcaraz, C.; Lopez, J. A survey of iot-enabled cyberattacks: Assessing attack paths to critical infrastructures and services. *IEEE Commun. Surv. Tutor.* **2018**, *20*, 3453–3495. [CrossRef]
76. Ghafur, S.; Kristensen, S.; Honeyford, K.; Martin, G.; Darzi, A.; Aylin, P. A retrospective impact analysis of the WannaCry cyberattack on the NHS. *npj Digit. Med.* **2019**, *2*, 98. [CrossRef] [PubMed]
77. Ghafur, S.; Grass, E.; Jennings, N.R.; Darzi, A. The challenges of cybersecurity in health care: The UK National Health Service as a case study. *Lancet Digit. Health* **2019**, *1*, e10–e12. [CrossRef] [PubMed]
78. Page, M.J.; McKenzie, J.E.; Bossuyt, P.M.; Boutron, I.; Hoffmann, T.C.; Mulrow, C.D.; Shamseer, L.; Tetzlaff, J.M.; Akl, E.A.; Brennan, S.E.; et al. The PRISMA 2020 statement: An updated guideline for reporting systematic reviews. *Int. J. Surg.* **2021**, *88*, 105906. [CrossRef] [PubMed]
79. Le, A.; Maple, C.; Watson, T. A Profile-Driven Dynamic Risk Assessment Framework for Connected and Autonomous Vehicles. 2018. Available online: https://digital-library.theiet.org/content/conferences/10.1049/cp.2018.0020 (accessed on 19 June 2023)
80. Kandasamy, K.; Srinivas, S.; Achuthan, K.; Rangan, V.P. IoT cyber risk: A holistic analysis of cyber risk assessment frameworks, risk vectors, and risk ranking process. *EURASIP J. Inf. Secur.* **2020**, *2020*, 8. [CrossRef]
81. Ksibi, S.; Jaidi, F.; Bouhoula, A. Cyber-Risk Management within IoMT: A Context-Aware Agent-Based Framework for a Reliable e-Health System. In Proceedings of the 23rd International Conference on Information Integration and Web Intelligence, Linz, Austria, 29 November–1 December 2021; pp. 547–552.
82. Kandasamy, K.; Srinivas, S.; Achuthan, K.; Rangan, V.P. Digital Healthcare-Cyberattacks in Asian Organizations: An Analysis of Vulnerabilities, Risks, NIST Perspectives, and Recommendations. *IEEE Access* **2022**, *10*, 12345–12364. [CrossRef]
83. Newaz, A.I.; Sikder, A.K.; Rahman, M.A.; Uluagac, A.S. A survey on security and privacy issues in modern healthcare systems: Attacks and defenses. *ACM Trans. Comput. Healthc.* **2021**, *2*, 1–44. [CrossRef]
84. Gressl, L.; Krisper, M.; Steger, C.; Neffe, U. Towards Security Attack and Risk Assessment during Early System Design. In Proceedings of the IEEE 2020 International Conference on Cyber Security and Protection of Digital Services (Cyber Security), Dublin, Ireland, 15–19 June 2020; pp. 1–8.
85. Mohsin, M.; Sardar, M.U.; Hasan, O.; Anwar, Z. IoTRiskAnalyzer: A probabilistic model checking based framework for formal risk analytics of the Internet of Things. *IEEE Access* **2017**, *5*, 5494–5505. [CrossRef]
86. Pal, D.; Funilkul, S.; Charoenkitkarn, N.; Kanthamanon, P. Internet-of-things and smart homes for elderly healthcare: An end user perspective. *IEEE Access* **2018**, *6*, 10483–10496. [CrossRef]
87. Craigen, D.; Diakun-Thibault, N.; Purse, R. Defining cybersecurity. *Technol. Innov. Manag. Rev.* **2014**, *4*, 13–21. [CrossRef]
88. Lu, Y.; Da Xu, L. Internet of Things (IoT) cybersecurity research: A review of current research topics. *IEEE Internet Things J.* **2018**, *6*, 2103–2115. [CrossRef]
89. Ginter, P.M.; Duncan, W.J.; Swayne, L.E. *The Strategic Management of Health Care Organizations*; John Wiley & Sons: Hoboken, NJ, USA, 2018.
90. Angst, C.M.; Block, E.S.; D'Arcy, J.; Kelley, K. When do IT security investments matter? Accounting for the influence of institutional factors in the context of healthcare data breaches. *Mis Q.* **2017**, *41*, 893–A8. [CrossRef]
91. Xu, S.; Yung, M.; Wang, J. Seeking Foundations for the Science of Cyber Security: Editorial for Special Issue of Information Systems Frontiers. *Inf. Syst. Front.* **2021**, *23*, 263–267. [CrossRef]
92. Tweneboah-Koduah, S.; Skouby, K.E.; Tadayoni, R. Cyber security threats to IoT applications and service domains. *Wirel. Pers. Commun.* **2017**, *95*, 169–185. [CrossRef]
93. *ANSI/AAMI/ISO 14971: 2007/(R) 2010*; Medical Devices—Application of Risk Management to Medical Devices. AAMI: Melbourne, Australia, 2007.
94. Mansfield-Devine, S. DevOps: Finding room for security. *Netw. Secur.* **2018**, *2018*, 15–20. [CrossRef]
95. Atzori, L.; Iera, A.; Morabito, G. The internet of things: A survey. *Comput. Netw.* **2010**, *54*, 2787–2805. [CrossRef]

96. Sicari, S.; Rizzardi, A.; Miorandi, D.; Coen-Porisini, A. A risk assessment methodology for the Internet of Things. *Comput. Commun.* **2018**, *129*, 67–79. [CrossRef]
97. Abie, H.; Balasingham, I. Risk-based adaptive security for smart IoT in eHealth. In Proceedings of the 7th International Conference on Body Area Networks, Oslo, Norway, 24–26 February 2012; pp. 269–275.
98. Jacobs, V.; Bulters, J.; van Wieren, M.; Koch, R.; Rodosek, G. Modeling the impact of cyber risk for major Dutch organizations. In Proceedings of the Deloitte Cyber Risk Services, European Conference on Cyber Warfare and Security, 2016; pp. 145–154.
99. Sieber, D.A.; Adams, W.P., Jr. What's your micromort? A patient-oriented analysis of breast implant-associated anaplastic large cell lymphoma (BIA-ALCL). *Aesthetic Surg. J.* **2017**, *37*, 887–891. [CrossRef]
100. Matheu-García, S.N.; Hernández-Ramos, J.L.; Skarmeta, A.F.; Baldini, G. Risk-based automated assessment and testing for the cybersecurity certification and labelling of IoT devices. *Comput. Stand. Interfaces* **2019**, *62*, 64–83. [CrossRef]
101. Ge, M.; Hong, J.B.; Guttmann, W.; Kim, D.S. A framework for automating security analysis of the internet of things. *J. Netw. Comput. Appl.* **2017**, *83*, 12–27. [CrossRef]
102. Duan, X.; Ge, M.; Le, T.H.M.; Ullah, F.; Gao, S.; Lu, X.; Babar, M.A. Automated security assessment for the internet of things. In Proceedings of the 2021 IEEE 26th Pacific Rim International Symposium on Dependable Computing (PRDC), Perth, Australia, 1–4 December 2021; pp. 47–56.
103. Stiawan, D.; Idris, M.; Malik, R.F.; Nurmaini, S.; Alsharif, N.; Budiarto, R. Investigating brute force attack patterns in IoT network. *J. Electr. Comput. Eng.* **2019**, *2019*, 4568368 . [CrossRef]
104. Mughal, A.A. Building and Securing the Modern Security Operations Center (SOC). *Int. J. Bus. Intell. Big Data Anal.* **2022**, *5*, 1–15.
105. Jalali, M.S.; Kaiser, J.P. Cybersecurity in hospitals: A systematic, organizational perspective. *J. Med. Internet Res.* **2018**, *20*, e10059. [CrossRef]
106. Zhang, G.; Navimipour, N.J. A comprehensive and systematic review of the IoT-based medical management systems: Applications, techniques, trends and open issues. *Sustain. Cities Soc.* **2022**, *82*, 103914. [CrossRef]
107. Riesco, R.; Villagrá, V.A. Leveraging cyber threat intelligence for a dynamic risk framework: Automation by using a semantic reasoner and a new combination of standards (STIX™, SWRL and OWL). *Int. J. Inf. Secur.* **2019**, *18*, 715–739. [CrossRef]
108. Antonello, F.; Buongiorno, J.; Zio, E. A methodology to perform dynamic risk assessment using system theory and modeling and simulation: Application to nuclear batteries. *Reliab. Eng. Syst. Saf.* **2022**, *228*, 108769. [CrossRef]
109. Collen, A.; Szanto, I.C.; Benyahya, M.; Genge, B.; Nijdam, N.A. Integrating Human Factors in the Visualisation of Usable Transparency for Dynamic Risk Assessment. *Information* **2022**, *13*, 340. [CrossRef]
110. Moustafa, N.; Adi, E.; Turnbull, B.; Hu, J. A new threat intelligence scheme for safeguarding industry 4.0 systems. *IEEE Access* **2018**, *6*, 32910–32924. [CrossRef]
111. Czekster, R.M. Leveraging Cyber Threat Intelligence in Smart Devices. In *Information Security and Privacy in Smart Devices: Tools, Methods, and Applications*; IGI Global: Hershey, PA, USA, 2023; pp. 71–95.
112. Bolhasani, H.; Mohseni, M.; Rahmani, A.M. Deep learning applications for IoT in health care: A systematic review. *Inform. Med. Unlocked* **2021**, *23*, 100550. [CrossRef]
113. Panch, T.; Szolovits, P.; Atun, R. Artificial intelligence, machine learning and health systems. *J. Glob. Health* **2018**, *8*, 020303. [CrossRef] [PubMed]
114. Lee, D.; Yoon, S.N. Application of artificial intelligence-based technologies in the healthcare industry: Opportunities and challenges. *Int. J. Environ. Res. Public Health* **2021**, *18*, 271. [CrossRef] [PubMed]
115. Manne, R.; Kantheti, S.C. Application of artificial intelligence in healthcare: Chances and challenges. *Curr. J. Appl. Sci. Technol.* **2021**, *40*, 78–89. [CrossRef]
116. Jamal, A.A.; Majid, A.A.M.; Konev, A.; Kosachenko, T.; Shelupanov, A. A review on security analysis of cyber physical systems using Machine learning. *Mater. Today Proc.* **2023**, *80*, 2302–2306. [CrossRef]
117. Mukati, N.; Namdev, N.; Dilip, R.; Hemalatha, N.; Dhiman, V.; Sahu, B. Healthcare assistance to COVID-19 patient using internet of things (IoT) enabled technologies. *Mater. Today Proc.* **2023**, *80*, 3777–3781. [CrossRef]
118. Quy, V.K.; Hau, N.V.; Anh, D.V.; Ngoc, L.A. Smart healthcare IoT applications based on fog computing: architecture, applications and challenges. *Complex Intell. Syst.* **2022**, *8*, 3805–3815. [CrossRef] [PubMed]
119. Balasamy, K.; Krishnaraj, N.; Ramprasath, J.; Ramprakash, P. A secure framework for protecting clinical data in medical IoT environment. In *Smart Healthcare System Design: Security and Privacy Aspects*; Wiley: Hoboken, NJ, USA, 2022; pp. 203–234.
120. Bruynseels, K.; Santoni de Sio, F.; Van den Hoven, J. Digital twins in health care: Ethical implications of an emerging engineering paradigm. *Front. Genet.* **2018**, *9*, 31. [CrossRef]
121. Ahmadi-Assalemi, G.; Al-Khateeb, H.; Maple, C.; Epiphaniou, G.; Alhaboby, Z.A.; Alkaabi, S.; Alhaboby, D. Digital twins for precision healthcare. In *Cyber Defence in the Age of AI, Smart Societies and Augmented Humanity*; Springer: Cham, Switzerland, 2020; pp. 133–158.
122. Laamarti, F.; Badawi, H.F.; Ding, Y.; Arafsha, F.; Hafidh, B.; El Saddik, A. An ISO/IEEE 11073 standardized digital twin framework for health and well-being in smart cities. *IEEE Access* **2020**, *8*, 105950–105961. [CrossRef]

applied sciences

MDPI

Article

MIDOM—A DICOM-Based Medical Image Communication System

Branimir Pervan [1,*], Sinisa Tomic [2], Hana Ivandic [1] and Josip Knezovic [1]

[1] Department of Control and Computer Engineering, Faculty of Electrical Engineering and Computing, University of Zagreb, 10000 Zagreb, Croatia; hana.ivandic@fer.hr (H.I.); josip.knezovic@fer.hr (J.K.)
[2] Information Support Centre, Faculty of Electrical Engineering and Computing, University of Zagreb, 10000 Zagreb, Croatia; sinisa.tomic@fer.hr
* Correspondence: branimir.pervan@fer.hr; Tel.: +385-1-6129-779

Abstract: Despite the existing medical infrastructure being limited in terms of interoperability, the amount of medical multimedia transferred over the network and shared through various channels increases rapidly. In search of consultations with colleagues, medical professionals with the consent of their patients, usually exchange medical multimedia, mainly in the form of images, by using standard instant messaging services which utilize lossy compression algorithms. That consultation paradigm can easily lead to losses in image representation that can be misinterpreted and lead to the wrong diagnosis. This paper presents MIDOM—**M**edical **I**maging and **D**iagnostics **o**n the **M**ove, a DICOM-based medical image communication system enhanced with a couple of variants of our previously developed custom lossless **C**lassification and **B**lending **P**redictor **C**oder (CBPC) compression method. The system generally exploits the idea that end devices used by the general population and medical professionals alike are satisfactorily performant and energy-efficient, up to a point to support custom and complex compression methods successfully. The system has been implemented and appropriately integrated with Orthanc, a lightweight DICOM server, and a medical images storing PACS server. We benchmarked the system thoroughly with five real-world anonymized medical image sets in terms of compression ratios and latency reduction, aiming to simulate scenarios in which the availability of the medical services might be hardly reachable or in other ways limited. The results clearly show that our system enhanced with the compression methods in the question pays off in nearly every testing scenario by lowering the network latency to at least 60% of the latency required to send raw and uncompressed image sets and 25% in the best-case, while maintaining the perfect reconstruction of medical images and, thus, providing a more suitable environment for healthcare applications.

Keywords: DICOM; medical imaging; lossless compression; network latency reduction

Citation: Pervan, B.; Tomic, S.; Ivandic, H.; Knezovic, J. MIDOM—A DICOM-Based Medical Image Communication System. *Appl. Sci.* **2023**, *13*, 6075. https://doi.org/10.3390/app13106075

Academic Editors: Stefano Silvestri and Francesco Gargiulo

Received: 7 April 2023
Revised: 8 May 2023
Accepted: 9 May 2023
Published: 15 May 2023

1. Introduction

The volume of medical data (mostly multi-dimensional, such as images, videos, and volumes) in modern hospital information systems (HIS) can easily exceed dozens of terabytes. Utilizing efficient compression techniques in these environments brings benefits from both a financial and functional perspective. In addition to reducing storage costs, exchanging medical data in distributed environments of connected and mobile devices is also required to increase efficiency and reduce communication costs (bandwidth, latency), battery consumption, user experience, etc. Lossless compression techniques are used in medical applications even though they result in a modest compression ratio compared to lossy compression. However, the reversibility of lossless compression is vital in remote diagnostic consultancy and diagnostic data archival since it does not introduce artifacts into stored data and provides perfect reconstruction of medical images when acquired from the underlying PACS (Picture Archiving and Communication System).

The European Union's General Data Protection Regulation (GDPR) came into effect on 25 May 2018, as a piece of data protection legislation within the EU and had much impact on the global technology development [1]. It is important to stress that GDPR considers health data as a particular category for data protection, together with its US counterpart, named the Health Insurance Portability and Accountability Act (HIPAA). These data protection laws even inspired some researchers to work on de-identification techniques to additionally protect the identity of subjects [2]. As GDPR applies only to EU health data and HIPAA covers the USA, patients' health data are not protected worldwide. Results of a study by Moris et al. [3] analyze the use of instant messaging apps showing these are still in use. One example is Botswana, where doctors use instant messaging apps such as WhatsApp for telepathology [4] even though WhatsApp does not comply with GDPR, which is further confirmed by the EU's second-largest GDPR fine of EUR 225m directly to WhatsApp [5].

As DICOM (**D**igital **I**maging and **Co**mmunications in **M**edicine) contains health data, its access is usually limited only inside the institution's network. There are several ways to make these data remotely available, such as the use of virtual private networks (VPN), sharing the images using CDs or online services, or using cloud PACS. There are several issues with these; a VPN requires configuration or even software installation on computers that users use to connect to the PACS; sharing the images using the CD or public online services usually does not provide enough privacy protection. Cloud PACS stores the private health data on other companies' servers which may be contrary to the laws such as GDPR or HIPAA.

Privacy is not the only issue when accessing the DICOM files remotely. Downloading a 1GB file which a modern CT scanner produces using a typical download speed for 2G (EDGE) of 0.1Mbit/s will take more than 22 h; using a 3G (HSPA+) at 4Mbit/s will take 44 min; using a 4G (LTE cat 4) at 15 Mbit/s will take 3 min; while on 5G at 150 MBit/s will take less than one minute. With no size reduction in such files and using a slow network speed, such as a 2G or 3G network, it will take too long to download them for fast analysis. Such network types are still the most common in some relatively underdeveloped parts of the world, where doctors use instant messaging apps for data sharing [6]. As instant messaging apps automatically use lossy image compression to decrease upload and download time, shared images are losing information, which may result in an incorrect diagnosis.

This paper demonstrates MIDOM, **M**edical **I**maging and **D**iagnostics **o**n the **M**ove, a complex system used for the efficient and secure exchange of medical images over a broad spectrum of connection profiles and devices. The system consists of a server component used as the hub for storing diagnostic data and providing functionalities to create studies (batches of diagnostic data), consultation requests, and responses. The system features two versions of a **C**lassification and **B**lending **P**redictor **C**oder (CBPC) lossless compression method that we developed as part of our previous research [7,8]. Depending on the client-side parameters, such as connection bandwidth, display size, and storage capacity, the exchange of consultation requests can be completed with or without the CBPC compression. The contributions of the paper are as follows:

1. A framework for exchange of DICOM-based medical images between remote medical professionals in heterogeneous environments with closed and isolated PACS systems and varying connectivity;
2. Reduction of transmission latency and cost through integration of our customized lossless image compression method (CBPC) into the system in question;
3. A system for the increase in the availability of medical care in underdeveloped parts of the world, dependent on low-grade mobile networks.

The rest of the paper is organized as follows. First, in Section 2 we provide the background needed to understand the paper completely, through theoretical concepts and related work. In Section 3, we describe the implementation of the MIDOM system, together with the integration of our custom compression method. Next, in Section 4 we describe the testing methodology and benchmarks, and present the results in terms of the compression ratio and latency reduction in the selected network environments. Section 5 finally concludes the paper.

2. Background

This section provides necessary technical background needed for the full understanding of the text. It also provides an overview of the compression methods used for medical images, and state of the art in the field of communication in health systems.

2.1. DICOM

Medical Imaging and Technology Alliance, a division of the National Electrical Manufacturers Association (NEMA), specifies the DICOM standard. It defines the communication and management of medical imaging information and related data. It establishes a set of protocols for network communication; commands' syntax and semantics for data exchange; file formats and folder structure for images and other information data storage; and information supplied for given DICOM standard. NEMA published version 1.0 of the DICOM in 1985, while it introduced the latest changes in 2019. DICOM standards led to high diagnostic criteria, such as:

- Universal standard of digital medicine—for its data and image transmission and storage.
- High image quality—up to 16 bits monochrome images.
- Support for various image-acquisition parameters—much information about the image is also stored, such as size, orientation, and number of layers.
- Encoding of medical data—it defines more than 2000 standardized attributes, such as patients name, age, or diagnosis.
- Well described imaging devices—it precisely describes the device and its functionality.

The structure of the DICOM is an object defined with standardized attributes—DICOM Information Object Definitions (IOD). It represents the patient's name, sex, height, name of the study, physician, and other similar attributes. There are 27 types of values, such as date, time, or age.

The speed of changes in the DICOM standard may not follow the pace of changes in devices. Therefore, DICOM allows the use of the Private Data Dictionaries as reserved values that manufacturers may use for their internal use to overstep this limitation. The problem is that manufacturers are not required to publish their Private Data Dictionaries, and the data are not available to other medical devices.

2.2. CBPC

Data compression is a process defined by storing information in a more compact form with an ultimate goal of lowering necessary space needed to store the data, or lowering time needed to transfer the data over a communication channel. CBPC [7,8] is a lossless image compression method based on error prediction coding. A phenomena that the aforementioned coder is based on is the fact that in natural images neighbouring image elements correlate, which alternatively means that the difference between two neighbouring elements is relatively small. If we turn this fact around, we can freely conclude that the value of a single element can be predicted by values of a few of the previous elements. The CBPC method, instead of encoding actual values of image elements, first tries to predict their values, followed by encoding the difference between the real and predicted value in entropy coder. By approaching the problem in such a manner, and assuming relatively high quality of prediction, model of the prediction errors will have smaller entropy than image elements values model whose larger entropy is mostly caused by the irregular distribution of their values. With fairly good prediction, most of the prediction errors will converge towards zero (0), with the small amount of cases with large prediction errors, e.g., borders between two different regions in image. Such a distribution is generally considered better for entropy coding, as entropy coders encode the most frequent values with the shortest code words, and the least frequent values with the longest code words. Out of that follows that such distribution of prediction errors yields a better compression level.

CBPC has also been implemented for heterogeneous systems featuring graphics processing units, as presented in [9]. The method itself can be divided in two steps:

- Predictive model,
- Entropy coder.

2.2.1. Predictive Model

Prediction error is being calculated for each image element sequentially, starting from the leftmost element in the first row, to the last one, which is the rightmost element in the last row. To predict values of the current image element, a small number of neighbouring elements called prediction context is being used. An example of such context can be observed in Figure 1. The current element whose value is being predicted is marked with $I(x, y)$.

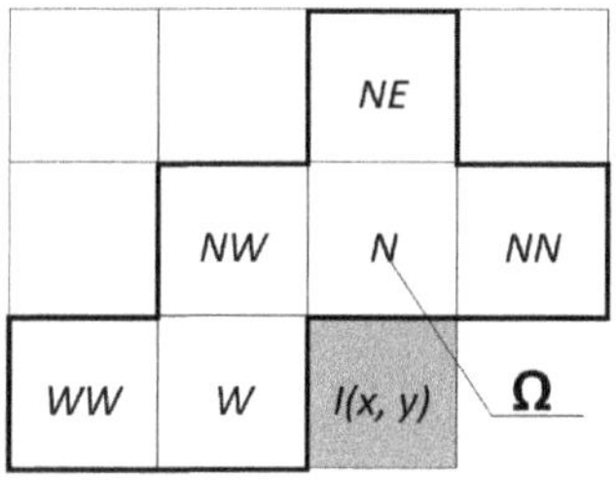

Figure 1. An example of the prediction context—processed element shaded gray.

CBPC compression methods defines and implements multiple prediction functions, ranging from simpler to more complex ones [7]. Simpler functions usually return one of the element from the context:

- **N**—returns value of the image element positioned **north** (up) from the current element.
- **W**—returns value of the image element positioned **west** (left) from the current element.
- **NW**—returns value of the image element positioned **northwest** (up-left) from the current element.
- **NE**—returns value of the image element positioned **northeast** (up-right) from the current element.

On the contrary, more complex functions return non-trivial values calculated by using individual values from the context:

- **GradW**—returns result of calculating $2N - NN$.
- **GradN**—returns result of calculating $2W - WW$.
- **L-JPEG4**—returns result of calculating $N + W - NW$.
- **MED**—returns result according to the function displayed in Equation (1).

$$\hat{I}(x,y) = \begin{cases} min(N, W) & \text{if } NW \geq max(N, W) \\ min(N, W) & \text{if } NW \leq min(N, W) \\ N + W + NW & \text{otherwise} \end{cases} \quad (1)$$

- **GAP**—chooses one of the previously mentioned functions based on the horizontal and vertical gradient around the current element.
- **FPG**—combines neighbouring elements based on the approximation of the gradients from the context.

These functions are used in a complex process of image elements classification and correction of the predicted values. Final prediction error is acquired at the end of the modelling, finally being sent to the Golomb–Rice entropy coder.

2.2.2. Entropy Coder

The CBPC compression method implements more entropy coding methods, namely Huffman, Arithmetic, and Golomb–Rice. The latter is being used as a primary method as it provides satisfactory performance while retaining ease of implementation. This method encodes only positive values, implying the necessity to mirror negative elements to the positive part of the set. Every code word produced by the Golomb–Rice coder consists of two parts separated by the separator. The first or unary part is a series of bits with length equal to the result of integer division of the value being coded and parameter m. In the current implementation, the first part is a series of logical 1 s, making 0 the separator. The second or binary part of the code word is a binary representation of the modulo of the aforementioned integer division, with length k. Prior to the coding process, parameters m and k need to be determined, such that the relation (2) is satisfied.

$$m = 2^k \tag{2}$$

While the length of the binary part is constant, the length of the unary part is variable and is growing with the increase in the value being coded. This implies that the most frequent values will be coded with the shortest coding word, thus making it particularly suitable for coding prediction errors which converge towards zero.

The original value is decoded by counting the number of 1 s prior to the separator, multiplying it by m and adding decade value of the next k bits. If n denotes the original value, u number of 1s in the unary part, b decade value of the binary part, original value reconstruction can be achieved by the relation (3).

$$n = u \times m + b \tag{3}$$

2.3. *CBPC2*

CBPC2 is an upgrade of the CBPC lossless image compression method. It uses the same procedure as the original version, but implements Run-Length Encoding (RLE) method in addition to Golomb-Rice coding to provide additional compression. Although the procedure is the same, the encoder is more complex and therefore it consumes more computing power.

RLE is a simple lossless data compression method. The core idea is to count the successively repeating elements of the original series and write them as a pair (element, consecutive repetition number). An example is shown in Figure 2 where the first four 0s are encoded as a pair (0, 4), then a single 1 as (1, 1) and, finally, three 4 s as (4, 3).

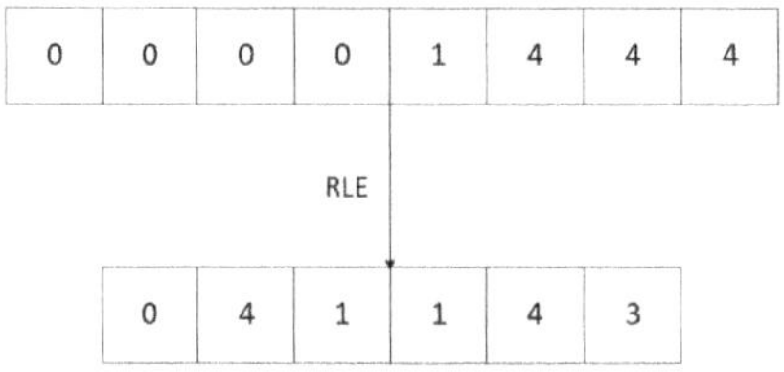

Figure 2. An example of run-length encoding.

This method is suitable only for series with a high number of successively repeating values since, on the contrary, it can lead to the expansion of the original series. Considering that medical images have a lot of large areas of uniform colour, with a fairly good prediction most of the values converge towards zero which makes RLE a suitable extension for CBPC.

Because of the aforementioned properties of the RLE, it is usually used as an auxiliary rather than a primary encoding method. It is activated when a region with a high number of successively repeating elements is found. The minimum number of element repetitions for activating the RLE method should be high enough to avoid expansion of the series and make the cost of switching the encoding methods acceptable. In this context, switching to RLE is called run-mode and is a part of the LOCO-I algorithm, which is accepted as a fundamental part of the JPEG-LS standard.

2.4. Related Work

Many modern medical imaging devices, such as CT scanners, MRIs, or X-rays, use DICOM for information sharing and standardized output. As Liu et al. [10] describe, the size of a typical CT exam had about 12 MB in the early 1990s. In 2017, a similar exam on a modern CT scanner increased the output size of the file between 600 MB and 1 GB. The size of a standard DICOM file may require higher bandwidth and storage, which is an issue even during the data migration [11].

Compression techniques for images stored in DICOM files are one approach to lowering the file size and bandwidth required. There are two main types of image compression, lossless, which retains complete image information, and lossy, which removes some information from the image. As lossy compression removes some data from the picture, it is questionable if that image is still valid for further analysis. Authors, such as García-Vílchez et al. in their paper [12], analyze the impact of lossy compression on hyperspectral image classification.

Authors, such as Li Z. et al. in their work [13], describe an optimized JPEG-XT method (OPT_JPEG_XT) that better compresses 16-bit medical images than JPEG-XT and JPEG 2000. They continue their efforts to increase the compression ratio and publish their upgraded work [14] in 2023.

Other authors, such as Nassef et al. [15], describe a lossy algorithm inspired by translating DNA sequences into protein sequences to store grayscale images, which they represent as promising compared to JPEG lossy image compression. The output file size is not the only limitation—another is computing power and running memory. Zhang et al. describe their approach [16] to lossy JPEG image compression. They use a new image compression algorithm based on a non-uniform partition and U-system designed for such devices. In their work [17], Kumar et al. propose lossless compression of CT images by an improved prediction scheme using the least square algorithm. Their implementation on Raspberry Pi shows a significant improvement compared to other algorithms, such as JPEG, JPEG lossless, BCOT, SPIHT, and Maxshift. In another work, Kumar et al. [18] propose Gaussian Hemite polynomial-based lossless medical image compression, which produces better results when compared with the Legendre polynomial-based compression and JPEG lossless compression. Authors, such as Aldemir et al. [19], suggest two new chain code approaches as solutions to the large data size required to store in PACS over time.

Some authors, such as Latha et al. [20], even suggest combining data compression with encryption for biomedical images to achieve better data security in telemedicine. They achieve lossless compression using the hybrid of Huffman coding, linear predictive coding, and discrete wavelet. Some, such as de Aguiar et al. in their work [21], suggest implementing a blockchain token mechanism stored in DICOM files to track access to the shared medical data.

PACS are generally used to store and access DCIM files. These systems are usually accessible only from inside medical institutions. There were several attempts to create mobile or web applications to facilitate peer-review data entry. In their work, Lewis et al. [22] analyze their responsive web application to support the logging of cases and conclude that it took much fewer clicks and screen taps than previous formalized data entry using an electronic spreadsheet.

O'Sullivan et al., in their work [23], researched the use of WhatsApp in health in 2017. They discovered that all health professionals in University Hospital Limerick (UHL), Ireland, who responded to their questionnaire (41/51) used WhatsApp. All of them participated in the group chat for clinical medicine at UHL.

In 2017, Mars et al. [6] examined the future of telehealth implementation in two cases. First is the usage of smartphones in rural areas of South Africa, where doctors take photographs of skin lesions and send them to dermatologists in regional hospitals using WhatsApp. This approach significantly reduced the travel time for many patients (an estimated 70%). The problem was that many doctors then contacted dermatologists directly by phone after they replied to a message. The second case was the support for burn victims, where doctors also used WhatsApp to transfer images. In both cases, the issue was that doctors contacted specialists during specialists' busiest times and their vacations or while they were on conferences.

Giansanti et al. [24] further improved on the work of Mars et al. They created software that uploads a video file from the PACS to the Google Drive cloud and sends links to cardiologists using WhatsApp Web. Experts responded with high grades for ease of use (3.8) and graded AVI quality with 3.1 out of 5 points in their feedback. As the authors note, this approach still requires work on compliance with adequate regulations.

Other authors, such as Pongkunakorn et al. in their work [25], use DCIM images to create a Keynote presentation on 6.5-inch iPhone to superimpose a preoperative template for hip replacement. They describe this method as accurate and reproducible for predicting the implant size of cementless THA. Experience in using iPads as Radiological Workstations and their creation of user interfaces was examined by Costa et al. in their work [26] in 2016. They concluded that the device and application were well accepted.

Some authors, such as Wattanapisit et al. [27], analyze the challenges of implementing a mHealth application. Even with no access to PACS data or other direct access to the medical data, they concluded that users mainly used the application for medical references (77.0%) and medical calculations (78.3%). It was less used to track health information (22.1%) and patient education (14.3%).

Authors, such as Ziegler et al. in their work [28], introduce Open Health Imagins Foundation Viewer—an Extensible Open-Source Framework for Building Web-Based Imaging Applications. Their work suggests that the viewer only uses a desktop browser, such as Chrome, Firefox, or Internet Explorer. Authors, such as Bai et al. in their work [29], analyze the 3D visualization of data using only web technologies as they recognize that most existing visualizations are desktop applications that may be challenging to use and maintain as they often rely on specific operating systems.

3. MIDOM

MIDOM is a software system mainly developed at the University of Zagreb, Faculty of Electrical Engineering and Computing, which aims to deliver a novel approach in medical diagnostics by allowing collaboration in distributed and mobile environments.

3.1. Overview

The system primarily targets medical specialists and enables inter-specialist consultations with colleagues from other institutions or locations, with focus on delivering healthcare to places which lack a wider range of medical specialists and to generally underdeveloped parts of the world. The novelty of MIDOM is the usage of mobile technologies to bridge the gap between a diagnosing physician and a specialist who provides the required expertise in the interpretation of the diagnostic medical data in the form of a medical image. Exchanged data are in the form of studies and consultation requests, which can be consisted of various types of multimedia content.

To completely describe MIDOM as a system, its components, and functionalities, we introduce the following keywords:

- **Study**—A basic set of diagnostic data created with the purpose of exchange in the system;
- **Consultation Request (CR)**—A request for medical advice, opinion, or feedback for the existing study;
- **Administrator**—A system user tasked with user administration, management of system settings, and application-specific tasks;
- **Study Provider (SP)**—A physician or other medical professional who is in charge of creating medical studies and issuing consultation requests for medical specialists;
- **Medical Specialist (MS)**—A physician or domain expert who can accept or reject consultation requests and provide feedback to the requesting study provider.

Block diagram in Figure 3 presents a high-level overview of MIDOM. Different Hospital Information Systems, HIS 1 and HIS 2, are connected to MIDOM, each with an independent PACS 1 and PACS 2 subsystems, and disjunct medical personnel, SP, MS 1, and MS 2. Medical professional outside HIS can still access MIDOM, and are depicted under acronyms MS 3, MS 4, and SP 3. Parts of the figure that are shaded in blue represent MIDOM, while orange-shaded parts represent PACS components. Green-shaded components and arrows are implemented as part of this work.

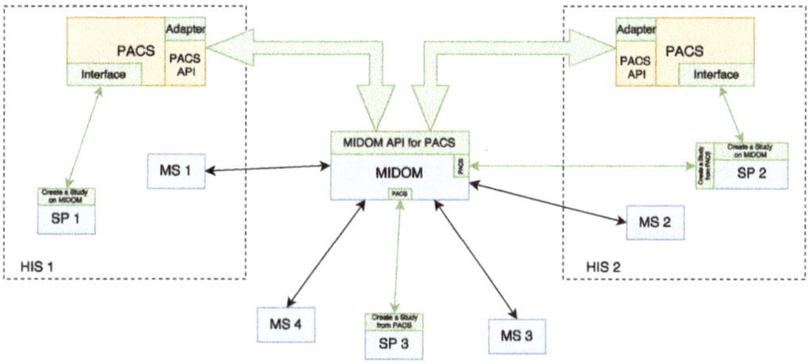

Figure 3. MIDOM in use.

In order to provide and support good performance and user experience, the system emphasizes these three aspects:

1. On-demand server-side compression of medical images of ultra-high-resolution—Algorithms for lossless compression of one or series of images comprising a study, adaptation of such algorithms for multicore and many-core systems, the performance of such algorithms for different compression levels;
2. Client-side decompression of medical images of ultra-high-resolution—Capabilities of Android mobile platform for high storage and computing requirements posed by the application;
3. Adaptation to current environmental characteristics—Strategies and techniques for different communication channel throughput and client platform capabilities. Adaptation mechanisms as a specific feature of MIDOM consider three main challenges, user experience, data transmission cost (in particular for clients connected through mobile networks), and throughput capabilities of client devices.

A collaborative environment has been realized in the form of a MIDOM application server and several client applications in a Web interface and mobile application for the Android platform.

3.2. MIDOM Components

A simple usage of the MIDOM in a medical institution can be observed in Figure 4. Four main components can be easily distinguished, namely:

- **MIDOM server**—The main component which facilitates the collaboration of medical specialists on sets of diagnostic procedure results, i.e., studies. This component hosts studies and related multimedia data, mainly in high-resolution images, and keeps track of the statuses of each study and consultation request. It also provides methods for system administration and performance monitoring, and performs computationally and storage-intensive operations in order to adjust to communication and processing power characteristics of the medical specialist and devices transparently to the system users;
- **PACS server**—This component, originally not an integrated part of MIDOM, is used for storage purposes, for efficient medical data accessing and fetching. By attaching PACS component with MIDOM, fast access to a large number of medical images and their import for usage was enabled;
- **Study Provider**—A component used by medical professionals seeking consultations with other colleagues. It allows inspection, selection, and extraction of diagnostic

imaging data from the PACS server to form a study. It also allows for requests for consultations and the collection of feedback returned by medical specialists. The study provider component can manage the study and associated consultation requests' lifecycle. The main goals of this work have been developed through this component by enabling the study provider to access the PACS server and allowing it to create a study using image data from that server;

- **Medical Provider**—This component is usually implemented as a mobile part of the system. A medical specialist offers consultation services to the study provider in a standard flow. The study provider assigns consultation requests to a medical specialist then they seek further consultations about a particular study. A single study usually consists of medical images paired with their description and further explanation of the problem. A medical specialist can accept or reject a consultation request. If the consultation request is accepted, a medical specialist can inspect image data from the study for which the consultation has been requested and provide either textual or audio feedback. Medical specialists' end devices can be connected through various types of networks, which can cause significant delays in terms of latency or time needed to pass studies through network channels. This aspect is thoroughly addressed in MIDOM by appropriate tooling and required logic for compressing exchanged imaging data to optimize user experience, throughput, and data communication costs associated with mobile networks.

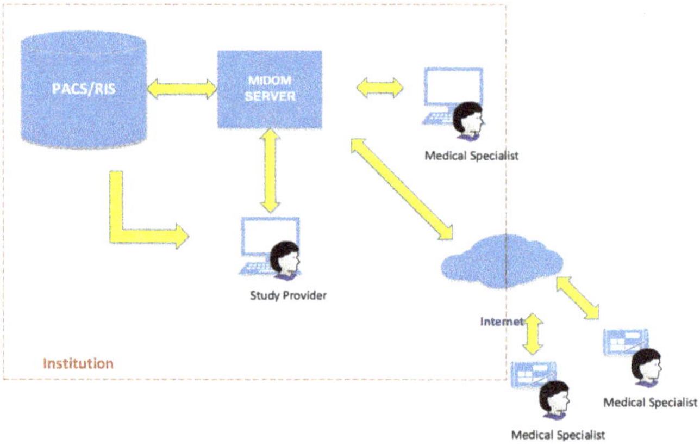

Figure 4. MIDOM components.

4. Evaluation

This section describes the evaluation we performed to assess if the integrations mentioned above benefit the end-users, mainly in terms of faster and, thus, cheaper data transfers.

4.1. Benchmarks and Methodology

All of the experiments were conducted in a controlled environment, measuring latency, i.e., the time needed to transfer medical images from MIDOM server to medical specialist's client application running on a mobile device with the Android operating system. We additionally measured and presented the size of the data that we worked with, in order to calculate appropriate compression rates. Although one could argue that file size and transfer latency are tightly coupled, i.e., proportional, we opted to present both the latency and compression rates, as the implied proportionality does not necessarily hold. Data transfers in conventional networks usually impose a certain amount of packet losses that incur re-transfers and thus further charges, as Internet service providers usually charge for the organic data traffic and not for the successful transfer of data granulated as data packages. Furthermore, we wanted to stress the latency reduction as it presents a major benefit for the users of our system.

The experiments were conducted in different simulated network environments nowadays, widely available. Those environments are 3G, Wi-Fi, and LTE whose throughputs are available in Table 1.

Table 1. Network link conditioner parameters.

Profile	Bandwidth		Delay	
	Download	Upload	Download	Upload
3G	780 Kbps	330 Kbps	100 ms	100 ms
Wi-Fi	40 Mbps	30 Mbps	1 ms	1 ms
LTE	50 Mbps	10 Mbps	50 ms	50 ms

We opted for the environments mentioned earlier to test our system in various environments. 3G was included not only because it is still widely used as a fallback network around the globe, but because one of the aims of our system is to widen medical care to places which lack a range of medical specialists, which includes some underdeveloped parts of the world. By that, we wanted to express the necessity for high-quality worldwide medical care to be as reachable as possible. Wi-Fi and LTE environments are de facto standards, and 5G was not included as its usage is still limited to the relatively developed parts of the world which directly counters our aim of delivering a globally applicable system.

As much as we wanted to conduct the experiments in a real-world environment, we opted for a simulated one due to the expenses related to the on-field testing, which further influenced our possibility to consider fading models. However, we argue that that does not present a shortcoming, as additionally incurred re-transmissions when considering fading effects would even more stress the benefit of using our customized compression methods. The measuring environment consisted of a personal computer running the Android emulator (manufactured by Google, Mountain View, USA) with Intel x86 Emulator Accelerator (manufactured by Intel, Santa Clara, USA) emulating a Google Nexus device running the Android operating system. Network Link Conditioner, a tool for simulating different network environments, was used to probe our system with different parameters by limiting download and upload bandwidths and delays.

The experiments have been conducted on medical studies in each of the aforementioned network environments and using CBPC2, CBPC, and ZIP compressions, paired with raw image experiments, i.e., without compression. To obtain results as reliable as possible, each measurement was conducted five times for faster networks (Wi-Fi and LTE) and three times for the slower, 3G network. Within each measurement we compressed and transferred each image from the respective datasets, calculated averages, and, finally, after all measurements were completed, we once again calculated average of every measurement. The results for ZIP, CBPC, and CBPC2 in both subsequent Sections 4.2 and 4.3 are displayed as relative percentages to raw data size and latencies measured when transferring raw images. The displayed result was rounded to two decimal places prior to multiplying with 100%.

Regarding compression methods, we primarily used CBPC2 and CBPC, both described in Section 2.2, as those two methods present a backbone of our work in general and key to delivering high-quality medical content to end devices. Although ZIP is not adapted and used for image compression, we used it as it was simple to implement in our solution, it is widely available, popular, and most importantly, lossless. We thus satisfied the need to add at least one more compression method.

Benchmarking sets, or studies, consist of multiple monochromatic images, namely:

1. **Angio**—One image, DICOM modality: XA, 1252×1200 pixels in size, 1.43 MB large;

2. **X-ray**—Two images, DICOM modality: PX, 2372 × 2372 and 2880 × 2372 pixels in size, total of 11.88 MB large;
3. **MR-1**—383 images, DICOM modality: MR, 512 × 512 pixels in size, total of 95.82 MB large;
4. **CT**—307 images, DICOM modality: CT, 512 × 512 pixels in size, total of 76.81 MB large;
5. **MR-2**—2534 images, DICOM modality: MR, 320 × 320 pixels in size, total of 486.83 MB large.

4.2. Compression Ratio

The first set of results we display in this section is compression ratios acquired by comparing compressed files' data sizes with uncompressed raw files' sizes. The results can be seen in Table 2 as sizes in Megabytes, and in Figure 5, grouped by individual benchmarks with each bar, but the black one, representing one compression method. Blue-shaded bars represent CBPC and CBPC2 compressions, while the grey-shaded bar represents the ZIP compression ratio. The black bar is fixed to 1 representing the raw and uncompressed image size. Both CBPC and CBPC2 compression methods significantly reduce uncompressed images, with compression levels ranging from 22% and 25% for the X-ray benchmark to 47% and 50% for CT benchmarks. When assessing compression ratios of CBPC and CBPC2 compression methods with respect to ZIP compression, results vary between more considerable reductions for Angio, X-ray, and MR-1 benchmarks and relatively minor reductions for CT and MR-2 benchmarks. When assessing the benefits of improvements of the CBPC2 compression method concerning CBPC, every benchmark shows an improvement of at least 2 percentage points, with MR-2 being an example of an improvement of 6 percentage points.

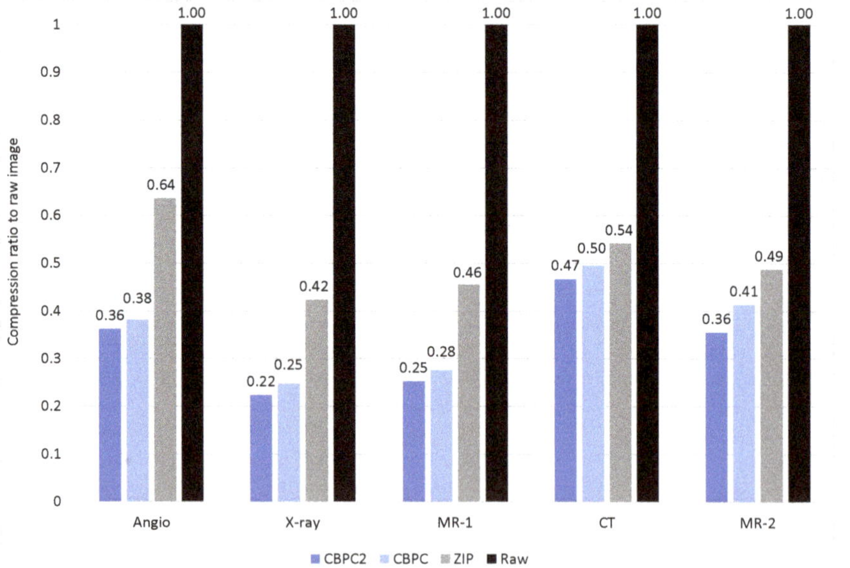

Figure 5. Reduction in terms of data size relative to raw image.

4.3. Latency Reduction

In this subsection, we display the second set of results, the network latency reduction when transmitting medical images over the various types of networks. The results are presented as transmission time ratios of the transmission time when using different data compression methods to the transmission time of raw data for different network environments. The results are grouped by the network type and each bar represents a different compression method. As in the previous result representation, the black-shaded bars are fixed to 1, representing raw and uncompressed data transmission time, while blue-shaded bars represent CBPC and CBPC2 compression, and grey-shaded ones represent ZIP compression. Additionally, raw data in terms of latencies in seconds are presented in Table 3.

Table 2. Raw sizes of the original and compressed data.

	Data Size [MB]			
	Original	**CBPC2**	**CBPC**	**ZIP**
Angio	1.43	0.52	0.55	0.91
X-ray	11.88	2.66	2.95	5.03
MR-1	95.82	24.23	26.48	43.62
CT	76.81	35.87	38.07	41.56
MR-2	486.83	173.41	201.52	237.37

Table 3. Raw latencies in miliseconds.

		Latency [s]				
		Angio	**X-ray**	**MR-1**	**CT**	**MR-2**
3G	Original	28.41	146.57	1108.39	879.66	6197.09
	CBPC2	12.01	41.97	286.48	415.87	2095.19
	CBPC	12.94	45.06	312.58	443.33	2242.86
	ZIP	20.15	68.61	506.64	483.02	2861.06
LTE	Original	3.28	10.46	58.29	43.58	532.27
	CBPC2	1.41	3.27	14.78	21.41	156.95
	CBPC	1.41	4.76	18.00	23.57	211.59
	ZIP	2.17	5.84	30.32	26.73	334.01
Wi-Fi	Original	1.06	5.94	36.24	28.58	224.94
	CBPC2	0.49	1.46	8.89	14.75	82.40
	CBPC	0.55	2.04	12.73	17.17	84.78
	ZIP	0.71	3.87	18.77	19.87	101.17

4.3.1. Angio

Figure 6 displays latency reduction results for Angio study. As expected, CBPC2 and CBPC compression methods achieve the best results for all three simulated network environments. For LTE, CBPC2, and CBPC results are identical, thus rendering CBPC2 unnecessary, as it lacks any benefits in terms of latency reduction while being more computationally expensive. The best result is achieved in the 3G environment for the CBPC2 method, with latency lowered down to 42% of the latency needed to transfer the raw study, which is particularly important as 3G is the network environment with the relatively smallest throughput used due to its wide applicability. In the context of the 3G network, a couple of percentage points gained by using CBPC2 make a significant difference. At the same time, analogously, that benefit can be disregarded in the context of a Wi-Fi network. Therefore, it can be concluded that, due to its added computational cost, CBPC2 pays off for the 3G network only. ZIP compression yields results close to 70% for all networks. Compared to ZIP, both CBPC2 and CBPC yield significantly better results and quickly pay off for every network environment.

4.3.2. X-ray

Unlike the previously described Angio benchmark, the X-ray benchmark fully displays the plausibility of using the CBPC2 compression method, as it achieved significantly better results than its simpler counterpart. This is depicted on Figure 7. For Wi-Fi and LTE, CBPC2 achieved better results for 9 and 15 percentage points, respectively, than CBPC. For 3G, that margin is smaller but can still be considered significant, as relatively low speeds of the 3G network could use each increase in latency reduction. When comparing our custom compression methods with ZIP compression, using CBPC and CBPC2 led to better results regarding latency reductions. The margin was the smallest on the LTE network and larger on Wi-Fi and 3G networks. For this benchmark, latency reduction varies greatly for ZIP compression, ranging from 65% for a Wi-Fi network to 47% for a 3G network. The largest margin is achieved on the Wi-Fi network as the CBPC2 compression method reduces latency to just 25%, relative to raw image transfer, and for 40 percentage points with respect to ZIP compression.

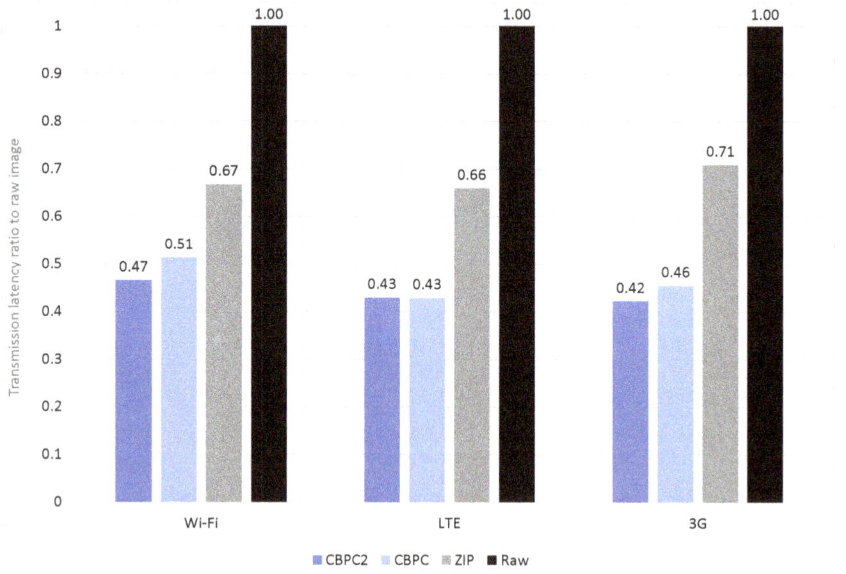

Figure 6. Latency reduction for Angio benchmark.

4.3.3. MR-1

When it comes to the MR-1 benchmark, results can be seen in Figure 8. Again, both CBPC2 and CBPC cause significant reductions in latency, with CBPC2 paying off better for Wi-Fi, due to a large increase in latency reduction, and for 3G, due to a minor yet not insignificant reduction in the context of this network type. CBPC2 gains the expected result in sense of additional latency reduction for LTE network. For each network profile, latency is reduced for approximately 25% relative to raw image transfer. ZIP compression is steady at around 50% for each network type but is still significantly worse than CPBC2 and CBPC for each network profile, again rendering them plausible for use.

4.3.4. CT

When putting all of the benchmarks performed in this paper in perspective, it cannot be avoided to state that this benchmark yielded the worst results for latency reduction. As can be observed in Figure 9, the significant difference between CBPC2 and CBPC compression methods can be observed for Wi-Fi and 3G, with the latter being significant due to relatively low throughput, which makes every percentage point essential to spare. CBPC2 compression method yields at most 47% reduction in latency for the 3G environment, 49% for the LTE environment, and 52% for the Wi-Fi environment. For the CBPC compression method, every environment yields up to 50% reduction in latency. When comparing reductions with ZIP compression, both CBPC2 and CBPC do not achieve significant reductions, especially for the 3G network with ZIP-reducing latency to 55%, CBPC to 50%, and CBPC2 to 47% of the raw image transfer latency, meaning that CBPC2 and CBPC are only 8 and 5 percentage points better than ZIP compression method. The margin between ZIP and CBPC2 compression methods is at least 18 percentage points for other benchmarks. Here, we again observe cases in which our compression methods do not achieve at least 50% of reduction in latency (CBPC2 and CBPC in Wi-FI environment, CBPC in LTE environment), which, in the context of other benchmarks, was observed only for Angio benchmark (CBPC in Wi-Fi environment).

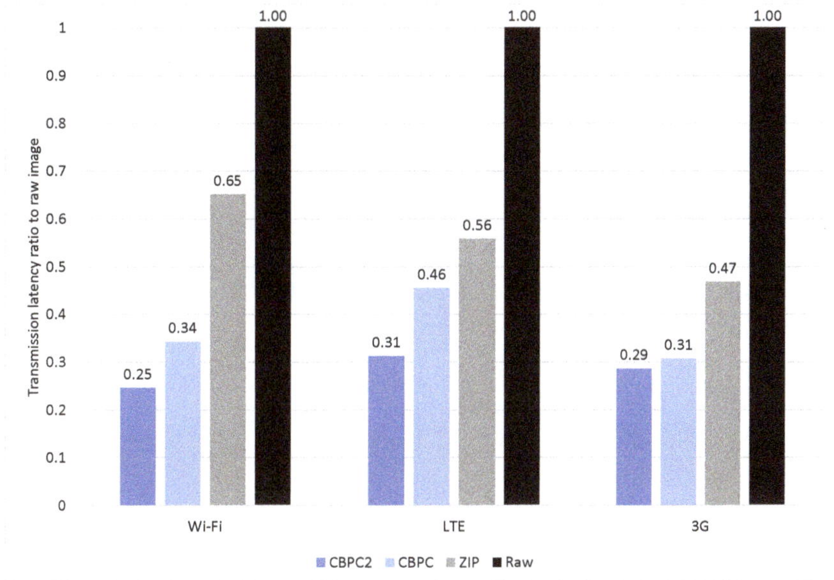

Figure 7. Latency reduction for the X-ray benchmark.

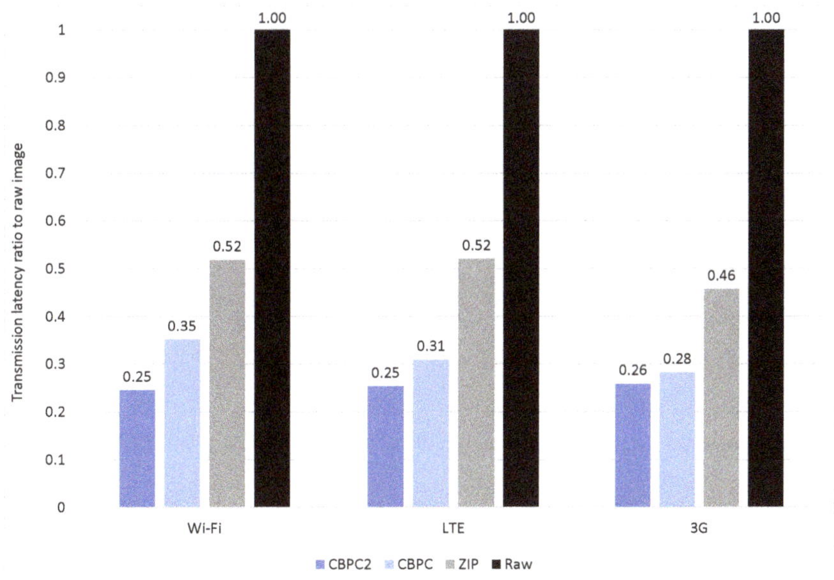

Figure 8. Latency reduction for MR-1 benchmark.

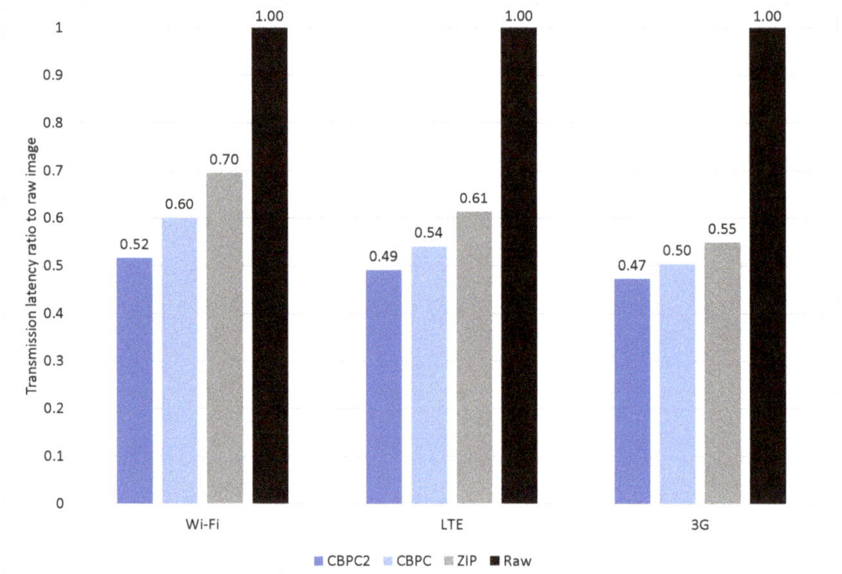

Figure 9. Latency reduction for CT benchmark.

4.3.5. MR-2

The latency reduction results for the MR-2 benchmark are available in Figure 10. The difference between CBPC2 and CBPC is negligible for the Wi-Fi network environment and significant for LTE and 3G environments, with particular significance in LTE environments with a gain in latency reduction of 11 percentage points. Compared to the ZIP compression method, CBPC2 and CBPC methods generate the best addition in the reduction for LTE and 3G networks. ZIP produces 45% reduction in latency regarding raw image transfer for the Wi-Fi network environment, which, paired with a relatively weak result of CBPC2 and CBPC compressions, renders them unplausible to use.

4.4. Discussion

MIDOM as a system for the exchange of DICOM-based medical images between remote medical professionals in heterogeneous environments with isolated PACS systems envisioned for underdeveloped parts of the world with limited connectivity, truly is one of a kind which makes it hard to find a system that is similar enough to compare with. We aimed to compare our work with the one found in Ziegler et al. [28], but their approach differs from ours since mobile phones are neither their primary target nor the lossless compression of the files to achieve smaller file sizes and latency, as in MIDOM.

On the other hand, Bai et al. [29] are focused primarily on 3D visualization and not on compression of the files for smaller file sizes and latency with the goal of developing a system for underdeveloped parts of the world, as in MIDOM.

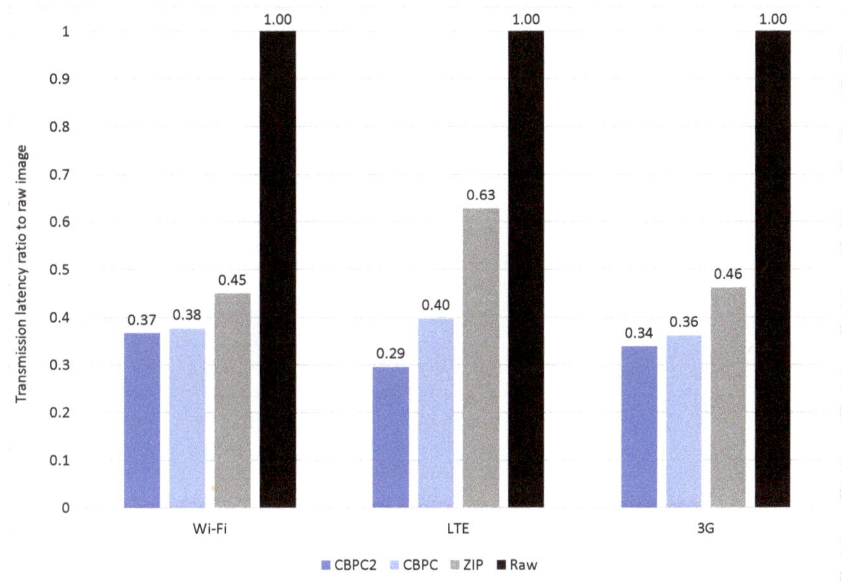

Figure 10. Latency reduction for MR-2 benchmark.

5. Conclusions

This section briefly discusses the outcomes of the research presented through this paper, evaluates the limitations, and proposes further work in this area.

5.1. Summary

In this paper, we proposed MIDOM, an e-health platform whose main aim is to increase the availability of medical care in underdeveloped parts of the world and, generally, in places with limited access to medical professionals. It does so mainly by increasing interoperability by acting as a man in the middle between different medical actors, devices, medical professionals, and inherently standards in electronic health. MIDOM enables the increase in communication reliability, confidence, and confidentiality by providing secure communication packed with a lossless compression method, which significantly reduces sizes, implying a reduction in network latencies and data savings. Implicitly, it provides mitigation mechanisms between various standards in electronic health systems, which are heavily limited in terms of interoperability.

In addition to MIDOM's implementation and integration with broader systems like PACS server, one of the main focuses of this paper is integration of the aforementioned custom compression method (CBPC), and its additional implementation (CBPC2) which features run-length coding enhancement. Higher compression rates with lossless compression methods are crucial in achieving the availability of electronic health systems, which is especially important for low throughput networks. The latter kind of network is still widely used as failover networks in developed parts of the world and as main networks in underdeveloped parts.

We demonstrate significant data reductions through experiments by using our custom compression methods, which implied latency reductions in the tested network. We performed five benchmarks on three different networks, namely Wi-Fi, LTE, and 3G, demonstrating that our compression methods pay off in nearly every testing scenario by lowering the network latency to at least 60% of the original latency measured when transferring equivalent uncompressed dataset. The best result is achieved by lowering network latency to mere 25% of uncompressed transfer latency for MR-1 benchmark on Wi-Fi and LTE networks and X-ray benchmark on the Wi-Fi network environment.

5.2. Limitations

We acknowledge the limitations regarding our simulation environment and commit to extend the benchmarks with on-field testing that will simulate real-world environment and provide the so much needed measurements of the signal fading effects. Furthermore, we were limited with the amount of the available medical data, mostly due to GDPR. An increased amount of data would further increase the reliability of the study. The implemented system was used in laboratory environment and may require additional improvements in terms of scalability and stability. The study does not consider the security aspect of the data transfer as we assume the use of the standard security protocols.

5.3. Suggestions for Future Research

As electronic health services keep developing, we see promising aspects for future work. Conceptually, medical imaging and consultation with a medical professional could vastly profit from 3D modelling. It is now possible to transfer complex 3D models by dissecting a model to multiple layers, encoding that layers as images, and transferring them accordingly. Future work in the field of compression will include the development of such an algorithm that explores and exploits space similarities to different layers with the ultimate purpose of increasing the compression ratios of such a model. By developing such an algorithm, the compression ratio of a complete model would be larger than the sum of disjunct compression ratios of each independent layer. We will further continue developing our system on a system level by increasing stability and reliability on low-throughput networks. We will additionally work on further expanding platforms that the system can target.

Author Contributions: Conceptualization, B.P. and J.K.; Funding acquisition, J.K.; Investigation, B.P. and S.T.; Methodology, B.P.; Resources, J.K.; Software, J.K.; Supervision, J.K.; Validation, B.P. and S.T.; Visualization, H.I.; Writing—original draft, B.P., S.T. and H.I.; Writing—review and editing, B.P. and J.K. All authors have read and agreed to the published version of the manuscript.

Funding: This research received no external funding.

Institutional Review Board Statement: Not applicable.

Informed Consent Statement: Not applicable.

Data Availability Statement: The availability of the images used in this work can be discussed with the corresponding author, as well as the data collected by simulating the described system in testing scenarios.

Acknowledgments: The authors would like to thank Eugen Druzin for implementing parts of the system and conducting the experiments while working on their Master's degree thesis at the University of Zagreb Faculty of Electrical Engineering and Computing.

Conflicts of Interest: The authors hereby declare that no interest that could be perceived as conflicting exist.

Abbreviations

The following abbreviations are used in this manuscript:

API	Application Programming Interface
CBPC	Classification and Blending Predictor Coder
CR	Consultation Request
CT	Computed Tomography
DICOM	Digital Imaging and Communications in Medicine
GDPR	General Data Protection Regulation
HIPAA	Health Insurance Portability and Accountability Act

HIS	Hospital Information System
IOD	Information Object Definitions
MIDOM	Medical Imaging and Diagnostics on the Move
MR	Magnetic Resonance
MS	Medical Specialist
NEMA	National Electrical Manufacturers Association
OPT_JPEG_XT	Optimized JPEG-XT
PACS	Picture Archiving and Communication System
RLE	Run-Length Encoding
SP	Study Provider
UHL	University Hospital Limerick
VPN	Virtual Private Network

References

1. Li, H.; Yu, L.; He, W. The Impact of GDPR on Global Technology Development. *J. Glob. Inf. Technol. Manag.* **2019**, *22*, 1–6. [CrossRef]
2. Jeong, Y.U.; Yoo, S.; Kim, Y.H.; Shim, W.H. De-identification of facial features in magnetic resonance images: Software development using deep learning technology. *J. Med. Internet Res.* **2020**, *22*, e22739. [CrossRef] [PubMed]
3. Morris, C.; Scott, R.E.; Mars, M. Whatsapp in clinical practice—The challenges of record keeping and storage. A scoping review. *Int. J. Environ. Res. Public Health* **2021**, *18*, 13426. [CrossRef]
4. Ncube, B.; Mars, M.; Scott, R.E. The need for a telemedicine strategy for Botswana? A scoping review and situational assessment. *BMC Health Serv. Res.* **2020**, *20*, 794. [CrossRef]
5. BBC News. WhatsApp Issued Second-Largest GDPR Fine of €225m. Available online: https://www.bbc.com/news/technology-58422465 (accessed on 8 May 2023).
6. Mars, M.; Scott, R.E. Being Spontaneous: The Future of Telehealth Implementation? *Telemed. J. Health Off. J. Am. Telemed. Assoc.* **2017**, *23*, 766–772. [CrossRef] [PubMed]
7. Knezovic, J. *Kompresija Slika Bez Gubitaka Metodom Predvidjanja;* Faculty of Electrical Engineering and Computing, University of Zagreb: Zagreb, Croatia, 2005.
8. Knezovic, J.; Kovac, M.; Mlinaric, H. Classification and Blending Prediction for Lossless Image Compression. In Proceedings of the MELECON 2006—2006 IEEE Mediterranean Electrotechnical Conference, Malaga, Spain, 16–19 May 2006; IEEE: Piscataway, NJ, USA, 2006; Volume 2006, pp. 486–489. [CrossRef]
9. Strizic, L.; Knezovic, J. Optimization of losless image compression method for GPGPU. In Proceedings of the 2016 18th Mediterranean Electrotechnical Conference (MELECON), Lemesos, Cyprus, 18–20 April 2016; IEEE: Piscataway, NJ, USA, 2016; number April, pp. 1–6. [CrossRef]
10. Liu, F.; Hernandez-Cabronero, M.; Sanchez, V.; Marcellin, M.W.; Bilgin, A. The current role of image compression standards in medical imaging. *Information* **2017**, *8*, 131. [CrossRef]
11. van Ooijen, P.M.; Aryanto, K.Y.; Broekema, A.; Horii, S. DICOM data migration for PACS transition: Procedure and pitfalls. *Int. J. Comput. Assist. Radiol. Surg.* **2015**, *10*, 1055–1064. [CrossRef]
12. García-Vílchez, F.; Muñoz-Marí, J.; Zortea, M.; Blanes, I.; González-Ruiz, V.; Camps-Valls, G.; Plaza, A.; Serra-Sagristà, J. On the impact of lossy compression on hyperspectral image classification and unmixing. *IEEE Geosci. Remote Sens. Lett.* **2011**, *8*, 253–257. [CrossRef]
13. Li, Z.; Ramos, A.; Li, Z.; Osborn, M.L.; Li, X.; Li, Y.; Yao, S.; Xu, J. An optimized JPEG-XT-based algorithm for the lossy and lossless compression of 16-bit depth medical image. *Biomed. Signal Process. Control* **2021**, *64*, 102306. [CrossRef]
14. Li, Z.; Ramos, A.; Li, Z.; Osborn, M.L.; Zaid, W.; Li, X.; Li, Y.; Xu, J. Nearly-lossless-to-lossy medical image compression by the optimized JPEGXT and JPEG algorithms through the anatomical regions of interest. *Biomed. Signal Process. Control* **2023**, *83*, 104711. [CrossRef]
15. Nassef, M.; Alkinani, M.H. A Novel Multilevel Lossy Compression Algorithm for Grayscale Images Inspired by the Synthesization of Biological Protein Sequences. *IEEE Access* **2021**, *9*, 149657–149680. [CrossRef]
16. Zhang, Y.; Cai, Z.; Xiong, G. A New Image Compression Algorithm Based on Non-Uniform Partition and U-System. *IEEE Trans. Multimed.* **2021**, *23*, 1069–1082. [CrossRef]
17. Kumar, S.N.; Fred, A.L.; Kumar, H.A.; Varghese, P.S. Lossless Compression of CT Images by an Improved Prediction Scheme Using Least Square Algorithm. *Circuits Syst. Signal Process.* **2020**, *39*, 522–542. [CrossRef]
18. Kumar, S.N.; Ahilan, A.; Haridhas, A.K.; Sebastian, J. Gaussian Hermite polynomial based lossless medical image compression. *Multimed. Syst.* **2021**, *27*, 15–31. [CrossRef]
19. Aldemir, E.; Dueñas, O.A.T.; Kavur, A.E.; Tohumoglu, G.; Sánchez-Cruz, H.; Selver, M.A. Chain code strategy for lossless storage and transfer of segmented binary medical data. *Expert Syst. Appl.* **2023**, *216*, 119449. [CrossRef]
20. Latha, H.R.; Ramaprasath, A. HWCD: A hybrid approach for image compression using wavelet, encryption using confusion, and decryption using diffusion scheme. *J. Intell. Syst.* **2023**, *32*, 20229056. [CrossRef]

21. de Aguiar, E.J.; dos Santos, A.J.; Meneguette, R.I.; Grande, R.E.D.; Ueyama, J. A blockchain-based protocol for tracking user access to shared medical imaging. *Future Gener. Comput. Syst.* **2022**, *134*, 348–360. [CrossRef]
22. Lewis, T.; Berkowitz, S.; Weinstein, J. Abstract No. 565 Smartphone and web-based interventional radiology case logging system to facilitate recording of procedures performed by interventional radiology residents. *J. Vasc. Interv. Radiol.* **2021**, *32*, S157. [CrossRef]
23. O'Sullivan, D.M.; O'Sullivan, E.; O'Connor, M.; Lyons, D.; McManus, J. WhatsApp Doc? *BMJ Innov.* **2017**, *3*, 238–239. [CrossRef]
24. Giansanti, D.; Cosentino, L. WhatsApp in mHealth: Design and evaluation of an mHealth tool to share dynamic images in hemodynamics. *mHealth* **2021**, *7*, 1–7. [CrossRef]
25. Pongkunakorn, A.; Aksornthung, C.; Sritumpinit, N. Accuracy of a New Digital Templating Method for Total Hip Arthroplasty Using Picture Archiving and Communication System (PACS) and iPhone Technology: Comparison with Acetate Templating on Digital Radiography. *J. Arthroplast.* **2021**, *36*, 2204–2210. [CrossRef] [PubMed]
26. Costa, P.; von Wangenheim, A.; von Wangenheim, C.; Inácio, A.; de Macedo, D. Usability Engineering of a Radiological Workstation for Mobile Devices: An Experience Report. *Soc. Bras. Comput. SBC* **2016**, *7*, 2471–2480. [CrossRef]
27. Wattanapisit, A.; Amaek, W.; Wattanapisit, S.; Tuangratananon, T.; Wongsiri, S.; Pengkaew, P. Challenges of implementing an mhealth application for personalized physical activity counselling in primary health care: A qualitative study. *Int. J. Gen. Med.* **2021**, *14*, 3821–3831. [CrossRef] [PubMed]
28. Ziegler, E.; Urban, T.; Brown, D.; Petts, J.; Pieper, S.D.; Lewis, R.; Hafey, C.; Harris, G.J. Open Health Imaging Foundation Viewer: An Extensible Open-Source Framework for Building Web-Based Imaging Applications to Support Cancer Research. *JCO Clin. Cancer Inform.* **2020**, *4*, 336–345. [CrossRef]
29. Bai, S.; Ma, C.; Wang, X.; Zhou, S.; Jiang, H.; Ma, L.; Jiang, H. Application of Medical Image 3D Visualization Web Platform in Auxiliary Diagnosis and Preoperative Planning. *J. Image Graph.* **2023**, *11*, 32–39. [CrossRef]

applied sciences

MDPI

Article

Chidroid: A Mobile Android Application for Log Collection and Security Analysis in Healthcare and IoMT

Stylianos Karagiannis [1,2,*,†], Luís Landeiro Ribeiro [1,†], Christoforos Ntantogian [2], Emmanouil Magkos [2] and Luís Miguel Campos [1]

1 PDM&FC, R. Fradesso da Silveira, 4-1B, 1300-609 Lisboa, Portugal
2 Department of Informatics, Ionian University, Plateia Tsirigoti 7, 49100 Corfu, Greece
* Correspondence: stylianos.karagiannis@pdmfc.com or skaragiannis@ionio.gr
† These authors contributed equally to this work.

Abstract: The Internet of Medical Things (IoMT) is a growing trend that has led to the use of connected devices, known as the Internet of Health. The healthcare domain has been a target of cyberattacks, especially with a large number of IoMT devices connected to hospital networks. This factor could allow attackers to access patients' personal health information (PHI). This research paper proposes Chidroid, an innovative mobile Android application that can retrieve, collect, and distribute logs from smart healthcare devices. The proposed approach enables the creation of datasets, allowing non-structured data to be parsed into semi-structured or structured data that can be used for machine learning and deep learning, and the proposed approach can serve as a universal policy-based tool to examine and analyse security issues in most recent Android versions by distributing logs for analysis. The validation tests demonstrated that the application could retrieve logs and system metrics from various assets and devices in an efficient manner. The collected logs can provide visibility into the device's activities and help to detect and mitigate potential security risks. This research introduces a way to perform a security analysis on Android devices that uses minimal system resources and reduces battery consumption by pushing the analysis stage to the edge.

Keywords: android security; log analysis; IoMT security; IoT security; artificial intelligence; IoMT

Citation: Karagiannis, S.; Ribeiro, L.L.; Ntantogian, C.; Magkos, E.; Campos, L.M. Chidroid: A Mobile Android Application for Log Collection and Security Analysis in Healthcare and IoMT. *Appl. Sci.* **2023**, *13*, 3061. https://doi.org/10.3390/app13053061

Academic Editors: Stefano Silvestri and Francesco Gargiulo

Received: 18 January 2023
Revised: 16 February 2023
Accepted: 21 February 2023
Published: 27 February 2023

1. Introduction

The world currently is heavily dependent on the Internet of Things (IoT) for our daily lives [1]. The IoT is a rapidly growing field and is expected to expand in the coming years. This growth is likely driven by various factors, including the increasing affordability and availability of smart devices and the growing demand for connected products and services.

Android is an operating system often used on the IoT, based on the Linux kernel, acquired initially and currently developed by Google, and was first released in 2008. The Android operating system supports the IoT, which means that it can be used to connect and control a wide range of smart devices. For example, an Android device can monitor and maintain smart home appliances, such as thermostats and lighting systems. In addition, many Android devices are equipped with sensors and other hardware to collect data from the environment and provide input to IoT applications. Overall, the combination of Android and the IoT offers many possibilities to create useful and innovative connected products and services [2–4]. Smartphones and other mobile devices are used for mobile health applications (mHealth applications) and recently have played an increasingly important role in the healthcare industry [5]. Android and mHealth applications are used for various purposes, including patient care, clinical decision support, exchange of health information, and remote patient monitoring [6]. In addition, Android devices are increasingly popular in the healthcare domain, but as they become more commonplace, so do their security and privacy risks.

According to ENISA and the report published in July 2022 (https://www.enisa.europa.eu/news/ransomware-publicly-reported-incidents-are-only-the-tip-of-the-iceberg), *"Between May 2021 and June 2022 about ten terabytes of data were stolen each month by ransomware threat actors. 58.2% of the stolen data included employees' personal data"*. The study reports that the most-affected sectors include heavy industry, information services, government, and healthcare [7]. A recent relevant example of cyberattacks in the healthcare domain was the case of the Ryuk ransomware [8], as mentioned by ENISA's Threat Landscape Report 2021 (ETL 2021) (https://www.enisa.europa.eu/publications/enisa-threat-landscape-2021, accessed 20 February 2023).

The healthcare domain has been a target of cyberattacks, especially with the growing use of connected devices known as the Internet of Medical Things (IoMT). Similarly, the IoT extends the threat landscape even further, with the most-common cyberattacks being denial-of-service (DoS) attacks or unauthorised access to sensitive health information [9]. In some cases, cyberattacks lead to the exposure of patient personal health information (PHI) [10,11]. To address these concerns, healthcare organisations should ensure that their IoT devices, infrastructure, and information systems are adequately secured. Furthermore, many IoMT devices are connected to hospital networks [12], a factor that could allow attackers to access patient health information or even disrupt medical care. There are several ways to perform security and privacy analysis in the IoMT. A common approach for conducting security assessments on Android is static analysis, which examines the source code of applications and operating systems for potential vulnerabilities. Another method is to use dynamic analysis to monitor the behaviour of these devices at runtime. Taking this into account, it is essential to devise mechanisms that retrieve logs and operating metrics to discover if an IoMT device is acting abnormally or has even been compromised [13–15].

The IoMT is characterised by the high interconnectivity of physical objects and devices embedded in sensors, software, and other technologies that enable them to collect and exchange data [16]. To protect patients' security and privacy and safeguard their medical data, healthcare organisations must take measures to secure all mobile devices that have access to PHI [17]. This includes both employee-owned and corporate-owned devices. IoMT devices often collect sensitive health data, making them attractive targets for attackers [18,19]. Patients' homes are also at risk if they have connected medical devices. According to research (ESET Threat Report T1 2022), the volume of IoT malware in the first six months of 2022 was higher than that recorded in the previous four years. This indicates a significant increase in the number of IoT devices targeted by attackers.

Considering the above, the security of the IoT and Android is essential, and research has been performed to enhance network authentication and mitigate attacks, contributing to the security of mobile health systems on 5G networks [20]. Therefore, it is critical to protect healthcare and IoMT devices from potential security threats, as these devices are used to handle sensitive medical and healthcare data. This research paper proposes Chidroid, an Android application that can retrieve, collect, and distribute logs for analysis on the cloud or on-premises servers.

Chidroid enables log collection and distribution to the cloud or other endpoints (servers, computers, Android devices) for analysis enabling edge computing. It can run on multiple edge devices, enabling edge computing and distributing the data to multiple endpoints for simultaneous management, allowing remote management of edge devices. Edge computing is a computational paradigm that brings computation and data storage closer to the network, where data are generated and used. Edge computing offers several advantages in the Internet of Medical Things (IoMT). Firstly, it enables the processing of large amounts of health-related data generated by various medical devices in real-time without overwhelming the back-end infrastructure. Secondly, edge computing can provide improved privacy and security as sensitive health information can be processed locally, reducing the risk of data breaches. Finally, edge computing can improve the overall system efficiency by reducing the amount of data transmitted to the cloud, thus reducing latency, bandwidth usage, and energy consumption.

1.1. Related Work

While there is a significant amount of research on the IoT and data and artificial intelligence (AI) in healthcare, it should be noted that the topics covered by these studies can vary greatly and do not directly relate to the context of this work. Some researchers study specific security or privacy issues, while others focus on reducing the cost of IoT sensors. To this end, we included the most-relevant research studies on Android security, the IoT, and edge computing with significant impacts on healthcare and eHealth. The selected related work is presented below and organised and summarised in a concise manner (Table 1).

Table 1. Table summarising the related work.

Topics	Paper Ref.	Description
Log Collection	[21]	Android security, log retrieval and analysis. Collection of system-generated logs at runtime and filtering for analysis.
	[22]	Log management tool to collect and display installation log files and track changes during the installation process.
Malware Analysis	[23]	Malware analysis and a framework combining machine learning and static analysis.
	[24]	Hybrid Android malware detection combining dynamic and static analysis.
	[25]	Framework for Android system call processing to detect malware early.
	[26]	BMD: bi-level malware detection using application programming interface (API) call sequences and co-evolutionary algorithm.
Permissions	[27]	Permission monitoring in Android security to categorise applications and use static analysis to detect malware.
	[28]	Permission classification as an information gain metric for improved detection accuracy.
Package Analysis	[29]	Review of the techniques combining static and dynamic analysis with studying Android applications.
	[30]	Static data flow analysis tool and library developed for the purpose of computing data flows in Android applications and Java programs.
	[31]	Python-based tool designed for reverse-engineering of Android applications by breaking down raw Android Package Kit (.apk) files.
	[32]	A static analysis framework for the security evaluation of Android apps.
HIDS	[33]	An HIDS system that runs on mobile devices and detects known and zero-day attacks using machine learning and statistical algorithms.
	[34]	A Review of system-call-based HIDS, including feature extraction, data mining algorithms, HIDS datasets, and applicability to embedded systems.

There are many research papers and studies on Android security, log retrieval, and analysis (Table 1). Some of these articles focused on specific aspects of Android security, such as the use of Logcat (https://developer.android.com/studio/command-line/logcat, accessed 20 February 2023) and Package Manager (https://developer.android.com/reference/android/content/pm/PackageManager, accessed 20 February 2023). In [21], the authors proposed an approach that involves collecting system-generated logs at runtime and filtering them for the application under analysis. These logs are then matched against generated signatures that account for the application's behaviour, such as information leakage, jailbreak attempts, privilege escalation attempts, and access to critical permissions. Another example is [22], where the authors proposed a log management tool to collect and display installation log files. These log files contain information about the installation process, such as the time and date of the installation, the user who installed the application, and the location of the installation files. Additionally, the tool can compare the contents of the log files before and after an application is installed, allowing users to see any changes that may have occurred during the installation process.

The field of malware analysis has seen the development of frameworks combining machine learning and static analysis ([23]) and hybrid Android malware detection approaches combining dynamic and static analysis [24]. One important aspect of malware analysis is the early detection of malicious activities to prevent harm to the system and its users.

A framework for system call processing has been proposed to address this issue, focusing on analysing system calls made by Android applications [25]. The bi-level malware detection method (BMD) was also introduced to improve detection accuracy by utilising API call sequences and a co-evolutionary algorithm [26]. The experiments performed on Android datasets showed that BMD outperforms existing state-of-the-art methods for malware detection.

Other articles focus on the role of permissions in Android security and permission monitoring to investigate access to the sensitive data and resources of the device [27]. In terms of permission monitoring, the researchers presented a method for classifying Android applications based on their access to private information and the abuse of this information. The method categorises applications into three types based on their access to private information. Then, a static analysis is used to detect Android malware utilising the information and permissions of the applications. In another study [28], the authors used the classification of permissions as an information gain metric to provide better detection accuracy.

In [29], the researchers proposed a technique that combines static and dynamic analysis to examine Android applications. This approach makes it possible to expand an application's method call graph (MCG) by capturing additional modules loaded at runtime and additional paths of execution concealed by reflection calls. The researchers also reported the analysis of recent state-of-the-art tools that should be taken into account, namely Flowdroid [30], AndroGuard [31], and Amandroid [32], among others. Other researchers [33] proposed using host-based intrusion detection systems (HIDSs) to run entirely on a mobile device without relying on a remote server. The application monitors the device by regularly sampling features that represent the overall use of the device's resources, such as the central processing unit (CPU), random access memory (RAM), battery, and others. The detection engine adopts machine learning and statistical algorithms to detect known and unprecedented (zero-day) attacks. Furthermore, in a review [34], various approaches were presented, including system-call-based host-based intrusion detection systems (HIDSs), examining various components. The research presented the extraction of features, the use of data-mining algorithms, the availability and utilisation of HIDS datasets, the implementation in current embedded systems, and future research directions.

Research on edge computing has also been considered and is not directly related to the current research. The literature includes studies on AI-based mechanisms for enhancing healthcare data security in the IoT-cloud and reducing the cost of IoT sensors [35]. A survey article [36] covered the edge architecture's security and privacy issues caused by heterogeneous device networking. Reference [37] provided a comprehensive analysis of data security and privacy in edge computing, including an overview of edge computing, security, and privacy requirements. Reference [38] explored the use of smart medical sensors and the IoT in healthcare and the limitations of cloud-based systems, highlighting the trend towards edge and fog computing as solutions. Reference [38] also provided an overview of the IoT in healthcare, covering early wearable-sensor-based health monitoring to recent advancements in fog/edge computing for smart health. Finally, Reference [38] comprehensively analysed data security and privacy in edge computing, including an overview of the fundamentals, challenges, mechanisms, state-of-the-art solutions, and proposed research directions.

In summary, prior research in the field of Android security has encompassed a range of approaches, including malware detection and security analysis techniques. However, the distribution of datasets to cloud or edge servers for monitoring and analysis of Android logs has not been sufficiently addressed. This study presents a new approach for conducting security analysis while reducing the impact on system resources and battery consumption. This was achieved by transferring the analysis stage to the edge and utilising the device's collected data. The current research paper is differentiated from prior research in the field of Android security by proposing a unique approach to the security analysis of edge devices, which focuses on the retrieval and distribution of log files for analysis.

The aim of this research was to minimise the impact on system resources and battery consumption by performing the analysis at the edge instead of on the device itself. This approach is supported by the proposed Chidroid, a software package that provides a comprehensive solution for log retrieval and data distribution from Android devices. The integrated toolchain, with Chidroid as the central component, enables the generation, collection, parsing, and distribution of datasets for the development of machine and deep learning models.

1.2. Contribution

The current study proposes a unique approach for conducting security analysis on edge devices, which involves the retrieval of logs from Android devices. The aim was to minimise the impact on system resources and battery consumption by transferring the computational workload off the device and executing the analysis at the edge.

Chidroid is a software package that provides a comprehensive solution for log retrieval and data distribution from Android devices. This package leverages a protected policy-driven decomposition technique to enable the generation and collection of logs and thus contribute to the development of detection and analysis tools. This study proposes a modular toolchain, with Chidroid as the central component for generating, collecting, parsing, and distributing datasets. The proposed approach was designed to be reusable and scalable and can be extended to address additional classes of vulnerabilities. Furthermore, Chidroid opens up several possibilities for further applications, such as permission monitoring. The contribution of this research paper and the characteristics of Childroid are summarised as follows:

- Chidroid is an Android log retrieval and data distribution process that enables the generation and collection of logs from Android devices.
- The evaluation process was conducted in the healthcare domain and interconnected devices such as the IoT and health wearables.
- Chidroid enables the creation of datasets, allowing non-structured data to be parsed into semi-structured or structured data that can be used for machine learning and deep learning. The proposed approach can be used as a universal policy-based tool to identify and analyse security issues in all recent versions of Android (https://www.appbrain.com/stats/top-android-sdk-versions, accessed 20 February 2023), approximately 95% of all active Android devices.
- A modular toolchain is proposed, with Chidroid as the main component to generate, collect, and distribute datasets. The approach is reusable, can be extended to detect additional classes of vulnerabilities, and can be applied to permission monitoring.
- Chidroid can retrieve the set of priorities for the applications and can also set the time duration and privileges used by the software packages. The detection rules can report on permissions if an application misbehaves due to the usage or to maintain excessive system resources.

Finally, the research paper provides practical examples of log retrieval from Android devices and details the ways in which these logs can be utilised to extract meaningful insights and behaviour patterns in device usage. A comprehensive examination of the feasibility and potential of this approach is also presented.

1.3. Structure

The rest of this paper is structured as follows. Section 2 presents the methodology employed to develop and assess Chidroid and the successive stages followed for this research. Section 3 provides a comprehensive analysis of Chidroid's architecture, including a thorough examination of its constituent components. Section 4 offers practical examples of Chidroid's usage and presents the findings from its evaluation. Finally, the conclusions and potential future avenues for this research are outlined in Section 5.

2. Methodology

In this section, the methodology followed during the development of Chidroid is described. The test and validation cycles (Figure 1) were as follows: (i) Chidroid development and versioning updates and the creation of the Android Package Kit (APK) file, (ii) the definition of the default configuration files and permissions granted required by the APK, (iii) enabling Chidroid to execute shell commands defined by the configuration, (iv) the definition of the commands that generate and create Android logs, (v) the creation of data type patterns, regular expressions, and corresponding log sources, and finally, (vi) the support of bash shell piped commands to be executed by Chidroid. These stages were followed sequentially, and multiple iterations were performed to provide better versions of the Chidroid to support the required functionalities. Figure 1 explains the structured methodology to ensure that the application met the functional requirements and performed as expected.

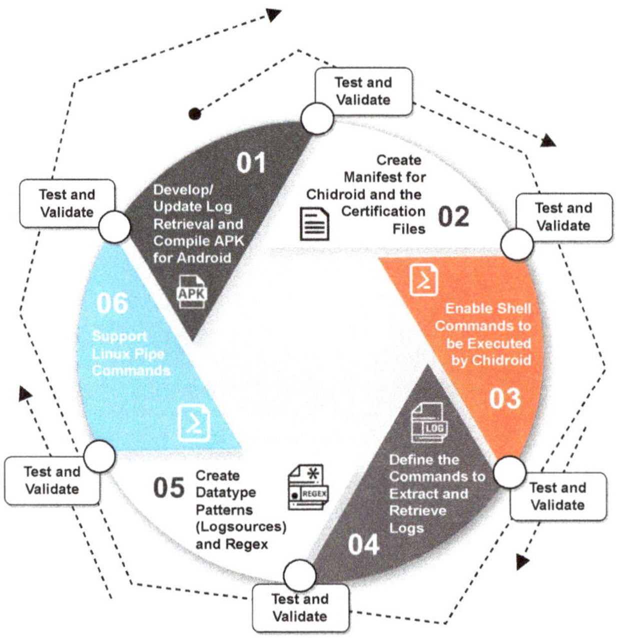

Figure 1. Methodology followed to develop, validate, and upgrade Chidroid.

The first step of the methodology (Figure 1) comprises the development of functional requirements, including log retrieval and log distribution. The test and validation steps were carried out to ensure correctness. Once the application was functional, the next step was to define the permissions needed by Chidroid and define the relevant files that should be included in the APK, for example the permissions that Chidroid needs to have to retrieve logs and configuration files that must be included in the APK to enable log collection and shipping by default.

The Chidroid system was derived from a previous iteration of a software application known as Metago, which was developed by the PDMFC organisation. The encoding protocols and formatting techniques utilised in Metago were retained in the development of Chidroid, with additional features incorporated to facilitate the collection and analysis of the log data from Android devices. Consequently, it may include different configuration options employing the encoding scheme characteristic of Metago, or the collected logs may be distributed in the raw format (Metago Raw).

The present study advanced this by incorporating the functionality of executing user-defined shell commands and specifying their usage in the configuration file. The implementation of the shell command execution enabled the collection and tracking of Android logs through the utilisation of relevant tools such as Logcat, Package Manager, and AppOpsManager (https://developer.android.com/reference/android/app/AppOpsManager, accessed 20 February 2023). The initial verification of the data collection accuracy was conducted, followed by the parsing of logs into a structured format, the creation of data type patterns, and the definition of regular expressions to extract specific fields. The implementation of shell pipe commands in Chidroid enabled the execution of multiple commands for searching and filtering logs prior to collection and distribution. A methodological validation was carried out at each step of the implementation process, utilising the following devices for testing purposes:

- Android smartphones and tablets were used for the validation steps (Android Version 6 to Version 12).
- Android IoT devices or gateways, such as routers and hubs for smart healthcare and IoMT devices, such as medical sensors and healthcare systems (the exact models are confidential due to licence agreements) (e.g., smart glasses, smartwatches, medical implants).

The individual testing of the devices was carried out to enhance compatibility and verify the functionalities of Chidroid. During the validation tests, no medical or healthcare data were collected. Chidroid collected logs and metrics from a variety of assets and devices to test and validate the functionalities. Validation tests were instrumental in discovering software flaws, bugs, or permission changes and in expanding the functionality of Chidroid and verifying its correctness. In general, the validation tests demonstrated that the application could retrieve logs and system metrics from various assets and devices.

To evaluate the performance impact of Chidroid on the device, a preliminary assessment was carried out to gather data on CPU and RAM utilisation. The assessment involved the usage of the Android Debug Bridge (ADB (https://developer.android.com/studio/command-line/adb), accessed 20 February 2023) shell and the execution of specific commands to obtain the relevant metrics. The commands in Listing 1 were used to retrieve the CPU and RAM usage of a specific process with the package name "com.github.lribeiro.metago.chidroid".

Listing 1: Example structure of TOML files.

```
cpu_usage=$(top -b -n 2 | awk '/com.github.lribeiro.metago.chidroid↩
    / {print $9}')
ram_usage=$(top -b -n 2 | awk '/com.github.lribeiro.metago.chidroid↩
    / {print $10}')
```

The output of the "top" command (Listing 1) provides a comprehensive representation of the processes running on the system. This information includes the process ID (PID), the user who initiated the process, and the CPU and memory utilisation of each process, among other details. In this study, the "top" command was utilised to retrieve the CPU and RAM usage of the Android process with the package name "com.github.lribeiro.metago.chidroid". The output of the top command was filtered to show only the information relevant to this process. The "awk" command was then utilised to extract the desired metric values, the CPU and RAM usage, from the filtered output. The instant values were stored, and the mean values were calculated by finding the minimum, average, and maximum values.

3. Chidroid Architecture

The Chidroid architecture is presented in Figure 2 and describes how the application collects data from Android devices and distributes them to other endpoints. Once the application is installed and configured, it collects logs and system metrics.

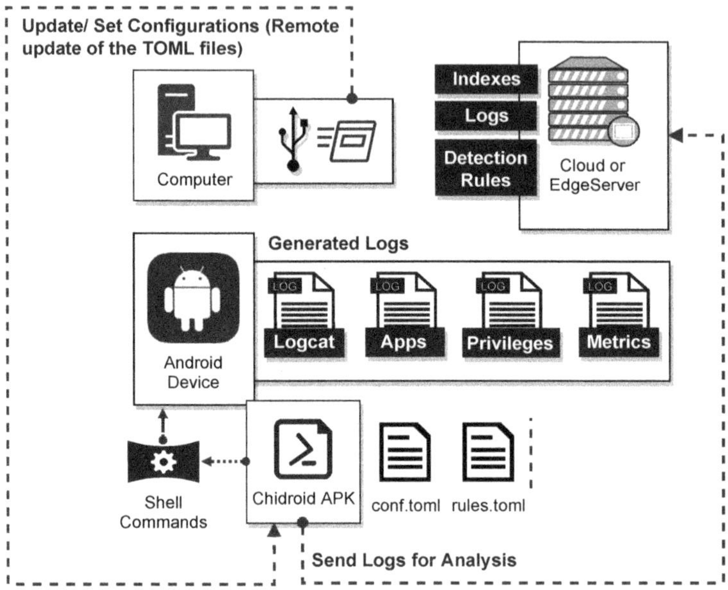

Figure 2. Chidroid architecture and deployment details.

The Chidroid architecture (Figure 2) allows the efficient collection and secure distribution of logs and system metrics from Android devices. By using shell commands and the API, Chidroid can provide valuable information for monitoring and optimising the performance and security of Android devices. Chidroid generates, collects, and distributes the following logs: (i) logcat.log, (ii) packages.log, and (iii) privileges.log, along with (iv) metrics. Internally, Chidroid uses a scheduler to run user-defined scripts or shell commands to generate the logs or data. This scheduler follows the familiar CRON syntax, extended to add seconds. After collecting logs and system metrics, Chidroid encodes them in JSON and distributes them to the chosen target collector for analysis. This collector can be a cloud service or another web server that is able to receive and process JSON data.

Chidroid can be remotely configured using the POST method, and the API can replace the configuration files, namely config.toml and rules.toml. When Chidroid starts up, it reads these configuration files and sets up the log input sources, internal settings, and output sinks from *config.toml*. From *config.toml*, Chidroid reads the processing and transforming rules, for example, regular expressions or event-breaking rules. It is noteworthy that the rules.toml file possesses the capability to integrate privacy-centric rules, which can be invoked during the course of log collection. Such rules serve to enable data transformation, which is geared towards privacy enhancement objectives. This is achieved through the application of anonymisation and other pertinent processes to the collected logs, adding privacy features. As for distribution, Chidroid can ship logs in the raw format or JSON encoded. If needed, traffic can be relayed on another Chidroid listener (peer-to-peer distribution).

3.1. Chidroid APK

Chidroid was developed using the Go programming language and compiled as APK (with the package name com.github.lribeiro.metago.chidroid) using Gomobile (https://pkg.go.dev/golang.org/x/mobile/cmd/gomobile, accessed 20 February 2023). The build process takes the source code and generates multiple binary files for a combination of operating systems (Linux, Windows, MacOS, and Android) and CPU instruction sets (x86_64, arm64, arm7). Chidroid currently supports the following CPU architectures: (i) Advanced RISC Machine (CPU architecture ARM and ARM64) and (ii) Intel Atom (x86_64). The APK file includes resources, assets, the manifest file, and the linked SO library (which contains the majority of the executable code). In the context of software development, manifest files are used to specify the requirements, dependencies, privileges, and other details that are needed to run the project or application. In Android application development, manifest files are an essential part of APK files. They are used by the Android operating system to determine how to run an application and the permissions that the application acquires from the Android system.

3.2. *Configuration Files (Conf.Toml, Rules.Toml, Certs, and Manifest Files)*

There are two main Chidroid configuration files included in the APK: (i) "config.toml" and (ii) "rules.toml". The first (config.toml) is used to set up sources and sinks (outputs), while the second (rules.toml) is used to define the privacy rules and to set up the needed transformations to parse the sources to the required format. Tom's Obvious, Minimal Language (TOML (https://toml.io/en/v1.0.0), accessed 20 February 2023) is a file format used to represent configuration data in a human-readable and easily editable format.

TOML files are commonly used in software development to store configuration data for applications and other tools. The files use a simple and consistent syntax, with key–value pairs separated by an equal sign (=) and sections indicated by square brackets ([and]). A generic example is provided in Listing 2 and contains two stanzas (i.e., block of text within a configuration file). In this example, the server section includes a single option, "port", which specifies the port number on which the server will listen for incoming connections.

Listing 2: Example structure of TOML files.

```
[server]
port = 8080

[database]
host = "localhost"
user = "admin''
password = "secret"
```

3.3. *Configuration of Endpoints*

A web API endpoint is a specific URL or location on a web server that provides access to a web API. Chidroid supports the distribution of raw data to remote HTTP or HTTPS endpoints. Alternatively, another Chidroid application can act as a gateway with a dedicated listener and receive and forward whatever data it receives to the specified final endpoint. Next, an example of configuring a remote output is presented (Listing 3).

Listing 3: Configuration of the outputs.

```
[outputs.AI4HEALTHSEC]
Urls = ["METAGOs://siem.AI4HEALTHSEC.pdmfc.com/dynamic-ports↩
    /10000/:80/"]
```

In Listing 3 a new output named "AI4HEALTHSEC" is defined and specifies that it will send data to a single endpoint using an HTTP Post over HTTPS, to a host where an SIEM is deployed. As an example, in Listing 4, the encoded JSON output is presented as an event retrieved from Logcat (see Section 3.4 for more details on Logcat).

Listing 4: Chidroid: METAGO-encoded JSON output.

```
{
  "header": {
  "agentId": "55bb84e8-b2ee-4af4-94f3-435826e14f98",
  "host": "Android8",
  "os": "Android",
  "architecture": "arm64",
```

```
  "source": "script://Logcat"
  "sourcetype": "logcat"
  "format": "METAGO"
  "timefield": "timestamp",
  "timeformat": "MM-DD hh:mm:ss.SSS"
  "timezone": "Europe/Lisbon"
  },
  "events": [
  {
   "timestamp": "12-05 17:48:28.215",
   "pid": 26458,
   "opid": 26458,
   "type": "V",
   "AppName": "GraphicsEnvironment",
   "Message": "ANGLE Developer option for 'com.google.android.apps.↩
       messaging' set to: 'default'"
  }
  ]
 }
```

3.4. *Logcat and Generation of System Logs in the Android Environment*

Logcat is a software tool that can retrieve logs available on Android devices. Android stores the kernel logs generated by the system and application logs generated by individual applications. In general, logs are an important source of information for detecting and troubleshooting problems on Android devices. By regularly checking the log data, security professionals can identify potential security threats and take the appropriate action to address them. Even if the main goal of Logcat is to be used as an essential debugging tool, the continuous stream of system messages and user-generated diagnostics is used to detect security issues.

Traditionally, to retrieve logs from an Android device, developers or advanced users connect their computers to the device using the ADB. The simpler way is to connect using USB, install the required drivers if necessary, and open a shell using the *adb shell* command. Inside that shell, the command *logcat* can be issued to retrieve the logs stored internally. The following taxonomy of events is retrievable by Logcat (Table 2).

The logs from Logcat contain information about the device's hardware and software, as well as any message that has been logged by the system or applications, such as the device's boot process, system events, and running applications. Logcat can be combined with arguments or other shell commands to search log data for specific keywords or phrases (e.g., *"adb logcat *:D"* or using the grep command). The logs from Logcat are, by default, stored as circular memory buffers on the device. Therefore, Chidroid can execute and collect the logs from Logcat and distribute the data for analysis. They are collected and shipped before being naturally erased by filling in all the reserved ring buffer sizes.

Several commands can be used on an Android device to generate logs and perform various actions. These commands are typically executed using a command-line interface, such as a terminal emulator application or the ADB tool. Chidroid uses an internal interpreter to execute shell commands that can be scheduled with CRON-like rules. The shell commands to execute Logcat are defined in the config.toml file (Listing 5).

Table 2. Logcat event types.

Event Type	Description
Log.Verbose	Verbose logs are detailed logs that provide a comprehensive record of an activity or system. In the context of Android, verbose logs may be used to troubleshoot issues with the operating system or a specific app.
Log.Debug	Debug logs are not intended for production environments, as they can contain sensitive information and may impact an app's performance. When an application is ready for release, debug logs should be removed or disabled to ensure that the application runs efficiently and securely.
Log.Info	Info refers to log messages that provide useful information about the state or behaviour of an application or the Android system.
Log.Warning	Warning log messages are typically used to alert the user or the developer to a potential problem or issue that may require attention. For example, a warning log message may be generated if an application receives invalid input from the user, if a network connection is lost, or if a critical system resource is running low.
Log.Error	Error log messages are typically used to alert the user or the developer to a serious problem or failure that has occurred within an application or the Android system. For example, an error log message may be generated if an application crashes or an important system function fails.
Log.Fatal	Fatal log messages should be used sparingly, as they indicate a critical failure or an error that requires immediate attention. When a fatal log message is printed, the application or system may be unable to continue running and may need to be restarted or shut down.

Listing 5: Android shell commands defined in the TOML configuration file.

```
[script.logcat]
Cmd = "logcat -t '#timestamp' -b all"
EvalArgsIndex = [1]
Outputs = ["AI4HEALTHSEC"]
Rules=["eventbreak.eventperm","rex.logcat"]
Index= "android_logs"
SourceType="logcatraw"
Debug=true
Cron="!*/15 * * * * *"
[script.logcat.Params]
timestamp='01-01 00:00:00.000'
```

There is much unpack here, and the snippet above (Listing 5) corresponds to the execution and log collection using *[script.logcat]*. The "Cmd" property specifies the command that will be executed to collect data. Here, the *logcat* command is executed with the "-t" and "-b" options to filter the output by timestamp and log buffer, respectively. Proper shell–argument parsing is performed on "Cmd", and all arguments are stored internally in a string array. The "EvalArgsIndex" property specifies the indexes of the script arguments that shall be evaluated as internal expressions. In this case, all but *#timestamp* are simple strings. The *#timestamp* represents the extracted timestamp field of the *rex.logcat* rule presented below.

"Outputs" specifies the names of the output streams that will receive the script's output. The "Rules" property specifies the names of the rules that will be applied to the script's output. The "Index" specifies the name of the index that will be used to store the processed log data. The "SourceType" option specifies the type of log data the script collects. The "Debug" option specifies whether debug information will be output to the internal log of Chidroid. The "Cron" option specifies the schedule and recurrence rule for executing the script. The "[script.logcat.Params]" section of the configuration file contains additional parameters passed to the script at runtime. In the example provided above, the "timestamp" parameter was set to "01-01 00:00:00.000", which for all intents and purposes sets the initial value for the timestamp.

3.5. AppOpsManager

AppOps includes a set of APIs within the Android operating system to manage the permissions granted to applications. These APIs effectively monitor and control software packages' permissions on an Android device, enabling the detection and prevention of potential security issues. The proposed methodology entails the utilisation of the "appops" command in the Chidroid software package to access the AppOps interface and retrieve the permissions assigned to each software package. By comprehensively analysing these permissions, Chidroid can identify any deviation or anomaly that may pose a security risk. For instance, if a software package is found to be requesting an excessive number of permissions or utilising permissions that are not congruent with its intended function, Chidroid can alert the user or administrator and take necessary measures to resolve the issue. This feature of Chidroid demonstrates the potential of utilising AppOps APIs to enhance the security of Android devices and safeguard against potential security threats.

Healthcare organisations must comply with the regulations set forth by the Health Insurance Portability and Accountability Act (HIPAA) when handling medical or healthcare data on Android devices. The use of AppOps can assist in enforcing these policies and regulations by tracking and managing the permissions of software packages that handle sensitive data. Chidroid can ensure that these packages are only granted the necessary permissions for their intended use and prevent the use of any permissions that could compromise the security of the device or its users. Using AppOps, Chidroid can monitor the permissions of software packages on Android devices and detect and prevent any security issues that may arise from their use. The privilege.log file generated by AppOps can also assist Chidroid in maintaining the security and HIPAA compliance of medical or healthcare data on Android devices in the eHealth environment.

3.6. Android Permission Retrieval

Overall, the config.toml file defines the behaviour and settings of the data collection inputs. Here, the shell commands that initiate the Package Manager (pm command) and the corresponding permission monitoring and retrieval are presented. The "pm" command (Listing 6) is a tool provided by the Android operating system for managing installed packages.

The Package Manager is an Android system internal application that performs actions and queries on applications and software packages installed on an Android device. The command pm is a Command-Line Interface (CLI) API to interact with Package Manager to enumerate or manage the installed packages on the device. It can also enable various actions on those packages. For example, the command can retrieve the full list of the software packages installed on the device, displaying the names of the software packages, along with the version number, process id, and other details for each of the installed software packages.

Internal filtering allows this command to display specific packages, such as associated files, enabled/disabled packages, system packages, third-party packages, and installer packages. For example, the -u flag can display a list of uninstalled packages. In summary, the command can be used to retrieve the lifecycle of installed software packages.

Listing 6: Command to retrieve the permissions given to the installed packages.

```
[script.permissions]
Cmd="pm list packages -u -3
  | cut -c 9-
  | while read line; do echo $line; appops get $line
  | sed 's/Uid mode: //' ; done"
Rules=["eventbreak.eventperm","rex.extract","zip.perms","str.j13","↩
    for.join13","zip.perms_time","str.j15","for.join15","zip.↩
    perms_duration","fields.remove_temp"]
Index="android_permissions"
Outputs = ["AI4HEALTHSEC"]
```

The "list packages" subcommand lists all installed packages on the device, including both user-installed and system packages. The output will include uninstalled packages using the "-u" option, and the "-3" option will include third-party packages. The "pm list packages" output is passed to the "cut" command, which extracts the package names from the output. Using a "while" loop, the script reads the package names one by one and runs the "appops" command to retrieve application permission data for each package. The "appops" command is another tool provided by Android for managing application permissions, and the "get" sub-command retrieves the application permission data for a specific package. The output from the "appops get" command is piped to the "sed" command, which removes the "Uid mode:" prefix from each line of output.

3.7. System Metrics

In addition to the aforementioned logs, Chidroid can directly retrieve system metrics from the Android device, including information about battery life, virtual memory usage, CPU usage, and network connections. These system metrics are important to monitor the performance and overall state of the device. Tracking these metrics makes it possible to identify software packages that consume a large number of system resources, such as CPU or memory. This is particularly important in IoMT and healthcare services, where the high usage of resources can lead to risky and critical safety conditions for patients. As a result, Chidroid can help identify and mitigate the potential security risks posed by software packages that consume a large number of system resources. This can help ensure the safety and security of patients and their data in the IoMT and healthcare domains if there is a malfunction, critical system, or security issue.

Chidroid retrieves various metrics, including CPU usage, virtual memory, disk counters, load average, network counters, connections, and running processes, on an Android device using the following stanza (Listing 7). Within this stanza, the index name, job frequency, and endpoint for log distribution are defined for each metric. The source-type settings are described in the following subsections (Sections 3.3 and 3.8).

Listing 7: Retrieve device metrics.

```
[metrics.all]
Metrics = [
  "cpu", # Cpu time consumed
  "cpuinfo", # Cpu version, and spec
  "virtualmem", # Memory used/free
  "disk", # Disk IO counters
  "loadavg", # CPU load average 1,5,15m
  "net", # Net IO Counters by interface
  "connections",
  "process",
]
Cron="!0 * * * * *"
Index="android_metrics"
Outputs = ["AI4HEALTHSEC"]
```

The stanza "[metrics.all]" specifies the settings for the "metrics" rule type and creates a new internal instance associated with the name "all". The "Metrics" property specifies the list of counters to be collected. In the example above (Listing 7), the rule set will collect metrics for CPU time consumed, CPU version and specification, memory usage, disk IO counters, CPU load average, network IO counters, network connections, and processes.

The "Cron" property specifies the schedule at which the metrics will be collected. Metrics will be collected every minute (0 * * * * *). The "Index" suggests the target database name where metrics should be stored. Log collectors have final control and can override this definition. The "Outputs" option specifies the next hop the collected metrics will be sent. Here, the metrics will be sent to the "AI4HEALTHSEC" as the configuration output (see Section 3, Listing 3).

3.8. Log Distribution for Analysis—Regex and Log Sourcetypes

Regular expressions are a powerful technique for matching and manipulating text and are widely used in various fields of study and industry. Regular expressions can be employed in log sources to search and filter data for specific patterns or messages. A regular expression is a string of characters that defines a pattern to be matched in a text string. These patterns are specified using a special syntax, which allows for the matching of a wide range of patterns in text. For example, regular expressions can be used to match a specific word or phrase in a log message or to identify a specific pattern of characters in a URL. To search for a specific pattern in a log message using a regular expression, the pattern can be defined using the regular expression syntax and then employed with a tool or program such as Chidroid, which has built-in support for regular expressions. The tool or program will highlight or indicate the matching text in the log data if the pattern is found. Chidroid also has the capability of utilising named captures, a feature of regular expressions, which allows for the capturing of text matched by the regular expression and the ability to reuse it within the same pattern or in a substitution. This feature allows for greater flexibility and precision in analysing and manipulating log data.

Each capture group in the example below (Listing 8) is defined using the following syntax: "(?P<name>pattern)", where "name" is the name of the capture group and "pattern" is the regex pattern that defines the contents of the group. The regex pattern in the example has five named capturing groups: "timestamp", "pid", "opid", "type", "AppName", and "Message". The "timestamp" capturing group matches a timestamp in the format "MM-DD hh:mm:ss.SSS". The "pid" and "opid" capturing groups match a string of digits representing a process ID and operation ID, respectively. The "type" capture group matches a single word character representing the type of the log message. The "AppName" capture group matches a string of characters representing the name of the application that generated the log message up to the first colon character. The "Message" capture group matches the remaining characters in the log message after the application name.

Listing 8: Configuration of the regular expressions and source types.

```
[rex.logcat]
Patterns=['(?P<timestamp>\d\d-\d\d \d\d:\d\d:\d\d.\d\d\d)\s+(?P<pid>\d+)\s+(?P<opid>\d+)\s+(?P<type>\w)\s+(?P<AppName>[^:]+):\s+(?P<Message>.*)']
Field="_raw"

[sourcetypes.logcat] #Define the Time Format of the logs
Format="METAGO"
TimeFormat="MM-DD hh:mm:ss.SSS"
TimeField="timestamp"
TimeZone="Europe/Lisbon"
```

The "[sourcetypes.logcat]" configuration stanza (Listing 8) creates a new SourceType named "logcat". The SourceType contains a set of properties that hint at how logs should be parsed, of particular importance for detecting and extracting correct timestamps for each entry. The timezone, timestamp format, and other configuration details are also defined.

3.9. Performance Assessment and Compatibility

Chidroid allows the usage of multiple pipelines and sends data in multiple outputs with one execution. Chidroid is compatible with Android smartphones running Version 8.0 or later and has been designed to have minimal impact on system resources. It was assessed through empirical analysis that the system under consideration exhibits a memory footprint of approximately 62 MB in terms of RAM consumption while displaying low CPU utilisation of approximately 1% on an Octa-core architecture comprised of 1 × 2.84 GHz Cortex-X1, 3 × 2.42 GHz Cortex-A78, and 4×1.80 GHz Cortex-A55 processors. The values in the outputs (Listing 9) represent the mean CPU and RAM usage of the Android process. The date and time of the results of the assessment are included in each output, along with the mean CPU usage and mean RAM usage in percentage. These metrics give information on the resource utilisation of the process at a specific moment.

Listing 9: Example structure of TOML files.

```
#Output from the lower CPU usage during the assessment
{ "date": "2023-02-11_18-59-45", "mean_cpu_usage": 3%, "↩
    mean_ram_usage": 1.8% }
#Output from the mean CPU usage during the assessment
{ "date": "2023-02-11_19-20-01", "mean_cpu_usage": 6.2%, "↩
    mean_ram_usage": 1.6% }
#Output from the higher CPU usage during the assessment
{ "date": "2023-02-11_18-48-44", "mean_cpu_usage": 10.3%, "↩
    mean_ram_usage": 1.8% }
```

4. Log Generation and Analysis: Examples, Results, and Discussion

In this section, a collection of sample log files is presented that was retrieved from various Android devices. These logs serve as exemplars of the Chidroid execution process and demonstrate the data types that can be obtained through this methodology. The log files can be extracted from Android devices and transmitted to the edge server for further analysis. Through the utilisation of regular expression matching, the data contained within the logs can be transformed into a structured format, enabling the ease of monitoring. Additionally, the data can be exported in a variety of formats, including JSON and CSV, for further analysis and manipulation.

4.1. Logcat Example

The following snippet presents an example output using Logcat. These logs contain different events, including system events, application events, and debugging messages. They can be useful for detecting security issues such as unauthorised access attempts or abnormal application behaviour. The default Logcat structure is explained below (Listing 10).

Listing 10: Explanation of the Logcat default structure.

```
[08-01-2022 10:15:23] [DEBUG] [MyApp] [MainActivity]: Starting activity: Intent { cmp=com.↩
    example.myapp/.MainActivity }
[08-01-2022 10:15:24] [INFO] [MyApp] [MainActivity]: Successfully connected to database
[08-01-2022 10:15:29] [WARNING] [MyApp] [MainActivity]: Invalid input detected
[08-01-2022 10:15:32] [ERROR] [MyApp] [MainActivity]: Failed to retrieve data from server
```

In the sample Logcat output, there are four log messages (DEBUG, INFO, WARNING, ERROR), each with a different log level. The first log message is a debug message indicating that the application is starting an activity. The second log message is an info log message, indicating that the application has successfully connected to a database. The third log message is a warning message indicating that the application has received invalid user input. The fourth log message is an error log message indicating that the application has failed to retrieve data from a server. In the Logcat output (Listings 10 and 11), each log message is printed on a separate line and includes the following information:

- Timestamp: The date and time at which the log message was generated, in the format YYYY-MM-DD HH:MM:SS.
- Log level: The severity of the log message, which can be one of the following: DEBUG, INFO, WARNING, ERROR, or FATAL.
- Application name: The name of the application or system that generated the log message.

- Log tag: A short string that provides additional context about the log message.
- Log message: The actual log message that provides information about the state or behaviour of the application or system.

Listing 11: Example output using Logcat.

```
12-05 17:48:28.215 26458 26458 V GraphicsEnvironment: ANGLE Developer option for 'com.google↩
    .android.apps.messaging' set to: 'default'
12-05 17:47:04.950 8113 8113 D IHansComunication: HansComunication::configCheckedUid-- ↩
    10302, type = 0
12-05 17:46:52.935 2058 3726 I OplusHansManager : uid=10302, pkg=com.spotify.music F exit(),↩
    reason=Broadcast
12-05 17:46:52.935 3801 3801 D DeviceInfoHidlClient: isRadioOn()=true
12-05 17:48:28.517 2058 7258 W PackageManager: package unknown uid 10223 pid 26458 call ↩
    SetEnabledSetting(com.google.android.apps.messaging component = com.google.android.ims.↩
    binding.SystemBindingService, 1, 0x1, 0)
12-05 17:48:28.519 26458 26492 I BugleRcsEngine: [1364] bdre.run: SystemBindingManager: ↩
    SystemBinding enabled: true
12-05 17:48:28.520 26458 26492 I BugleRcsEngine: [1364] bdrf.b: System Binding updated
12-05 17:47:04.022 3872 7096 E Battery : AppStats: Uid = 10317; pkgName = gr.winbank.↩
    mobilenext; GpsPower = 1.253625 mAh; GpsTotalPower = 0.0 mAh
```

By regularly checking logs (Listing 11), it is possible to identify potential security risks and take the appropriate actions to mitigate them. For example, if the log contains a message like "User logged in successfully", this indicates that a user has successfully logged into the app. However, if the log contains a message like "User login failed", this may indicate a potential security risk, such as an incorrect password or username used in an attempted login. In this case, it would be important to investigate the issue further and take appropriate action to secure the system, such as requiring the user to reset his/her password or blocking the device's IP address that made the failed login attempt.

4.2. Package Manager

The Package Manager is a system service on Android devices and is used to manage the installation, removal, and updating of software packages. One of the tasks that can be performed using the Package Manager is to enumerate the list of software packages installed on the device. To do this, the following command can be used (Listing 12):

Listing 12: Enumerate installed packages.

```
pm list packages
```

This command (Listing 12) will display a list of all software packages installed on the device, along with their package names and versions (Listing 13). For example, the output of the command "pm list packages" might look as follows.

Listing 13: Installed software packages.

```
com.skype.raider:8.66.0.123
cn.wps.xiaomi.abroad.lite:6.2.2
com.aviapp.translator:1.3.5
com.adobe.reader:20.6.0
com.linkedin.android:16.0.0.226
com.termux:0.115
```

In this example, the package names are listed on the left, followed by the version numbers in parentheses. The version number consists of three or four parts, separated by periods. The first number indicates the major version, the second the minor version, and the third the patch level. The fourth number, if present, indicates a build number.

The command "pm list packages" can be used to obtain a list of all installed packages on the device, or the "-f" flag can filter the output based on a specific package name or part of a package name. For example, to list all installed packages that contain the word "skype" in the package name, use the following command (Listing 14).

Listing 14: Filter by package name.

```
pm list packages -f "skype"
```

To retrieve detailed information about a package, you can use the following command (Listing 15).

Listing 15: Retrieve package information.

```
pm dump <package_name>
```

The "<package_name>" argument should be replaced with the application's package name to obtain the relevant information. The package name is a unique identifier for each application that the Android operating system uses to identify and manage the application. The "pm dump" command will display detailed information about the specified package, including its permissions, version, and signature. This information can be helpful when debugging issues with the application or when trying to understand its behaviour. Here are some examples of package names and the applications to which they correspond:

com.skype.raider This is the package name for the Skype (https://www.skype.com/, accessed 20 February 2023) application, which is a messaging and video calling application developed by Skype.

cn.wps.xiaomi.abroad.lite This is the package name for the WPS Office (https://www.wps.com/, accessed 20 February 2023) application, which is a productivity suite developed by Kingsoft Office Software Corporation.

com.adobe.reader This is the package name for the Adobe Acrobat Reader (https://get.adobe.com/reader/), a PDF reader and annotator developed by Adobe Systems.

com.linkedin.android This is the package name for LinkedIn (https://www.linkedin.com/, accessed 20 February 2023), which is a professional networking and job searching application developed by LinkedIn Corporation.

com.termux This is the package name for Termux (https://github.com/termux/, accessed 20 February 2023), which is a terminal emulator and Linux environment for Android.

The package names can provide a way to identify and manage the applications installed on an Android device.

4.3. AppOpsManager and Privilege Extraction

The following stanza (Listing 16) includes sample logs retrieved from an Android smartphone using the Package Manager to enumerate the installed software packages. These logs display the package names, version numbers, and permissions of the packages installed on the device. Package names are unique identifiers assigned to each application by the developer, while version numbers indicate the current version of the application installed on the device. The permissions indicate the actions and data the application can access on the device.

Listing 16: Example output from the permission parser.

```
com.linkedin.android
Uid mode: COARSE_LOCATION: ignore
FINE_LOCATION: ignore
READ_CONTACTS: ignore
WRITE_CONTACTS: ignore
READ_CALENDAR: ignore
```

```
CAMERA: ignore
RECORD_AUDIO: ignore
READ_PHONE_STATE: ignore
SYSTEM_ALERT_WINDOW: default; rejectTime=+2d18h29m18s525ms ago
READ_CLIPBOARD: allow; time=+71d4h26m24s53ms ago
WAKE_LOCK: allow; time=+10h57m51s192ms ago; duration=+265ms
USE_BIOMETRIC: allow; time=+1h41m59s218ms ago
```

The logs show the permissions of LinkedIn (https://www.linkedin.com/, accessed 20 February 2023), namely "com.linkedin.android". By tracking the permissions of these packages, it is possible to detect any abnormal usage of permissions, such as a game requesting permission to write to external storage when it should not. This can help ensure that the software packages are not violating any regulations or policies and do not present any security risks to the device or its users. Another example (Listing 17) follows for the Termux application.

Listing 17: Permissions on the Termux package.

```
com.termux
Uid mode: LEGACY_STORAGE: allow
ACCESS_MEDIA_LOCATION: ignore
SYSTEM_ALERT_WINDOW: ignore
READ_CLIPBOARD: allow; time=+38d16h15m20s598ms ago
WRITE_CLIPBOARD: allow; time=+38d16h21m13s703ms ago
START_FOREGROUND: allow; time=+20d16h15m12s687ms ago; duration=+40s7ms
MANAGE_EXTERNAL_STORAGE: default; rejectTime=+64d2h40m4s128ms ago
```

The above logs (Listing 17) present the permissions requested by the Termux application for Android. The application has been granted the "LEGACY_STORAGE", "READ_CLIPBOARD", "WRITE_CLIPBOARD", and "START_FOREGROUND" permissions by the user, but has not been granted the "ACCESS_MEDIA_LOCATION" or "MANAGE_EXTERNAL_STORAGE" permission. The application requests the following permissions:

- LEGACY_STORAGE: This permission allows the application to access the device's legacy storage directories, which may be used to store data compatible with older versions of Android.
- ACCESS_MEDIA_LOCATION: This permission allows the application to access the location metadata associated with media files on the device, such as photos and videos.
- SYSTEM_ALERT_WINDOW: This permission allows the application to display windows on top of other applications, which may be used to display important information or to provide additional functionality.
- READ_CLIPBOARD: This permission allows the application to read from the device's clipboard, which may be used to paste text or other data into the app.
- WRITE_CLIPBOARD: This permission allows the application to write to the device's clipboard, which may be used to copy text or other data from the app.
- START_FOREGROUND: This permission allows the application to start a foreground service, which will continue to run even if the application is not in the foreground.
- MANAGE_EXTERNAL_STORAGE: This permission allows the application to manage the device's external storage, such as an SD card, which may be used to store application data or other files.

The temporal metrics "time" and "duration" for the permissions "READ_CLIPBOARD", "WRITE_CLIPBOARD", and "START_FOREGROUND" serve to record the point in time when the user granted the permission, as well as the duration for which the application has utilised the permission. As an illustration, the "time" value for the "READ_CLIPBOARD" permission reveals that the user authorisation was granted 38 days, 16 h, 15 min, 20 s, and 598 ms prior to the current time. Conversely, the "duration" value for the "START_FOREGROUND" permission demonstrates that the application has been in possession of the permission for a period of 40 s and 7 ms. In conclusion, these values furnish insight into the manner in which applications obtain the permissions granted by the user.

The "Uid mode" values for each permission indicate how the application will handle the permission. For example, the "ignore" value for the "ACCESS_MEDIA_LOCATION" permission indicates that the application will not use the permission, even if it is granted by the user. The "default" value for the "MANAGE_EXTERNAL_STORAGE" permission indicates that the application will use the default system behaviour for permission, which may be to ask the user for permission when the application attempts to access the protected data or resource.

4.4. System Metrics

System or device metrics (Listing 18) are essential for monitoring the performance and general status of an Android device. These metrics can provide valuable information about various aspects of the device's hardware, software, and network configuration, which can be useful for troubleshooting issues, identifying trends, and optimising performance.

Listing 18: Example output of the system metrics retrieved from Android.

```
1  2022-11-28 15:19:00 @date :11/28/2022 CoreID :0Cores :1Flags :fp asimd evtstrm aes pmull ↩
     sha1 sha2 crc32Mhz :1872Model :0xd03Stepping :4VendorID :ARMmetric :cpuinfo
2  2022-11-28 15:19:00 @date :11/28/2022 CPU :1CoreID :1Cores :1Flags :fp asimd evtstrm aes ↩
     pmull sha1 sha2 crc32Mhz :1872Model :0xd03Stepping :4VendorID :ARMmetric :cpuinfo
3  2022-11-28 15:19:00 @date :11/28/2022 CPU :2CoreID :2Cores :1Flags :fp asimd evtstrm aes ↩
     pmull sha1 sha2 crc32Mhz :1872Model :0xd03Stepping :4VendorID :ARMmetric :cpuinfo
4  2022-11-28 15:19:00 @date :11/28/2022 CPU :3CoreID :3Cores :1Flags :fp asimd evtstrm aes ↩
     pmull sha1 sha2 crc32Mhz :1872Model :0xd03Stepping :4VendorID :ARMmetric :cpuinfo
5  2022-11-28 15:19:00 @date :11/28/2022 available :1526226944free :133947392metric :↩
     virtualmemtotal :2952015872used :1327394816
6  2022-11-28 15:19:00 @date :11/28/2022 load1 :4.78955078125load15 :5.0224609375load5 :4.78125↩
     metric :loadavg
7  2022-11-28 15:19:00 @date :11/28/2022 bytesRecv :288737228bytesSent :11125292metric :netname↩
      :wlan0packetsRecv :234757packetsSent :81621
8  2022-11-28 15:19:00 @date :11/28/2022 bytesRecv :176bytesSent :176metric :netname :↩
     lopacketsRecv :2packetsSent :2
9  2022-11-28 15:19:00 @date :11/28/2022 metric :netname :rmnet2
10 2022-11-28 15:19:00 @date :11/28/2022 dst_ip :213.63.130.243dst_port :443family :2fd :75↩
     metric :connectionspid :21859src_ip :192.168.1.88src_port :48582status :SYN_SENTtype :1
```

The log messages (Listing 18) provide information about the device's CPU, including the core ID, the number of cores, the CPU flags, the CPU speed, and the CPU vendor ID (Lines 1 to 5 in Listing 18). Other log messages provide information about the device's memory usage, load average (Line 6), network traffic (Line 7), and network connections (Line 10). For example, one of the log messages indicates that the device has four CPU cores, each with a speed of 1872 MHz. The log message also indicates that the CPU supports various instruction sets, and details regarding the CPU (ARMv8-A) are provided. Other log messages provide information about the device's memory usage, including the total amount of memory, free memory, and used memory. The log message indicates that the device has 2.952.015.872 bytes of memory, with 1.327.394.816 bytes currently in use.

Finally, the log messages provide information about the device's network connections, including the source and destination IP addresses, the port numbers, the protocol family, and the connection status. For example, one of the log messages indicates that the device has established a network connection to the IP address 213.63.130.243 on port 443 using the TCP protocol. The connection is currently in the "SYN_SENT" state, which indicates that the device has sent a synchronisation request, but has not yet received a response.

Each log message includes a timestamp indicating the date and time the message was generated. The messages include fields such as the CPU core ID, the number of CPU cores, the CPU flags, the CPU speed, and the CPU vendor ID. Other log messages provide information about device memory usage, load average, network traffic, and network connections:

- CPU usage: This metric indicates the percentage of CPU currently being used by the device. High CPU usage can indicate that the device is under heavy load and may be experiencing performance issues.
- Memory usage: This metric indicates the amount of memory the device uses. High memory usage can indicate that the device is running low on memory and may be experiencing performance issues.
- Battery status: This metric indicates the device's current battery level and charging status. A low battery level can indicate that the device may need to be charged more often or consumes a large amount of power.
- Network usage: This metric indicates the amount of data currently being transferred over the network by the device. High network usage can indicate that the device is transmitting or receiving a large amount of data, which can affect performance and battery life.

Overall, these log messages provide a snapshot of the device's performance and configuration, which can be useful for troubleshooting issues and monitoring the device's health. By tracking and analysing these metrics, it is possible to monitor the performance and overall status of an Android device. For example, if the device has high CPU usage and a low battery level, it may be experiencing performance issues and may need to be charged. Similarly, if memory usage is high, it could indicate that the device is running low on memory or that a specific software package consumes a large amount of memory. Regularly checking system metrics makes it possible to identify and address potential performance and security issues on the device. Monitoring the system metrics makes it possible to identify and address potential problems and ensure that the device runs smoothly and securely.

5. Conclusions

This research paper presented Chidroid, an innovative mobile Android application for collecting and distributing logs from smart healthcare and IoMT devices. With this cutting-edge tool, healthcare professionals and IT administrators can easily gather critical log data from a wide range of medical devices, including wearable fitness trackers and remote monitoring systems. The intuitive interface allows users to view, filter, and analyse log data in real-time, enabling them to quickly identify and address any potential security issues or performance problems. Additionally, the application's compatibility for distributing data to cloud-based architectures allows for the easy distribution of logs to multiple stakeholders, ensuring that everyone has access to vital information. This way, it is possible to transform how healthcare and IoMT devices are managed. It is important to note that future applications that utilise the collected log data may necessitate the sanitisation and anonymisation of the logs to address privacy concerns. Chidroid includes such functionalities, which are not finalised and were not explained in the context of this research paper. Considering that, this research paper assumed that the edge devices involved in log collection and analysis are secured by implementing appropriate security protocols.

Chidroid enables a novel Android security system that can serve as a universal policy-based tool to examine and find security issues in most Android versions by distributing logs for analysis. The logs can contain valuable information about the device and its applications, such as hardware and software information, system events, and running applications. The metrics collected include battery status, network connections, virtual memory, and CPU usage. These metrics are important for monitoring the performance and overall state of the device. Logs and metrics are retrieved from the Android device using the Logcat and Package Manager tools. Logs from Android devices can be useful for improving the security of Internet of Medical Things (IoMT) devices in a number of ways. For example, logs can be used for security analysis as follows:

- Detect and diagnose security issues, such as unauthorised access or malicious activity on the device.
- Track changes to the device's configuration and identify potential security risks, such as installing unauthorised software or enabling unsafe permissions.
- Monitor device usage and identify unusual or suspicious activity that may indicate a security threat.
- Assist forensic investigations in the event of a security breach by providing a record of events that can help identify the cause of the issue and the steps taken to resolve it.

Overall, logs can be an important resource for improving the security of IoMT devices by providing visibility into the device's activities and helping to detect and mitigate potential security risks. In addition to logs, Chidroid directly retrieves various system metrics from the Android device, including information about battery status, virtual memory usage, and CPU usage. These metrics are important to monitor the performance and overall state of the device. By regularly retrieving and analysing logs and system metrics, Chidroid can help identify and mitigate potential security and privacy risks for devices and the sensitive data they handle. It can also be used to extract datasets from logs and use them to improve device performance and reliability. In general, Chidroid is a powerful and versatile tool that can help ensure the safety and security of Android devices in the smart healthcare and IoMT domains.

Future Work

There are several directions in which the Chidroid tool could be improved and extended in the future. Some potential areas of future work include the following:

- Improved log collection and analysis: The Chidroid system aims to enhance its security posture by collecting and analysing logs. Currently, the focus is on securing and protecting the privacy of Android devices. However, further analysis is needed to define detection rules for security incidents. Advanced log analysis techniques such as machine learning algorithms or statistical analysis could potentially provide insight into the performance and security of the device. The security analysis of collected logs represents a promising area for future research.
- Enhanced security and privacy: The Chidroid system is designed to identify and mitigate security and privacy risks in Android devices. However, further analysis is necessary to determine additional ways to improve protection. A key future milestone will be to conduct a security analysis to support the development of more robust detection rules.
- Extended testbed: An eHealth testbed will be established as a platform for conducting experiments and evaluating the performance of the Chidroid system in real-world eHealth applications. The testbed will be flexible and scalable, allowing for the testing of various configurations and parameters.
- Performance assessment: A comprehensive evaluation method will be developed to measure the impact of the Chidroid system in a more comprehensive manner regarding the resource utilisation and performance. This will provide valuable information on the potential of Chidroid as a solution for edge computing applications. Towards this direction, more research will be conducted to examine the feasibility of reducing the resource requirements by scaling down the continuous log retrieval process. The goal is to decrease the CPU utilisation requirements and optimise the resource utilisation of Chidroid.
- Compatibility: While there is potential to extend the Chidroid system to support iOS devices, the current focus will remain solely on Android devices. This is due to the greater opportunity for researching and addressing security and privacy challenges on the open Android platform, as opposed to the closed architecture of iOS.

In general, there are many opportunities to extend and improve the Chidroid tool to make it an even more powerful and effective tool to track the performance, security, and privacy of Android devices in the smart healthcare and IoMT domains.

Author Contributions: Conceptualisation, S.K. and L.L.R.; methodology, S.K.; software, L.L.R.; validation, S.K. and L.L.R.; formal analysis, L.L.R.; writing—original draft preparation, S.K.; writing—review and editing, L.L.R., E.M., C.N. and L.M.C.; supervision, E.M. and L.M.C. All authors have read and agreed to the published version of the manuscript.

Funding: This work was funded by European Union's Horizon 2020 Research and Innovation Programmes under Grant Agreement No. 883273 (AI4HEALTHSEC) and No. 101007273 (DAIS).

Institutional Review Board Statement: Not applicable.

Informed Consent Statement: Not applicable.

Data Availability Statement: Sample logs can be obtained by contacting the authors.

Acknowledgments: The authors would like to acknowledge the support and funding provided by the AI4HEALTHSEC and DAIS projects. These projects have played a crucial role in the development and execution of the research presented in this paper. We are grateful for the opportunity to collaborate with the esteemed members of these projects and for the resources provided to us throughout the course of our research.

Conflicts of Interest: The authors declare no conflict of interest.

Abbreviations

The following abbreviations are used in this manuscript:

ADB	Android Debug Bridge
ARM architecture	Advanced RISC Machine architecture
API	Application programming interface
AI	Artificial intelligence
APK	Android Package Kit
ARM	Advanced RISC Machine
BMD	Bi-level malware detection
CPU	Control processing unit
CLI	Command0Line Interface
DoS	Denial of service
HIDS	Host intrusion detection system
HIPAA	Health Insurance Portability and Accountability Act
IoMT	Internet of Medical Things
IoT	Internet of Things
MCG	Method call graph
mHealth	mobile Health
PHI	Personal health information
RAM	Random access memory
TOML	Tom's Obvious Minimal Language

References

1. Vermesan, O.; Friess, P.; Guillemin, P.; Giaffreda, R.; Grindvoll, H.; Eisenhauer, M.; Serrano, M.; Moessner, K.; Spirito, M.; Blystad, L.; et al. Internet of things beyond the hype: Research, innovation and deployment. In *Building the Hyperconnected Society-Internet of Things Research and Innovation Value Chains, Ecosystems and Markets*; River Publishers: New York, NY, USA, 2022; pp. 15–118. [CrossRef]
2. Almomani, I.; Al Khayer, A. A comprehensive analysis of the android permissions system. *IEEE Access* **2020**, *8*, 216671–216688. [CrossRef]
3. Sarkar, A.; Goyal, A.; Hicks, D.; Sarkar, D.; Hazra, S. Android application development: A brief overview of android platforms and evolution of security systems. In Proceedings of the 2019 Third International Conference on I-SMAC (IoT in Social, Mobile, Analytics and Cloud)(I-SMAC), Palladam, India, 12–14 December 2019; pp. 73–79. [CrossRef]
4. Garg, S.; Baliyan, N. Comparative analysis of Android and iOS from security viewpoint. *Comput. Sci. Rev.* **2021**, *40*, 100372. [CrossRef]

5. He, D.; Naveed, M.; Gunter, C.; Nahrstedt, K. Security concerns in Android mHealth apps. *AMIA Annu. Symp. Proc.* **2014**, *2014*, 645. [PubMed]
6. Jang, J.; Colletti, A.; Ricklefs, C.; Snyder, H.; Kardonsky, K.; Duggan, E.; Umpierrez, G.; O'Reilly-Shah, V. Implementation of App-Based Diabetes Medication Management: Outpatient and Perioperative Clinical Decision Support. *Curr. Diabetes Rep.* **2021**, *21*, 50. [CrossRef] [PubMed]
7. Halouzka, K.; Burita, L.; Kozak, P. Overview of Cyber Threats in Central European Countries. In Proceedings of the 2021 Communication and Information Technologies (KIT), Vysoke Tatry, Slovakia, 13–15 October 2021; pp. 1–6. [CrossRef]
8. Ramsdell, K.; Esbeck, K. MITRE, Health Cyber, EVOLUTION OF RANSOMWARE (2021). Available online: https://healthcyber.mitre.org/wp-content/uploads/2021/08/Ransomware-Paper-V2.pdf (accessed on 20 February 2023).
9. Kettani, H.; Cannistra, R. On cyber threats to smart digital environments. In Proceedings of the 2nd International Conference on Smart Digital Environment, Rabat, Morocco, 18–20 October 2018; pp. 183–188. [CrossRef]
10. Bhosale, K.; Nenova, M.; Iliev, G. A study of cyber attacks: In the healthcare sector. In Proceedings of the 2021 Sixth Junior Conference on Lighting (Lighting), Gabrovo, Bulgaria, 23–25 September 2021; pp. 1–6. [CrossRef]
11. Binbusayyis, A.; Alaskar, H.; Vaiyapuri, T.; Dinesh, M. An investigation and comparison of machine learning approaches for intrusion detection in IoMT network. *J. Supercomput.* **2022**, *78*, 17403–17422. [CrossRef] [PubMed]
12. Razdan, S.; Sharma, S. Internet of Medical Things (IoMT): Overview, emerging technologies, and case studies. *IETE Tech. Rev.* **2022**, *39*, 775–788. [CrossRef]
13. Hatzivasilis, G.; Soultatos, O.; Ioannidis, S.; Verikoukis, C.; Demetriou, G.; Tsatsoulis, C. Review of security and privacy for the Internet of Medical Things (IoMT). In Proceedings of the 2019 15th International Conference on Distributed Computing in Sensor Systems (DCOSS), Santorini, Greece, 29–31 May 2019; pp. 457–464. [CrossRef]
14. Vaiyapuri, T.; Binbusayyis, A.; Varadarajan, V. Security, privacy and trust in IoMT enabled smart healthcare system: A systematic review of current and future trends. *Int. J. Adv. Comput. Sci. Appl.* **2021**, *12, 731–737.* [CrossRef]
15. Koutras, D.; Stergiopoulos, G.; Dasaklis, T.; Kotzanikolaou, P.; Glynos, D.; Douligeris, C. Security in IoMT communications: A survey. *Sensors* **2020**, *20*, 4828. [CrossRef]
16. Zhang, Y.; Deng, R.; Zheng, D.; Li, J.; Wu, P.; Cao, J. Efficient and robust certificateless signature for data crowdsensing in cloud-assisted industrial IoT. *IEEE Trans. Ind. Inform.* **2019**, *15*, 5099–5108. [CrossRef]
17. Martinez, A.; Pérez, M.; Ruiz-Martinez, A. A comprehensive review of the state of the art on security and privacy issues in Healthcare. *ACM Comput. Surv.* **2022**. [CrossRef]
18. Otoum, Y.; Chamola, V.; Nayak, A. Federated and Transfer Learning-Empowered Intrusion Detection for IoT Applications. *IEEE Internet Things Mag.* **2022**, *5*, 50–54. [CrossRef]
19. Wright, A.; Aaron, S.; Bates, D. The big phish: Cyberattacks against US healthcare systems. *J. Gen. Intern. Med.* **2016**, *31*, 1115–1118. [CrossRef] [PubMed]
20. Divakaran, J.; Prashanth, S.; Mohammad, G.; Shitharth, D.; Mohanty, S.; Arvind, C.; Srihari, K.; Abdullah, R.Y.; Sundramurthy, V.F. Improved handover authentication in fifth-generation communication networks using fuzzy evolutionary optimisation with nanocore elements in mobile healthcare applications. *J. Healthc. Eng.* **2022**, *2022*, 2500377. [CrossRef] [PubMed]
21. Sihag, V.; Swami, A.; Vardhan, M.; Singh, P. Signature based malicious behavior detection in android. In Proceedings of the International Conference on Computing Science, Communication and Security, Gujarat, India, 26–27 March 2020; pp. 251–262. [CrossRef]
22. Lee, J.; Lee, Y.; Jin, M.; Kim, J.; Hong, J. Analysis of application installation logs on android systems. In Proceedings of the 34th ACM/SIGapplication Symposium on Applied Computing, Limassol, Cyprus, 8–12 April 2019; pp. 2140–2145. [CrossRef]
23. Sasidharan, S.; Thomas, C. ProDroid—An Android malware detection framework based on profile hidden Markov model. *Pervasive Mob. Comput.* **2021**, *72*, 101336. [CrossRef]
24. Wang, H.; Zhang, W.; He, H. You are what the permissions told me! Android malware detection based on hybrid tactics. *J. Inf. Secur. Appl.* **2022**, *66*, 103159. [CrossRef]
25. Zhang, X.; Mathur, A.; Zhao, L.; Rahmat, S.; Niyaz, Q.; Javaid, A.; Yang, X. An early detection of android malware using system calls based machine learning model. In Proceedings of the 17th International Conference on Availability, Reliability and Security, Vienna, Austria, 23–26 August 2022; pp. 1–9. [CrossRef]
26. Jerbi, M.; Dagdia, Z.; Bechikh, S.; Said, L. Android malware detection as a bi-level problem. *Comput. Secur.* **2022**, *121*, 102825. [CrossRef]
27. Ito, K.; Hasegawa, H.; Yamaguchi, Y.; Shimada, H. Detecting privacy information abuse by android apps from API call logs. In Proceedings of the Advances in Information and Computer Security: 13th International Workshop on Security, IWSEC 2018, Sendai, Japan, 3–5 September 2018; pp. 143–157._10. [CrossRef]
28. Khariwal, K.; Singh, J.; Arora, A. IPDroid: Android malware detection using intents and permissions. In Proceedings of the 2020 Fourth World Conference on Smart Trends in Systems, Security and Sustainability (WorldS4), London, UK, 27–28 July 2020; pp. 197–202. [CrossRef]
29. Ahmad, M.; Costamagna, V.; Crispo, B.; Bergadano, F.; Zhauniarovich, Y. StaDART: Addressing the problem of dynamic code updates in the security analysis of android applications. *J. Syst. Softw.* **2020**, *159*, 110386. [CrossRef]
30. Arzt, S.; Rasthofer, S.; Fritz, C.; Bodden, E.; Bartel, A.; Klein, J.; Le Traon, Y.; Octeau, D.; McDaniel, P. Flowdroid: Precise context, flow, field, object-sensitive and lifecycle-aware taint analysis for android apps. *ACM Sigplan Not.* **2014**, *49*, 259–269. [CrossRef]

31. Androguard: Reverse Engineering, Malware and Goodware Analysis of Android Applications. Available online: https://code.google.com/p/androguard/ (accessed on 20 February 2023).
32. Wei, F.; Roy, S.; Ou, X. Amandroid: A precise and general inter-component data flow analysis framework for security vetting of android apps. *ACM Trans. Priv. Secur. (TOPS)* **2018**, *21*, 1–32. [CrossRef]
33. Ribeiro, J.; Saghezchi, F.; Mantas, G.; Rodriguez, J.; Shepherd, S.; Abd-Alhameed, R. An autonomous host-based intrusion detection system for android mobile devices. *Mob. Netw. Appl.* **2020**, *25*, 164–172._14. [CrossRef]
34. Liu, M.; Xue, Z.; Xu, X.; Zhong, C.; Chen, J. Host-based intrusion detection system with system calls: Review and future trends. *ACM Comput. Surv. (CSUR)* **2018**, *51*, 1–36. [CrossRef]
35. Khadidos, A.; Shitharth, S.; Khadidos, A.; Sangeetha, K.; Alyoubi, K. Healthcare data security using IoT sensors based on random hashing mechanism. *J. Sens.* **2022**, *2022*, 8457116. [CrossRef]
36. Singh, S.; Sulthana, R.; Shewale, T.; Chamola, V.; Benslimane, A.; Sikdar, B. Machine-learning-assisted security and privacy provisioning for edge computing: A survey. *IEEE Internet Things J.* **2021**, *9*, 236–260. [CrossRef]
37. Zhang, J.; Chen, B.; Zhao, Y.; Cheng, X.; Hu, F. Data security and privacy-preserving in edge computing paradigm: Survey and open issues. *IEEE Access* **2018**, *6*, 18209–18237. [CrossRef]
38. Greco, L.; Percannella, G.; Ritrovato, P.; Tortorella, F.; Vento, M. Trends in IoT based solutions for health care: Moving AI to the edge. *Pattern Recognit. Lett.* **2020**, *135*, 346–353. [CrossRef]

applied sciences

MDPI

Article

A Maximum-Entropy Fuzzy Clustering Approach for Cancer Detection When Data Are Uncertain

Mario Fordellone [1,†], Ilaria De Benedictis [2,*,†], Dario Bruzzese [3] and Paolo Chiodini [1]

1 Medical Statistics Unit, Universitiy of Campania "Luigi Vanvitelli", 81100 Naples, Italy
2 Universitiy of Campania "Luigi Vanvitelli", 81100 Naples, Italy
3 Department of Public Health, University of Naples Federico II, 80131 Naples, Italy
* Correspondence: ilaria.debenedictis@gmail.com
† These authors contributed equally to this work.

Abstract: (1) Background: Cancer is a leading cause of death worldwide and each year, approximately 400,000 children develop cancer. Early detection of cancer greatly increases the chances for successful treatment, while screening aims to identify individuals with findings suggestive of specific cancer or pre-cancer before they have developed symptoms. Precise detection, however, often mainly relies on human experience and this could suffer from human error and error with a visual inspection. (2) Methods: The research of statistical approaches to analyze the complex structure of data is increasing. In this work, an entropy-based fuzzy clustering technique for interval-valued data (EFC-ID) for cancer detection is suggested. (3) Results: The application on the Breast dataset shows that EFC-ID performs better than the conventional FKM in terms of AUC value (EFC-ID = 0.96, FKM = 0.88), sensitivity (EFC-ID = 0.90, FKM = 0.64), and specificity (EFC-ID = 0.93, FKM = 0.92). Furthermore, the application on the Multiple Myeloma data shows that EFC-ID performs better than the conventional FKM in terms of Chi-squared (EFC-ID = 91.64, FKM = 88.26), Accuracy rate (EFC-ID = 0.71, FKM = 0.60), and Adjusted Rand Index (EFC-ID = 0.33, FKM = 0.21). (4) Conclusions: In all cases, the proposed approach has shown good performance in identifying the natural partition and the advantages of the use of EFC-ID have been detailed illustrated.

Keywords: cancer detection; cancer classification; unsupervised classification; entropy regularization procedure; penalized classification model; interval-valued data; imprecise data

Citation: Fordellone, M.; De Benedictis, I.; Bruzzese, D.; Chiodini, P. A Maximum-Entropy Fuzzy Clustering Approach for Cancer Detection When Data Are Uncertain. *Appl. Sci.* **2023**, *13*, 2191. https://doi.org/10.3390/app13042191

Academic Editors: Stefano Silvestri and Francesco Gargiulo

Received: 31 December 2022
Revised: 2 February 2023
Accepted: 6 February 2023
Published: 8 February 2023

1. Introduction

Cancer is a leading cause of death worldwide, accounting for nearly 10 million yearly deaths. Moreover, each year, approximately 400,000 children develop cancer. Cancer mortality is reduced when cases are detected and treated early. There are two components of early detection: early diagnosis and screening. Early detection of cancer greatly increases the chances for successful treatment, while screening aims to identify individuals with findings suggestive of specific cancer or pre-cancer before they have developed symptoms. Precise detection, however, often mainly relies on human experience and this could suffer from human error and error with a visual inspection. To try to solve these problems there is a demand for statistical/mathematical algorithms (e.g., supervised and unsupervised classification models, machine learning approaches, latent class analysis, etc.) for the early detection of tumors. Then, the efficiency and effectiveness of early diagnosis and screening can be increased if tumors are detected and classified automatically through computers [1].

In the conventional statistical data analysis, usually point data are analyzed, i.e., exact results of measurements that consist of features of the reference sample. These values can be either directly observed as results of measurements (e.g., systolic and/or diastolic blood pressure of a person) or can be observed as counts of a category (i.e., group) representing called events (e.g., the gender of that person). However, in many real life applications, the results of these measurements are never precise, and some degree of uncertainty that characterizes them exists.

The uncertainty of a measurement can be defined as the interval on the measurement scale within which the true value lies with a specified probability when all sources of error have been taken into account [2]. The quantification of this uncertainty could become an important issue to treat in the area of the statistical quality of data. In the medical field, chemists/biologists should be expected as standard practice to provide a statement of the uncertainty alongside their estimated measure to make it into account in the data analysis step [2,3]. In other words, a measurement cannot be properly interpreted without knowledge of its uncertainty. In clinical practice, many rules and guidelines have been proposed aiming to provide a general overview of the uncertainty concept in the measurement step and make it into account for the data interpretation [4]. For some example, the reader can refer to [5] which provided a review where a rule-based approach is suggested with a number of the more common rules tabulated for the routine calculation of measurement uncertainty, and [6] which provided a systematic review regarding uncertainty tolerance in the health and healthcare-related outcomes.

The research of statistical approaches to analyze the complex structures of data is increasing. A lot of attention is focused on the methodologies to treat complex datasets where the data features are uncertain (called *imprecise data*). The simplest structure of *imprecise data* is the *interval-valued data* [7–9]. An interval-valued data can be formalized as $x_{ij} = [\underline{x}_{ij}, \bar{x}_{ij}]$, $i = 1, \ldots, n$ and $j = 1, \ldots, J$, where x_{ij} is the j-th interval-valued variable observed on the i-th observation, $\underline{x}_{ij}$ and $\bar{x}_{ij}$ denote the lower and upper bounds of the interval, respectively, (i.e., the extreme values registered for the j-th interval-valued variable on the i-th observation). Then, in a $n \times J$ interval-valued data matrix, each observation is represented as a hyperrectangle (in $\mathbb{R}^J$) having 2^J vertices [10]. However, in this work, we use a simpler notation of interval-valued data, consisting to consider centers and radii, separately. In particular *i* for the centers we indicate $\mathbf{C}$ the $n \times J$ *centers matrix* whose generic element $c_{ij} = 2^{-1}(\underline{x}_{ij} + \bar{x}_{ij})$ is the center (i.e., the midpoint) of the associated interval; *ii* for the radii we define $\mathbf{R}$ the $n \times J$ *radii matrix* whose generic element $r_{ij} = 2^{-1}(\bar{x}_{ij} - \underline{x}_{ij})$ is the radius of the associated interval. Then, by considering this reformulation of the interval-valued data, the complete interval-valued matrix can be formalized as follows:

$$\mathbf{X} \equiv \{x_{ij} = [c_{ij}, r_{ij}] : i = 1, \ldots, n; j = 1, \ldots, J\}. \quad (1)$$

In Figure 1, a bi-dimensional artificial dataset is represented. In this dataset two groups of 50 subjects classified as normotensive (black color with $\mu' = [75, 140]$) and hypertensive (red color with $\mu' = [100, 210]$) have been simulated. In the left plot of Figure 1, the dataset is represented in ordinary form (i.e., with a radius equal to zero), while in the right one, the dataset is represented in interval-valued form (i.e., with a radius bigger than zero). In the literature on data analysis, a great deal of attention is paid to statistical methods to treat interval-valued data, in different research areas [7–9,11–13].

In a classical cluster analysis framework different interesting methods have been suggested. In particular, Ref. [14] proposed a clustering method for symbolic data; Ref. [15] proposed a similarity measure for comparing interval-valued data and a modified agglomerative method for clustering symbolic data. Ref. [16] proposed a partitional dynamic clustering method for interval data based on adaptive Hausdorff distances; Ref. [17] suggested clustering methods for interval data based on single adaptive distances.

However, an interesting line of research has focused on clustering of interval-valued data based on fuzzy approaches, where the weighting exponent m controls the extent of membership sharing between fuzzy clusters [7,18–21]. Ref. [22] remarked that this "strange" parameter is unnatural and has no physical meaning. Then, in the above objective function, we may remove m, but in this case, the procedure cannot generate the membership update Equations [23]. To this purpose, Refs. [22,24] suggested a new approach to fuzzy clustering by proposing the so-called Maximum Entropy Inference Method. The idea underlies the paper by [25] where the trade-off between fuzziness and compactness is dealt with by introducing a unique objective function reformulating the maximum entropy method in terms of regularization of the fuzzy c-means (FCM) function.

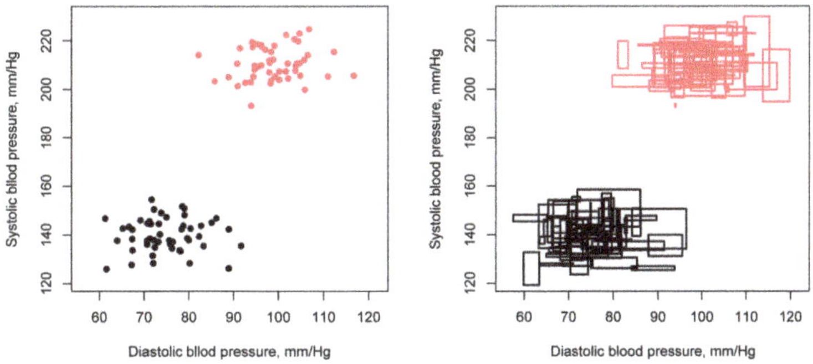

Figure 1. Artificial data generated by two bi-variate Normal distributions. To the left we have a dataset in an ordinary form; to the right, we have an interval-valued dataset.

In the literature, many authors proposed the entropy-based approach as regularization in fuzzy clustering modeling. In particular, Ref. [26] proposed an entropy-based fuzzy clustering method that automatically identifies the number and initial locations of cluster centers. Successively, it removes all data points having a similarity larger than a threshold with the chosen cluster center. The procedure is repeated till all data points are removed; Refs. [27,28] suggested a generalized objective function with additional variables. These authors consider a covariance matrix and show an equivalence between their Kullback–Leibler (KL) fuzzy clustering and the Gaussian mixture model. The method of fuzzy clustering using the KL information is called the entropy-based method of FCM; Ref. [29] suggested an axiomatic derivation of the Maximum Entropy Inference (and also of the possibilistic) clustering approach, based on a unifying principle of physics, that of Extreme Physical Information (EPI) defined by [30]; Ref. [23] suggest fuzzy unsupervised clustering models based on Shannon entropy regularization in order to classify time-varying data; Ref. [31] proposed a new fuzzy clustering method based on FCM and the relative entropy is added to its objective function as a regularization function to maximize the dissimilarity between clusters; Ref. [32] presented an entropy-based FCM segmentation method that incorporates the uncertainty of classification of individual pixels within the classical framework of FCM; Ref. [33] showed a novel method considering noise intelligently based on the existing FCM approach, called adaptive-FCM and its extended version (adaptive-REFCM) in combination with relative entropy; more recently, Ref. [34] proposed an entropy-based regularization approach to fuzzify the partition and to weight features, enabling the method to capture more complex patterns, identify significant features, and yield better performance facing high-dimensional data. Notice that the here-cited proposals on the models with entropy-based regularization, regard applications on ordinary point data.

Following this research line, in this work, an entropy-based fuzzy clustering technique for interval-valued data for cancer detection is suggested. The novelty of this statistical approach is to consider the uncertainty of the data in the classification procedure using the standard deviation of data variables as a measure of the uncertainty. Moreover, the presence of an entropy-based regularization redresses the uncertainty among the statistical units, especially in the boundary region guarantying a more precise classification with respect to the other competitor models. The model is named entropy-based fuzzy clustering for interval-valued data (EFC-ID). Since for all kinds of cancer, it is particularly important to improve the accuracy of early diagnosis, and that conventional early diagnosis mainly relies on human experience, an automatic classification procedure can be improved the cancer detection in screening stages.

The paper is organized as follows: in Section 2 the principal ingredients of EFC-ID approach are provided; in Section 3 the mathematical structure and the algorithm of the model are described; in Section 4 a detailed simulation study and comparison with other fuzzy and not fuzzy clustering models for interval-valued data is proposed; in Section 5 the results obtained by the EFC-ID application on empirical data are shown; finally, in Section 6 some concluding remarks and the lines for future research in this field are provided.

2. Principal Ingredients

In this section, the principal ingredients of the entropy-based fuzzy clustering approach for interval-valued data (EFC-ID) are provided. The fundamental ingredients of this classification model are *(i)* the dissimilarity/distance measure to consider, and *(ii)* the entropy regularization approach applied in the fuzzy clustering framework.

2.1. Euclidean Distance

The generic interval-valued data pertaining to the i-th observation with respect to the j-th interval-valued feature can be shown as the pair (c_{ij}, r_{ij}), $i = 1, \ldots, n$ and $j = 1, \ldots, J$, where c_{ij} denotes the center and r_{ij} the radius of the interval.

In the literature, several metrics have been suggested for interval-valued. In this paper, we adopt a weighted distance measure, proposed by [35]. In this case, the distance between each pair of observations is measured by separately considering the distances for the centers and the radii of the interval-valued data and using a suitable weighting system for such distance components. Formally, by considering the i-th and i'-th observations, we have

$$d(\tilde{\mathbf{x}}_i, \tilde{\mathbf{x}}_{i'}) = \left[w_c^2 d^2(\mathbf{c}_i, \mathbf{c}_{i'}) + w_r^2 d^2(\mathbf{r}_i, \mathbf{r}_{i'})\right]^{\frac{1}{2}}, \tag{2}$$

where $d^2(\mathbf{c}_i, \mathbf{c}_{i'}) = \|\mathbf{c}_i - \mathbf{c}_{i'}\|^2$ is the squared Euclidean distance between the centers and $d^2(\mathbf{r}_i, \mathbf{r}_{i'}) = \|\mathbf{r}_i - \mathbf{r}_{i'}\|^2$ is the squared Euclidean distance between the radii, while w_c and w_r are suitable weight for the center component and the radius component, respectively.

Moreover, we assume the following conditions: *(i)* $w_c + w_r = 1$ (*normalization condition*) and *(ii)* $w_c \geq w_r \geq 0$ (*coherence condition*). In particular, by means of the *coherence condition* we manage to exclude the anomalous case where the radius component, which represents the uncertainty around the centers of the interval-valued data, has more importance than the center component, which represents the core information of each interval-valued datum. Furthermore, through the *normalization condition* we can easily assess, in a comparative fashion, the contributions of the center and radius components in the distance computation.

The distance measure shown in Equation (2) has the following properties:

1. $d(\tilde{\mathbf{x}}_i, \tilde{\mathbf{x}}_{i'})$ is a metric, i.e., the properties of identity, non-negativity, symmetry, and the triangular inequality are satisfied (for details see [8]).
2. $d(\tilde{\mathbf{x}}_i, \tilde{\mathbf{x}}_{i'})$ is computationally easy and theoretically intuitive.
3. $d(\tilde{\mathbf{x}}_i, \tilde{\mathbf{x}}_{i'})$ tunes suitable the contribution of the (squared) distance measures of the center and radius components of the interval-valued data by means of a weighting system capable to assign objectively (by means of an optimization process) or subjectively (by means of the expertise and experience of the researcher) weights to the two distance components.

2.2. Shannon Entropy Regularization

In this paper, we focus on the entropy regularization approach in a fuzzy clustering framework because is known that the maximum entropy principle, as applied to fuzzy clustering, provides a new perspective to face the problem of fuzzifying the clusterization of the units, while ensuring the maximum of compactness of the obtained clusters [23,33]. The former objective is achieved by maximizing the entropy (i.e., the uncertainty) of the classification of the units into the various clusters. The latter objective is obtained by constraining the above maximization process in such a way as to minimize the overall distance of the units from the cluster prototypes (i.e., to maximize cluster compactness). In other words, we use an entropy-based FCM segmentation method that incorporates the uncertainty of classification of individuals within the classical framework of FCM [32].

Through this technique, the Shannon entropy measure is employed in the objective function of FCM to redress the uncertainty among the statistical units, especially in the boundary region. Additionally, given the nature of our data (i.e., interval-valued), a weighted distance measure proposed by [35] is adopted. In this case, the distance between each pair of observations is measured by separately considering the distances for the centers and the radii of the interval-valued data and using a suitable weighting system for such distance components.

3. Model and Algorithm

The proposed model has been processed through the statistical software R Studio release 2022.02.0. The algorithm and dataset used in the simulation study and empirical applications are uploaded on the following web page: https://github.com/mfordellone/EFC-ID (accessed on 1 February 2023).

3.1. Optimization Problem

Let $\mathbf{X}$ be a $n \times J$ interval-valued data matrix. Given the distance measure shown in Equation (2), in which we assume that the weights (i.e., w_c and w_r) are objectively computed during the clustering process, we can classify observations within a fuzzy framework, by means of the entropy-based fuzzy clustering (EFC-ID) model, characterized as follows:

$$\begin{aligned} \min \quad & J_{EFC-ID}(\mathbf{U},\tilde{\mathbf{X}},w) = \sum_{i=1}^{n}\sum_{g=1}^{k} u_{ig}\left[w_c^2 d^2(\mathbf{c}_i,\mathbf{c}_g) + w_r^2 d^2(\mathbf{r}_i,\mathbf{r}_g)\right] + \\ & + p\sum_{i=1}^{n}\sum_{g=1}^{k} u_{ig} log(u_{ig}) \\ \text{s.t.} \quad & \sum_{g=1}^{k} u_{ig} = 1, u_{ig} \geq 0, \\ & w_c \geq w_r \geq 0, w_c + w_r = 1. \end{aligned} \tag{3}$$

where u_{ig} indicates the membership degree of the i-th unit in the g-th cluster; $d^2(\tilde{\mathbf{x}}_i,\tilde{\mathbf{x}}_g)$ is the squared version of Equation (2) between the i-th unit and the centroid in the g-th cluster; $\mathbf{c}_i$ and $\mathbf{r}_i$ are the centers and radii of the i-th unit, respectively; $\mathbf{c}_g$ and $\mathbf{r}_g$ are the centroids of the centers and radii in the g-th cluster, respectively; $p\sum_{i=1}^{n}\sum_{g=1}^{k} u_{ig} log(u_{ig})$ is the *fuzzy entropy function*; p is a weight factor, called *degree of fuzzy entropy*, similar to the weight exponent m used in the fuzzy k-means approach and represents the uncertainty associated with each statistical unit which is defined as the Shannon entropy [22–24]. To simplify things, we can set $w_c = (1 - w)$ and $w_r = w$. In this way, the *normalization condition* is satisfied and the *coherence condition* turns into $0 \leq w \leq 0.5$. Then, the objective function became:

$$\begin{aligned} \min \quad & J_{EFC-ID}(\mathbf{U},\tilde{\mathbf{X}},w) = \sum_{i=1}^{n}\sum_{g=1}^{k} u_{ig}\left[(1-w)^2 d^2(\mathbf{c}_i,\mathbf{c}_g) + w^2 d^2(\mathbf{r}_i,\mathbf{r}_g)\right] + \\ & + p\sum_{i=1}^{n}\sum_{g=1}^{k} u_{ig} log(u_{ig}) \\ \text{s.t.} \quad & \sum_{g=1}^{k} u_{ig} = 1, u_{ig} \geq 0, \\ & 0 \leq w \leq 0.5 \end{aligned} \tag{4}$$

By solving the constrained quadratic minimization problem shown in Equation (4) *via* Lagrangian multiplier method, we obtain the optimal solutions u_{ig} and w. In particular, by considering the following Lagrangian function:

$$L_m(u_{ig},\lambda,w) = \sum_{i=1}^{n}\sum_{g=1}^{k} u_{ig}\Big[(1-w)^2 d^2(\mathbf{c}_i,\mathbf{c}_g) + w^2 d^2(\mathbf{r}_i,\mathbf{r}_g)\Big] + \\ + p\sum_{i=1}^{n}\sum_{g=1}^{k} u_{ig} log(u_{ig}) - \lambda\left(\sum_{g=1}^{k} u_{ig} - 1\right), \tag{5}$$

and setting the first partial derivatives with respect u_{ig} and λ equal zero, we obtain

$$\frac{\partial L_m(u_{ig},\lambda,w)}{\partial u_{ig}} = 0 \Leftrightarrow \Big[(1-w)^2 d^2(\mathbf{c}_i,\mathbf{c}_g) + w^2 d^2(\mathbf{r}_i,\mathbf{r}_g)\Big] + \\ + p(log(u_{ig})+1) - \lambda = 0, \tag{6}$$

$$\frac{\partial L_m(u_{ig},\lambda,w)}{\partial \lambda} = 0 \Leftrightarrow \sum_{g=1}^{k} u_{ig} - 1 = 0. \tag{7}$$

From Equation (6), we obtain

$$log(u_{ig}) = \frac{1}{p}\Big[\lambda - \Big[(1-w)^2 d^2(\mathbf{c}_i,\mathbf{c}_g) + w^2 d^2(\mathbf{r}_i,\mathbf{r}_g)\Big]\Big] - 1, \tag{8}$$

and then

$$u_{ig} = \exp\left[\frac{\lambda}{p} - \frac{1}{p}\Big[(1-w)^2 d^2(\mathbf{c}_i,\mathbf{c}_g) + w^2 d^2(\mathbf{r}_i,\mathbf{r}_g)\Big] - 1\right]. \tag{9}$$

By considering Equation (7):

$$\exp\left(\frac{\lambda}{p} - 1\right) = \frac{1}{\sum_{g=1}^{k}\left[\dfrac{1}{\exp\big[(1/p)[(1-w)^2 d^2(\mathbf{c}_i,\mathbf{c}_g) + w^2 d^2(\mathbf{r}_i,\mathbf{r}_g)]\big]}\right]}, \tag{10}$$

and by replacing Equation (10) in Equation (9), we obtain

$$u_{ig} = \frac{1}{\sum_{g'=1}^{k}\left[\dfrac{\exp\big[(1/p)[(1-w)^2 d^2(\mathbf{c}_i,\mathbf{c}_g) + w^2 d^2(\mathbf{r}_i,\mathbf{r}_g)]\big]}{\exp\big[(1/p)[(1-w)^2 d^2(\mathbf{c}_i,\mathbf{c}_{g'}) + w^2 d^2(\mathbf{r}_i,\mathbf{r}_{g'})]\big]}\right]}. \tag{11}$$

The normalization condition for w is implicitly satisfied. To take into account the *coherence condition*, observing that Equation (5) is a parabola with respect to w, the optimum value of w results in the minimum between the abscissa of its vertex and 0.5 [8], i.e.,

$$w = \min\left\{\frac{\sum_{i=1}^{n}\sum_{g=1}^{k} u_{ig}\left[d^2(\mathbf{c}_i,\mathbf{c}_g)\right]}{\sum_{i=1}^{n}\sum_{g=1}^{k} u_{ig}\left[d^2(\mathbf{c}_i,\mathbf{c}_g) + d^2(\mathbf{r}_i,\mathbf{r}_g)\right]}, 0.5\right\}. \tag{12}$$

Finally, we compute the centroids for the centers and radii through the steps shown in Equations (13) and (14), respectively.

$$
\begin{aligned}
&\frac{\partial J_{EFC-ID}(\mathbf{U},\tilde{\mathbf{X}},w)}{\partial \mathbf{c}_g} = 0 \Leftrightarrow \\
&\sum_{i=1}^{n} u_{ig}\left[(1-w)^2 d^2(\mathbf{c}_i,\mathbf{c}_g) + w^2 d^2(\mathbf{r}_i,\mathbf{r}_g)\right] + p\sum_{i=1}^{n} u_{ig}log(u_{ig}) = 0 \Leftrightarrow \\
&\sum_{i=1}^{n} u_{ig}\left[(1-w)^2(\mathbf{c}_i^2 + 2\mathbf{c}_i\mathbf{c}_g + \mathbf{c}_g^2) + w^2(\mathbf{r}_i^2 + 2\mathbf{r}_i\mathbf{r}_g + \mathbf{r}_g^2)\right] \\
&+ p\sum_{i=1}^{n} u_{ig}log(u_{ig}) = 0 \Leftrightarrow \\
&\sum_{i=1}^{n} u_{ig}\left[(1-w)^2(\mathbf{c}_i + \mathbf{c}_g)\right] = 0 \Leftrightarrow \\
&\mathbf{c}_g = \frac{\sum_{i=1}^{n} u_{ig}\mathbf{c}_i}{\sum_{i=1}^{n} u_{ig}}.
\end{aligned}
\tag{13}
$$

$$
\begin{aligned}
&\frac{\partial J_{EFC-ID}(\mathbf{U},\tilde{\mathbf{X}},w)}{\partial \mathbf{r}_g} = 0 \Leftrightarrow \\
&\sum_{i=1}^{n} u_{ig}\left[(1-w)^2 d^2(\mathbf{c}_i,\mathbf{c}_g) + w^2 d^2(\mathbf{r}_i,\mathbf{r}_g)\right] + p\sum_{i=1}^{n} u_{ig}log(u_{ig}) = 0 \Leftrightarrow \\
&\sum_{i=1}^{n} u_{ig}\left[(1-w)^2(\mathbf{c}_i^2 + 2\mathbf{c}_i\mathbf{c}_g + \mathbf{c}_g^2) + w^2(\mathbf{r}_i^2 + 2\mathbf{r}_i\mathbf{r}_g + \mathbf{r}_g^2)\right] \\
&+ p\sum_{i=1}^{n} u_{ig}log(u_{ig}) = 0 \Leftrightarrow \\
&\sum_{i=1}^{n} u_{ig}\left[w^2(\mathbf{r}_i + \mathbf{r}_g)\right] = 0 \Leftrightarrow \\
&\mathbf{r}_g = \frac{\sum_{i=1}^{n} u_{ig}\mathbf{r}_i}{\sum_{i=1}^{n} u_{ig}}.
\end{aligned}
\tag{14}
$$

In order to show an example of application we consider the bi-dimensional interval-valued dataset described in Introduction. In Table 1 are shown the mean and variance of centers and radii used to generate 300 observations of a bi-dimensional interval-valued data with a structure of three groups (i.e., 100 observations for each cluster).

Table 1. Clusters mean and variance of an artificial interval-valued dataset.

	Centers				*Radii*		
	Cluster 1	Cluster 2	Cluster 3		Cluster 1	Cluster 2	Cluster 3
μ_1	0	−10	10	μ_1	0	−3	3
μ_2	−10	10	10	μ_2	−3	3	3
σ_1^2	5	5	5	σ_1^2	2	2	2
σ_2^2	5	5	5	σ_2^2	2	2	2

By applying the EFC-ID model on this dataset, we have the results shown in Figure 2. Then, the centroids of centers and radii have been correctly identified with the Adjusted Rand index (ARI) value equal to 1.

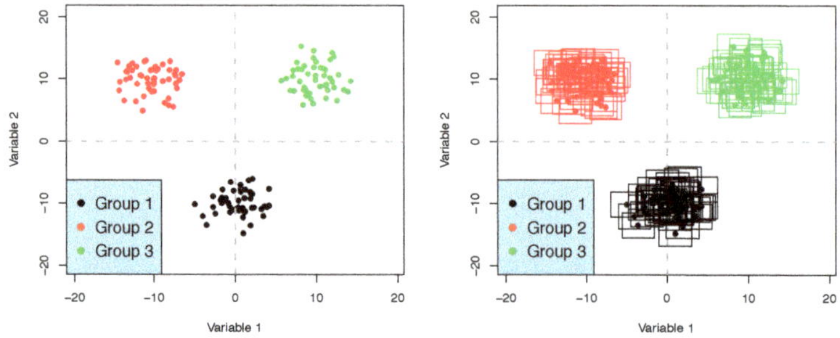

Figure 2. Partition identified by the EFC-ID model of an artificial interval-valued data. The clusters are highlighted through different colors.

3.2. Entropy-Based Fuzzy Clustering Algorithm

In the following, we show the algorithm for the EFC-ID model. Fixed p (*degree of fuzzy entropy*), k (the number of clusters) and $maxiter$ (the maximum number of iterations), and set iter = 0, the EFC-ID Algorithm 1 is composed of the following steps:

Algorithm 1 Entropy-based fuzzy clustering algorithm.

1: Randomly generate the membership matrix $\mathbf{U}^{iter}$ subject to constraints shown in (4);
iter = iter+1
2: Given $\mathbf{U}^{iter-1}$, compute the centroids for the centers and radii $\mathbf{C}^{iter-1}$ and $\mathbf{R}^{iter-1}$;
3: Compute w^{iter-1} according Equation (12);
4: Update the membership matrix $\mathbf{U}^{iter}$ according Equation (11);
5: **if** $\|\mathbf{U}^{iter} - \mathbf{U}^{iter-1}\| > \epsilon$ & **iter** $<$ maxiter ;
go to step 2.
6: **else**
exit loop.
7: **Return**: the membership matrix **U**,
the centroids for the centers and radii **C** and **R**,
the weight w,
the number of iteration *iter*.

Notice that, given the constraints on **U**, the algorithm can be expected to be rather sensitive to *local optima*. For this reason, it is recommended the use of some randomly started runs to find the best solution.

3.3. Cluster Validity Indices

The first step of the EFC-ID application is the choice of the optimal *degree of fuzzy entropy*. For this purpose, two cluster validity indices are considered: the *partition coefficient* index (V_{PC}) and the *partition entropy* measure (V_{PE}). The former one can be viewed as a mean over the n units of Onicescu's *information energy* [36] in a fuzzy setting:

$$V_{PC} = \frac{1}{n} \sum_{i=1}^{n} \sum_{g=1}^{k} u_{ig}^2, \tag{15}$$

the latter one is the same measure in an entropy-based setting [23]:

$$V_{PE} = -\frac{1}{n} \sum_{i=1}^{n} \sum_{g=1}^{k} u_{ig} log(u_{ig}). \tag{16}$$

Both V_{PC} and V_{PE} measure the degree of the overlapping among clusters. Moreover, V_{PC} is a decreasing function of p in the fuzzy entropy objective function, while V_{PE} is an increasing function of this parameter.

Then, given the number of clusters k, an optimal value of p is the value at which $V_{PC} = V_{PE}$, obtaining a good compromise between maximizing the separation of clusters (i.e., the V_{PC} minimization), and optimizing the *fuzziness* degree of classification (i.e., the V_{PE} maximization). This criterion can be used to choose the optimal number of clusters also.

4. Simulation Study

To investigate the performance of the entropy-based fuzzy clustering (EFC-ID) model, a simulation study has been carried out. The aim of this simulation study is to study the behavior of EFC-ID in different cases that could be occurred in empirical applications (e.g., well-separated and not well-separated clusters, presence of fuzzy points, groups structure applied on centers, on radii, or on both, etc.). In particular, is very interesting to study the EFC-ID model in terms of weights (w) estimate and identification of the natural partition for different *degrees of entropy*.

The proposed model has also been compared with other fuzzy clustering models for interval-valued data, i.e., fuzzy k-means clustering (FKM) proposed by [35] and fuzzy relational clustering (FRC), and with other crisp models, i.e., hierarchical clustering (HC). Moreover, EFC-ID has been also compared with another version of the entropy-based clustering model, i.e., the entropy-based fuzzy clustering model for point data (here called EFC) and the entropy-based clustering for interval-valued data (EC-ID).
For FRC and HC a dissimilarity measure for interval-valued data based on OR proposed by [37] has been used.

Regarding the simulation scheme, three data generation scenarios have been considered. In each scenario, the simulated dataset is constructed in such a way that two well-separated clusters ($k = 2$) with the same size are generated (i.e., cluster 1: $1, \ldots, n/2$, cluster 2: $n/2 + 1, \ldots, n$). Following the simulation line proposed by [8,19,21], we have:

- *centers-radii scenario*, where the centers and the radii of the interval-valued data generated have a group structure.
- *centers scenario*, where the radii of the interval-valued data are all randomly generated, while the centers of the data generated have a group structure.
- *radii scenario*, where the centers of the interval-valued data are all randomly generated, while the radii of the data generated have a group structure.

In Table 2, the details on the simulated scheme are shown.

Table 2. Data generation in the simulation scheme.

Scenario	Centers	Radii
centers-radii	Cluster 1: U[0, 1]	Cluster 1: U[0, 1]
	Cluster 2: U[3.5, 4.5]	Cluster 2: U[1.5, 2.5]
centers	Cluster 1: U[0, 1]	Cluster 1: U[0, 2]
	Cluster 2: U[3.5, 4.5]	Cluster 2: U[0, 2]
radii	Cluster 1: U[0, 2]	Cluster 1: U[0, 1]
	Cluster 2: U[0, 2]	Cluster 2: U[1.5, 2.5]

Each simulated dataset is composed of one hundred objects ($n = 100$) and two interval-valued variables ($J = 2$). Moreover, for the purpose of evaluating the fuzzy clustering performances of the proposed model in presence of fuzzy points (i.e., data points with memberships degree for each cluster equal to 0.5), three different percentages of fuzzy points (1, 5, and 10%) have been included in the 100 objects. In this way, we have 4 different datasets for each scenario. Note that for each scenario the data-generating process has been replicated 300 times. Finally, we have also set three values of the fuzziness parameter m (1.1, 1.5, and 2, respectively) and three values of the fuzzy entropy parameter p (0.10, 0.20, and 0.40), to detect how the clustering performance is affected by these parameters. For the hierarchical clustering model, HC (i.e., hard clustering), the *single linkage* and the *complete linkage* approaches have been considered.

For evaluating the performance of the model the Frobenius distance (Fdist) computed between the natural (generated) memberships matrix $\mathbf{U}_c$ and the memberships matrix $\hat{\mathbf{U}}$ obtained by the model, has been used. This approach is often used as a stopping rule in some fuzzy clustering algorithms [38]. The Frobenius distance has been then averaged over the 300 simulation runs.

The results are presented in Table 3 with respect to different percentages of fuzzy points, different fuzziness/fuzzy entropy parameters, and different linkage methods. Table 3 shows that the average values of Fdist recorded for EFC-ID and HC are exactly equal to zero in the case of well-separated clusters (i.e., the natural partition is correctly identified by the model), whereas FKM shows Fdist values slightly higher. Another remarkable finding is that the clustering performance of our proposed model is slightly affected by the percentage of fuzzy points with respect to the other models, especially when the *degree of fuzzy entropy* increases. Moreover, EFC-ID shows better performance than all the other approaches especially in the *radii scenario*. Notice that all the results of the not fuzzy approaches can be compared with EFC-ID when $p = 0.2$ (i.e., the medium *fuzziness degree*).

Table 3. Clustering models performance with well-separated clusters (0% of fuzzy points) and not well-separated clusters (1%, 5%, 10% of fuzzy points).

		Centers-Radii		*Centers*		*Radii*	
	Fuzzy Points	**Fdist**	w	**Fdist**	w	**Fdist**	w
	Entropy-based fuzzy clustering for interval-valued data (EFC-ID)						
$p = 0.10$	0%	0.000	0.490	0.000	0.200	0.023	0.500
	1%	0.000	0.500	0.158	0.254	0.140	0.500
	5%	1.578	0.500	1.581	0.380	0.665	0.500
	10%	2.236	0.500	2.236	0.445	1.664	0.500
$p = 0.20$	0%	0.000	0.490	0.000	0.200	0.522	0.492
	1%	0.014	0.500	0.043	0.254	0.513	0.493
	5%	1.480	0.500	1.544	0.381	0.580	0.496
	10%	2.231	0.500	2.232	0.445	0.902	0.500
$p = 0.40$	0%	0.000	0.490	0.000	0.200	7.062	0.338
	1%	0.006	0.500	0.017	0.254	7.028	0.340
	5%	0.996	0.500	1.205	0.388	6.887	0.350
	10%	2.092	0.500	2.097	0.452	6.707	0.364
	Fuzzy *k*-means clustering (FKM)						
$m = 1.10$	0%	0.000	0.490	0.000	0.200	0.021	0.500
	1%	0.016	0.500	0.171	0.254	0.284	0.500
	5%	1.593	0.500	1.623	0.382	1.275	0.500
	10%	2.236	0.500	2.239	0.445	2.178	0.500
$m = 1.50$	0%	0.002	0.492	0.005	0.202	0.632	0.500
	1%	0.014	0.500	0.048	0.257	0.641	0.500
	5%	1.556	0.500	1.729	0.407	0.730	0.500
	10%	2.475	0.500	2.527	0.490	1.112	0.500
$m = 2.00$	0%	0.176	0.500	0.533	0.500	7.071	0.338
	1%	0.178	0.500	0.540	0.500	7.036	0.340
	5%	0.995	0.500	1.603	0.500	6.892	0.350
	10%	2.245	0.500	2.574	0.500	6.708	0.364

Table 3. *Cont.*

	Fuzzy Points	*Centers-Radii* Fdist	w	*Centers* Fdist	w	*Radii* Fdist	w
		Fuzzy relational clustering (FRC)					
$m = 1.10$	0%	5.584	-	5.670	-	5.257	-
	1%	5.815	-	5.630	-	5.315	-
	5%	5.773	-	5.606	-	5.275	-
	10%	5.769	-	5.480	-	5.955	-
$m = 1.50$	0%	0.125	-	3.428	-	4.433	-
	1%	0.496	-	2.565	-	4.232	-
	5%	1.554	-	2.765	-	4.112	-
	10%	2.428	-	2.548	-	4.233	-
$m = 2.00$	0%	0.796	-	1.673	-	8.342	-
	1%	0.827	-	1.842	-	8.661	-
	5%	1.234	-	1.662	-	7.844	-
	10%	2.139	-	1.992	-	7.645	-
		Hierarchical clustering (HC)					
Single linkage	0%	0.000	-	1.400	-	2.144	-
	1%	0.707	-	3.659	-	2.558	-
	5%	1.581	-	8.483	-	2.799	-
	10%	2.283	-	9.105	-	2.721	-
Complete linkage	0%	0.000	-	0.009	-	2.144	-
	1%	0.707	-	0.723	-	2.558	-
	5%	1.581	-	1.613	-	2.799	-
	10%	2.236	-	2.286	-	2.721	-

Concerning the weights, we can note that $wc = ws = 0.5$ in the *centers-radii scenario* (i.e., when the variability of data is balanced between centers and radii) and in the *radii scenario* (i.e., when the variability of radii is higher than the variability of centers and then, ws assume the maximum value). Finally, $wc \geq ws$ when the variability of centers is higher than the variability of radii (i.e., in the *centers scenario*).

In order to complete the evaluation of the proposed model, we have compared the EFC-ID results with the entropy-based fuzzy clustering model for point data (EFC) and the entropy-based clustering (EC-ID) model (i.e., the crisp version for interval-valued data). In Table 4, all the results are reported. The results in Table 4 show that the EFC-ID performance is better also than other entropy-based clustering models.

Table 4. Clustering models performance with well-separated clusters (0% of fuzzy points) and not well-separated clusters (1%, 5%, 10% of fuzzy points).

	Fuzzy Points	*Centers-Radii* Fdist	w	*Centers* Fdist	w	*Radii* Fdist	w
		Entropy-based fuzzy clustering for interval-valued data (EFC-ID)					
$p = 0.10$	0%	0.000	0.490	0.000	0.200	0.023	0.500
	1%	0.000	0.500	0.158	0.254	0.140	0.500
	5%	1.578	0.500	1.581	0.380	0.665	0.500
	10%	2.236	0.500	2.236	0.445	1.664	0.500
$p = 0.20$	0%	0.000	0.490	0.000	0.200	0.522	0.492
	1%	0.014	0.500	0.043	0.254	0.513	0.493
	5%	1.480	0.500	1.544	0.381	0.580	0.496
	10%	2.231	0.500	2.232	0.445	0.902	0.500
$p = 0.40$	0%	0.000	0.490	0.000	0.200	7.062	0.338
	1%	0.006	0.500	0.017	0.254	7.028	0.340
	5%	0.996	0.500	1.205	0.388	6.887	0.350
	10%	2.092	0.500	2.097	0.452	6.707	0.364

Table 4. *Cont.*

	Fuzzy Points	*Centers-Radii* Fdist	w	*Centers* Fdist	w	*Radii* Fdist	w
		Entropy-based fuzzy clustering for point data (EFC)					
$p = 0.10$	0%	0.000	-	0.000	-	9.387	-
	1%	0.547	-	0.547	-	9.360	-
	5%	1.581	-	1.581	-	9.269	-
	10%	2.236	-	2.236	-	9.145	-
$p = 0.20$	0%	0.000	-	0.000	-	9.136	-
	1%	0.100	-	0.100	-	9.108	-
	5%	1.581	-	1.581	-	9.015	-
	10%	2.236	-	2.236	-	8.886	-
$p = 0.40$	0%	0.000	-	0.000	-	8.480	-
	1%	0.030	-	0.030	-	8.452	-
	5%	1.572	-	1.572	-	8.348	-
	10%	2.236	-	2.236	-	8.213	-
		Entropy-based clustering for interval-valued data (EC-ID)					
	0%	0.000	0.490	0.000	0.200	0.566	0.500
	1%	0.706	0.500	0.707	0.254	0.625	0.500
	5%	1.581	0.500	1.581	0.380	1.571	0.500
	10%	2.236	0.500	2.236	0.445	2.236	0.500

5. Empirical Applications

In this section, we show the results obtained by the entropy-based fuzzy clustering (EFC-ID) model in two empirical applications. For replication purposes, the reader can refer to the R-scripts and datasets uploaded on the following web page: https://github.com/mfordellone/EFC-ID (accessed on 1 February 2023). Notice that for the classification we assume that the observed diagnosis groups are unknown (i.e., unsupervised classification), and subsequently, we use the natural partitions of datasets to evaluate the diagnostic performance of the models.

5.1. Breast Cancer Wisconsin Data

In this subsection an analysis of the Breast Cancer Wisconsin (Diagnostic) dataset is performed (https://archive.ics.uci.edu/ml/datasets/breast+cancer+wisconsin+(diagnostic), accessed on 1 February 2023). This data set was created by [39] and it has been very used for training of statistical methods (e.g., [40]). The endpoint of this statistical analysis is to unsupervised classify the kind of breast cancer (i.e., benign or malignant). The dataset consists of 569 patients: 357 with benign diagnosis and 212 with malignant status. Table 5 shows the features average by a breast cancer diagnosis.

Table 5. Breast Cancer Wiscosin: features average by diagnosis.

	Benign (n = 357)	**Malignant (n = 212)**	***p*-Value**
radius	12.1 ± 1.78	17.5 ± 3.20	<0.001
texture	17.9 ± 4.00	21.6 ± 3.78	<0.001
perimeter	78.1 ± 11.8	115 ± 22	<0.001
area	463 ± 134	978 ± 368	<0.001
smoothness	0.09 ± 0.01	0.10 ± 0.01	<0.001
compactness	0.08 ± 0.03	0.15 ± 0.05	<0.001
concavity	0.05 ± 0.04	0.16 ± 0.07	<0.001
concave points	0.02 ± 0.01	0.09 ± 0.03	<0.001
symmetry	0.17 ± 0.02	0.19 ± 0.03	<0.001
fractal dimension	0.06 ± 0.01	0.06 ± 0.01	0.880

For each feature we have the average ± standard deviation.

In order to include the variability/uncertainty that characterizes the dataset in the classification procedure, the radii have been fixed equal to the standard deviation of data-features and then the EFC-ID model for malignant breast cancer diagnosis has been applied to the obtained interval-valued dataset. For comparison purposes, also the conventional fuzzy k-means clustering (FKM) for interval-valued data has been applied. This is because FKM is the major competitor model of EFC-ID, showing the best results in the simulation study. Figure 3a,b show the ROC curves obtained by the EFC-ID and FKM approaches, respectively. From Figure 3 we can see that EFC-ID outperforms the FKM with the AUC value equal to 0.9647 (CI 95% 0.9495–0.9778) against the 0.8770 (CI 95% 0.8621–0.9066) obtained by FKM.

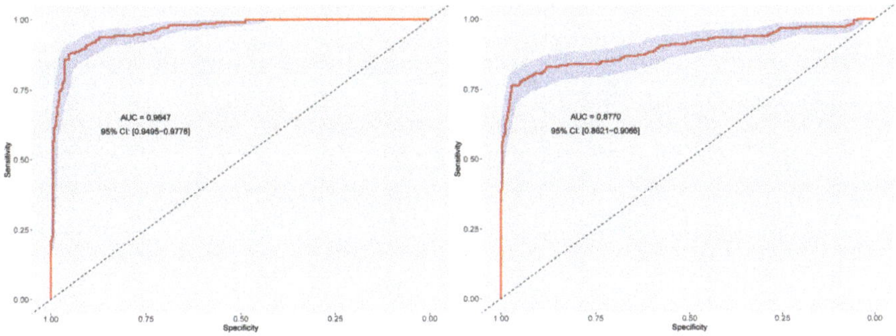

(**a**) (**b**)

Figure 3. ROC curves obtained by the EFC-ID and FKM approaches. (**a**) ROC curve obtained by EFC-ID approach; (**b**) ROC curve obtained by FKM approach.

Table 6 shows the performance indexes computed on the results obtained by the two approaches. Notice that, in this application, the optimal entropy parameter p has been fixed to 0.5.

Table 6. Performance indexes obtained by EFC-ID and FKM for malignant breast cancer diagnosis.

	EFC-ID			**FKM**		
	Estimate	Lower *	Upper *	Estimate	Lower *	Upper *
Sensitivity	0.896	0.847	0.934	0.643	0.596	0.738
Specificity	0.934	0.895	0.955	0.916	0.903	0.977
Pos.Pred.Val.	0.864	0.811	0.906	0.898	0.821	0.963
Neg.Pred.Val.	0.937	0.906	0.960	0.666	0.614	0.743
Youden index	0.812	0.762	0.862	0.546	0.411	0.658
Accuracy	0.909	0.882	0.931	0.845	0.800	0.877
Error rate	0.091	0.069	0.118	0.177	0.132	0.188

* 95% exact confidence interval.

From the performance table, we can see that EFC-ID showed better performance than FKM in terms of global performance, Sensibility, Specificity, and Negative Predictive Value. However, the Specificity and the Positive Predictive Value obtained by FKM are better but, unfortunately, also the false negative rate increases. In this case, it seems that FKM unbalances the weights in favor of *centers* ($w_c = 0.97$), providing a result similar to the simple FCM for point data (i.e., when $w_c = 1$), and showing a high rate of false negative events. Conversely, the entropy regularization of EFC-ID guarantees a better balancing of weights ($w_c = 0.65$). Moreover, we think that the high rate of false negative events obtained by FKM is a serious problem in the cancer detection field. In particular, false negative event tests at diagnosis of early disease and of relapse resulted in diagnostic and therapeutic delays.

5.2. Multiple Myeloma Data

In this subsection, an analysis of the Multiple Myeloma Data available in survminer R-package is performed (https://cran.r-project.org/web/packages/survminer/survminer.pdf, accessed on 1 February 2023). Multiple Myeloma data is extracted from publicly available gene expression data (GEO Id: GSE4581). The endpoint of this statistical analysis is to unsupervised classify the molecular groups of Multiple Myeloma. The original dataset consists of 256 patients with the IMWG molecular cytogenetic classification as shown in Table 7. However, since there is a large number of groups, we have selected a sub-sample including in the analysis only three molecular groups: Hyperdiploid, MAF, and MMSET (i.e., 131 patients). In this dataset, we have six features that correspond to six different gene expressions (i.e., CCND1, CRIM1, DEPDC1, IRF4, TP53, and WHSC1). Table 8 shows the gene expression average by molecular groups of Multiple Myeloma.

Table 7. Multiple Myeloma Data: IMWG molecular cytogenetic classification.

Molecular Group	# Patients
Cyclin D-1	22
Cyclin D-2	43
Hyperdiploid	66
Low bone disease	31
MAF	21
MMSET	44
Proliferation	29

Table 8. Multiple Myeloma Data: gene expression average by molecular groups.

	Hyperdiploid (n = 66)	MAF (n = 21)	MMSET (n = 44)	p-Value
CCND1	1280 ± 1500	434 ± 765	427 ± 602	<0.001
CRIM1	73 ± 174	59 ± 91	482 ± 392	<0.001
DEPDC1	169 ± 111	382 ± 356	311 ± 236	0.006
IRF4	14,500 ± 3850	12,700 ± 4930	12,300 ± 3950	0.013
TP53	1880 ± 669	1350 ± 1040	1240 ± 475	<0.001
WHSC1	139 ± 136	481 ± 454	8100 ± 4560	<0.001

For each feature we have the average ± standard deviation.

Furthermore, in this case, in order to include the variability/uncertainty that characterizes the dataset in the classification procedure, the radii have been fixed equal to the standard deviation of data-features and then the EFC-ID model has been applied for molecular group identification. Such as the previous subsection, the conventional fuzzy k-means (FKM) for interval-valued data has been applied for comparison purposes. Notice that, in this application, the optimal entropy parameter p has been fixed to 0.25. In order to evaluate the performance of both approaches, three different evaluation criteria have been used (i.e., the Chi-Squared Index [41], the Accuracy rate and the Adjusted Rand Index [42]). The results obtained are shown in Table 9.

Table 9. Performance indexes obtained by EFC-ID and FKM for Multiple Myeloma classification.

	EFC-ID	FKM
Chi-Squared	91.636	88.257
Accuracy	0.710	0.601
Adjusted Rand Index	0.329	0.211

Furthermore, in this case, the three evaluation criteria show an EFC-ID performance gain than the conventional FKM. In particular, both the empirical applications show that FKM, unlike EFC-ID, unbalances the weights in favor of centers ($wc = 0.97$), providing a result similar to the simple FCM for point data (i.e., when $wc = 1$), and then neglecting the information included in the uncertainty of data. Therefore, the important contribution of this proposal is the use of entropy regularization which improves the separability of groups and their homogeneity without neglecting the degree of uncertainty characterized by the data.

6. Concluding Remarks

Following a fuzzy approach, in this paper, a new fuzzy clustering technique for interval-valued data is suggested. In particular, by considering a suitable weighted distance, we propose a fuzzy clustering model with entropy regularization (i.e., the EFC-ID model). Moreover, an approach has been proposed where the uncertainty that characterizes the data has been considered in the classification procedure using the degree of variability to estimate it.

The principal advantages of this approach consist of *(i)* the use of entropy regularization approach in a fuzzy clustering framework is the maximum entropy principle that provides a new perspective to facing the problem of fuzzifying the clusterization of the units while ensuring the maximum of compactness of the obtained clusters; *(ii)* including the uncertainty of the data in the classification procedure leads more homogeneous and separated groups partitions; *(iii)* the multi-group approach facilitates the use of this approach for other purposes as stages detection, response classes identification, prognosis classification, etc.); *(iv)* the external procedure of uncertainty recognition leads to fix a different kind of interval measures (e.g., specific percentile differences); *(v)* the weighted distance guarantees that the point data has a bigger weight than the radii. In this way, the risk to associate the biggest relevance to the uncertainty in the classification procedure is reduced.

Conversely, the principal disadvantages consist of *(i)* the unknown membership function of the imprecise data; *(ii)* the approach could suffer in the case of a small sample size which inflates the radii.

To investigate the performance and effectiveness of the proposed model a simulation study has been carried out. In particular, the aim of the simulation study has been to study the behavior of the EFC-ID model in terms of weights (w) estimate and identification of the natural partition for different degrees of entropy in different cases that could be occurred in empirical applications: *(i)* well-separated clusters, *(ii)* not well-separated clusters (i.e., when fuzzy points there are in the data structure), *(iii)* groups structure applied on centers only, on the radii only, or on both. Results have shown that the proposed approach is more able to distinguish the natural clusters as well as to identify prototypes with respect to other methodologies. The proposed model has been compared with crisp and fuzzy models for interval-valued data. We have also analyzed two real case studies. In all cases, the proposed approach has shown good performance in identifying the natural partition and the advantages of the use of EFC-ID have been detailed illustrated.

For future research could be interesting to embed a cross-validation approach in EFC-ID to select different uncertainty measures with respect to the standard deviation (e.g., inter-quartile range) in order to obtain also non-symmetrical imprecise data (e.g., trapezoidal data [43].

Author Contributions: Conceptualization, M.F.; methodology, M.F., I.D.B. and P.C.; software, M.F. and I.D.B.; validation, D.B. and P.C.; formal analysis, M.F., D.B. and P.C.; writing—original draft preparation, P.C.; writing—review and editing, P.C.; visualization, M.F. and I.D.B.; supervision, P.C. All authors have read and agreed to the published version of the manuscript.

Funding: This research received no external funding.

Institutional Review Board Statement: Not applicable.

Informed Consent Statement: Not applicable.

Data Availability Statement: Not applicable.

Conflicts of Interest: The authors declare no conflict of interest.

References

1. Fordellone, M.; Chiodini, P. Unsupervised Hierarchical Classification Approach for Imprecise Data in the Breast Cancer Detection. *Entropy* **2022**, *24*, 926. [CrossRef] [PubMed]
2. Oosterhuis, W.P.; Bayat, H.; Armbruster, D.; Coskun, A.; Freeman, K.P.; Kallner, A.; Koch, D.; Mackenzie, F.; Migliarino, G.; Orth, M.; et al. The use of error and uncertainty methods in the medical laboratory. *Clin. Chem. Lab. Med. (CCLM)* **2018**, *56*, 209–219. [CrossRef] [PubMed]
3. Analytical Methods Committee. Uncertainty of measurement: Implications of its use in analytical science. *Analyst* **1995**, *120*, 2303–2308. [CrossRef]
4. White, G.H.; Farrance, I. Uncertainty of measurement in quantitative medical testing: A laboratory implementation guide. *Clin. Biochem. Rev.* **2004**, *25*, S1. [PubMed]
5. Farrance, I.; Frenkel, R. Uncertainty of measurement: A review of the rules for calculating uncertainty components through functional relationships. *Clin. Biochem. Rev.* **2012**, *33*, 49. [PubMed]
6. Strout, T.D.; Hillen, M.; Gutheil, C.; Anderson, E.; Hutchinson, R.; Ward, H.; Kay, H.; Mills, G.J.; Han, P.K. Tolerance of uncertainty: A systematic review of health and healthcare-related outcomes. *Patient Educ. Couns.* **2018**, *101*, 1518–1537. [CrossRef]
7. Denoeux, T.; Masson, M. Multidimensional scaling of interval-valued dissimilarity data. *Pattern Recognit. Lett.* **2000**, *21*, 83–92. [CrossRef]
8. D'Urso, P.; De Giovanni, L. Robust clustering of imprecise data. *Chemom. Intell. Lab. Syst.* **2014**, *136*, 58–80. [CrossRef]
9. D'Urso, P.; Leski, J. Fuzzy c-ordered medoids clustering for interval-valued data. *Pattern Recognit.* **2016**, *58*, 49–67. [CrossRef]
10. D'Urso, P.; De Giovanni, L. Midpoint radius self-organizing maps for interval-valued data with telecommunications application. *Appl. Soft Comput.* **2011**, *11*, 3877–3886. [CrossRef]
11. Coppi, R.; Giordani, P.; D'Urso, P. Component models for fuzzy data. *Psychometrika* **2006**, *71*, 733. [CrossRef]
12. D'Urso, P.; Giordani, P. A possibilistic approach to latent component analysis for symmetric fuzzy data. *Fuzzy Sets Syst.* **2005**, *150*, 285–305. [CrossRef]
13. Giordani, P.; Kiers, H.A. Principal component analysis of symmetric fuzzy data. *Comput. Stat. Data Anal.* **2004**, *45*, 519–548. [CrossRef]
14. Gowda, K.C.; Diday, E. Symbolic clustering using a new dissimilarity measure. *Pattern Recognit.* **1991**, *24*, 567–578. [CrossRef]
15. Guru, D.; Kiranagi, B.B.; Nagabhushan, P. Multivalued type proximity measure and concept of mutual similarity value useful for clustering symbolic patterns. *Pattern Recognit. Lett.* **2004**, *25*, 1203–1213. [CrossRef]
16. De Carvalho, F.d.A.; Lechevallier, Y. Partitional clustering algorithms for symbolic interval data based on single adaptive distances. *Pattern Recognit.* **2009**, *42*, 1223–1236. [CrossRef]
17. De Carvalho, F.d.A.; de Souza, R.M.; Chavent, M.; Lechevallier, Y. Adaptive Hausdorff distances and dynamic clustering of symbolic interval data. *Pattern Recognit. Lett.* **2006**, *27*, 167–179. [CrossRef]
18. De Carvalho, F.d.A.; Tenório, C.P. Fuzzy K-means clustering algorithms for interval-valued data based on adaptive quadratic distances. *Fuzzy Sets Syst.* **2010**, *161*, 2978–2999. [CrossRef]
19. D'Urso, P.; De Giovanni, L.; Massari, R. Trimmed fuzzy clustering for interval-valued data. *Adv. Data Anal. Classif.* **2015**, *9*, 21–40. [CrossRef]
20. D'Urso, P.; Giordani, P. A robust fuzzy k-means clustering model for interval valued data. *Comput. Stat.* **2006**, *21*, 251–269. [CrossRef]
21. D'Urso, P.; Massari, R.; De Giovanni, L.; Cappelli, C. Exponential distance-based fuzzy clustering for interval-valued data. *Fuzzy Optim. Decis. Mak.* **2017**, *16*, 51–70. [CrossRef]
22. Li, R.P.; Mukaidono, M. A maximum-entropy approach to fuzzy clustering. In Proceedings of the 1995 IEEE International Conference on Fuzzy Systems, Yokohama, Japan, 20–24 March 1995; Volyme 4, pp. 2227–2232.
23. Coppi, R.; D'Urso, P. Fuzzy unsupervised classification of multivariate time trajectories with the Shannon entropy regularization. *Comput. Stat. Data Anal.* **2006**, *50*, 1452–1477. [CrossRef]
24. Li, R.P.; Mukaidono, M. Gaussian clustering method based on maximum-fuzzy-entropy interpretation. *Fuzzy Sets Syst.* **1999**, *102*, 253–258. [CrossRef]
25. Sadaaki, M.; Masao, M. Fuzzy c-means as a regularization and maximum entropy approach. In Proceedings of the 7th International Fuzzy Systems Association World Congress (IFSA'97), Prague, Czech Republic, 25–30 June 1997.
26. Yao, J.; Dash, M.; Tan, S.; Liu, H. Entropy-based fuzzy clustering and fuzzy modeling. *Fuzzy Sets Syst.* **2000**, *113*, 381–388. [CrossRef]
27. Ichihashi, H. Gaussian mixture PDF approximation and fuzzy c-means clustering with entropy regularization. In Proceedings of the 4th Asian Fuzzy Systems Symposium, Tsukuba, Japan, 31 May–3 June 2000; pp. 217–221.
28. Miyagishi, K.; Yasutomi, Y.; Ichihashi, H.; Honda, K. Fuzzy Clustering with regularization by KL information. In Proceedings of the 16th Fuzzy System Symposium, Akita, Japan, 6–8 September 2000; pp. 549–550.
29. Ménard, M.; Eboueya, M. Extreme physical information and objective function in fuzzy clustering. *Fuzzy Sets Syst.* **2002**, *128*, 285–303. [CrossRef]
30. Frieden, B.R. Physics from Fisher information: A unification. *Am. J. Phys.* **2000**, *68*, 1064. [CrossRef]
31. Zarinbal, M.; Zarandi, M.F.; Turksen, I. Relative entropy fuzzy c-means clustering. *Inf. Sci.* **2014**, *260*, 74–97. [CrossRef]

32. Kahali, S.; Sing, J.K.; Saha, P.K. A new entropy-based approach for fuzzy c-means clustering and its application to brain MR image segmentation. *Soft Comput.* **2019**, *23*, 10407–10414. [CrossRef]
33. Gao, Y.; Wang, D.; Pan, J.; Wang, Z.; Chen, B. A novel fuzzy c-means clustering algorithm using adaptive norm. *Int. J. Fuzzy Syst.* **2019**, *21*, 2632–2649. [CrossRef]
34. Ashtari, P.; Haredasht, F.N.; Beigy, H. Supervised fuzzy partitioning. *Pattern Recognit.* **2020**, *97*, 107013. [CrossRef]
35. D'Urso, P.; Giordani, P. A weighted fuzzy c-means clustering model for fuzzy data. *Comput. Stat. Data Anal.* **2006**, *50*, 1496–1523. [CrossRef]
36. Lepădatu, C.; Nitulescu, E. Information energy and information temperature for molecular systems. *Acta Chim. Slov* **2003**, *50*, 539–546.
37. Kabir, S.; Wagner, C.; Havens, T.C.; Anderson, D.T.; Aickelin, U. Novel similarity measure for interval-valued data based on overlapping ratio. In Proceedings of the 2017 IEEE International Conference on Fuzzy Systems (FUZZ-IEEE), Naples, Italy , 9–12 July 2017; pp. 1–6.
38. Leski, J. Towards a robust fuzzy clustering. *Fuzzy Sets Syst.* **2003**, *137*, 215–233. [CrossRef]
39. Mangasarian, O.L.; Street, W.N.; Wolberg, W.H. Breast cancer diagnosis and prognosis via linear programming. *Oper. Res.* **1995**, *43*, 570–577. [CrossRef]
40. Agarap, A.F.M. On breast cancer detection: An application of machine learning algorithms on the wisconsin diagnostic dataset. In Proceedings of the 2nd International Conference on Machine Learning and Soft Computing, Phuoc Island, Vietnam, 2–4 February 2018; pp. 5–9.
41. Jin, X.; Xu, A.; Bie, R.; Guo, P. Machine learning techniques and chi-square feature selection for cancer classification using SAGE gene expression profiles. In *International Workshop on Data Mining for Biomedical Applications*; Springer: Berlin/Heidelberg, Germany, 2006; pp. 106–115.
42. Steinley, D. Properties of the Hubert-Arable Adjusted Rand Index. *Psychol. Methods* **2004**, *9*, 386. [CrossRef]
43. Hüllermeier, E. Learning from imprecise and fuzzy observations: Data disambiguation through generalized loss minimization. *Int. J. Approx. Reason.* **2014**, *55*, 1519–1534. [CrossRef]

applied sciences

MDPI

Review

Fractal Analysis Applied to the Diagnosis of Oral Cancer and Oral Potentially Malignant Disorders: A Comprehensive Review

Maria Contaldo [1,*], Federica Di Spirito [2], Maria Pia Di Palo [2], Alessandra Amato [3], Fausto Fiori [1,*] and Rosario Serpico [1]

[1] Multidisciplinary Department of Medical-Surgical and Dental Specialties, University of Campania Luigi Vanvitelli, Via Luigi de Crecchio, 6, 80138 Naples, Italy; rosario.serpico@unicampania.it

[2] Department of Medicine, Surgery and Dentistry, University of Salerno, 84084 Salerno, Italy; fdispirito@unisa.it (F.D.S.); mariapia140497@gmail.com (M.P.D.P.)

[3] Department of Neuroscience, Reproductive Science and Dentistry, University of Naples Federico II, 80131 Naples, Italy; aale.amato@gmail.com

* Correspondence: maria.contaldo@unicampania.it (M.C.); fausto.fiori@outlook.com (F.F.)

Citation: Contaldo, M.; Di Spirito, F.; Di Palo, M.P.; Amato, A.; Fiori, F.; Serpico, R. Fractal Analysis Applied to the Diagnosis of Oral Cancer and Oral Potentially Malignant Disorders: A Comprehensive Review. *Appl. Sci.* **2024**, *14*, 777. https://doi.org/10.3390/app14020777

Academic Editor: Bruno Chrcanovic

Received: 23 November 2023
Revised: 15 January 2024
Accepted: 15 January 2024
Published: 16 January 2024

Abstract: In nature, everything is regular and orderly arranged. The degree of derailment from geometry is related to the disarrangement of living tissues associated with diseases. In the diagnostic field, fractal analysis calculates the fractal dimension (FD), a numerical measure of the degree of regularity of a tissue or structure. As for oral lesions, fractal analysis has been reported to determine the degree of irregular tissue/vascularization derailment mathematically, and this event has been correlated with the nature of the lesion. The purpose of this paper is to evaluate the scientific literature on the fractal analysis of oral cancer and its precursors (oral potentially malignant disorders, OPMDs) to convey whether the specific fractal dimension may be predictive of cancer or the cancerous progression of OPMDs. For this purpose, three databases (PubMed, Scopus, and ISI Web of Science) were investigated according to the PRISMA checklist to answer the following query: "Is fractal analysis a support method to diagnose oral cancer and distinguish it from its precursors?" The risk of biases was also assessed. All original articles published in English were considered; letters, reviews, editorials, and proceedings were excluded.

Keywords: fractal dimension; fractal analysis; oral oncology; oral carcinoma; OPMDs; OSCC

1. Introduction

Cancers of the lips and oral cavity (ICD C00-06) (oral cancer, OC) are a significant global health concern, with rising incidence in many parts of the world. The last statistics available from the International Agency for Cancer Research (IARC) are related to 2020 and reported 377,713 new cases, a 5-year prevalence of 959,248, and a mortality of 177,757 [1]. OC may arise on apparently healthy oral mucosa or from precursor lesions and conditions with an increased risk of malignancy, collectively named "oral potentially malignant disorders" (OPMDs) [2]. The heterogeneous clinical patterns of OPMDs and OC at its early stages, together with their misdiagnosis, lead to the diagnosis of OC often at its advanced stages, when lymph nodal and distant metastases are already present, and thus are responsible for high mortality and morbidity (related to poor life expectancy and quality) [3–5].

Biopsy procedures and related histopathological assessments are still the gold standard for diagnosing oral lesions suspected of OC [6]. However, various methods (salivary markers, liquid biopsies) and tools (imaging systems) have been developed to obtain more accurate, noninvasive, and timely diagnoses for effective treatments and improved patient outcomes [7–10].

In recent years, rising numbers of digitally assisted medical procedures have been born, as eHealth has irrupted our lives. eHealth, by the definition given by the World Health Organization, is "the cost-effective and secure use of information and communications technologies (ICT) in support of health and health-related fields" [11].

One such innovative approach to oral-health-related challenges is fractal analysis. Fractal analysis (FA) is a mathematical and computational tool that quantitatively assesses the so-called fractal dimension (FD) of a natural or artificial thing called a "fractal object", whose irregular and highly intricate structures repeat at different scales, with the peculiar phenomenon of "self-similarity" [12]. Indeed, the shape of a fractal object is usually given by the repetition of regular shapes reproducing its geometry at different scales, thus having a peculiar FD. Another critical point of FA is the "measuring complexity": FA quantifies the intricate and complex nature of objects that may not have a well-defined, smooth geometry, thus providing a more nuanced understanding of irregular shapes and patterns.

Last, it must be considered that various methods can be employed to calculate fractal dimensions. Each method emphasizes different aspects of the fractal structure. The more common method to measure FD is the box-counting method and its variants, as follows [13]:

- The box-counting method is based on a grid of multiple small boxes at different scales superimposed on the fractal object to analyze and count the boxes needed to cover the object; the relationship between box size and the number of boxes gives the FD.
- Box-counting in 2D (Minkowski–Bouligand dimension) is an extension of the box-counting method wherein the box size is varied, and the relationship between box size and the number of boxes is analyzed.
- Box-counting in 3D is an extension of the box-counting method to three-dimensional objects. Three-dimensional boxes are used to cover the fractal, and the relationship between box size and the number of boxes is analyzed.

Independently from these methods, to simplify, the higher the FD, the more chaotic and irregular the geometry of an object. An example of the application of FA in medicine is when the fractal object is a histopathological specimen: healthy tissues have low FD due to the regularity of their shapes, but the progressive derailment that occurs during pathology or cancerization leads to the disarrangement of their fractal geometry, which will be more complex and is expressed as an increase in its FD [14,15].

On these bases, fractal analysis, when applied to clinical and histological images, can quantitatively assess the complexity and irregularity of structures within these images, thus allowing characterizing and distinguishing patterns, textures, and structures in various medical applications such as diagnosing diseases and evaluating tissue properties [16]. In oncology, fractal analysis has shown its utility for diagnosing, staging, or prognosis of various cancer types, including those of the oropharynx area [17]. This approach can enhance diagnostic accuracy and improve the understanding of the disease's progression at a microscopic level. Through a comprehensive review, this work aims to explore the application of fractal analysis to diagnose oral cancer and OPMDs to provide scientific evidence to determine whether fractal dimensioning can improve oral cancer diagnosis.

2. Research Methods

2.1. Protocol, Focused Question

This review was performed according to the Preferred Reporting Items for Systematic Reviews and Meta-Analysis (PRISMA) [18]. The search was conducted by investigating three different databases (PubMed, Scopus, and the ISI Web of Science, or WoS) to answer the following focused question: "Is fractal analysis a valid support method to diagnose oral cancer or its precursors in humans?"

2.2. Search and Selection Strategy

The research strategy consisted of the following terms and their synonyms, used in a single query and combined with the Boolean operators (AND, OR): fractal dimension, fractal analysis, oral oncology, oral carcinoma, oral squamous cell carcinoma, oral cancer, oral potentially malignant disorders, lip cancer, actinic cheilitis, leukoplakia, erythroplakia, oral lichen planus, oral ulcers, oral submucous fibrosis, reverse smokers, lupus erythematosus, dyskeratosis congenita, epidermolysis bullosa, chronic hyperplastic candidiasis, oral lichenoid lesions, exophytic verrucous hyperplasia, oral lesions of graft vs. host disease.

The search was conducted in all databases without any restrictions on year of publication, type of publication, language, or species studied. The research and export phase ended on 31 July 2023, and a re-check for novel published articles was performed on 20 September.

The PICO strategy was considered to focus the question [19]:

- The study population (P) consists of humans with oral cancer and oral potentially malignant disorders;
- The intervention (I) was fractal analysis for diagnostic purposes;
- The comparison (C) was with the conventional gold standard diagnosis;
- The outcome (O) was the evaluation of the capability of fractal analysis to diagnose oral cancer and distinguish among oral cancer, oral potentially malignant disorders, and non-neoplastic oral lesions and diseases;
- The study designs (S) included cross-sectional studies, retrospective cohort studies, prospective comparative studies, case-control studies, case series, and case reports.

The following articles were eligible: original studies on humans that underwent fractal analysis (from different kinds of sources, later reported), available full text, and published in English. The exclusion criteria were studies on animal or cellular models. All the reviews, letters, proceedings, meeting abstracts, and editorials were excluded from qualitative analysis but were read for searching the eventually cross-referenced eligible articles. Further exclusion criteria included languages different from English and lack of full-text availability. Two authors performed the quality assessment of the articles (M.C. and F.F.) while, in case of disagreement, a third reviewer was involved (F.D.S.). Data from the eligible papers were organized in tables summarizing, for any study, the reference, the aims, the methods, the sample source that had undergone fractal analysis (clinical macroscopic photographs of the lesions, histological samples at microscopic resolution, vessel architecture, and so on...), the main findings, and the conclusions.

3. Characteristics of the Studies

A total of 110 articles were identified. After removing 57 duplicates and 16 articles considered ineligible because of a language different from English or the type (reviews, systematic reviews, editorials, letters, proceedings, and meeting abstracts), the remaining 37 records were screened for inclusion/exclusion criteria by considering their title/abstract. According to this screening, two works not meeting the inclusion criteria were excluded. In total, 35 full texts were read, and 27 of them, fulfilling all the requirements, were considered eligible at the end of the selection (Figure 1).

The 27 eligible studies were published over 30 years (1993–2022) from different countries of origin. Forty-four percent of them were published by Indian research groups [20–31], followed by, per number, four works from Greece [32–35], three from Italy [36–38], and the remaining papers from different countries, such as the UK [39], Romania [40], Germany [41], Canada [42], Taiwan [43], China [44], Poland [45], and Spain [46]. All the main characteristics of the studies are reported in Table 1.

Table 1. Main characteristics of the studies.

	First Author, (Year), Country	Aims of the Study	Sample Source (Fractal Object)	Method of Fractal Dimension Calculation	Methods, Number of Cases, and Type of Lesion	Main Findings	Conclusions
1	Landini (1993), UK [39]	To quantitatively investigate nFD of normal and cancerous oral epithelial cell nuclei	Histological specimens for nuclei assessment in OC	Yardstick method for fractal dimension estimation	Total of 762 nuclei of 10 OC and normal oral mucosa, digitalized images from transmission electron microscope (×1400)	Statistically significant differences in FD of OC nuclei vs. normal cells' nuclei	Confirmed potential use of FA for diagnosis and prognosis of malignancy.
2	Goutzanis (2008), Greece [32]	To evaluate the nFD in tissue specimens from patients with OC	Histological specimens for nuclei assessment in OC	Implementation of box-counting algorithm in a specially designed application (Fractalyser)	Histological sections from 48 OC and 17 healthy controls to quantify nFD using box-counting method	nFD mean values significantly increased from healthy mucosa to well differentiated and poorly differentiated OC. OC-nFD mean values were higher than normal mucosa. Patients with FD lower than the median value of the sample had statistically significant higher survival rates.	nFD was proved to be an independent prognostic factor of survival in oral cancer patients.
3	Goutzanis, (2009), Greece [33]	To evaluate the vascular FDs in OC to assess their potential value as factors reflecting angiogenesis	Histological specimens for vascular assessment in OC	Box-counting algorithm using the Fractalyser software	Histologic sections from 48 OC and 17 healthy controls to quantify vascular FD	OC presented statistically significant higher mean values of vascular FD compared with normal mucosa.	Vascular FD was a reliable indicator of angiogenesis in oral malignant tumors.
4	Margaritescu, (2010), Romania [40]	To assess the geometry of the lymphatic vessels in oral mucosa utilizing fractal analysis	Histological specimens for lymphatic vessels assessment in OC	Perimeter stepping algorithm using Image-Pro Plus software (Media Cybernetics, Inc., Bethesda, MD, USA)	Comparison between immunohistochemistry images of 20 OC with tumor-free resection margins	Comparison between contour FD values of different pathological conditions of the same area showed no statistically significant difference.	Results not statistically significant
5	Krishnan, (2011), India [30]	To improve the classification accuracy based on different textural features for the development of computer-assisted screening of OSF	Histological specimens for fibrosis in OSF	Modified differential box-counting with sequential algorithm	Involved 45 OSF patients and 10 healthy controls for a total of 90 images of normal oral mucosa, 42 OSF without dysplasia, and 26 OSF with dysplasia. Compared textual features obtained using FA and other textural techniques.	The combination of FD with other textural analyses led to the highest accuracy of 88.38% for classification.	Combining more than two texture measures is most effective in characterizing OSF subtypes.
6	Krishnan, (2012), India [20]	To analyze collagen fibers in the subepithelial connective tissue for accurate OSF screening and classification	Histological specimens for FA of fibrosis in OSF	Differential box-counting	Used 60 normal and 59 OSF images taken from histopathological samples. The segmentation of collagen fibers from histological images was performed using neural networks on color channels. Textural features were extracted from collagen areas using fractal methods like differential box-counting.	F fractal features of collagen under Gaussian transformation improves classification performance from 80.69% to 90.75%.	FA significantly improved the classification of healthy and OSF tissues.
7	Raja, (2012), India [21]	To investigate the usefulness of texture analysis in the OC characterization To evaluate its effectiveness in distinguishing between different grades of tumors	Computed tomography of OC	Differential box-counting	Compared 21 computed tomography images of OC patients. Two ROIs were identified: one at the site of the lesion and the other on the normal, unaffected side of the buccal mucosa. Texture analysis measures, specifically FD and gray level co-occurrence matrix (GLCM), in both ROIs.	Statistically significant differences between the mean FD and GLCM parameters of the lesion ROI and the normal ROI	FD demonstrated its usefulness in distinguishing between normal and pathological tissues, but it could not play a role in tumor grading detection.

Table 1. *Cont.*

	First Author, (Year), Country	Aims of the Study	Sample Source (Fractal Object)	Method of Fractal Dimension Calculation	Methods, Number of Cases, and Type of Lesion	Main Findings	Conclusions
8	Klatt, (2014), Germany [41]	To assess the potential of calculated fractal dimension FD of time-resolved autofluorescence in discriminating tumors from healthy tissues of the oral cavity	Histological fluorescence in OC	Fractal dimension based on time-resolved autofluorescence spectra	Histological samples from 15 OC and 22 healthy controls. After time-resolved fluorescence measurements, the FD was calculated by using an algorithm based on the non-exponential decay behavior of autofluorescence.	FD was significantly higher in OC than in healthy tissues, at 86% specificity and 100% sensitivity.	FD, based on time-resolved autofluorescence spectra, had promising potential in real-time detection of OC.
9	Spyridonos, (2014), Greece [34]	To quantify the morphological irregularities of the lower lip border, to validate its discriminative power in solar cheilosis diagnosis, and to provide supportive tools toward cost effective, noninvasive disease monitoring	Clinical picture of actinic cheilitis	Box-counting method and Sevcik approximation	Clinical pictures from 50 subjects were used. Two different methods for estimating FD were employed: the box-counting method (FDbc) and a method proposed by Sevcik (FDs).	FD yielded the highest accuracy in discriminating patients from controls, resulting in 98% sensitivity and 94% specificity.	FA to evaluate lip contour irregularities might be effective in distinguishing healthy lips from solar cheilosis-affected lips.
10	Bose, (2015), Canada [42]	To propose a method that integrates multiple histopathological features of the tumor microenvironment into a single, digital pathology-based biomarker using nFD analysis	Microarray nuclei evaluation DAPI-stained images of tissue microarray (TMA) cores	Box-counting	A total of 107 consecutive OC patients were classified using nFD scores of nuclei stained with DAPI from TMA.	High nFD was significantly associated with pT-stage and RT. High nFD of the total tumor microenvironment was significantly associated with improved disease-specific survival. High nFD was significantly associated with high tumor proliferation and lymphatic invasion.	nFD analysis integrates known prognostic factors from the tumor microenvironment, such as proliferation and immune infiltration, into a single digital pathology-based biomarker.
11	Lucchese, (2015), Italy [36]	To assess local vascular architecture in atrophic-erosive OLP	OPL capillaroscopy	Box-counting	Used 31 OLP patients and 32 healthy controls. The images captured with capillaroscopy were converted to 8-bit grayscale, and the box-counting method was used to assess the FD.	Statistically significant differences in the FD of vessels' density in OLP and healthy controls	Microvessel density analysis could be used as a parameter in determining potential malignant progression of OLP lesions, but more studies are needed.
12	Mincione, (2015), Italy [37]	To investigate FD as an OC prognostic tool by correlating FD values with clinicopathological features and survival of OC patients	Immunohistochemistry of podoplanin in OC	Box-counting	Used 64 OC and 10 healthy controls. Postproduction analysis of the specimen images was performed, and the box-counting method was used to assess FD. Podoplanin expression in tumor-free resection margins of OC	The mean FD values difference was statistically significant between the control and test groups. Increasing value of FD statistically correlated with different stages, grades, and survival of OC.	FD correlates with OC histological grade and stage and can be used for prognosticating OC survival.
13	Ou-Yang, (2015), Taiwan [43]	To develop a combination of textural and spectral methods for diagnosing OC	Histological images from an inverted microscope	Morphology-based fractal dimension method for tissue discrimination	Total of 34 OC and 34 patient-related healthy mucosa	FD had 90% sensitivity and 88% specificity in distinguishing among OC and healthy mucosa.	FD was effective in detecting OC in biopsies with high sensitivity and specificity.
14	Pandey, (2015), India [22]	To evaluate the FD of OL compared with normal oral mucosa and the changes during and after treatments	Clinical pictures of OL	Box-counting	Clinical pictures of 50 OL and 50 normal mucosa considered for FA after postproduction ROI selection.	The difference between the two groups was statistically significant. The difference in FDs between pretreated and post-treated lesions was observed and was suggestive of decreased FD.	FA can be an effective, economical, and noninvasive diagnostic and prognostic tool for OL.
15	Spirydonos, (2015), Greece [35]	To determine robust macro-morphological descriptors of the vermilion border from non-standardized digital photographs	Clinical picture of actinic cheilitis	Box-counting method and Sevcik approximation	Clinical images from 75 AC and 75 healthy controls. Lip borders quantified on the basis of the extent of vermilion retraction and the degree of border irregularity employing fractal features.	The different FD values were related with individual variabilities other than the status (AC vs. healthy lips).	The proposed method opens new perspectives toward a cost-effective, noninvasive monitoring of AC.

Table 1. *Cont.*

	First Author, (Year), Country	Aims of the Study	Sample Source (Fractal Object)	Method of Fractal Dimension Calculation	Methods, Number of Cases, and Type of Lesion	Main Findings	Conclusions
16	Yinti, (2015), India [23]	To assess nuclear morphologic complexity with nFD obtained from computer-aided image analysis and correlate the fractal dimension with clinical features	Histological specimens for nuclei assessment in OC	Sarkar box-counting method	Histopathological and postproduction analysis of 14 OC and 6 healthy controls. After hematoxylin and eosin for histopathological assessment, Feulgen staining was performed to evaluate nuclear complexity. Using Adobe Adobe PhotoShop CS and ImageJ software 1.43u (Wayne Rasband, National Institutes of Health, Bethesda, USA), postproduction analysis was performed.	Higher mean nFD was observed in the OC group compared with the control group. Significant difference in the average value of nFD between the four stages of the disease. Patients with FD value $\leq$ 1.71 showed a higher survival period of 72 months, while patients with FD > 1.71 showed a lower survival period of 36 months.	nFD seemed a reliable diagnostic tool that need standardization to be validated, but the data collected suggest the possible use of FD also as a prognostic factor.
17	Phulari, (2016), India [24]	To compare the morphometric complexity using nFD in normal, epithelial dysplasia, and OC cases and to verify the differences among the various histological grades of dysplasia and OC	Histological specimens for assessment for distinguishing OC and various degrees of dysplasia	Box-counting	Used 70 histological samples of normal mucosa, mild dysplasia, moderate dysplasia, severe dysplasia, well-differentiated OC, moderately differentiated OC, and poorly differentiated OC. The images were analyzed using ImageJ and the box-counting algorithm.	Progressive increase in mean FD from healthy mucosa to poorly differentiated OC.	FA could be a reliable tool for distinguishing the normal, dysplastic, and neoplastic tissues.
18	Das, (2017), India [25]	To develop a microscopic image analytics approach for automated recognition of mitotic cells and its count for assisting pathological evaluation of OC	Histological specimens for assessment of mitotic cells	Modified differential box-counting method	Five histological slides for each grade, fifteen slides, and ten images for every region of interest. FD was calculated using the box-counting method.	Found 89% precision in mitotic cell segmentation.	The proposed methodology was effective for mitotic cell detection in OC histopathological images.
19	Yang, (2017), China [44]	To quantitatively examine the DNA content and nuclear morphometry status of OL and investigate their association with the degree of dysplasia	Cytology study to assess DNA content amount, nuclear shape, area, radius, intensity, sphericity, entropy, and nFD	Not specified	Cytobrush samples from 70 OLs, before the scalpel biopsy, were stained with Feulgen-thionin.	A total of 48.6% of the OLs had a DNA content abnormality; positive correlation was observed between the degree of oral dysplasia and DNA content status.	DNA content and nuclear morphometric status using cytobrush biopsy with image cytometry contribute to diagnosing high-grade dysplasia within OL.
20	Daddazio, (2018), Italy [38]	To consider a possible correlation between the intensity of expression of osteopontin and grading in OC To correlate the increase in FD and osteopontin	Histological OC	Box-counting	Used 64 OC and 14 healthy controls and immunohistochemical stain to identify and localize osteopontin. Postproduction analysis was performed using ImageJ and the box-counting method.	Statistically significant differences found in the FD values between the test group and controls. Correlation between FD and OPN expression was visually more considerable when divided by tumor grading, especially in the G3 group.	The study suggests a potential correlation between osteopontin expression, FD values, and OC grading. Combining these factors may enhance diagnostic accuracy and prognostic evaluation.
21	Jurczyszyn, (2018), Poland [45]	To distinguish OL and OLP using FA in a classical examination with white light and PDD	Clinical photos and photodynamic diagnosis photos of OL and OLP	Modified box-counting	In 41 patients with OL or OLP, photodynamic therapy (PDT) with 5-ALA was administered, and FA was conducted using the Fractalyse program to evaluate the efficacy of PDT in treating oral lesions.	No significant differences were observed between the FDs of OL and OLP.	Variations within groups were noted, although its utility in distinguishing between LP and leukoplakia without histopathological examination remains inconclusive.

Table 1. *Cont.*

	First Author, (Year), Country	Aims of the Study	Sample Source (Fractal Object)	Method of Fractal Dimension Calculation	Methods, Number of Cases, and Type of Lesion	Main Findings	Conclusions
22	Iqbal, (2020), India [26]	To assess the efficacy of FA in detecting the malignancy potential of OL	Clinical photo after toluidine blue staining of OL	Box-counting	In 121 OL and healthy controls, digital images of normal mucosa and lesions were taken before and after staining with toluidine blue. Postproduction analysis performed using the box-counting method.	FD values showed a significant difference between dysplastic and nondysplastic cases. FD values based on age and the type of tobacco product used indicated an increasing trend with advancing age. Surti/khaini abusers showed a significant difference in FD values. The correlation of FD values with age and the duration of smoking and smokeless tobacco was highly significant.	FD analysis could be used as a noninvasive, cost-effective diagnostic tool for the early detection of malignant conversion.
23	Nawn, (2021), India [27]	To explore and analyze oral differences in FD among normal mucosa, OSF, OSF with dysplasia, OL, and OC	Histopathological images	Not specified	Histological sections of healthy mucosa, OSF, OSF with dysplasia, OL, and OC were considered for tissue grading and FA.	Discriminative multifractal signatures for healthy and pathological tissues	FA was useful to distinguish alterations in the singularity spectrum width across healthy, pre-cancerous, and cancerous tissues.
24	Sharma, (2021), India [28]	To understand the crystallization patterns in saliva and their relation to oral potentially malignant disorders in male patients	Salivary specimens for assessment of crystallization pattern in OSF, OL, and OC	Not specified	Dried salivary films from patients with OSF, OL, and OC were examined under a stereo-zoom microscope to select ROIs for fern structure analysis.	Significant differences in FD among normal individuals and those with OSF, OL, and OC	Saliva could serve as a potential imaging biomarker for the early-stage, noninvasive diagnosis of OPMDs and OC.
25	Guerrero-Sánchez, (2022), Spain [46]	To assess dysplasia	Histological specimens for assessment of FD of in OL	Modified box-counting	A total of 29 OL and 10 normal oral mucosa biopsies were analyzed using FA for the epithelial and the connective layer.	In the OL group, the FD median value was higher compared with the control group, with statistically significant differences. Significant differences were observed between the non-dysplasia vs. high-grade and low-grade vs. high-grade groups.	FD is an effective tool for diagnosing OL when evaluating the epithelial layer.
26	Rahman, (2022), India [31]	To evaluate differences in nFD values of epithelial cells of normal tissue, fibroepithelial hyperplasia, verrucous carcinoma, and OSCC. Also, the correlation between these features and the cervical lymph node metastasis was assessed.	Histological specimens for assessment of epithelial cells from fibroepithelial hyperplasia, verrucous carcinoma, and OSCC	Box-counting	Photo of samples underwent postproduction analysis with Image J. All the clinical features were then compared with the image analysis results.	Significant difference between the mean nFD of healthy cells and malignant epithelial cells. nFD and grading together demonstrated significant predictive potential for lymph node metastasis.	nFD combined with grading may predict lymph node metastasis.
27	Santolia, (2022), India [29]	To assess the fractal dimension (FD) and radiomorphometric indices (RMIs) in the mandible from orthopantomographic radiographs in patients with oral lesions	Radiological images in patients with tobacco and areca-nut-associated oral lesions	Box counting method by White and Rudolph	FD and radiomorphometric indices were assessed, along with participant habits, BMI, and statistical analyses.	Mean FD was significantly reduced in patients with oral lesions compared with controls. FD and RMI values were significantly altered in patients with oral lesions associated with tobacco and areca nut habits.	These imaging parameters could potentially serve as indicators or markers for assessing oral health in individuals with specific tobacco and areca nut habits in the North Indian population.

AC, actinic cheilitis; DAPI, 4′,6-diamidino-2-phenylindole; FA, fractal analysis; FD, fractal dimension; nFD, nuclear fractal dimension; OC, oral cancer; OL, oral leukoplakia; OLP, oral lichen planus; OSCC, oral squamous cell carcinoma; OSF, oral submucous fibrosis; PDD, photodynamic diagnosis; pT, pathological state grade; ROI, region of interest; RT, radiation treatment; TMA, tissue microarray.

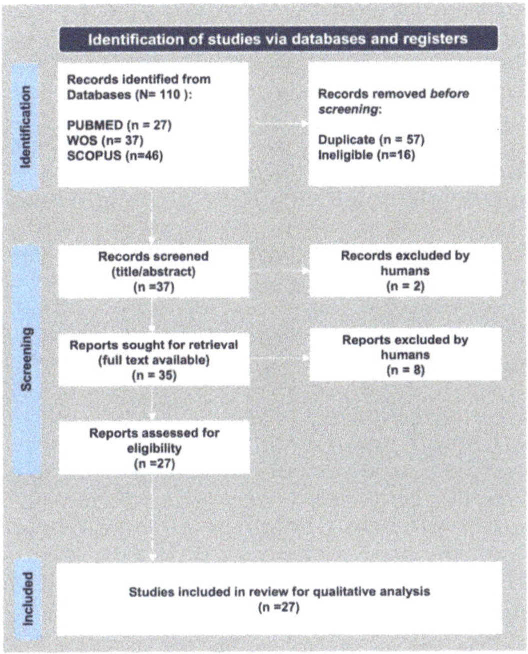

Figure 1. PRISMA flowchart.

3.1. *FA Methodologies and Tools*

The first method reported to measure the fractal dimension was the "yardstick method" used in 1993 by Landini et al. [39] and consisting of a ruler to manually measure the perimeters of nuclei from normal and cancerous keratinocytes from histological specimens that were magnified up to ×1400, photographed and further enlarged 2.6 times, with a black-and-white scanned photograph at a final resolution of 1 pixel equal to 35 nm.

Then, Goutzanis et al. [32,33] adopted the box-counting method to measure the nuclear periphery, its inner structure complexity, and the tumor-associated vasculature FD. In their works, the authors reported a significant positive correlation between FD and the size of the neoplastic nuclei, with FD values generally higher in carcinomas than in the control group and a statistically significant difference in FD between well-differentiated tumors and moderately or poorly differentiated ones.

Since then, the box-counting method and its variants have become the most used method. Box-counting was refined year after year, owing to the rising technological and informatics improvements of specific tools to acquire high-definition images, such as CDD cameras, which replaced scanned analog conventional photographs. Image processing software is consistently more accurate and precise in performing textural analysis in the RGB channel; this is then transformed into grayscale and later into binary images for better definition through semi-automatized and automatized image analyses with neural network supports.

3.2. *Fractal Objects*

The sample source objects for the fractal analyses comprised histological specimens, clinical pictures, radiological images, salivary samples, and cytobrushes. The main application of the FD was to perform textural features for improved classification of oral histopathological images. The most frequent purpose that emerged from the studies was diagnosis to discriminate among normal mucosa, various degrees of dysplasia, OPMDs, and OC. Other research focused on the prognostic significance of nuclear fractal dimensions among oral squamous cell carcinoma (OSCC), thus relating to other classical prognostic factors such as lymphatic invasion or tumoral neovascularization. Other works explored multifractal alterations in the oral subepithelial connective tissue during the progression of pre-cancer and cancer or else integrated tumor and stromal features into a single prognostic factor of the oral cancer microenvironment [38]. Some reports further explored the nuclear fractal dimension in oral squamous cell carcinoma to evaluate grading, staging, and survival.

Fractal analysis was predominantly applied to the analysis of the nuclear fractal dimension [23,24,31,32,39,43], in some cases supported by adjunct methods such as fluorescent or immunohistochemical staining [37,38,41,42], while other authors considered the fractal analysis to detect mitotic cells [25]. In some works, the vascular fractal dimension [33] or the geometry of the lymphatic vessels [40] was considered instead.

Additionally, other works focused on the textural features of the epithelial-connective interface and its regularity or irregularity in healthy specimens compared with oral submucous fibrosis (OSF), dysplastic, and cancerous specimens [20,27,30,46], or they studied the OC-associated vasculature [33,36].

Furthermore, apart from the classical nuclear fractal dimension, some researchers used immunohistochemical and fractal analysis to focus on specific OC-related cell markers according to their nuclear localization and quantification, such as D'Addazio et al. [38], who investigated osteopontin, or Margaritescu et al. [40], who investigated podoplanin expression.

Some cumulative methods added to conventional histology were variously considered, from time-resolved autofluorescence to discriminate tumors from healthy tissues in the oral cavity [41] to tissue microarrays to differentiated nuclear/cytoplasmic biomarkers localization [42].

Apart from histological samples, some research groups considered alternative sources to be analyzed via fractal analysis. Sharma et al. [28] conducted multifractal texture analysis of salivary fern patterns for oral pre-cancers and cancer assessment. Alternatively, Raja et al. [21] performed texture analysis of CT images to characterize oral cancers involving the buccal mucosa. Similarly, Santolia et al. [29] investigated fractal dimension and radiomorphometric analysis of orthopanoramic radiographs in patients with tobacco- and areca-nut-associated oral mucosal lesions. The Greek group of Spyridonos et al. [34,35] compared the fractal dimension of actinic cheilitis and healthy lips from clinical pictures of the vermilion borders.

Apart from actinic cheilitis, among the OPMDs, FD was widely and preponderantly investigated in oral leukoplakia [22,26,44–47] and oral submucous fibrosis (OSF) [20,27,28,30], mainly by the Indian groups, where OSF is endemic [47]. Regarding OLP, different preliminary studies investigated fractal analysis of mucosal microvascular patterns [36] and fractal dimension analysis to differentiate between lichen planus and leukoplakia [45].

4. Fractal Analysis to Support Oral Cancer and OPMDs Diagnosis and Prognosis

From the analysis of the results presented in the selected literature, fractal analysis can be globally considered to be a valid supporting method to diagnose oral cancer or its precursors in humans.

The most frequently investigated parameter that gave, in general, supportive robust results was the nuclear fractal dimension (nFD). nFD was statistically significantly different in OC nuclei than in normal cell nuclei [23,24,26,38,39]. In detail, a progressive increase in the mean FD was shown from healthy mucosa to poorly differentiated OC. These pieces of evidence were strengthened by the statistical analysis of Klatt et al., who reported that nFD was significantly higher in tumors than in healthy tissues, with an 86% specificity and 100% sensitivity [41], and confirmed by Ou-Yang et al. [43], who reported a similar high sensitivity rate (correctly identifying cancerous cells) and high specificity rate (correctly identifying normal cells). Furthermore, the nuclear fractal dimension was also proved to be an independent prognostic factor of survival in oral cancer patients, while, in synergy with the grading, it demonstrated significant predictive potential for lymph node metastasis [31–33].

Furthermore, nFD also correlated with prognostic factors from the tumor microenvironment, such as proliferation and immune infiltration, into a single digital pathology-based biomarker [22,32,42].

The exact significance was also reported in those studies in which the fractal object was a histological section. In these cases, the FD of histological architecture and the epithelial-connective interface of healthy mucosa compared with OC or OPMDs significantly differed [21,27].

Moreover, fractal analysis applied to vasculature also revealed its efficacy as a prognostic parameter to determine the potential malignant progression of OLP lesions based on the microvessel density analysis [36]. Statistically significant differences were also reported concerning the vascular fractal dimension of OC compared with normal mucosa [33].

Limitations of the Studies

Not all applications of fractal analysis to support OC and OPMD diagnosis were successful. In some cases, the results did not reach statistical significance; in others, they failed.

As an example, the studies on actinic cheilitis did not find the fractal analysis to be effective in distinguishing healthy lips from solar cheilosis-affected lips [34]. However, it must be considered that clinical pictures instead of histological samples were used for fractal analysis in these cases.

In fact, a key point first highlighted by Landini et al. [39] was that "the irregularity is not fully reproduced at all scales". They noticed that the same nuclear borders appeared more irregular at lower magnification and smoother at higher magnification.

Hence, the fractal object and methodology must be accurately chosen, from the acquisition mode, to the image magnification and processing, up to the fractal analysis methods.

Furthermore, it is not always true that "more is better": in some cases, combining fractal analysis with other texture measures did not reveal significant advantages over fractal analysis alone in discerning subtypes and grades of similar histopathological diseases [30] or among different OPMDs such as oral lichen planus and leukoplakia [45].

5. Discussion and Conclusions

Modern medicine and dentistry require the growing support of digital technologies to improve the diagnostic, therapeutic, and follow-up processes in patient management, including and especially cancer patients, where the timeliness and precocity of diagnosis and intervention, and knowledge of the prognosis related to novel parameters, can make the difference between life and death.

Digital aid is conveyed by the practice of eHealth, recently regulated by the World Health Organization [48].

One such innovative approach to oral health-related challenges in oral oncology is fractal analysis to assess quantitatively the regularity/irregularity of patterns mathematically and digitally in healthy mucosa compared with OC and OPMDs.

The present review affirmatively answered whether fractal analysis could be considered a valid support method to diagnose oral cancer or its precursors in humans.

Indeed, fractal analysis succeeded in the measurement and quantification of changes in the morphological complexity of the epithelial, connective, and vascular components of the tumor.

In detail, the box-counting method was the most frequently used. However, it was possible to assist, year after year, in the refinement of the method and the increasing support of digital processes for image analysis, from conventional photographs scanned and manually segmented up to the acquisition through CDD cameras and integrated software, thus resulting in more accurate and standardized textural analyses.

The keratinocyte nuclear boundary was the most frequently considered and most significative fractal object. The mean nuclear fractal dimension (nFD) progressively increased from healthy oral keratinocytes to those from poorly differentiated OC, thus being considered an independent prognostic factor of survival in oral cancer patients. Furthermore, the nFD prognostic significance was enhanced when grading, immune infiltration, and tumoral neovascularization were correlated.

Other works focused on this last feature, the pattern of tumor-associated neovascularization, thus reporting statistically significant differences between the vascular density of OC compared with healthy mucosa.

A third most frequent fractal object was the epithelial-subepithelial interface, whose FD statistically significantly differed between healthy mucosa and OC and between healthy mucosa and OPMDs.

Last, the fractal analyses failed in some works, such as those on solar cheilitis. In these cases, it was unclear whether the failure to discriminate was due to the fractal object considered (a clinical picture) or to the pathological features not adequately investigated through fractal analysis.

Furthermore, few works—only 27—have emerged from the literature. They are very heterogeneous, considering the source analyzed (mainly clinical pictures or histological specimens), the diseases investigated, the methodologies of fractal analysis, and the significance of the results.

These limitations are mainly related to the preliminary nature of these works, which, although pioneering, need more extended and standardized studies to be consolidated and considered for clinical applications.

6. Future Directions

In summary, fractal analysis provides a powerful tool for characterizing and understanding complex, irregular patterns and structures that may not fit well within traditional geometric frameworks. It has broad applications across various scientific disciplines and has contributed to a deeper understanding of the complexity inherent in natural and artificial systems.

In oral oncology, fractal analysis is worthy of consideration because it can be an effective and noninvasive diagnostic and prognostic tool for various premalignant lesions and conditions. It is economical, less time-consuming, and an accurate tool for measuring the progression of premalignant lesions [22], mainly when applied to clinical pictures, thus opening new perspectives toward cost-effective, noninvasive monitoring of OPMDs and suspicious lesions to support the patients' management [35].

Indeed, the fractal analysis could be applied virtually to all clinical and histological procedures to obtain significant progress in managing oral cancer and its precursors, to offer the capability to distinguish among oral lesions that are similar in shape but different in prognosis.

At this point, it is reasonable to hypothesize the future directions for fractal analysis in oral oncology and modern dentistry.

First, fractal analysis could be investigated for benefits in association with other digitally assisted imaging systems, such as in vivo microscopy, thus improving the qualitative assessment of in vivo-detected histological and cytological differences among OPMDs and OSCCs with mathematical analysis. In this case, in vivo confocal microscopy itself already has proven to be dramatically helpful, for diagnosing the early signs of malignancies/pathology in living tissues before biopsy, offering digital pictures of living tissues at microscopic resolution that could be fit to be considered appropriate fractal objects in future works, and for measuring the fractals of nuclear shapes, cellular borders, and/or other parameters easily visible and defined through this in vivo technique [49,50].

Second, apart from histological samples and clinical photographs, it could be interesting to test the fractal analysis applied to innovative imaging procedures, which could fit well with the application of fractal analysis of vascular patterns, already proven to be distinct through conventional capillaroscopy, which will benefit from a mathematical analysis for diagnostic and prognostic purposes.

Third, fractal analysis could be used to estimate responsiveness to treatments.

Although the present review focused on the diagnostic and prognostic value of fractal analysis in oral oncology, the literature reported some sporadic and preliminary works dealing with the monitoring of treatments as reported by the Polish group of Jurczyszyn et al. [51,52], who applied fractal dimension and texture analysis of lesion autofluorescence in the evaluation of oral lichen planus treatment effectiveness and in estimating the effectiveness of oral leukoplakia treatment using the LiteTouch™ Er:YAG Dental laser, or by Varsha et al., who recently explored the pre- and post-treatment objective evaluation of remission in oral lichen planus using fractal analysis and compared it with the visual analog (VAS) scale [53].

Moreover, it could be interesting to understand if fractal analysis could also be valuable for characterizing, distinguishing, and evaluating HPV-related oral and oropharyngeal lesions due to the evidence that HPV DNA integrates with human keratinocytes' DNA, giving origin to HPV-associated cancers.

Last, to revolutionize oral cancer diagnosis and make the most of the potential of fractal analysis in oral oncology, it could be integrated with machine learning and other artificial intelligence-enhanced tools, as demonstrated in the case of breast and colon cancers [54,55].

Author Contributions: Conceptualization, M.C. and R.S.; methodology, M.C. and F.D.S.; investigation, F.F. and A.A.; data curation, M.C. and M.P.D.P.; writing—original draft preparation, M.C. and F.D.S.; writing—review and editing, M.C. and F.F.; supervision, M.C. and R.S. All authors have read and agreed to the published version of the manuscript.

Funding: This research received no external funding.

Institutional Review Board Statement: Not applicable.

Informed Consent Statement: Not applicable.

Data Availability Statement: Not applicable.

Conflicts of Interest: The authors declare no conflicts of interest.

References

1. Miranda-Filho, A.; Bray, F. Global Patterns and Trends in Cancers of the Lip, Tongue and Mouth. *Oral Oncol.* **2020**, *102*, 104551. [CrossRef] [PubMed]
2. Warnakulasuriya, S. Oral Potentially Malignant Disorders: A Comprehensive Review on Clinical Aspects and Management. *Oral Oncol.* **2020**, *102*, 104550. [CrossRef] [PubMed]
3. Mauceri, R.; Bazzano, M.; Coppini, M.; Tozzo, P.; Panzarella, V.; Campisi, G. Diagnostic Delay of Oral Squamous Cell Carcinoma and the Fear of Diagnosis: A Scoping Review. *Front. Psychol.* **2022**, *13*, 1009080. [CrossRef] [PubMed]
4. Contaldo, M.; Di Napoli, A.; Pannone, G.; Franco, R.; Ionna, F.; Feola, A.; De Rosa, A.; Santoro, A.; Sbordone, C.; Longo, F.; et al. Prognostic Implications of Node Metastatic Features in OSCC: A Retrospective Study on 121 Neck Dissections. *Oncol. Rep.* **2013**, *30*, 2697–2704. [CrossRef]
5. Mascitti, M.; Togni, L.; Caponio, V.C.A.; Zhurakivska, K.; Bizzoca, M.E.; Contaldo, M.; Serpico, R.; Lo Muzio, L.; Santarelli, A. Lymphovascular Invasion as a Prognostic Tool for Oral Squamous Cell Carcinoma: A Comprehensive Review. *Int. J. Oral Maxillofac. Surg.* **2021**, *51*, 1–9. [CrossRef]
6. Chasma, F.; Pedr King, R.; Ker, S.Y. Are There Diagnostic Alternatives to Histopathology in Detecting Oral Cancer? *Evid. Based Dent.* **2022**, *23*, 24–25. [CrossRef]
7. Anders, P.L.; Davis, E.L.; Reuland-Bosma, W.; Van Dijk, J.; Nakagawa, I.; Amano, A.; Ohara-Nemoto, Y.; Endoh, N.; Morisaki, I.; Kimura, S.; et al. Electronic Cigarette: Users Profile, Utilization, Satisfaction and Perceived Efficacy. *Spec. Care Dent.* **2015**, *11*, 30–35. [CrossRef]
8. Mauceri, R.; Coppini, M.; Vacca, D.; Bertolazzi, G.; Panzarella, V.; Di Fede, O.; Tripodo, C.; Campisi, G. Salivary Microbiota Composition in Patients with Oral Squamous Cell Carcinoma: A Systematic Review. *Cancers* **2022**, *14*, 5441. [CrossRef]
9. Romano, A.; Di Stasio, D.; Petruzzi, M.; Fiori, F.; Lajolo, C.; Santarelli, A.; Lucchese, A.; Serpico, R.; Contaldo, M. Noninvasive Imaging Methods to Improve the Diagnosis of Oral Carcinoma and Its Precursors: State of the Art and Proposal of a Three-Step Diagnostic Process. *Cancers* **2021**, *13*, 2864. [CrossRef]
10. Sreeshma, B.; Sivakumar, D.; Maiti, D.; Devi, A. Biomarkers in the Progression and Metastasis of Oral Squamous Cell Carcinoma. *J. Stem Cells* **2022**, *16*, 127–161.

11. Penedo, F.J.; Oswald, L.B.; Kronenfeld, J.P.; Garcia, S.F.; Cella, D.; Yanez, B. The Increasing Value of EHealth in the Delivery of Patient-Centred Cancer Care. *Lancet Oncol.* **2020**, *21*, e240–e251. [CrossRef] [PubMed]
12. Lopes, R.; Betrouni, N. Fractal and multifractal analysis: A review. *Med. Image Anal.* **2009**, *13*, 634–649. [CrossRef] [PubMed]
13. Bisoi, A.K.; Mishra, J. On calculation of fractal dimension of images. *Pattern Recognit. Lett.* **2001**, *22*, 631–637. [CrossRef]
14. Salwaji, S.; Pasupuleti, M.K.; Manyam, R.; Pasupuleti, S.; Alapati, N.S.; Birajdar, S.S.; Mounika, R. Nuclear Fractal Dimension in Diagnosing Oral Cancer-A Systematic Review. *Uttar Pradesh J. Zool.* **2023**, *44*, 47–55. [CrossRef]
15. Panigrahi, S.; Rahmen, J.; Panda, S.; Swarnkar, T. Fractal Geometry for Early Detection and Histopathological Analysis of Oral Cancer. In Proceedings of the 7th International Conference, MIKE 2019, Goa, India, 19–22 December 2020; Volume 11987, pp. 177–185.
16. Sahoo, G.R.; Bharti, D.; Pradhan, A. Multifractal Analysis of Low Coherence Spectra for Oral Cancer Detection. In Proceedings of the SPIE BiOS, San Francisco, CA, USA, 1–6 February 2020; Volume 11253.
17. Delides, A.; Panayiotides, I.; Alegakis, A.; Kyroudi, A.; Banis, C.; Pavlaki, A.; Helidonis, E.; Kittas, C. Fractal Dimension as a Prognostic Factor for Laryngeal Carcinoma. *Anticancer Res.* **2005**, *25*, 2141–2144.
18. Page, M.J.; McKenzie, J.E.; Bossuyt, P.M.; Boutron, I.; Hoffmann, T.C.; Mulrow, C.D.; Shamseer, L.; Tetzlaff, J.M.; Akl, E.A.; Brennan, S.E.; et al. The PRISMA 2020 Statement: An Updated Guideline for Reporting Systematic Reviews. *BMJ* **2021**, *372*, n71. [CrossRef]
19. Saaiq, M.; Ashraf, B. Modifying "Pico" Question into "Picos" Model for More Robust and Reproducible Presentation of the Methodology Employed in A Scientific Study. *World J. Plast. Surg.* **2017**, *6*, 390–392.
20. Krishnan, M.M.R.; Shah, P.; Chakraborty, C.; Ray, A.K. Statistical Analysis of Textural Features for Improved Classification of Oral Histopathological Images. *J. Med. Syst.* **2012**, *36*, 865–881. [CrossRef] [PubMed]
21. Raja, J.V.; Khan, M.; Ramachandra, V.K.; Al-Kadi, O. Texture Analysis of CT Images in the Characterization of Oral Cancers Involving Buccal Mucosa. *Dentomaxillofac. Radiol.* **2012**, *41*, 475–480. [CrossRef]
22. Pandey, P.; Kandakurti, S.; Saxena, V.; Tripathi, P.; Pamula, R.; Yadav, M. Fractal Analysis in Oral Leukoplakia. *J. Indian Acad. Oral Med. Radiol.* **2015**, *27*, 354–358. [CrossRef]
23. Yinti, S.R.; Srikant, N.; Boaz, K.; Lewis, A.J.; Ashokkumar, P.J.; Kapila, S.N. Nuclear Fractal Dimensions as a Tool for Prognostication of Oral Squamous Cell Carcinoma. *J. Clin. Diagn. Res.* **2015**, *9*, EC21–EC25. [CrossRef] [PubMed]
24. Phulari, R.; Rathore, R.; Talegaon, T. Nuclear Fractal Dimension: A New Objective Approach for Discriminating Normal Mucosa, Dysplasia and Carcinoma. *J. Oral Maxillofac. Pathol.* **2016**, *20*, 400–404. [CrossRef]
25. Das, D.K.; Mitra, P.; Chakraborty, C.; Chatterjee, S.; Maiti, A.K.; Bose, S. Computational Approach for Mitotic Cell Detection and Its Application in Oral Squamous Cell Carcinoma. *Multidimens. Syst. Signal Process.* **2017**, *28*, 1031–1050. [CrossRef]
26. Iqbal, J.; Patil, R.; Khanna, V.; Tripathi, A.; Singh, V.; Munshi, M.A.I.; Tiwari, R. Role of Fractal Analysis in Detection of Dysplasia in Potentially Malignant Disorders. *J. Fam. Med. Prim. Care* **2020**, *9*, 2448–2453. [CrossRef]
27. Nawn, D.; Pratiher, S.; Chattoraj, S.; Chakraborty, D.; Pal, M.; Paul, R.R.; Dutta, S.; Chatterjee, J. Multifractal Alterations in Oral Sub-Epithelial Connective Tissue during Progression of Pre-Cancer and Cancer. *IEEE J. Biomed. Health Inform.* **2021**, *25*, 152–162. [CrossRef]
28. Sharma, N.; Nawn, D.; Pratiher, S.; Shome, S.; Chatterjee, R.; Biswas, K.; Pal, M.; Paul, R.R.; Dutta, S.; Chatterjee, J. Multifractal Texture Analysis of Salivary Fern Pattern for Oral Pre-Cancers and Cancer Assessment. *IEEE Sens. J.* **2021**, *21*, 9333–9340. [CrossRef]
29. Santolia, D.; Dahiya, S.; Sharma, S.; Khan, M.A.; Mohammed, N.; Priya, H.; Gupta, S.R.; Bhargava, S.; Gupta, D.S.R. Fractal Dimension and Radiomorphometric Analysis of Orthopanoramic Radiographs in Patients with Tobacco and Areca Nut Associated Oral Mucosal Lesions: A Pilot in-Vivo Study in a North Indian Cohort. *Oral Surg. Oral Med. Oral Pathol. Oral Radiol.* **2022**, *134*, 627–638. [CrossRef]
30. Krishnan, M.M.R.; Shah, P.; Choudhary, A.; Chakraborty, C.; Paul, R.R.; Ray, A.K. Textural Characterization of Histopathological Images for Oral Sub-Mucous Fibrosis Detection. *Tissue Cell* **2011**, *43*, 318–330. [CrossRef]
31. Rahman, J.; Panda, S.; Panigrahi, S.; Mohanty, N.; Swarnkar, T.; Mishra, U. Perspective of Nuclear Fractal Dimension in Diagnosis and Prognosis of Oral Squamous Cell Carcinoma. *J. Oral Maxillofac. Pathol.* **2022**, *26*, 127. [CrossRef]
32. Goutzanis, L.; Papadogeorgakis, N.; Pavlopoulos, P.M.; Katti, K.; Petsinis, V.; Plochoras, I.; Pantelidaki, C.; Kavantzas, N.; Patsouris, E.; Alexandridis, C. Nuclear Fractal Dimension as a Prognostic Factor in Oral Squamous Cell Carcinoma. *Oral Oncol.* **2008**, *44*, 345–353. [CrossRef]
33. Goutzanis, L.P.; Papadogeorgakis, N.; Pavlopoulos, P.M.; Petsinis, V.; Plochoras, I.; Eleftheriadis, E.; Pantelidaki, A.; Patsouris, E.; Alexandridis, C. Vascular Fractal Dimension and Total Vascular Area in the Study of Oral Cancer. *Head Neck* **2009**, *31*, 298–307. [CrossRef] [PubMed]
34. Spyridonos, P.; Gaitanis, G.; Tzaphlidou, M.; Bassukas, I.D. Spatial Fuzzy C-Means Algorithm with Adaptive Fuzzy Exponent Selection for Robust Vermilion Border Detection in Healthy and Diseased Lower Lips. *Comput. Methods Programs Biomed.* **2014**, *114*, 291–301. [CrossRef]
35. Spyridonos, P.; Gaitanis, G.; Bassukas, I.D.; Tzaphlidou, M. Evaluation of Vermillion Border Descriptors and Relevance Vector Machines Discrimination Model for Making Probabilistic Predictions of Solar Cheilosis on Digital Lip Photographs. *Comput. Biol. Med.* **2015**, *63*, 11–18. [CrossRef] [PubMed]

36. Lucchese, A.; Gentile, E.; Capone, G.; De Vico, G.; Serpico, R.; Landini, G. Fractal analysis of mucosal microvascular patterns in oral lichen planus: A preliminary study. *Oral Surg. Oral Med. Oral Pathol. Oral Radiol.* **2015**, *120*, 609–615. [CrossRef] [PubMed]
37. Mincione, G.; Di Nicola, M.; Di Marcantonio, M.C.; Muraro, R.; Piattelli, A.; Rubini, C.; Penitente, E.; Piccirilli, M.; Aprile, G.; Perrotti, V.; et al. Nuclear fractal dimension in oral squamous cell carcinoma: A novel method for the evaluation of grading, staging, and survival. *J. Oral Pathol. Med.* **2015**, *44*, 680–684. [CrossRef]
38. D'Addazio, G.; Artese, L.; Traini, T.; Rubini, C.; Caputi, S.; Sinjari, B. Immunohistochemical study of osteopontin in oral squamous cell carcinoma allied to fractal dimension. *J. Biol. Regul. Homeost. Agents* **2018**, *32*, 1033–1038.
39. Landini, G.; Rippin, J.W. An "asymptotic fractal" approach to the morphology of malignant cell nuclei. *Fractals* **1993**, *1*, 326–335. [CrossRef]
40. Margaritescu, C.; Raica, M.; Pirici, D.; Simionescu, C.; Mogoanta, L.; Stinga, A.C.; Stinga, A.S.; Ribatti, D. Podoplanin Expression in Tumor-Free Resection Margins of Oral Squamous Cell Carcinomas: An Immunohistochemical and Fractal Analysis Study. *Histol. Histopathol.* **2010**, *25*, 701–711.
41. Klatt, J.; Gerich, C.E.; Gröbe, A.; Opitz, J.; Schreiber, J.; Hanken, H.; Salomon, G.; Heiland, M.; Kluwe, L.; Blessmann, M. Fractal Dimension of Time-Resolved Autofluorescence Discriminates Tumour from Healthy Tissues in the Oral Cavity. *J. Cranio-Maxillo-Facial Surg. Off. Publ. Eur. Assoc. Cranio-Maxillo-Facial Surg.* **2014**, *42*, 852–854. [CrossRef]
42. Bose, P.; Brockton, N.T.; Guggisberg, K.; Nakoneshny, S.C.; Kornaga, E.; Klimowicz, A.C.; Tambasco, M.; Dort, J.C. Fractal Analysis of Nuclear Histology Integrates Tumor and Stromal Features into a Single Prognostic Factor of the Oral Cancer Microenvironment. *BMC Cancer* **2015**, *15*, 409. [CrossRef]
43. Ou-Yang, M.; Hsieh, Y.-F.; Lee, C.-C. Biopsy Diagnosis of Oral Carcinoma by the Combination of Morphological and Spectral Methods Based on Embedded Relay Lens Microscopic Hyperspectral Imaging System. *J. Med. Biol. Eng.* **2015**, *35*, 437–447. [CrossRef] [PubMed]
44. Yang, X.; Xiao, X.; Wu, W.; Shen, X.; Zhou, Z.; Liu, W.; Shi, L. Cytological Study of DNA Content and Nuclear Morphometric Analysis for Aid in the Diagnosis of High-Grade Dysplasia within Oral Leukoplakia. *Oral Surg. Oral Med. Oral Pathol. Oral Radiol.* **2017**, *124*, 280–285. [CrossRef]
45. Jurczyszyn, K.; Kazubowska, K.; Kubasiewicz-Ross, P.; Ziółkowski, P.; Dominiak, M. Application of fractal dimension analysis and photodynamic diagnosis in the case of differentiation between lichen planus and leukoplakia: A preliminary study. *Adv. Clin. Exp. Med.* **2018**, *27*, 1729–1736. [CrossRef] [PubMed]
46. Guerrero-Sánchez, Y.; Gómez García, F.; Chamorro-Petronacci, C.M.; Suárez-Peñaranda, J.M.; Pérez-Sayáns, M. Use of the Fractal Dimension to Differentiate Epithelium and Connective Tissue in Oral Leukoplakias. *Cancers* **2022**, *14*, 2697. [CrossRef] [PubMed]
47. Singh, G.; Preethi, B.; Chaitanya, K.K.; Navyasree, M.; Kumar, T.G.; Kaushik, M.S. Prevalence of Oral Mucosal Lesions among Tobacco Consumers: Cross-Sectional Study. *J. Pharm. Bioallied. Sci.* **2023**, *15*, S562–S565. [CrossRef]
48. Seventhy-First World Health Assembly mHealth. Use of Appropriate Digital Technologies for Public Health. Available online: https://apps.who.int/gb/ebwha/pdf_files/WHA71/A71_R7-en.pdf (accessed on 21 November 2023).
49. Contaldo, M.; Lauritano, D.; Carinci, F.; Romano, A.; Di Stasio, D.; Lajolo, C.; Della Vella, F.; Serpico, R.; Lucchese, A. Intraoral confocal microscopy of suspicious oral lesions: A prospective case series. *Int. J. Dermatol.* **2020**, *59*, 82–90. [CrossRef]
50. Contaldo, M.; Di Stasio, D.; Petruzzi, M.; Serpico, R.; Lucchese, A. In vivo reflectance confocal microscopy of oral lichen planus. *Int. J. Dermatol.* **2019**, *58*, 940–945. [CrossRef]
51. Jurczyszyn, K.; Kozakiewicz, M. Application of Texture and Fractal Dimension Analysis to Estimate Effectiveness of Oral Leukoplakia Treatment Using an Er:YAG Laser-A Prospective Study. *Materials* **2020**, *13*, 3614. [CrossRef]
52. Jurczyszyn, K.; Trzeciakowski, W.; Kozakiewicz, M.; Kida, D.; Malec, K.; Karolewicz, B.; Konopka, T.; Zborowski, J. Fractal Dimension and Texture Analysis of Lesion Autofluorescence in the Evaluation of Oral Lichen Planus Treatment Effectiveness. *Materials* **2021**, *14*, 5448. [CrossRef]
53. Varsha, K.S.; Krithika, C.L.; Ganesan, A.; Chandraveni, A.; Jothi, A. Pre and post treatment objective evaluation of remission in oral lichen planus using fractal analysis and comparison with visual analog (vas) and thongprasom scale-a cohort study. *Int. J. Chem. Biochem. Sci.* **2023**, *23*, 177–184.
54. Chan, A.; Tuszynski, J.A. Automatic prediction of tumour malignancy in breast cancer with fractal dimension. *R. Soc. Open Sci.* **2016**, *3*, 160558. [CrossRef] [PubMed]
55. Chang, A.; Prabhala, S.; Daneshkhah, A.; Lin, J.; Subramanian, H.; Roy, H.K.; Backman, V. Early screening of colorectal cancer using feature engineering with artificial intelligence-enhanced analysis of nanoscale chromatin modifications. *Res. Sq.* **2023**, 1–25. [CrossRef]

applied sciences

MDPI

Review

The Importance of Conceptualising the Human-Centric Approach in Maintaining and Promoting Cybersecurity-Hygiene in Healthcare 4.0

Kitty Kioskli [1,2,*], Theofanis Fotis [3], Sokratis Nifakos [4] and Haralambos Mouratidis [1]

1 Institute of Analytics and Data Science (IADS), School of Computer Science and Electronic Engineering, University of Essex, Colchester SO4 3SQ, UK
2 Trustilio B.V., 681017 Amsterdam, The Netherlands
3 Centre for Secure, Intelligent and Usable Systems (CSIUS), School of Sport & Health Sciences, University of Brighton, Brighton BN2 4AT, UK
4 Department of Learning, Management and Ethics, Karolinska Institute, 17177 Solna, Sweden
* Correspondence: kitty.kioskli@essex.ac.uk

Abstract: The cyberspace depicts an increasing number of difficulties related to security, especially in healthcare. This is evident from how vulnerable critical infrastructures are to cyberattacks and are unprotected against cybercrime. Users, ideally, should maintain a good level of cyber hygiene, via regular software updates and the development of unique passwords, as an effective way to become resilient to cyberattacks. Cyber security breaches are a top priority, and most users are aware that their behaviours may put them at risk; however, they are not educated to follow best practices, such as protecting their passwords. Mass cyber education may serve as a means to offset poor cyber security behaviours; however, mandatory education becomes a questionable point if the content is not focused on human factors, using human-centric approaches and taking into account end users' behaviours, which is currently the case. The nature of the present paper is largely exploratory, and the purpose is two-fold: To present and explore the cyber hygiene definition, context and habits of end users in order to strengthen our understanding of users. Our paper reports the best practices that should be used by healthcare organisations and healthcare professionals to maintain good cyber hygiene and how these can be applied via a healthcare use case scenario to increase awareness related to data privacy and cybersecurity. This is an issue of great importance and urgency considering the rapid increase of cyberattacks in healthcare organisations, mainly due to human errors. Further to that, based on human-centric approaches, our long-term vision and future work involves facilitating the development of efficient practices and education associated with cybersecurity hygiene via a flexible, adaptable and practical framework.

Keywords: cyber hygiene; cyberattacks; healthcare; human factors

Citation: Kioskli, K.; Fotis, T.; Nifakos, S.; Mouratidis, H. The Importance of Conceptualising the Human-Centric Approach in Maintaining and Promoting Cybersecurity-Hygiene in Healthcare 4.0. *Appl. Sci.* **2023**, *13*, 3410. https://doi.org/10.3390/app13063410

Academic Editors: Stefano Silvestri and Francesco Gargiulo

Received: 7 February 2023
Revised: 3 March 2023
Accepted: 6 March 2023
Published: 7 March 2023

1. Introduction

The rapid evolution of cyberspace, over the last two decades, has had an impact on every facet of human life. The increase in the range, volume and speed of communications, which are offered within the cyberspace, have beyond doubt affected the way people are governed, how companies deliver their services and, overall, how societies interact. The cyberspace also depicts an increasing number of difficulties related to security. This is evident from how vulnerable critical infrastructures are to cyberattacks, while the global economy is unprotected against cybercrime and cyber-espionage. Damages of great value occur from spam, sophisticated Distributed Denial of Service (DDoS) attacks, viruses and worms. As a result, member states have a well-defined cyberspace in their security doctrines and military as a new domain of protection, investigation and conflict. Organisations, for example EU and NATO, treat cybersecurity as an issue of great importance affecting the defence and security of member states and the organisations per se [1].

The terms Healthcare 4.0, Health 4.0, Medical Industry 4.0 and Healthcare Industry 4.0 are associated with 4IR in healthcare [2]. Technologies related to 4IR are manufacturing systems, cloud-based design and the industrial Internet of Things. The common major challenge with these internet technologies is the applicability of cyber security and data privacy [3].

Users, ideally, should maintain a good level of cyber hygiene, via regular software updates and development of unique passwords, as an effective way to become resilient to cyberattacks. Cyber hygiene refers to keeping proper guidelines and norms and involves establishing healthy cyber behaviours within the cyberspace to protect any available data from hackers [4]. However, it is evident from the high volume of attacks that many users keep poor cyber hygiene, as they share personal information via social networks and freely share passwords as well [5]. Hackers know well that the easiest way to access a system is to find a technical vulnerability or steal an individual's information. There is an urgent need to help individuals improve their behavioural responses and cyber hygiene.

Weak cybersecurity has a detrimental financial cost on society. More specifically, the Ponemon Institute [6] conducted the Second Annual Cost of Cyber Crime Study showing that US organisations' average cost of cyberattacks is $17.36 million, Japan's is 8.39 million, Germany's $7.84 million, United Kingdom's $7.21 million, Brazil's $5.27 million and Australia's $4.3 million. These average estimated values of the attacks are only increasing since 2014. The study indicated that the reasons that the organisations experience the attacks are 98% associated with malware, 70% associated with social engineering and phishing, 63% web-based attacks, 61% associated with malicious code, 55% associated with botnets, 50% associated with stolen devices, 49% associated with denial of services and 41% associated with malicious insiders. It is worth noting that the organisations that experienced social engineering and phishing-related attacks have risen by 8% from 2015 to 2016.

Besides organisations, which are clearly affected by cyberattacks, end users are also greatly impacted by major losses from these cybersecurity breaches. The FBI's Internet Crime Complaints Center (IC3) [7] has provided useful data on cybercrimes reported by American citizens. Only in 2015, 288,012 complaints of cybercrimes were filed in by the FBI and more than 40% of those complaints were followed by monetary losses. The same year, the total amount of losses was officially reported as $1,070,711,522, with $8421 being the average report of a loss. Even though gender and age are not detrimental factors influencing cybercrimes, it has been recorded that males aged 50–59 years had a high victim count of 31,473 and for females aged 40–49 years, 29,559 reported cybercrimes. Meanwhile, there were 1648 women and men in all age groups, who reported over $100,000 in losses.

Humans are often characterised as the weakest link in cyber security [8,9]. This is particularly accurate when it comes to personal computing environments since they are the target of 95% of the malicious attacks [10]. This may be explained by the fact that personal and home computing devices are not guarded by security staff, who also keep software and hardware up to date [11]. The rapid increase of cyber threats and cyberattacks make defensive behaviours from users extremely important. This is because, regardless of how secure a system may be, the user is frequently a critical backdoor into the data and entire network [12]. Hackers look for vulnerabilities to exploit, which may come from end users who are maintaining poor cyber hygiene, such as, for example, by revealing personal information or not complying with best practices [5].

Cyber security breaches are a top priority, and most users are aware that their behaviours may put them at risk; however, they are not educated to follow best practices, such as protecting their passwords. Even though there is a vast variety of available security options, users often do not know how to access those options, understand them and implement them [13]. Furthermore, end users lack an understanding of the essential cyber security actions that can be taken, and this can feed inappropriate behaviours and attitudes [14]. Nevertheless, good cyber hygiene can enhance safe behaviours and can protect against upcoming threats and attacks [15].

Mass cyber education may serve as a means to offset poor cyber security behaviours; however, mandatory education becomes a questionable point if the content is not focused on human factors, using human-centric approaches and taking into account end users' behaviours, which is currently the case [16]. Many cybersecurity, information system and computer science courses do not include content, particularly addressing the weaknesses related to human factors in end users. On the one hand, in several institutions, coursework associated with human behaviour and cognition is not required of information systems or computer science students. This is frankly problematic since a human user will be the handler in a computer-based product. On the other hand, there is an evident shift, in many programs of study, in multidisciplinary approaches [17]. This significant shift in the cyber educational system represents a unique opportunity to set frameworks and guidelines related to good cyber hygiene, human-centric and multidisciplinary approaches. This will strengthen the content of the curricula and make their delivery more effective, while it will further provide practical implications in other fields where training in cybersecurity remains essential for all members of staff, such as governance [18].

It is worth noting that there is a strong connection between cybersecurity and the deep learning approach, as deep learning has shown significant potential in addressing many cybersecurity challenges. Deep learning is a subset of machine learning that involves training artificial neural networks with multiple layers to learn patterns and features from large amounts of data [19]. In the context of cybersecurity, deep learning algorithms can be used to identify and classify threats based on patterns and behaviours that are difficult to detect using traditional signature-based approaches.

One of the key applications of deep learning in cybersecurity, for example, is in the area of threat detection. Deep learning models can analyse large volumes of network traffic, log data and other security data to identify patterns and anomalies that may indicate a security threat. This can help security teams to detect and respond to threats more quickly and effectively. Deep learning is also being used in the development of advanced authentication and access control systems. These systems use deep learning algorithms to analyse user behaviour and identify anomalies that may indicate unauthorised access. This can help organisations to prevent insider threats and protect sensitive data.

Previous research has investigated this topic from various angles, such as by identifying attack paths and showing how a recommendation method can be used to classify potential future cyberattacks, from a risk management perspective [20]. Other additions from the literature include a contribution towards vulnerabilities and effective threats analysis by using machine learning models (i.e., BERT neural language model and XGBoost) to withdraw the most relevant information from the Natural Language documents mostly available online [21]. Another useful proposal is a deep learning technique presented for reliable classification and accurate detection of organic pollutants. This paper refers to water pollutants [19].

Overall, the deep learning approach has shown great promise in addressing many of the challenges associated with cybersecurity. As cyber threats continue to evolve and become more sophisticated, deep learning algorithms will likely play an increasingly important role in helping organisations to detect and respond to these threats.

The nature of the present paper is largely exploratory, and the purpose is two-fold: to present and explore the cyber hygiene definition, context and habits of end users in order to strengthen our understanding of users. Our paper reports the best practices that should be used by healthcare organisations to maintain cyber hygiene. To our knowledge, this is the first paper which collects and presents a concrete set of best practices and directly addresses healthcare organisations and the healthcare staff. Further to that, based on human-centric approaches, to facilitate the development of efficient practices and education associated with cybersecurity hygiene via a flexible, adaptable and practical framework.

2. Cyber Hygiene in the Cyberspace

Cyber hygiene originates from the concept of personal hygiene in the public health domain. In an extensive report exploring cyber hygiene practices across various nations, the European Union Agency for Network and Information Security (ENISA) [22] introduced that "cyber hygiene should be viewed in the same manner as personal hygiene and, once properly integrated into an organisation will be simple daily routines, good behaviours and occasional check-ups to make sure the organisations online health is in optimum condition".

Research in social sciences on cyber security has been focused on the security behaviours and risk factors of the end–end users, while there is limited research on developing measurements of cyber hygiene. In particular, according to previous approaches that assume that the end users are aware of cyber safety behaviours, they, therefore, focus on measuring the frequency of enactment of these behaviours [23].

It is of high importance to understand the role of how end users are processing information and their interpretation within a cybersecurity framework in an organisation. For instance, researchers have empirically demonstrated that individuals who systematically process information are less likely to get victimised during a spear phishing attack [24]. Therefore, plenty of cybersecurity awareness programs aim to enhance the ability of the users to process better information.

The lack of cyber hygiene leads to a number of cyber threats and cyberattacks, as described below. The recent WannaCry Ransomware cyberattack [25], which targeted, on a large scale, the Microsoft Windows operating system, had a severe impact on the systems. This occurred due to the organisations and individuals not having updated their software security versions as of the month of March, even though the more recent version had been released in 2014. This is why unlicensed Windows software and systems with outdated software versions became vulnerable and easy to exploit in this attack. The healthcare ecosystem was particularly affected by CT and MRI scanners being exploited in hospitals, among banking, business and corporate sectors worldwide. Around 300,000 computer systems in 150 countries were affected.

Ransomware refers to a cyber malware, which blocks the access to data and related information. However, it impaired the access over data with vulnerable ports. Sometimes, a ransomware needs an amount to be paid in order to access the infected data and when the individual clicks on that attachment or link, it activates on that email. In addition, it can infiltrate the system when the individual visits some webpages. A cyber malware blocks the internal files, encrypts according to itself and makes the documents inaccessible or inactive for the user while it may infect the server attached to that system and also lock up the whole computer network system.

Firstly, in this process, the attacker develops a key pair and puts the public key in the malware, and following that, the malware is released. Then, the malware develops a random symmetric key, which then encrypts the individual's data with it. This is referred to as hybrid encryption in which the public key is used in the malware in order to encrypt the symmetric key. This procedure results in the formulation of small symmetric and asymmetric ciphertext of the individual's data. It also places a message to the individual involving the asymmetric ciphertext and the amount that should be paid as ransom by the individual to get rid of this attack. If the end user sends back the asymmetric ciphertext along with the ransom amount to the cyber attacker, then the hacker decrypts the asymmetric ciphertext with his/her private key and sends back the symmetric key to the end user. Following that, the end user, with the help of the symmetric key, will be able to decrypt the encrypted data. Lastly, this crypto virological attack will have been completed [4].

However, there is no such evidence of computer systems getting deciphered after making the required ransom payments. There has been a recorded mitigation of one attack by Marcus Hutchin battling accusations of involvement in a malware scam. They discovered a "kill switch", which the malware itself had coded [26]. For the DNS sinkhole, he registered a space name; a DNS provides inaccurate data about a domain and made the spreading of the infection work, such as a worm. At the same time, the spread of malware was backing off and offering time to the end users to prepare protective measures. After that, Adrian Guinet created a solution to the WannaCry Ransomware cyberattack by providing a "wannakey", which was based on its flaws. This worked only if the decryption key was not overwritten by any malware, or the infected computer was not being rebooted.

These are just examples highlighting how ignorance in cyber hygiene could lead to critical cyber threats and cyberattacks [27,28]. Some of the prevention measures that should be adopted are as follows: in order to avoid unwanted searches, activate Google Opt-Out while logged into Google, delete cookies on a daily basis, use PayPal and credit cards instead of debit cards, turn off Google's web history, use a hard drive to back up your data, and bring counterfeit for your online purchases. If the end users keep updating their software regularly, such major cyberattacks would have been avoided efficiently and easily.

3. Human Behaviours: The Weakest Link in Cyberattacks

A significant number of cyberattacks are directed towards the users through distorted means, such as malicious emails and masqueraded applications. Though cyberattacks are aiming to exploit either the technical vulnerabilities of networks and systems, or the errors due to human behaviour, it is the latter that remains as the weakest link in these cyberattacks [29,30]. Attackers most often employ methods exploiting weak cyber behaviours, defined as social engineering.

Studies historically confirm that social engineering approaches account for the majority of total cyber security attacks. Bowen et al. [31] showed that 28% of the total attacks were due to social engineering, and in 2016, 97% of malware attacks targeted human behaviour. A more recent report estimated that 95% of cyberattacks were again attributed to human errors and risky behaviour [32].

Looking in the literature at the types of risky behaviours and human errors, one can identify the most common, including the use of infected memory disks, sharing of passwords, reusing the same passwords for different platforms, not updating software, unauthorised disclosure of personal information, accessing fake emails and installing software from unverified sources [33–37].

Early research exploring the reasons for risky behaviour found these to be due to an employee's lack of knowledge and poor decision making due to staff shortage, fatigue and heavy workload, as well as avoidance of human behaviour where the end user does not perceive the risk as related to them [37].

Exploring further the human behaviours that raise the risks of errors and increase the cybersecurity vulnerabilities, it seems there is a direct link between individual personalities and behavioural traits. Moustafa et al. [38] identified the following traits playing a key role in behavioural cybersecurity: (a) procrastination, where research has shown that individuals who procrastinate are less likely to adhere to security policies; (b) impulsivity, where research demonstrated that addictive behaviour is directly linked to risky cyber behaviour and ignorance of information security policies [14]; (c) future thinking, where it was shown that individuals who are interested in their future have higher rates on following cybersecurity guidelines [39–41], but at the same time those that are more optimistic may fall easier victims to cybersecurity attacks; and (d) risk taking behaviours, where it seems that according to some research studies, individuals that are taking high risks in their lives, are more likely to make cybersecurity errors.

4. Cyber Threats and Countermeasures in Healthcare 4.0

There are several attacks that occur daily within healthcare 4.0. However, as found in the literature, there are six main types of cyber threats that can be identified in the cyberspace, and are directly applied in healthcare 4.0, accompanied by appropriate countermeasures [4], which are presented in detail in Table 1.

Table 1. Cyber Threats in the Cyberspace.

Cyber Threat	Description
Attacks on Hosted Components	These types of attacks include destructive software injection to a targeted system, for example, cross-site scripting, SQL injection and related techniques, which threaten the access and/or authentication controls. This may occur in cloud-based control systems handling big volumes of sensitive data. Here, the countermeasures include mainly role-based approaches, creating awareness in order to protect towards impersonation at the cloud level and API authentication.
Social Engineering	It refers to the attacks performed on the "weakest link" in the security supply chain. This is achieved by psychologically manipulating individuals to perform malicious actions or share confidential information. Common techniques used for this manipulation are shoulder surfing, diversion theft, "dumpster diving", impersonation of help desk calls, phishing and/or personal blackmailing [38,39]. Social engineering is one of the major reasons why even security-aware and well-equipped companies fall victims to cyberattacks. Hackers identify the weakest link in the security supply chain in which they can insert the malicious software or the virus into the targeted system. Therefore, it is of great importance to identify and further secure the weakest link in the security chain. Some of the initial countermeasures, which can be adopted to prevent upcoming attacks, include block Wi-Fi connections to unsecured networks, block network connections related to malicious content, stop using non-secure web pages and websites and performing actions on them. Further approaches, which can be taken to reduce the high level of cyberattacks, include mitigating known threats in the systems and applications, regularly patching vulnerable systems and/or keeping the company's devices up-to-date with the latest version.
Physical Attack	Physical attacks are mostly carried out in fields involving several Internet of Things (IoT) applications since they are connected to a number of components and hardware devices. These are easily located by hackers since they cannot be monitored at a single location and are kept far away from each other [42,43]. The main countermeasures in such cases include trusted platform modules to enable storage of the data on separate platforms securely, file system encryption meaning proper algorithms and encryption decryption techniques shall be used so the data can be stored and secured properly, and lastly remote attestation meaning attesting a remote to each hardware device, which is located far in order to be controlled from faraway locations as well.
Network Compromise	These attacks are known as 'middle way attacks' where the hackers use a number of techniques, for example, altering or blocking communications between hardware devices and their cloud-based controller session and/or hijacking to enter and disrupt a network. The countermeasures that can be offered here include performing regular updates on the software and use of proper file decryption and encryption techniques while sending and receiving sensitive data between the end-to-end users.
Hacked Device Software	In these attacks, the hacker accesses the software at the device level and then it carries out several fraudulent activities and techniques. Such activities and techniques target to take control of the data in the system and include elevation of privileges, denial of service, malware injection and/or false identification [44]. These types of attacks can be tackled by carrying out countermeasures, as for example, software isolation; "secured boot", meaning that when any malicious activities are carried out in the system, after rebooting the system, it then does not turn on and all the available data in the system becomes resilient to the attacker; and/or software update, which maintains the software and its system updated with the latest version available on the market.
Security Misconfiguration	This type of attack is being performed due to inattentiveness or carelessness. The moment when it has been observed to occur is when handling the security changes of the software, as the security changes become misconfigured and provide the attackers with the right opportunity to attack the devices and extract the available data from them. Hence, the most significant countermeasure is that the security changes ought to be carried out with extreme care and with proper decryption encryption techniques as well [42].

It is essential to ensure aspects, such as higher confidentiality, resilience, and integrity levels, to tackle such attacks. Consideration of the human aspects would be key to build these aspects within healthcare 4.0.

5. Towards a Human-Centric Approach to Security

As we discussed earlier, human behaviour is the weakest link in cybersecurity; it is the employees of any organisation that should be involved and engaged within cybersecurity awareness and the development of mitigation approaches. Furthermore, it is important to accept that these individuals can be simultaneously the point of risk but also the point of success. Holland (2020), suggests as a response, the development of an interaction of trust between the end user and the systems especially as the cybersecurity landscape is vast and continuously expanding with the proliferation of new smarter and interconnected devices and networks [45].

Furthermore, as a result of the global COVID-19 pandemic, new working trends have been introduced, where employees working flexibly use their own devices or are using work devices outside the office, resulting in blurred lines between personal and business limits, exacerbating the risky behaviours. As a result, any measures to mitigate the cyber risks need to go beyond the software updating and hardware maintenance to a more human-centric approach.

Human-centric cyber security is still a new domain, which is an intangible concept and is challenging to define and to be understood, not only by the lay end user, but also by specialists in cyberspace. The reason is that it sits at the intersection of human behaviour, computing and security systems. Grobler et al. (2021) [46] defined human-centric cyber security as involving all aspects of cyber security, with a particular focus on the human involvement in the system and processes. They propose for the design, implementation and assessment of holistic human centric cyber security systems, three components of what they define as the 3U's, User, Usage and Usability, with each one of them including further subsections, as seen in Table 2.

Table 2. Design, implementation and assessment of holistic human-centric cyber security systems.

Component	Description
User	• Demography and Culture • Situational Awareness • Psychology and Behaviour • Cognitive Factors
Usage	• Functional Measures • Technical Measures • Legislation, Regulations and Policies
Usability	• Experience Factors • Interaction Factors

The authors suggest that the consideration of all these factors in the development of human-centric cybersecurity approaches can lead to automated functions and, at the same time, keep the end user engaged with the technology in an interaction of what they call 'collaborative intelligence'.

Furthermore similar and relevant components are proposed to be considered when organisations wish to build a human-centred security culture by following specific steps, including the assessment of the organisation's information handling, the testing of the employee's awareness, the review of their interactions and the promotion of their critical thinking, the identification of threats, the reflection on past mistakes, the revision of the processes and training and the automation of security functions [47].

Regarding the future and the way forward, similarly to Grobler et al. (2021) [46], relevant literature suggests that further research and a paradigm shift is required to validate and test such approaches (i.e., 3Us) addressing the need for a human-centric approach to cybersecurity. The paradigm shift suggests moving away from quantitative data collection of human behaviour to an observational approach, increasing the number of participants in projects with diverse samples rather than segmented groups and be 'Belief-Driven' where the cybersecurity researchers start considering end users perspectives rather than instructing them only what to do [48].

A human-centric, co-produced approach would lead and inform:

(a) Education tailormade to the demographics and needs of the audience with regularly updated messages to avoid desensitisation of the audience [49].
(b) Automation, whereby users would not need to proactively undertake cyber practices, reducing their workload and resulting in increased engagement and adherence to regulations [50].

This approach will inform the development of both best practices and education for cybersecurity hygiene that we will discuss below.

6. Best Practices and Education of Cybersecurity Hygiene for Healthcare Professionals

Cyber threats are rapidly increasing across various business sectors and the incidents in data privacy and cybersecurity breaches are also rising alongside them, particularly in the healthcare domain. In response to the rising threats and incidents, healthcare organisations adopt technical measures, such as the use of firewalls, antivirus and software/firmware patches, aiming to preserve and protect the business continuity of healthcare services. Regardless of such efforts, cybersecurity threats are rising, and the adopted measures have been proven insufficient to respond to cyberattacks. This is often because the important role that the personnel play in this supply chain, related to cyber defence, is not being considered.

In practice, healthcare organisations are encouraged to adopt general data privacy and cybersecurity guidelines that have, as a focal point, the human factor. Nevertheless, there is limited research within the literature on collective practical cyber hygiene guidelines and best practices, which can help healthcare organisations to apply specific interventions, such as training programs and awareness activities, which at the same time are measurable to the healthcare professionals. With that being said, structured best practices that would assist the higher management to choose the optimal number of security controls that will be most efficient for healthcare organisations and professionals are yet not available and, at the same time, are highly desirable.

The importance of developing best practices in order to maintain cybersecurity hygiene has been highlighted with the COVID-19 pandemic through the increased usage of cyberspace and worldwide connection via a simple click [51]. In similar ways, cyberspace has become the main means of working, which makes businesses and individuals particularly vulnerable to cyber threats and risks [4]. The high usage levels of cyberspace make individuals' lives easy; meanwhile, it exposes their personal and professional information to cyber threats. It is beyond doubt that end users are vulnerable to a number of cyber risks [51]. The most optimal way to secure cyberspace usage requires education and proper adoption of the cyber hygiene best practices. Acceptable and accessible practices are necessary to proactively protect, improve, monitor, secure and maintain user's information on the Internet [14,19]. The continuous development and application of such best practices should be the standard route that ensures user's safety, identity and information. These best practices help reduce the impact of corruption and loss of information, resource damage and data breach while improving cyber hygiene [17]. The repeated use of the best practices to maintain proper cybersecurity hygiene results in peace of mind with the prospective of reaching an excellent outcome overall.

Cybersecurity hygiene best practices and education are linked to individual differences aiming to improve cybersecurity. Even though Internet security guidelines for users are widely available, it is doubtful how many consumers understand and apply these reports and if the available security guidelines are written in a lay language for both tech laggards and tech savvy users [52]. One feasible solution in order to overcome the educational gap in cybersecurity would be to establish best practices and mandatory cyber hygiene education for users, including both non-cyber and cyber professionals [17,53].

Best practices and mass cyber education may contribute to discourage poor cybersecurity behaviours; however, to achieve the most optimal results, the content should shift its focus to human factors and use behaviours. It is evident that most available courses and/or training do not address explicitly human cognition and behaviours. In this section, we will present best practices for cyber hygiene, as found in the literature, which are suggested to be applied in the context of healthcare to improve security overall.

The baseline cyber hygiene involves several basic steps that are required for cyber defence. The baseline practices are mostly rooted in frameworks, such as, for example, the NIST cybersecurity framework. It helps organisations, including the healthcare supply chain, to have a detailed and clear set of best practices to show and modify how cybersecurity is being performed and measured regularly [19]. While there are not standardised best practices for healthcare, a basic set of methods to maintain cyber hygiene in business has been presented in the literature [54,55]. All organisations and cyber users need to take responsibility for their browsing in both their personal and professional space. Individuals must take ownership of maintaining sufficient cyber hygiene and safeguarding, by using best practices, against cyberattacks [4]. Best practices, as collected from the literature, are presented in Figure 1.

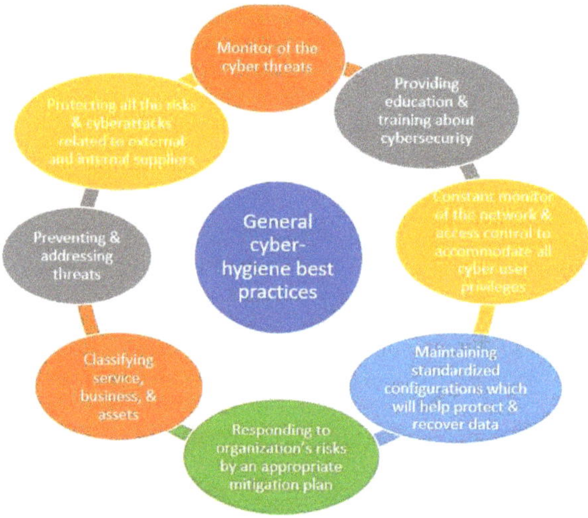

Figure 1. Best practices for general cyber hygiene.

Jointly with other best practices, the deficiency of essential techniques, such as the above, may lead to poor cyber hygiene. Additional recommended set of best practices for small business enterprises targeting cyber risks have been introduced [53]. Meanwhile, cyber hygiene best practices, which can be used by healthcare staff to maintain privacy and security, are illustrated in Figure 2 [56,57].

These practices should be constantly implemented to prevent data breach, unauthorised access and loss of information. The effects of using best practices for cyber hygiene will ultimately provide safe cyber surfing and improve cyber health. The baseline practice as compiled with the National Institute of Standards and Technology's (NIST) cybersecurity framework (CSF) will be explained below.

The current literature suggests the need [54,55] for organisations to align and comply with the NIST's cybersecurity framework in order to promote cyber hygiene. The NIST Framework's main aim is to provide a detailed outline for businesses and organisations to improve ways to identify, prevent and mitigate various cyber incidents [58]. The NIST framework includes five fundamental categories and functions for cyber threats, which are to identify, detect, protect, respond and recover [59].

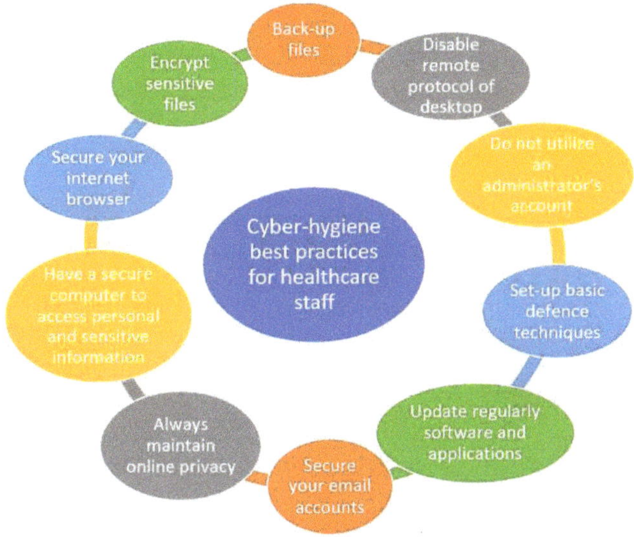

Figure 2. Cyber hygiene best practices for healthcare staff.

Every fundamental component plays a crucial role in promoting good practice while maintaining a balanced cyber hygiene at all levels. In order to comply with the "identify" main element, the asset's responsibility, leading role and vulnerability and risks to cyberattacks need to be understood. With this implementation of this fundamental function, each organisation would more easily establish the rules and policies that will help them improve good cyber hygiene and remain protected against cyber threats [54,55].

The second fundamental element is to "protect" the organisations by applying sufficient counter measures to safeguard against potential malicious cybersecurity attacks. In this phase, organisations should provide essential education and training related to cybersecurity measures. The third phase includes steps to continuously "detect" cybersecurity incidents and to monitor cyber threats. The fourth phase involves the development of a "response" plan, which will establish the communication channels, clearly mitigating the cyber incidents. The last phase is to "recover" the damaged services whose damages were caused by cyber incidents and to prioritise cyber-related activities [60].

When organisations and businesses are not compliant with the five fundamental elements of the NIST CSF, it becomes extremely challenging to properly handle cyber incidents. In addition, organisations and businesses tend to become vulnerable to cyber incidents, which could potentially affect their continuity. It is suggested that all organisations adopt human-centric approaches alongside with a detailed and clear mitigation plan to promote cyber hygiene and address cyber incidents.

From the analysis above, it is evident that cybersecurity is important for healthcare professionals because they deal with sensitive patient information and medical records, which must be kept confidential and secure. To deepen and summarise our analysis, the best hands-on practices for cyber hygiene are identified as follows:

- Use strong passwords: Healthcare professionals should use strong passwords for all their accounts, including their electronic medical record (EMR) system. Passwords should be long and include a mix of uppercase and lowercase letters, numbers and special characters.
- Use two-factor authentication: Two-factor authentication provides an extra layer of security for healthcare professionals. They should enable two-factor authentication for all their accounts, especially for EMR systems.

- Keep software updated: Healthcare professionals should keep all software, including operating systems and applications, up to date with the latest security patches and updates. This helps to protect against known vulnerabilities and exploits.
- Use secure networks: Healthcare professionals should only use secure networks, such as their workplace network or a trusted VPN, when accessing sensitive patient information or medical records. They should avoid using public Wi-Fi networks or unsecured networks.
- Be cautious of phishing scams: Healthcare professionals should be cautious of phishing scams, which are fraudulent emails or messages designed to steal personal information or infect computers with malware. They should avoid clicking on links or downloading attachments from unknown sources.
- Encrypt sensitive data: Healthcare professionals should encrypt sensitive patient information and medical records to protect against unauthorised access. Encryption helps to ensure that only authorised individuals can access the data.
- Regularly backup data: Healthcare professionals should regularly backup their data, including patient information and medical records, to ensure that it can be recovered in the event of a data breach or system failure.
- Use secure messaging: Healthcare professionals should use secure messaging platforms to communicate with colleagues and other healthcare professionals. They should avoid using unsecured messaging apps or SMS messages, which can be intercepted and read by unauthorised individuals.
- Educate staff: Healthcare professionals should educate their staff on cybersecurity best practices and provide regular training to ensure that everyone is aware of the risks and how to prevent them.
- Use a reputable IT provider: Healthcare professionals should work with a reputable IT provider to ensure that their systems and networks are secure and up to date with the latest security protocols. The IT provider can also provide support and guidance on cybersecurity best practices.

It is important to also highlight the advantages and disadvantages of the existing methods. Advantages of existing cyber hygiene methods are as follows:

1. Regular updates and patches—Keeping software, operating systems and applications up to date with the latest patches and updates can help prevent cyberattacks that exploit vulnerabilities in the system.
2. Strong passwords and authentication—Using strong and unique passwords, along with multi-factor authentication, can help prevent unauthorised access to accounts and data.
3. Backups—Regular backups of important data can help ensure that data is not lost in the event of a cyberattack or system failure.
4. Security awareness training—Educating employees about cybersecurity risks and best practices can help prevent human errors that could lead to cyberattacks.
5. Firewall and antivirus protection—Firewalls and antivirus software can help prevent unauthorised access to a network and protect against viruses and malware.

Disadvantages of existing cyber hygiene methods:

1. Complexity—Some cybersecurity practices can be complex and require technical expertise to implement and maintain, which can be challenging for small businesses or individuals.
2. Cost—Implementing robust cybersecurity measures can be costly, especially for small businesses or individuals with limited budgets.
3. False sense of security—Relying solely on cybersecurity measures can create a false sense of security and lead to complacency, which could make an organisation or individual more vulnerable to cyberattacks.

4. Lack of standardisation—Cybersecurity practices and standards are not always consistent across different organisations and industries, which could create gaps in cybersecurity coverage.
5. Evolving threat landscape—The threat landscape is constantly evolving, and new cyber threats are emerging all the time. Cybersecurity measures that were effective in the past may not be sufficient to protect against new threats.

Overall, cyber hygiene is critical in today's digital world, and adopting best practices and measures can help individuals and organisations protect themselves against cyber threats; this is why this piece of research is considered essential as a complete review of the literature on the topic has not been conducted before. However, it is important to be aware of the limitations of existing methods and to continuously evaluate and update cybersecurity practices to stay ahead of evolving threats.

7. Deployment, Demonstration and Implementation of a Healthcare Use-Case Scenario for Raising Data Privacy and Cybersecurity Awareness

The chosen scenario, which is described in this section, is mainly based on a user-centred Digital Health Living lab. This Living Lab provides a real-life setting with a systematic co-production and user co-creation approach while incorporating research and innovation processes. The key involved stakeholders are councils, residents, service providers, technology companies and academic institutions, and are active in every step from the creation to commercialisation of a product or service. This scenario aims to demonstrate the real-world applicability of best cybersecurity hygiene practices, aiming to raise data privacy and cybersecurity awareness.

More specifically, the involved stakeholders in the Living Lab are contributing to health innovation in an innovative way and have the opportunity to help individuals and society. They are being key partners in inspiring and creating health innovations based on their perceptions, needs and user experience. This is characterised as an open innovation ecosystem and the Living Lab plays the role of a unique testbed for the development and testing of prototypes or mature digital healthcare solutions. The scenario, presented here, is based on Tier 3 test and trial category in accordance with the UK National Institute for Health and Care Excellence (NICE) for Digital Health Technologies (DHTs). Particularly, Tier 3 is targeted on helping people who are diagnosed with a long or short-term condition with treatment and management. It involves clinical management tools for treatment and diagnosis via active monitoring or calculation. For example, a symptom tracking function, which transfers patients' records to the healthcare team to support the clinical decision process.

All involved stakeholders, such as service providers, patients, residents, and healthcare practitioners, are engaging with the Living Lab using their own network connections and infrastructures. As an extent, they connect to the internet through their own routers (WiFi) and communicate through online means, such as emails via their personal devices (i.e., PCs, mobile devices, tablets, laptops). It is worth noting that there is a lot of big data involved, such as personal information. In addition, the Living Lab includes several medical healthcare devices, such as infusion and/or insulin pumps and IoT devices for healthcare diagnosis, management and treatment. The scenario presented below is used to demonstrate the importance to maintain and promote cybersecurity hygiene in such an environment.

Vulnerabilities in the healthcare sector differentiate compared to the other sectors. This is due to the lack of security measures related to connectivity of the network and medical devices. The healthcare information infrastructure includes a huge number of legacy systems and threat actors are always looking for ways to exploit the systems. It has been noted in the literature that the most common attack path is found by hackers via social engineering and lack of cybersecurity hygiene by the involved actors. For example, healthcare professionals collect patient data (i.e., financial, personal), hence breaches of this data would provide additional benefits to the attackers.

This scenario is making a number of assumptions for the purpose of implementation. More specifically, the home patients use an insulin pump for their diabetes treatment and the pump is configured and managed by their healthcare practitioner. In addition, there are IT devices, such as servers and applications software, computers, operating systems and routers that are essential for the system infrastructure as a whole. The security of medical devices mainly relies on the cybersecurity hygiene and best practices adopted by the patient, healthcare professional and IT staff involved. Security is required to protect patient data and to safeguard the healthcare service delivery, as the medical devices are connected to the internet.

8. Conclusions

This paper shows the importance of human-centric and multidisciplinary approaches in cyber hygiene education and practices, and how specific end users are targeted through social engineering attacks. For example, males have the tendency to show greater trust in technological tools, which could act as a bias in their cyber hygiene practices and behaviours. Even though there is not a single theoretical framework or model for best practices in cyber hygiene, this piece of work, in combination with previous studies performed (i.e., [61]), is a start to develop and apply a holistic empirical educational framework. The present research sets the scene to utilise an articulated and flexible model of cyber hygiene education, which connects behaviours, human factors, knowledge, individual differences and attitudes. It is an extension of the existing literature and may be employed to cultivate and support current theories of cyber hygiene.

For reasons as such, the findings of the present research could better inform information technology courses, cybersecurity, computer science and didactical approaches in cybersecurity practices. This would be achieved by providing awareness of possible biases, and students may become prepared for future social engineering attacks in their professional and personal lives, while also grasping a better understanding of these principles as a whole.

Individual differences and human-centric approaches associated with cyber hygiene are essential to disseminate in mathematics (STEM), science, health, technology and engineering classes. They are an important addition into the curriculum of cyber education, since humans are the biggest threat to efficient cybersecurity. Hence, the practical application of this piecework is its application to education. Last, but not least, by personalising cyber hygiene training to fit the individual's needs based on their attitudes, behaviours and knowledge [62], greater efficacy and transfer are expected, especially related to the protection of confidential and personal information [63].

In conclusion, cyber education, at the moment, is not effectively preparing individuals to take into consideration human factors, which are strongly associated with cybersecurity. The human factor can be the main cause of security violations and malicious attacks and remains the weakest link in cyber resiliency.

The novelty of the present research is:

- As far as we are concerned, this is the first research paper that presents a holistic, hands-on set of best practices in cyber hygiene, specifically addressing the healthcare staff.
- It facilitates the identification as to why humans are the weakest link, due to their lack of awareness, training, education, errors and complexity of technology.
- It accomplishes the presentation of important theoretical and practical applications within cyber education.

Author Contributions: Conceptualization, H.M., T.F. and K.K.; methodology, H.M., T.F. and K.K.; investigation, T.F. and K.K.; resources, T.F., S.N. and K.K.; writing—original draft preparation, K.K.; writing—review and editing, T.F., S.N. and K.K.; visualization, H.M., T.F. and K.K.; supervision, H.M. and T.F.; project administration, K.K.; funding acquisition, H.M. All authors have read and agreed to the published version of the manuscript.

Funding: The research conducted in this paper was funded by the project 'A Dynamic and Self-Organized Artificial Swarm Intelligence Solution for Security and Privacy Threats in Healthcare ICT Infrastructures' (AI4HEALTHSEC) under grant agreement No. 883273. The project was funded by the European Union's Horizon 2020 research and innovation programme.

Institutional Review Board Statement: Ethical approval was not required for this study.

Informed Consent Statement: Not applicable.

Data Availability Statement: Not applicable.

Acknowledgments: The authors are grateful for the financial support of this project that has received funding from the European Union's Horizon 2020 research and innovation programme. The views expressed in this paper represent only the views of the authors and not of the European Commission or the partners in the above-mentioned project.

Conflicts of Interest: The authors declared no potential conflict of interest with respect to the research, authorship and/or publication of this article.

References

1. Liaropoulos, A. A Human-Centric Approach to Cybersecurity: Securing the Human in the Era of Cyberphobia. *J. Inf. Warf.* **2015**, *14*, 15–24.
2. Javid, T.; Faris, M.; Beenish, H.; Fahad, M. Cybersecurity and data privacy in the cloudlet for preliminary healthcare big data analytics. In Proceedings of the 2020 International Conference on Computing and Information Technology, Tabuk, Saudi Arabia, 9–10 September 2020; pp. 1–4. [CrossRef]
3. Thuemmler, C.; Bai, C. Health 4.0: Application of industry 4.0 design principles in future asthma management. In *Health 4.0: How Virtualization and Big Data Are Revolutionizing Healthcare*; Springer: Berlin/Heidelberg, Germany, 2017; pp. 23–37.
4. Singh, D.; Mohanty, N.; Swagatika, S.; Kumar, S. Cyber-hygiene: The key Concept for Cyber Security in Cyberspace. *Test Eng. Manag.* **2020**, *83*, 8145–8152.
5. Cain, A.; Edwards, M.; Still, J. An exploratory study of cyber hygiene behaviors and knowledge. *J. Inf. Secur. Appl.* **2018**, *42*, 36–45. [CrossRef]
6. Ponemon Institute. 2016. Available online: http://www.ponemon.org/li-brary/2016-cost-of-cyber-crime-study-the-risk-of-business-innovation (accessed on 1 January 2023).
7. FBI. 2015. Available online: https://www.ic3.gov/media/annualreports.aspx (accessed on 15 December 2022).
8. Long, R. Using Phishing to Test Social Engineering Awareness of Financial Employees. Ph.D. Thesis, Eastern Washington University, Cheney, WA, USA, 2013.
9. Russell, J.D.; Weems, C.F.; Ahmed, I.; Richard, G.G. Self-reported secure and insecure cyber behaviour: Factor structure and associations with personality factors. *J. Cyber Secur. Technol.* **2017**, *1*, 1–12. [CrossRef]
10. Talib, S.; Clarke, N.L.; Furnell, S.M. An analysis of information security aware-ness within home and work environments. In Proceedings of the International Conference on Availability, Reliability, and Security, Krakow, Poland, 15–18 February 2010; Volume 1, pp. 196–203.
11. Anderson, C.L.; Agarwal, R. Practicing safe computing: A multimedia empirical examination of home computer user security behavioral intentions. *MIS Q.* **2010**, *34*, 613–643. [CrossRef]
12. Konieczny, F. USAFR NJT. SEADE: Countering the futility of network security. *Air Space Power J.* **2015**, *29*, 1–11.
13. Furnell, S. Why users cannot use security. *Comput. Secur.* **2005**, *24*, 274–279. [CrossRef]
14. Henshel, Q.; Hart, P.; Cooke, D. The role of external influences on organizational information security practices: An institutional perspective. In Proceedings of the 39th Annual Hawaii International Conference on System Sciences 2006, Kauia, HI, USA, 4–7 January 2006; Volume 6, pp. 1–10. [CrossRef]
15. Almeida, V.A.F.; Doneda, D.; Abreu, J.S. Cyberwarfare and digital governance. *IEEE Internet Comput.* **2017**, *21*, 68–71. [CrossRef]
16. Neigel, A.R.; Claypoole, V.L.; Waldfogle, G.E.; Acharya, S.; Hancock, G.M. Holistic cyber hygiene education: Accounting for the human factors. *Comput. Secur.* **2020**, *92*. [CrossRef]
17. Dupuis, M.J. Cyber security for everyone: An introductory course for nontechnical majors. *J. Cybersecur. Educ. Res. Pract.* **2017**, *3*, 1–17.
18. Cone, B.D.; Irvine, C.E.; Thompson, M.F.; Nguyen, T.D. A video game for cyber security training and awareness. *Comput. Secur.* **2007**, *26*, 63–72. [CrossRef]
19. Molinara, M.; Cancelliere, R.; Di Tinno, A.; Ferrigno, L. A Deep Learning Approach to Organic Pollutants Classification Using Voltammetry. *Sensors* **2022**, *22*, 8032. [CrossRef] [PubMed]
20. Polatidis, N.; Pimenidis, E.; Pavlidis, M.; Papastergiou, S.; Mouratidis, H. From product recommendation to cyber-attack prediction: Generating attack graphs and predicting future attacks. *Evol. Syst.* **2020**, *11*, 479–490. [CrossRef]
21. Silvestri, S.; Islam, S.; Papastergiou, S.; Tzagkarakis, C.; Ciampi, M. A Machine Learning Approach for the NLP-Based Analysis of Cyber Threats and Vulnerabilities of the Healthcare Ecosystem. *Sensors* **2023**, *23*, 651. [CrossRef] [PubMed]

22. European Union Agency for Network and Information Security (ENISA). Review of Cyber Hygiene Practices. 2016. Available online: https://www.enisa.europa.eu/publications/cyber-hygiene (accessed on 30 November 2022).
23. Trevors, M. Mapping Cyber Hygiene to the NIST Cybersecurity Framework. 2019. Available online: https://insights.sei.cmu.edu/insider-threat/2019/10/mapping-cyber-hygiene-to-the-nist-cybersecurity-framework.html (accessed on 3 January 2023).
24. Vishwanath, A.; Neo, L.S.; Goh, P.; Lee, S.; Khader, M.; Ong, G.; Chin, J. Cyber hygiene: The concept, its measure, and its initial tests. *Decis. Support Syst.* **2020**, *128*, 113–160. [CrossRef]
25. Ehrenfeld, J.M. Wannacry, cybersecurity and health information technology: A time to act. *J. Med. Syst.* **2017**, *41*, 104. [CrossRef] [PubMed]
26. Independent. 2017. Available online: https://www.independent.co.uk/news/uk/home-news/marcus-hutchins-arrested-latest-us-authorities-wannacry-cyberattack-nhs-las-cegas-mccaran-a7875761.html (accessed on 3 January 2023).
27. Rader, M.; Rahman, S. Exploring Historical And Emerging Phishing Techniques And Mitigating The Associated Security Risks. *Int. J. Netw. Secur. Appl.* **2013**, *4*, 50–69.
28. Aparajita, A.; Swagatika, S.; Singh, D. Comparative Analysis of Clustering Techniques in Cloud for Effective Load Balancing. *Int. J. Eng. Technol.* **2018**, *7*, 47–51. [CrossRef]
29. Kelly, R. Almost 90% of Cyber Attacks Are Caused by Human Error or Behaviour. 2017. Available online: https://chiefexecutive.net/almost-90-cyber-attacks-caused-human-error-behavior/ (accessed on 5 December 2022).
30. Annarelli, A.; Nonino, F.; Palombi, G. Understanding the management of cyber-resilient systems. *Comput. Ind. Eng.* **2020**, *149*, 43–59. [CrossRef]
31. Bowen, B.; Devarajan, R.; Stolfo, S. Measuring the human factor of cyber security. In Proceedings of the 2011 IEEE International Conference on Technologies for Homeland Security (HST), Waltham, MA, USA, 13–16 November 2011; Volume 1, pp. 198–207.
32. Nobles, C. Botching human factors in cybersecurity in business organizations. *Holistica* **2018**, *9*, 71–88. [CrossRef]
33. Dragana, C.; Pattinson, M.R.; Parsons, K.; Butavicius, M.A.; McCormac, A. Naïve and Accidental Behaviours that Compromise Information Security: What the Experts Think. In Proceedings of the 10th International Symposium of Human Aspects of Information Security and Assurance, Frankfurt, Germany, 19–21 July 2016; Volume 1, pp. 32–52.
34. Baillon, A.; Bruin, J.; Emirmahmutoglu, A.; Veer, E.; Dijk, B. Informing, simulating experience, or both: A field experiment on phishing risks. *PLoS ONE* **2019**, *14*, e0224216. [CrossRef] [PubMed]
35. Hakim, Z.; Ebner, N.; Oliveira, D.; Getz, S.; Levin, B.E.; Lin, T.; Wilson, R.C. The phishing email suspicion test (PEST) a lab-based task for evaluating the cognitive mechanisms of phishing detection. *Behav. Res. Methods* **2021**, *53*, 1342–1352. [CrossRef] [PubMed]
36. Kobis, P. Human factor aspects in information security management in the traditional IT and cloud computing models. *Oper. Res. Decis.* **2021**, *31*, 61–76. [CrossRef]
37. Richardson, M.D.; Lemoine, P.A.; Stephens, W.E.; Waller, R.E. Planning for Cyber Security in Schools: The Human Factor. *Educ. Plan.* **2020**, *27*, 23–39.
38. Moustafa, A.A.; Bello, A.; Maurushat, A. The Role of User Behaviour in Improving Cyber Security Management. *Front. Psychol.* **2021**, *12*, 224–231. [CrossRef]
39. Moustafa, A.A.; Morris, A.N.; Elhaj, M. A review on future episodic thinking in mood and anxiety disorders. *Rev. Neurosci.* **2018**, *30*, 85–94. [CrossRef]
40. Moustafa, A.A.; Morris, A.N.; Nandrino, J.; Misiak, B.; Szewczuk-Boguslawska, M.; Frydecka, D.; El Haj, M. Not all drugs are created equal: Impaired future thinking in opiate, but not alcohol, users. *Exp. Brain Res.* **2018**, *236*, 2971–2981. [CrossRef]
41. Wikipedia. Available online: https://en.mwikipedia.org/wiki/social_engineering(security) (accessed on 18 January 2023).
42. Chen, H.; Zhongchuan, F.; Dongyan, Z. Security and trust research in M2M system. In Proceedings of the 2011 IEEE International Conference on Vehicular Electronics and Safety, Beijing, China, 10–12 July 2011; Volume 1, pp. 286–290.
43. Sung-Ming, Y.; Kim, S.; Lim, S.; Moon, S. A countermeasure against one physical cryptanalysis may benefit another attack. In Proceedings of the International Conference on Information Security and Cryptology, Seoul, Republic of Korea, 6–7 December 2001; pp. 414–427.
44. Gregory, R.G.; Fitzgerald, J.; Hunsperger, N.; Lavine, J.; Nguyen, V.; Tellado, J. Service Processor Configurations for Enhancing or Augmenting System Software of a Mobile Communications Device. U.S. Patent Application 14/083,324, 3 March 2014.
45. Holland, N. The Human-Centered Cybersecurity Stance. 2020. Available online: https://www.bankinfosecurity.com/human-centric-cybersecurity-stance-a-13897 (accessed on 1 October 2022).
46. Grobler, M.; Gaire, R.; Nepal, S. Usage and Usability: Redefining Human Centric Cyber Security. *Front. Big Data* **2021**, *4*, 344–452. [CrossRef]
47. Durbin, S. Eight Steps to Building a Human-Centered Security Culture. 2020. Available online: https://www.forbes.com/sites/forbesbusinesscouncil/2020/11/25/eight-steps-to-building-a-human-centered-security-culture/ (accessed on 5 January 2023).
48. Renaud, K.; Flowerday, S. Contemplating human-centred security & privacy research: Suggesting future directions. *J. Inf. Secur. Appl.* **2017**, *34*, 76–81. [CrossRef]
49. Khader, M.; Chai, W.; Neo, L.S. *Introduction to Cyber Forensic Psychology: Understanding the Mind of the Cyber Deviant Perpetrators*, 1st ed.; World Scientific Publishing: Singapore, 2021; 404p.
50. Blau, A. Better Cybersecurity Starts with Fixing Your Employees Bad Habits. 2017. Available online: https://hbr.org/2017/12/bettercybersecurity-starts-with-fixing-your-employees-badhabits (accessed on 1 December 2022).

51. Ncubukezi, T.; Mwansa, L.; Rocaries, F. A review of the current cyber hygiene in small and medium sized businesses. In Proceedings of the 15th International Conference for Internet Technology and Secured Transactions (ICITST), London, UK, 8–10 December 2020; Volume 15, pp. 283–288.
52. Symantec, C.D. Internet Security Threat Report: 2011 Trends. *Symantec Corp.* **2012**, *17*, 977–999.
53. Sobiesk, E.; Blair, J.R.; Conti, G.; Lanham, M.; Taylor, H. Cyber education: A multilevel, multi-discipline approach. In Proceedings of the 16th Annual Conference on Information Technology Education, London, UK, 4–8 September 2015; Volume 1, pp. 43–47.
54. Ncubukezi, T.; Mwansa, L. Best practices used by businesses to maintain good cyber hygiene during COVID-19 pandemic. *J. Internet Technol. Secur. Trans.* **2021**, *9*, 714–721. [CrossRef]
55. Trevors, M.; Wallen, C.M. *Cyber Hygiene: A Baseline Set of Practices*; Software Engineering Institute, Carnegie Mellon University: Pittsburgh, PA, USA, 2017; pp. 1–17.
56. Cyber Essentials. 2020. Available online: https://www.gov.uk/gov (accessed on 26 January 2023).
57. Such, J.M.; Cholas, P.; Rashid, A.; Vidler, J.; Seabrook, T. Basic cyber hygiene: Does it work? *Computer* **2019**, *52*, 21–31. [CrossRef]
58. NIST Special Publication 800–181. 2017. Available online: https://www.nist.gov/itl/applied-cybersecurity/nice/nice-framework-resource-center (accessed on 3 October 2022).
59. Mehravari, N. Resilience management through the use of CERT-RMM and associated success stories. In Proceedings of the IEEE, International Conference on Technologies for Homeland Security (HST), Vienna, Austria, 17–20 October 2013; Volume 1, pp. 119–125.
60. Martin, R.A. Non-Malicious Taint: Bad Hygiene Is as Dangerous to the Mission as Malicious Intent. 2014; Volume 1, pp. 19–30. Available online: https://apps.dtic.mil/sti/pdfs/AD1107757.pdf (accessed on 4 November 2022).
61. Parsons, K.; Calic, D.; Pattinson, M.; Butavicius, M.; McCormac, A.; Zwaans, T. The human aspects of information security questionnaire (HAIS-Q): Two further validation studies. *Comput. Secur.* **2017**, *66*, 40–51. [CrossRef]
62. Hancock, P.A.; Billings, D.R.; Schaefer, K.E.; Chen, J.Y.C.; Visser, E.J.; Parasuraman, R. A Meta-Analysis of Factors Affecting Trust in Human-Robot Interaction. *J. Hum. Factors Ergon. Soc.* **2011**, *53*, 517–527. [CrossRef]
63. Bansal, G.; Zahedi, F.; Genfen, D. The impact of personal dispositions on in-formation sensitivity, privacy concern and trust in dis-closing health information online. *Decis. Support Syst.* **2010**, *49*, 138–150. [CrossRef]

applied sciences

MDPI

Review

Recent Advances in Artificial Intelligence and Wearable Sensors in Healthcare Delivery

Sahalu Balarabe Junaid [1], Abdullahi Abubakar Imam [2], Muhammad Abdulkarim [1,*], Yusuf Alhaji Surakat [3], Abdullateef Oluwagbemiga Balogun [4,5], Ganesh Kumar [5], Aliyu Nuhu Shuaibu [6], Aliyu Garba [1], Yusra Sahalu [7], Abdullahi Mohammed [1], Tanko Yahaya Mohammed [1], Bashir Abubakar Abdulkadir [8], Abdallah Alkali Abba [9], Nana Aliyu Iliyasu Kakumi [10] and Ahmad Sobri Hashim [5]

1 Department of Computer Science, Ahmadu Bello University, Zaria 810107, Nigeria
2 School of Digital Science, Universiti Brunei Darussalam, Brunei Darussalam, Jalan Tungku Link, Gadong BE1410, Brunei
3 Department of Family Medicine, University Medical Centre, Ahmadu Bello University, Zaria 810107, Nigeria
4 Department of Computer Science, University of Ilorin, Ilorin 1515, Nigeria
5 Department of Computer and Information Sciences, Universiti Teknologi PETRONAS, Sri Iskandar 32610, Malaysia
6 Department of Electrical Engineering, University of Jos, Bauchi Road, Jos 930105, Nigeria
7 SEHA Abu Dhabi Health Services Co., Abu Dhabi 109090, United Arab Emirates
8 Department of Chemistry, Gombe State University, Gombe 760253, Nigeria
9 Institute of Health Science, Kaduna State University, Tafawa Balewa Way, 800283 Kaduna, Nigeria
10 Patient Care Department, General Ward, Saudi German Hospital Cairo, Taha Hussein Rd, Huckstep, El Nozha, Cairo 4473303, Egypt
* Correspondence: amuhd@abu.edu.ng

Citation: Junaid, S.B.; Imam, A.A.; Abdulkarim, M.; Surakat, Y.A.; Balogun, A.O.; Kumar, G.; Shuaibu, A.N.; Garba, A.; Sahalu, Y.; Mohammed, A.; et al. Recent Advances in Artificial Intelligence and Wearable Sensors in Healthcare Delivery. *Appl. Sci.* **2022**, *12*, 10271. https://doi.org/10.3390/app122010271

Academic Editor: Stefano Silvestri

Received: 3 September 2022
Accepted: 30 September 2022
Published: 12 October 2022

Abstract: Artificial intelligence (AI) and wearable sensors are gradually transforming healthcare service delivery from the traditional hospital-centred model to the personal-portable-device-centred model. Studies have revealed that this transformation can provide an intelligent framework with automated solutions for clinicians to assess patients' general health. Often, electronic systems are used to record numerous clinical records from patients. Vital sign data, which are critical clinical records are important traditional bioindicators for assessing a patient's general physical health status and the degree of derangement happening from the baseline of the patient. The vital signs include blood pressure, body temperature, respiratory rate, and heart pulse rate. Knowing vital signs is the first critical step for any clinical evaluation, they also give clues to possible diseases and show progress towards illness recovery or deterioration. Techniques in machine learning (ML), a subfield of artificial intelligence (AI), have recently demonstrated an ability to improve analytical procedures when applied to clinical records and provide better evidence supporting clinical decisions. This literature review focuses on how researchers are exploring several benefits of embracing AI techniques and wearable sensors in tasks related to modernizing and optimizing healthcare data analyses. Likewise, challenges concerning issues associated with the use of ML and sensors in healthcare data analyses are also discussed. This review consequently highlights open research gaps and opportunities found in the literature for future studies.

Keywords: artificial intelligence; machine learning; vital signs; wearable sensors

1. Introduction

As in many other research fields, the landscape of healthcare research is being progressively reshaped by the trending use of artificial intelligence (AI) techniques [1]. This can be attributed to the radical progression in the development of new machine learning (ML) algorithms. In recent years, ML algorithms have demonstrated an ability to significantly achieve or exceed human-level performance when it comes to computational tasks [2]. Particularly, the availability of big datasets and computing power improvements are partly responsible for these achievements by ML algorithms [3]. The discovery of beneficial healthcare knowledge brought by the application of AI techniques in analyzing medical datasets has attracted immense attention [4]. Clinicians are widely inclined to adopt the application of ML algorithms to process clinical datasets for their accuracy, robustness, and interpretability [5]. Often, the atmosphere for delivering medical care by health professionals is hasty, with the availability of boundless arrays of technologies and varying individual conclusions and judgments [6]. During a patient's examination, important information is continuously collected by health professionals either automatically or manually using appropriate devices.

Different approaches are being used worldwide to gather patients' vital information [7]. However, the situation in an intensive care unit (ICU) differs as it requires more devices for medical diagnoses and the continuous monitoring of each subject [8]. Accordingly, the electronic health form (EHF) system accepts and stores the volume of measured medical data in real-time [9,10]. Health forms might contain high-dimensional health data ranging from vital signs data such as blood glucose level, blood pressure, heart rate, oxygen saturation level, and body temperature, to other demographic data such as family medical history, laboratory tests, and medication records [11]. Thus, volumes of such high-dimensional health data pose an interpretational challenge to health professionals during the diagnosis and treatment of patients [12].

Amongst the health data parameters are vital signs, also referred to as bioindicators. These are important pieces of clinical information used to objectively measure and assess the general physical health of a person. These vital signs give clues to possible diseases and show progress toward recovery. Likewise, acute, and protracted diseases can also be monitored via vital signs. Thus, they serve as tools for crucial communication concerning the health status of patients [13,14], and they are usually the first intervention commonly observed by health professionals. However, some concerns still exist regarding general health practice issues, such as which health parameters must be measured, the frequency of the optimal measurements and the performance measure of the new health technologies for observing patients [15–17]. Consequently, ML techniques can be used to effectively analyze and efficiently generate actionable insights from vital signs data or through the combination of additional data from the patient's health records. It has been established in medical studies that timely discovery and prompt intervention are very crucial measures to avoid declining a patient's medical condition [18]. Both the cost and optimization of healthcare systems could be achieved through the early prediction of patient health outcomes.

Similarly, the availability of Electronic Health Record (EHR) systems offers abundant and unique prospects for biomedical studies, whereby analytics and predictive modelling are at the core [19]. Disease existence prediction or recognition [20], critical condition assessment [21], evaluating a condition that may require the intervention of life-support [22] and the existence of a specific medical outcome [23,24] are a few examples of tasks that are related to health that could be the objectives of such models. Additionally, it is possible to integrate these with EHR systems to automate real-time health warning systems [25]. There exist several instances where AI techniques are implemented in a variety of medical-care-related fields [26–28]. Many studies are available on the application of AI techniques for a particular disease, environment, health domain and outcome, and in some cases, specific ML algorithms are simply the focus.

For instance, Alanazi et al. [29] reviewed the application of ML techniques in medicine and healthcare. Xiao et al. [30] in their study investigated the usage of deep learning (DL) techniques to process EHR datasets. Several DL techniques for exploring different sources of data and their targeted applications were analyzed. Likewise, Gnaneswar and Jebarani [31] studied the use of data mining techniques for the diagnosis and prediction of heart diseases while Kavakiotis et al. [32] investigated the deployment of data mining techniques for the diagnosis and prediction of diabetes.

Hence, the objective of this review is to investigate and analyze the process of integrating AI techniques with clinical data acquired through wearable sensors. Consequently, a unique taxonomy is developed to highlight the benefits and challenges associated with the application of wearable sensors and AI techniques in the conventional healthcare delivery system.

The remainder of this paper is arranged as follows: the research approach and methods are explained in Section 2. The application of wearable sensors in healthcare is presented in Section 3. Section 4 discusses the deployment of AI in healthcare, while the benefits and challenges of the application of AI in healthcare are addressed in Section 4. The limitations encountered in this study are explained in Section 5, and finally, the conclusions of this review are presented in Section 6.

2. Research Methods

This review used the Preferred Reporting Items for Systematic reviews and Meta-Analyses (PRISMA) methodology to identify research articles for inclusion in the study.

2.1. Inclusion and Exclusion Criteria

This review endeavours to illustrate strategically the need for and the application of AI and wearable sensors in the current healthcare domain, providing a complete evaluation of these technologies as well as the benefits and challenges of their implementation in healthcare. This study focuses on articles and survey papers specifically related to the implementation of AI and wearable sensors in healthcare. This provides insight into hundreds of the papers included in this analysis, as well as the methods used in previous research.

In this research, the paper selection criterion technique is divided into three subsections: keyword selection, inclusion and exclusion, and the final results created by using these methods. In the sections that follow, specifics about these selection criteria are provided.

2.1.1. Selection of Keywords

Multiple well-known research databases and repositories, including IEEE, Science Direct, PubMed, Wiley, Taylor & Francis, JSTOR, ACM Digital Library, EBSCOhost, Springer, Emerald and IET, were searched exhaustively for research publications. The papers in the aforementioned databases were searched using keywords like sensors, wearable sensors, biosensors, AI, ML, healthcare, telemedicine, and e-health.

2.1.2. Inclusion

The study was limited to journals published between 2018 and 2022, with the remainder omitted. These publications were selected for evaluation based on a reexamination of the abstracts and papers that highlighted the applicability of wearable technologies and AI to this research. This study includes an examination of research publications, current review papers, technical notes, and other materials arranged in a logical order and related to the latest developments in wearable sensors, AI, and healthcare.

2.1.3. Exclusion

During the search for research publications, there are many stringent criteria for excluding studies, such as duplication, language (only English), and irrelevance (subject and material). Additionally, papers were eliminated if they were unrelated to wearable technology, AI and healthcare, and had previously published information on the same topic. Also removed were case series and reports, brief communications, and editorial comments resources.

2.2. Quality Assessment and Data Extraction

It is essential to keep in mind that the amount of research papers, notably surveys pertinent to the healthcare field, has been increasing, with more scholars striving to contribute to the body of knowledge. Nevertheless, such research (reviews or surveys) is susceptible to certain problems, besides a rising number of nonrandomized interventional studies.

Researchers are required to recognize high-quality reviews and surveys. Numerous techniques for examining specific parts of feedback have been developed, but there are not many structured tools for comprehensive review [33].

In this regard, the PRISMA approach is used in this study to assess the quality of the selected articles and ensure that only high-quality papers are considered for the research. Moreover, the PRISMA approach is utilized to evaluate objectively the material that is significant to the various selected publications [33]. Articles were chosen using inclusion and exclusion criteria, particularly publication year (as established by the PRISMA checklist). Figure 1 displays the PRISMA methodology used in this study.

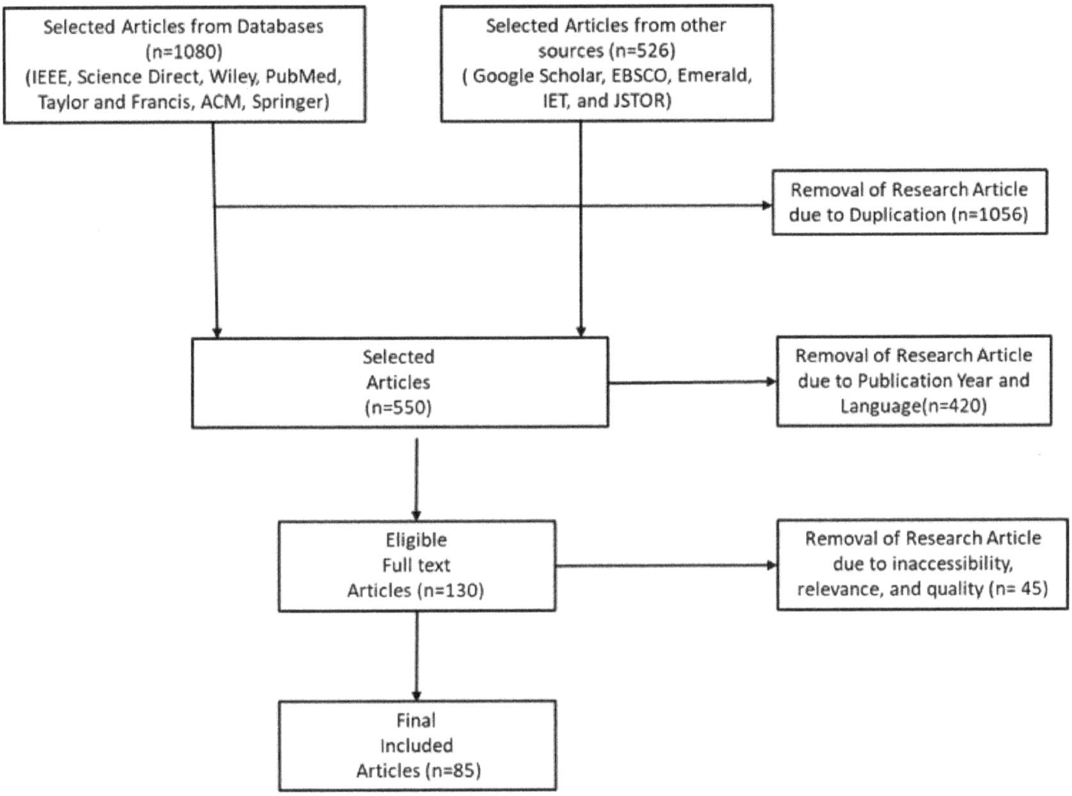

Figure 1. PRISMA flowchart of the study methodology.

After an in-depth evaluation of 1606 papers acquired from numerous sources (IEEE, Science Direct, PubMed, Wiley, Taylor & Francis, JSTOR, ACM Digital Library, EBSCOhost, Springer, Emerald and IET) in the first stage, 1056 duplicates were eliminated. Additional 420 papers were omitted due to their publication year and language, and 45 articles were discarded owing to their inaccessibility, lack of relevance, and poor quality. In the end, 85 papers are chosen upon thorough evaluation and analysis.

3. Wearable Sensors in Healthcare

The biosensing concept started around the early 20th century. It is a simple concept where potential electrical proportionality is viewed across the membrane [34]. However, the real biosensor device for the detection of oxygen was developed by L.C. Clark, Jr. in 1956. Henceforward, the development of a variety of biosensor platforms and devices was initiated, ranging from glucose [35] and the fibre-optic-based detection of carbon dioxide

(CO_2) and oxygen, to utilizing surface plasmon resonance (SPR) [36] to detect gas through inventing the first hand-held (i-STAT) blood biosensor in 1992 [37].

At present, biosensor technology is used in wearable devices for different aspects of our daily life activities. For instance, its use ranges from a simple daily steps counter with a fitness band to a highly complicated multiplexed device capable of detecting non-abundant biochemical body fluid markers. Undoubtedly, the evolution of wearable sensors has revolutionized the monitoring of healthcare as wearable sensors technology has made it possible for clinicians and users to obtain dynamic and real-time health-related information on the body's physiological function with a simple click, scan or tap while sitting at home or resting.

Wearable sensor devices can capture different kinds of biosignals such as motion, pulse rate and temperature changes. Furthermore, several biosensors are presently used as quick, point-of-care tools capable of being used on a large scale to screen the populace or to detect viruses such as the latest SARS-CoV-2 [38]. Nonetheless, the competition between giant technology industries has revealed a sneak peek of the wearable sensors' commercial market. Recently, a study from CBINSIGHTS stressed that wearables, telehealth and virtual reality (VR) will champion a clash of industries and technologies that can lead the post-pandemic world [39]. This is based on the premise that sensor devices that are easy to fabricate and most economical with high multimodal throughput and biocompatibility superiority would certainly attain substantial growth in the technology industry, especially when the finished products are readily available and are capable of having a significant impact on the remote monitoring of healthcare. Likewise, comfortability and compatibility with the surfaces and living tissues of human skin are important factors to consider when these devices are used in clinical routines for the constant gathering of biosignals to generate computable results. Furthermore, in dealing with delicate interfaces, wearable sensors require better sensitivity materials to accurately recognize as well as a higher discrimination power to identify specific forms of environmental stimuli in a specified period [40].

There has been a paradigm shift from the period of inflexible electrochemical devices to the current evolution period of flexible, printable and soft functional materials able to adhere to rough skin surfaces regarding the fabrication and utilization of biosensing systems [41]. For example, an ear-worn sensor capable of tracking actions and degrees of energy in patients with chronic obstructive pulmonary disease (COPD) was created by Fennedy, et al. [42]. The researchers were able to use the ear-worn sensor and an efficient ML technique to diagnose different types of physical actions along with the energy used in those actions. Also, Steele, et al. [43,44] conducted a 3D measurement experiment of human (patient) movements. Findings from their experiments showed that patient status measures were correlated with the level of acceleration vectors such as the force expiratory volume in one second (FEV1), distance walk of six minutes, severity of dyspnea and domain of physical function in a health-related quality of life gauge shown in patients with COPD.

Furthermore, Shashikumar, Stanley, Sadiq, Li, Holder, Clifford and Nemati [20] developed a novel ML algorithm for health-related data collection from a single unit to study the minute-by-minute activity levels of patients. A sample of 22 patients was used for 14 days to test the method. The developed algorithm was employed to assess whether the sensing device is active on the patient and to keep track of compliance.

The automation of wearable sensors experienced a fast evolution from what looks like a science fiction concept to a wide range of fine-established devices for medical use [45]. The fast evolution of wearable sensors might be connected but not limited to their affordability, user-friendliness, portability, the existence of mobile smartphones plus other connected devices and the increase in consumer desire for health awareness [46]. Regardless of the initial achievement, there is still a need for advancement in wearable sensors. The current wearable modalities for sensing are non-specific, hence, the wish remains unmet. For instance, the number of factors responsible for increasing one's pulse or causing one to perspire is still unknown. Additionally, most wearable sensor devices are still using techniques that have existed for years. Even the continuous transdermal glucose monitors that appear to be more-complex wearables take advantage of the advancements in enzyme electrodes from over three decades, including the discovery of basic and ultra-low-cost finger-prick glucose test strips. The assessment of transdermal glucose is likely the most widely engaged wearable sensor to regularly monitor the state of a severe condition (diabetes) [47,48]. Figure 2 is an illustration of a conceptual remote surveillance system.

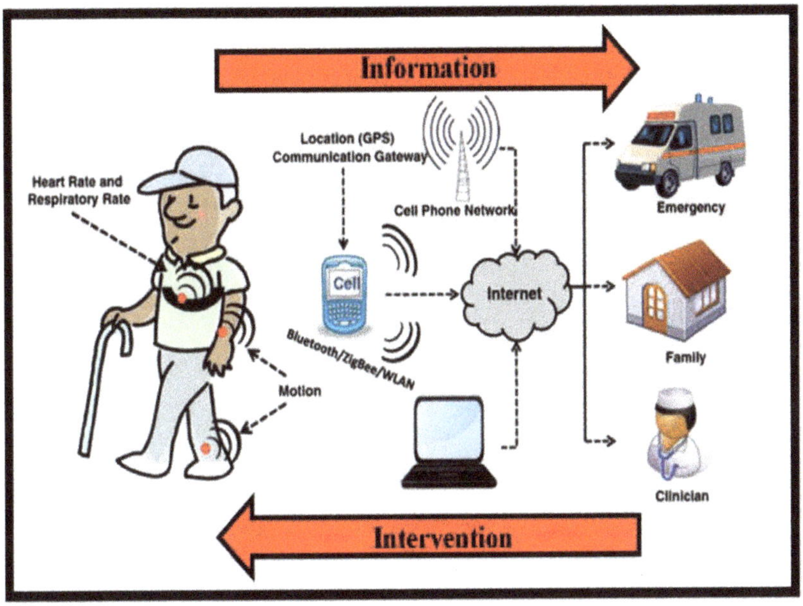

Figure 2. A conceptual picture of a remote surveillance system [45].

Wearable sensors are used to collect movement and physiological data, which allows for the monitoring of the patient's health status. There are different ways in which sensors are employed depending on the therapeutic routine of interest. For example, when monitoring congestive heart failure or COPD patients, vital signs monitoring sensors would be deployed.

Likewise, movement-data-recording sensors would be employed to monitor the efficacy of a home-based stroke survivor's recovery program or the usage of mobility assistance gears among elderly people. The data collected from patients or users are transmitted to an access point or mobile phone over wireless transmission before being communicated to a data center or cloud storage via the internet. The ML model embedded in the device detects an emergency and delivers an alert message to the trauma service center to promptly assist the patient. Invariably, in sensor-based healthcare systems, the patient's relatives and caregivers can be contacted in the case of an emergency or whenever the patient needs assistance with taking his/her prescriptions. Clinicians can examine the patient's condition remotely and can be alerted if there is a need to make a medical decision.

3.1. Design of Biosensors

According to Liu, et al. [49], a biosensor is an analytical integrated functional device capable of analyzing particular quantitative or semi-quantitative data using a biological recognition component. The device broadly consists of three main components. First is the biorecognition component often called a bioreceptor. This is the component that uses biomolecules from receptors or organisms modelled after biological systems to interact with an analyte of interest. Subsequently, a transducer will measure the interaction and outputs a quantifiable signal that is proportional to the target analyte present in the sample.

The overall aim of the biosensor design is to enable convenient and quick testing at the point of care or concern where the sample was acquired [50–52]. Second is the transducer, which is an electronic device that converts energy into an electrical current or voltage signal for transmission. The third is the signal amplifier, which simply refers to an electrical circuit that uses electrical power to increase the amplitude of an incoming current or voltage signal and outputs the higher amplitude version at its output terminals.

Figure 3 illustrates the biosensor's basic parts with their working mechanisms. Normally, the analyte is a biomolecule recognizable by a highly specific biorecognition element. Different transduction platforms are used for the reaction, which generates signals that are detectable by transducers and are converted to displayable data.

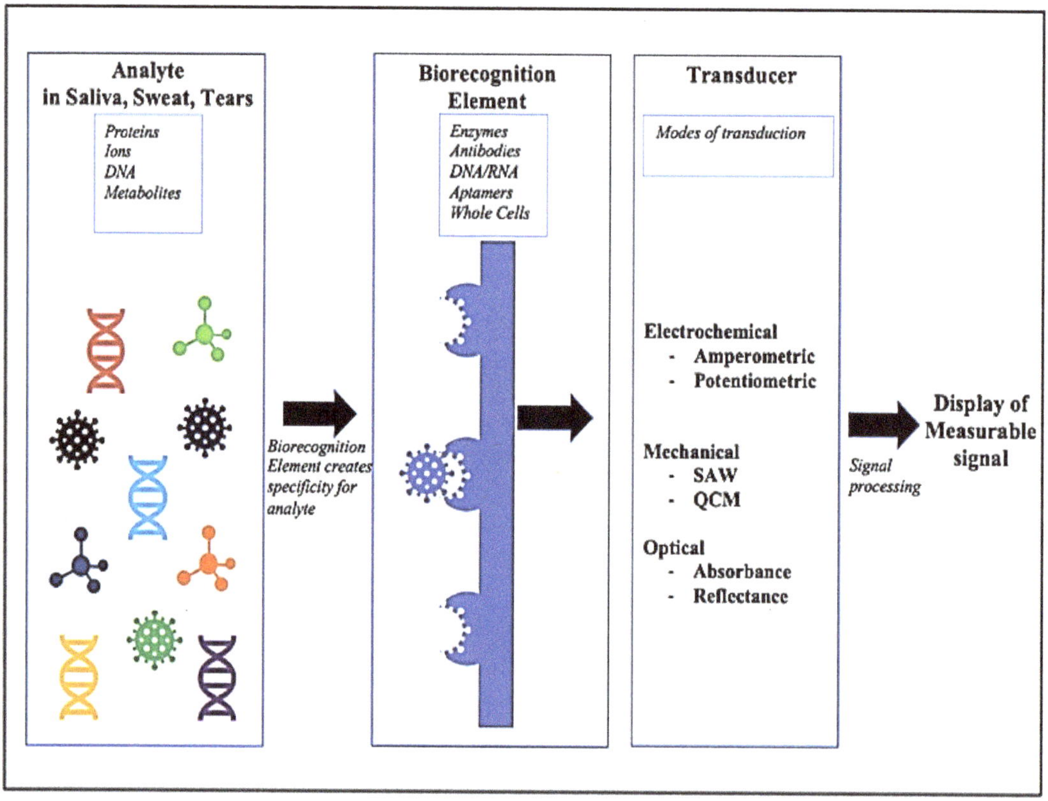

Figure 3. Basic parts of biosensors [39].

3.2. Categories of Wearable Biosensors

Wearable biosensors in the literature are categorized depending on the bio-analyte/biofluid used, the material of choice, the transduction platform, design, and utility. Several authors are inclined to categorize biosensors based on the bio-analyte/biofluid used, such as saliva, sweat and tears. Likewise, on an invasiveness basis, authors include implantable biosensors, which use other physiological biomarkers to observe health and subcutaneous injections. Based on design and utility, wearable biosensors can further be divided as arm and wrist-based, face and head-based or oral-cavity-based, food-mounted and textile-based (Figure 4).

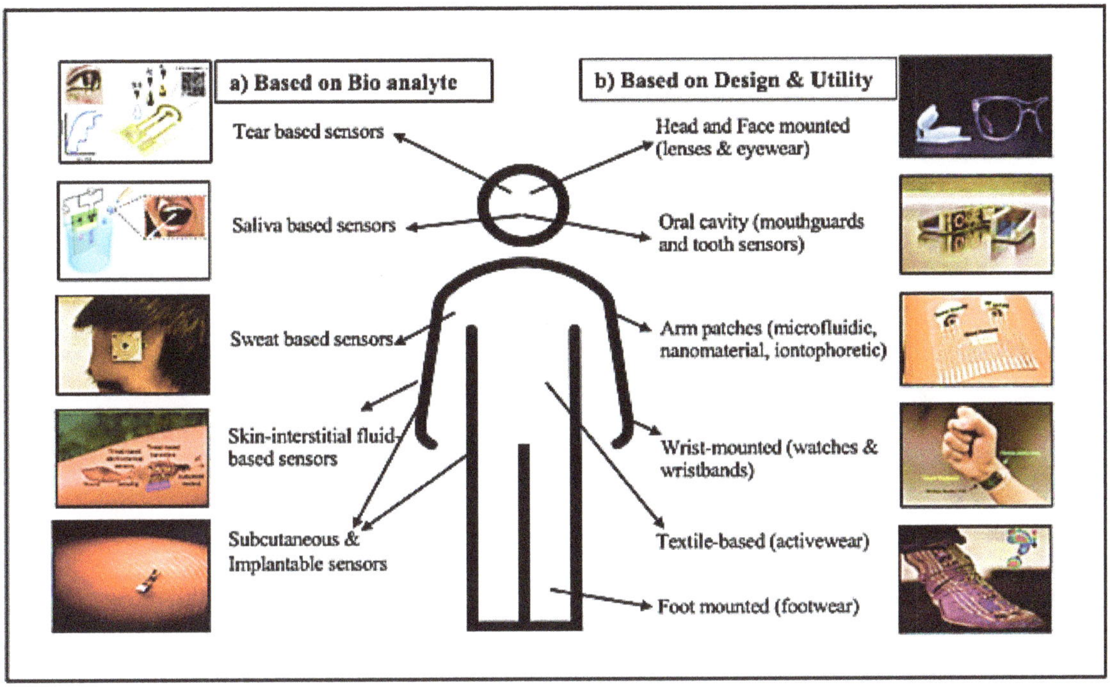

Figure 4. Different wearable biosensor devices are categorized based on: (**a**) bio-analytes and (**b**) design and utility [39].

Similarly, wearable biosensors can be categorized as biocompatible, biodegradable, carbon-based, inorganic biomaterials or polymer sensors depending on the source material used for their production. Although the electrochemical, electro-mechanical and optoelectrical/photo-sensing platforms of wearable biosensors all have a similar general mechanism for biorecognition, the transduction mode is what makes them differ. This review mainly focuses on electro-mechanical wearable biosensors.

3.3. Electromechanical Biosensors

The principle of sensing in electromechanical biosensors is fairly like that of electrochemical biosensors, though the generation of electrical responses is the variation between the two. This variation is primarily the result of the strain recorded due to an electrical bias or due to a mechanical force.

Electromechanical transduction does not depend on molecule labelling, which gives it a significant advantage over electrochemical and optical sensors. It also facilitates a wide range of identification and quantification parameters for biomolecules. Accordingly, the most essential feature that dictates the finest operation of electromechanical biosensors is their capability to sense the physical variations that occur on the human skin surface at a macroscale, such as movements in the arm, leg and wrist or slight changes such as stifling or the stretching of the epidermis, which occurs during actions such as breathing [53]. Typically, electromechanical transduction mechanisms are based on any of the following: (a) piezo-capacitive, (b) piezo-electric, (c) piezo-resistive, (d) iontronic or triboelectric nano-generation (TENG) effects [40,54] (Figure 5).

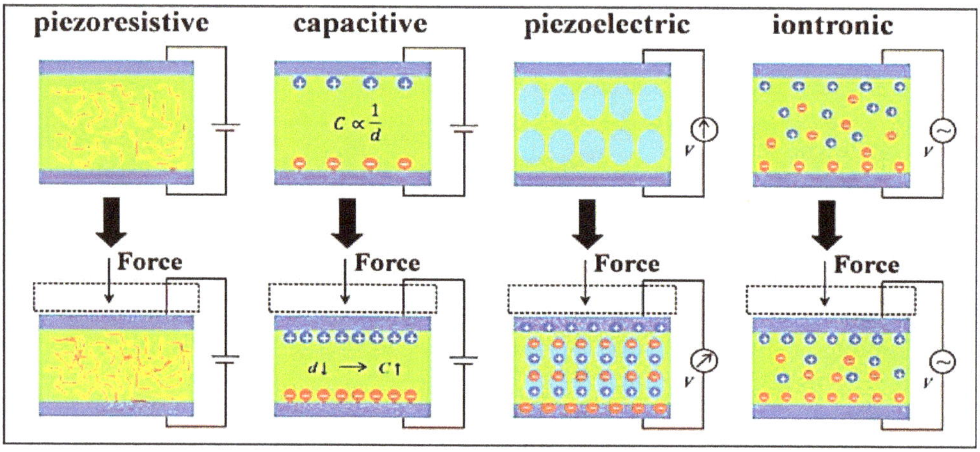

Figure 5. Illustration of different categories of electro-mechanical transduction mechanisms [39].

The function of a strain sensor is the quantification of the mechanical deformation concerning the corresponding changes in electrical signals. This can either be piezo-electric (when changes in surface potential due to polarization are captured) or piezo-resistive (when changes in the resistance produced by external forces are captured) [55,56]. The function of wearable strain sensors is the quantification of mechanical deformation for the corresponding changes in electrical signals. This could be in the form of capturing changes in surface potential due to polarization (also known as piezo-electric) or piezo-resistive, which means capturing variations in the resistance produced by exterior forces [53,55].

Capacitive wearable biosensors react to changes in capacitance and have superior sensitivity due to forces that cause geometrical deformations. However, surrounding noise is known to affect the sensors and may consequently impact their performance [57]. Iontronic wearable biosensors use a platform with super-capacitance. This is approximately 1000 times greater than a capacitor with a metal oxide platform. It forms an ion–electric interface between the electrolytes and electrodes, which causes a high capacitance per unit area and ion accumulation on the electrodes [54]. Triboelectric transduction operates on a simple principle known as frictional charges. This is a result of the interaction between two different materials. The principle was used in developing TENG [56]. Surface separation produces potential differences whenever friction is interrupted; hence, without the use of external power, this is used to develop sensors [58].

A flexible functional design that requires a high gauge factor is needed for the detection of minor movements by stretchable strain sensors, which arise on irregular skin surfaces. For example, a strain biosensor was designed by Tang, et al. [59] and was built by aligning a nanowire using a ratio with a high surface-to-volume ratio to monitor intangible human motion. In their study, they succeeded by achieving a high gauge factor of approximately 35.8 that could detect an incitement of deformation with less than 200μm in under 230ms. This achieved result was five times better in comparison with a comparable microwire-based biosensor [59].

Similarly, a stretchable ion-based biosensor was created by Wang, et al. [60]. It was built on surface strain redistributed elastic fiber (SSRE-fiber) where a wrinkle construct was used to improve the surface area together with an island bridge design [60]. Though the principle of the electro-mechanical mode of sense was not used, the strain was minimized on big sizes of the stretch by making the SSRE platform a notable choice in a textile-based wearable biosensor. Likewise, textile-based mechanical biosensors are becoming an attractive tool for detecting human motion and they are paving the way for the personalization of healthcare by working analogously to how the choice of our outfit adapts to our physical attributes.

Nevertheless, there are still challenges; for instance, there is a technology requirement for the fabric to have high conductivity and to be equally strain resistant.

Typically, to improve conductivity in textiles, carbonization is the first line of choice, which can either be performed by adding metal nanoparticles, dip-coating or vacuum filtration [61–65]. An instance of such a wearable biosensor was invented by Yang, et al. [66] using available commercial spandex, in which polyamide was dipped into carbonic pigment inks to fabricate the conductive strain sensor with high fidelity [66]. Figure 6 presents a schematic diagram illustrating the process of fabricating an ink-decorated fabric strain sensor.

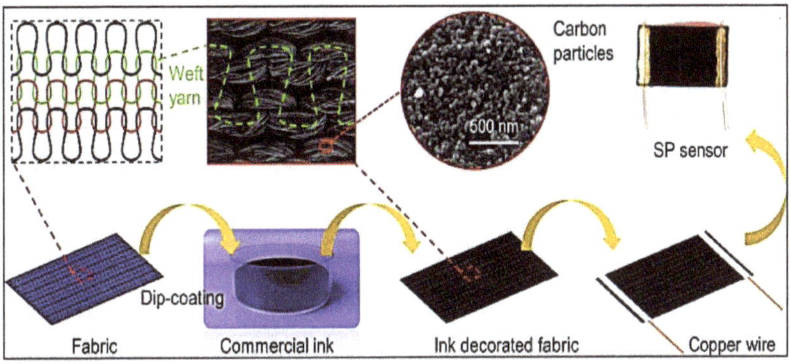

Figure 6. Schematic diagram illustrating the process of fabricating ink-decorated fabric strain sensor.

To begin with, deionized water is used to wash the fabric three times; then, after dip coating the fabric into commercial ink, the fabric is then absorbed and dried at 60 °C for about an hour in the oven. Next, silver paste is used to mount two copper wires on the fabric strip's two ends to improve integration, and again the setup is dried and is then ready to use with textiles [39]. Their study effort points to a potential proposed application of the smart textiles by (i) using any of the joints (arm, fingers, wrist) to fix them for pulse rates collection; (ii) sewing or otherwise printing the strain biosensors on the fabrics to capture the functions associated with respiration and breathing; or (iii) applying them in producing protecting devices to monitor joint activities in posture-related illnesses such as Parkinson's disease [66]. Table 2 presents a summary of the application of wearable sensors in healthcare.

Thus, AI will most likely play an important role in healthcare delivery over the next few years due to its capability to handle and process large amounts of information at an effective rate through numerous forms of AI systems. This includes both software-based (such as apps) and hardware-based (such as smartphones) systems. However, as mentioned earlier, technologies of wearable devices already exist, which offer similar functionality with improved accuracy. Therefore, consumers are the ones who will decide what technology to select.

Further, both AI and wearable sensors have an impact on our daily lives and certainly, between them, there is always going to be some overlap. The integration of AI with wearable devices is gaining momentum toward creating smarter devices for consumers (such as smartphones). Wearable devices are also integrating AI systems into their mobile applications to better analyze their abilities for use in predictive analytics applications. Another aspect where wearable devices complement AI is location tracking in smartphones, where wearable devices can be used to determine the location of a person at home or otherwise based on the signal from their smartphone's location when matched with historical records from preceding phone calls made using a similar device.

Table 1. A summary of the application of wearable sensors in healthcare.

Application	Analyte Parameter	Materials	Mode of Transduction	Challenges	Wearable Platform	Reference
Motion detection	Surface deformation	Aligned nanowires	Electrochemical–mechanical	Proof-of-concept sensor needs integration into wearable device	Mountable sensor	[59]
Sweat monitoring	Sodium	Ion-based SSRE-fiber	Electrochemical–mechanical	The lack of on-body trials needs optimization for integration to textiles	Textile-based	[60]
Breathing, motion detection and pulse rate	Strain and conductivity	Commercial spandex and carbon ink pigment-coated polyamides	Electromechanical	Cleaning, multistep fabrication process and textile/coated ink shelf life	Textile-based	[66]
Tactile communication	Vibro-tactile feedback	Velostat-polymer impregnated with carbon black	Electromechanical	Lacks longitudinal study to predict the interface success	Finger–hand based	[67]
Motion and pulse detection	Pressure sensations	Ni-coated core-sheath nanofiber yarn with CNT-embedded polyurethane	Electromechanical	Proof-of-concept design needs optimization and authentication for textile integration	Textile-based	[68]
Motion detection	Tactile sensations	3D-printed nanocomposites	Electromechanical	Needs miniaturization to fabricate the skin-compatible, compressible device	Skin-mounted	[69]
Patient Monitoring	Sensors used for pulse rate, respiration rate and temperature sensor	-	Sensor operation: measure body temperature, pulse rate and monitor the breath rate of a person	-	-	[70]
Stress Detection	-	Sensors used for ECG monitoring sensors and three-axis accelerometer		Sensor operation: collects ECG signals using three lead and measures the tilt angles between the user and the object	-	[71]
Position Alerting	-	Sensors are used as an accelerometer, pulse and ultrasonic sensor	-	Sensor operation: measures the angle between objects measures the heart rate and finds the tilt angle between the object and the user	-	[72]

Table 1. *Cont.*

Table 2. *Cont.*

Application	Analyte Parameter	Materials	Mode of Transduction	Challenges	Wearable Platform	Reference
Paralyzed	-	Infrared sensor	-	Sensor operation: it encloses an amplifier that acts as a comparator	-	[73]
Visually Challenged	-	Ultrasonic sensor		Sensor operation: uses the SONAR technique for identifying the distance between objects. Not affected by black materials or sunlight	-	[74]
Home Monitoring	-	MHZ-19(CO2 sensor)	-	Sensor operation: measure CO2 content levels	-	[75]
Elderly	-	Light, nasal airflow and pulse oximeter sensor		Sensor operation: measure the breathing rate of the user, the amount of oxygen dissolved in the blood, detect haemoglobin content and detect the light	-	[76]
Detecting Alcohol Content	–	PID sensor	-	Sensor operation: detects chemical content	-	[77]
Diabetes Monitoring	-	Pressure and weight sensor	-	Sensor operation: measures the pressure points in the human body and detects body weight	-	[78]

4. Artificial Intelligence (AI) in Healthcare

AI is fast becoming a catchword globally as it aims to simplify human work and make it more efficient. Thus, AI is playing a critical role in strengthening and transforming industries including the healthcare sector [79]. Moreover, in the healthcare sector, AI technology plays a significant role in minimizing human errors and complementing conventional healthcare processes. The application of AI techniques in healthcare can be done in several ways such as advanced patient diagnostics, disease prevention, medical therapy and informed clinical decision-making [80]. Based on this premise, the application of AI techniques in healthcare delivery has remarkably increased. This section reviews the use of ML, a subfield of AI, in clinical analytics using wearable sensor data. Different types of wearable sensors are available to collect clinical data. Thus, these datasets can often be processed using appropriate ML techniques. Figure 7 presents an ML-based healthcare system modelled with data from wearable sensors.

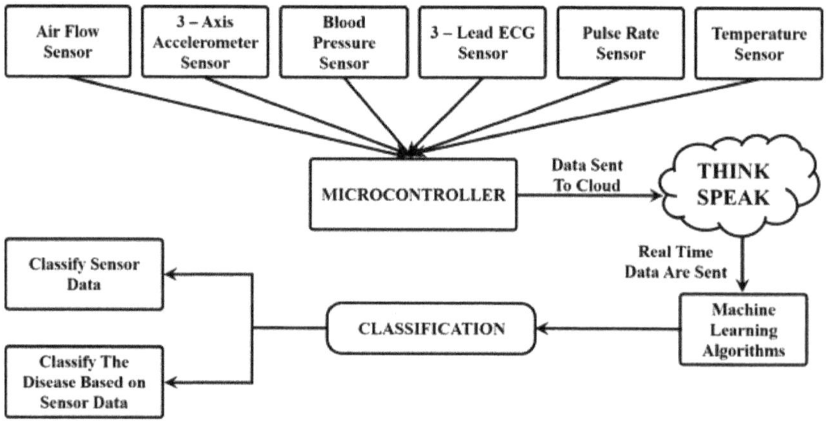

Figure 7. Machine Learning-based model via wearable sensors data for healthcare systems.

Wearable sensors enable the monitoring of vital health parameters, which can be used to detect many illnesses such as chronic clinical disorders, diabetes, hypertension, and some others. A patient's vital health signs such as blood glucose level, blood pressure, body temperature, oxygen saturation and pulse rate are measured using a variety of clinical-related sensors. Then, Internet of Things (IoT)-based platforms such as "Think speak" are utilized to send the data values measured from these sensors to the cloud. Think speak is an open IoT platform enabled by Arduino or Arduino-compatible hardware for data visualization. It allows writing or reading data to be put into or taken from the platform. This supports the data storage from the API or sensors in the cloud for either a private or public channel. ML techniques are then used to analyze the stored data in the channel. The diagnosis of the symptoms to identify the disease(s) affecting the patient can be performed using the data collected with the sensor. ML algorithms are hence used to classify and identify the disease. Undoubtedly, the classification capacity of ML algorithms is known to be effective, and the reason for their broad use in the health industry is their ability to classify and predict diseases based on their symptoms (health-related data).

Currently, many technologies are using ML algorithms for data analytics to obtain useful insights [81–84]. Supervised and unsupervised learning algorithms are the two broad classifications of ML algorithms. When the prediction of the values for the training dataset is the goal, supervised learning algorithms are used, while unsupervised learning algorithms are used for the identification of a specific label from the clustered labels [85–87].

Classification and regression are the most commonly used supervised learning algorithms [88]. Some examples of classification algorithms include Naïve Bayes (NB), k-Nearest Neighbor (kNN), Artificial Neural Network (ANN), Decision Tree (DT) and

Support Vector Machines (SVM) [89–92]. Discriminant Analysis (DA), Logistic Regression (Log) and Linear Regression (LR) are prominent regression algorithms. C-Means, K-Means, BIRCH, DBSCAN and X-Means algorithms are examples of clustering techniques which are classified as unsupervised learning algorithms [93–96]. Figure 8 provides a detailed classification of ML techniques.

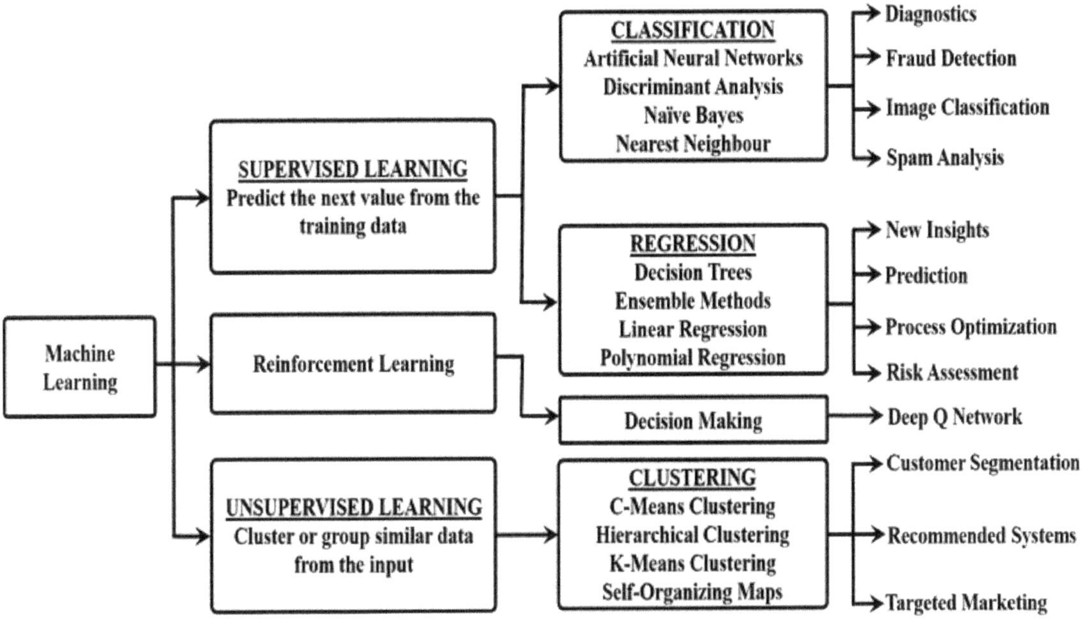

Figure 8. Classification of ML techniques into various sub-categories.

In practice, all these ML algorithms can be employed to address problems concerning medical image recognition, prediction and detection of diseases, behavioural adjustments and so on. The recent technological advancement that brought about wearable sensors has prompted several researchers to explore their potential in the concept of integrating AI with wearable sensors in the healthcare domain. Similarly, the affordability and availability of both wearable sensors and smartphones appear to be veritable devices to quickly drive the accumulation of human medical data, whereas an emerging subfield of AI (ML techniques) is also available to map those medical data to provide clinical predictions [97].

The proof-of-concept for an accurate, automatic, patient-specific system that is tunable to a person's needs presented by [98–101] is an example of a seizure-prediction system that can increase an epileptic patient's independence and allow for preventative treatment. A robust classification algorithm in ML (a DL classifier) was used to train a model to distinguish between interictal and preictal signals. DL is an ML technique and is a great computational tool that supports attributes to be automatically learnt from training data [102]. Generally, the use of DL is for training a class of algorithms termed deep neural networks to accomplish specific tasks. The use of neuromorphic hardware in combination with DL models can offer a basis for an always-on, real-time, patient-specific, wearable-sensor seizure early warning system with marginal power consumption with reliable and durable performance.

Furthermore, a different study by [103] aimed at automatic scoring Parkinsonian tremors. The study proposed ML algorithms to predict the Unified Parkinson's Disease Rating Scale (UPDRS). In their study, a wristwatch-type wearable sensor device fitted with an accelerometer and a gyroscope was used to measure the tremor signals of eighty-five Parkinson's disease patients. The number of features initially extracted from each signal was nineteen, but eventually, the dimension of the features was strategically abridged using a pairwise correlation approach. Five commonly used ML algorithms, such as the DT, DA, kNN, RF and SVM, were applied to the selected features to explore the automatic scoring of the severity of Parkinsonian disease tremors. Accuracy, precision, and recall were the metrics used to gauge the performance of the classifiers and compare the findings with similar studies.

These use-cases of successful implementations and applications of AI and wearable sensors has made it critical and necessary to complement conventional healthcare system with these disruptive technologies. The technologies among many things can assist in informed clinical decision-making processes since imprecise results can misinform both clinicians and patients.

Hence, an AI-based sensor healthcare system can assist in diagnosing disease symptoms and obtaining timely aid from clinicians and caregivers. The system will equally be of assistance to elderly or young people for regular in-home-based health monitoring and diagnosis.

5. Challenges and Benefits of AI

The field of AI currently appears to be a promising area that can act as an instrument to grow and transform the public health service sector drastically. Although the adoption of AI appears to be momentary, there is a continuous increase in its use largely because of the strong potential at the core of healthcare delivery. AI is anticipated to replace the face-to-face consultation experiences of clinicians and patients. Engaging AI technology to remodel the healthcare sector in many respects has been widely considered possible. EHR, physician-active supervision in clinical decisions and detailed knowledge processing aimed at health management systems constitute concerns at the center of the AI virtual systems [104]. The assistance derived from AI systems by clinical experts to diagnose patients has received research attention recently. Certainly, soon, advancements in technology sophistication with more comprehensive AI data systems will be able to detect many other diseases.

There is a clear benefit to using AI in healthcare, as the choices of patient management and outcomes are improved. Costs reduction, fewer referrals and time saving are other prospective secondary benefits. Additionally, professional isolation, recruitment, promotion and retention in rural areas can be reduced with the application of AI in healthcare [105]. This can in turn contribute toward a more balanced and equitable system of basic medical care in poor-resource locations of low- and high-income countries.

5.1. Benefits and Challenges of Artificial Intelligence in Healthcare

AI is rapidly dominating healthcare systems by replacing the conventional routine work/tasks conducted by personnel in medical services with an automated health system. Nevertheless, the digitization of health services through the application of AI systems in medical care practice comes with benefits and can also pose new associated technical challenges. The following sub-sections discuss the key benefits and challenges of AI in healthcare.

5.1.1. Benefits

The enhancement in patient management choices and outcomes are the primary benefit of technology applications in the healthcare system, while cost efficacy, time-saving, and fewer referrals may as well be the potential secondary benefits. Again, it can assist in health facility retention and promote recruitment in rural areas. Eventually, this can contribute to an equitable global healthcare delivery system [106,107], which addresses the challenges of enabling early acceptability and feasible implementation in the healthcare system and a lack of reflection from the perspective of users. AI adoption in the public healthcare system offers a blueprint for the flow of research that centers on diverse aspects of AI adoption in public healthcare systems [83,108].

5.1.2. Challenges

AI is projected to soon be incorporated into routine clinical care due to its proven efficacy in refining the administrative aspect of health services. However, ethical and privacy implications are reservations that have been expressed about introducing AI into the healthcare system. These reservations include AI application tasks in clinical situations, the fuzziness of some AI algorithms, privacy concerns for the data used in training the AI model, the likelihood of bias and security concerns. Similarly, access, consent, costs, efficacy, information, the right to decide and the right to try are some examples of the ethical concerns faced in clinical applications of AI techniques [107,109]. AI application is the preferable and right approach for progress in the health sector, particularly health services, despite its impact on ethical concerns, regulations, and systems error. The following are some of the open challenges of AI in healthcare.

1. Equity

Clinical datasets for training AI models should be well-structured and in an appropriate format that can make it easy to derive knowledge and actionable insights from it. That is, there should be adequate representations of instances in the datasets via the harmonization of different health-related data of patients [110]. Otherwise, this can cause the AI models to be biased, make imprecise predictions or even large-scale discrimination [111].

2. Transparency

Although the performance of the AI techniques, especially DL models in the prediction of clinical risk and medical image analysis has been significantly promising, nevertheless explaining and interpreting the DL models is difficult. This difficulty is a cause of serious concern in the medical world, where the ability to explain medical decisions and transparency are very vital [111,112].

3. Trust

To apply AI, matters including the cause and effect of a disease, the ML techniques and the models used to support the decision-making process of the medical experts needs to be considered by clinicians. The future of AI applications' autonomous roles and the conceivable exposure to the accidental or mischievous tampering of these applications to yield unjustifiable results may cause a critical obstacle for clinicians to admit AI in their clinical practice [111,113].

4. Accountability

The accountability begins with AI model development and then extends to the level where the model is used in medical care until eventual retirement. Many stakeholders are involved in this scope, which includes software developers, healthcare experts, patient advocacy groups and government officials [114]. The application of AI in healthcare services is not limited to increasing clinical capability but can also be for upgrading administrative capacity. As an example, the distribution of information and services related to health can be conducted using AI in the form of telemedicine by employing communication technology. Certainly, the implementation of telemedicine will impressively affect business models in hospitals [115].

5.2. Problems in the Application of AI in Health Services

1. Bias data: Large-scale data inputs related to clinical health records are a requirement for training or developing a robust AI model. Otherwise, bias can occur when incomplete or insufficient health-related data are used for training the AI models. Likewise, the output from training data that do not truly reflect the target population is usually biased. Under-representative data may occur as a result of accessibility to healthcare services (social discrimination) and/or comparatively lesser samples (such as with data from minority groups) [116].

2. Privacy: Medical service data are one of the most sensitive records that can be kept by an individual about another. Therefore, the principle of respecting the privacy of a patient is of vital importance in the medical care profession. This is also because privacy is bounded by the autonomy of the patient's well-being and a private identity [111]. Accordingly, ethics and moral practices must be deployed to respect the confidentiality of the patient's data as well as to safeguard adequate measures for obtaining the right consent.

5.3. Problem of Ethics Related to Biomedical and Health Sciences

As applicable to all new techniques in health sciences, the principles governing biomedical ethics must be followed by AI in medical care applications. This includes security and privacy regarding the available health-related data. They remain manifest as autonomous decision-making, consensus, privacy and safety, deliberate participation, etc., which must be reflected and practised in any implementation [107].

6. Conclusions

The recent trend of using AI techniques and wearable sensors in the medical field has progressively reshaped healthcare delivery systems. The adoption of these evolving technologies in healthcare delivery has truly attracted the attention of many researchers. This study proposes a distinctive taxonomy that illuminates the process of integrating AI techniques with the clinical data acquired through wearable sensors. For simplicity, the process is broadly divided into three major sections: wearable biosensors, AI, and the challenges and benefits of AI in healthcare. Wearable biosensors are IoT-enabled devices that facilitate the transmission of health-related data to the cloud for further processing. Of the various AI concepts, ML is utilized to automatically process and visualize the recorded health-related data for clinical decision-making. In this review, various forms of ML techniques were explored. This is to provide a concise and complete review and analysis of the application of AI in healthcare, which is of key importance in this article.

The efforts by the authors will certainly assist researchers and experts in academics and the healthcare domain respectively. For instance, a scholar may obtain an appropriate direction on different kinds of wearable biosensors and ML algorithms that may be engaged for the detection of a particular disease. An additional innovative aspect of this study is highlighting the benefits and challenges yet to be cleared in prospective studies on the application of AI to improve patient medical outcomes. The open research challenges addressed in this study may also offer researchers some clear future research prospects. By investigating further into these technologies and their integration, the future of AI and wearable biosensors is quite promising in healthcare delivery systems, essentially in remote healthcare monitoring.

Author Contributions: Conceptualization, S.B.J., A.A.I., A.O.B., M.A. and A.N.S.; data curation, A.O.B., G.K., Y.A.S. and A.G.; formal analysis., A.O.B., A.M., T.Y.M., Y.S. and B.A.A.; funding acquisition, S.B.J., A.A.I., A.S.H. and M.A.; investigation, S.B.J., A.A.I., A.O.B., M.A. and A.N.S.; methodology, S.B.J., A.A.I., A.O.B., M.A. and A.N.S.; Project administration, S.B.J., A.A.A., N.A.I.K., M.A., A.M. and A.G.; resources, S.B.J., A.A.A., N.A.I.K., A.S.H., A.G., T.Y.M., Y.S. and B.A.A.; software, M.A., Y.A.S. and G.K.; supervision, A.A.I., A.A.A. and N.A.I.K.; validation, A.M., T.Y.M., G.K., A.S.H. and B.A.A.; visualization, A.A.I., A.O.B., M.A., Y.S. and A.N.S.; writing—original draft, A.A.I., A.O.B., M.A. and A.N.S.; writing—review & editing, S.B.J., A.S.H. and A.A.A. All authors have read and agreed to the published version of the manuscript.

Funding: This research received no external funding.

Acknowledgments: This research paper was supported by the Faculty of Integrated Technologies, Universiti Brunei Darussalam, Brunei, and Tertiary Education Trust Fund (TETFund) Nigeria, via National Research Fund (NRF) with Ref. No.TETF/DR&D/CE/NRF/2020/SET1/65/VOL.1.

Conflicts of Interest: The authors declare no conflict of interest.

References

1. Yu, K.H.; Beam, A.L.; Kohane, I.S. Artificial intelligence in healthcare. *Nat. Biomed. Eng.* **2018**, *2*, 719–731. [CrossRef] [PubMed]
2. Goodfellow, I.; McDaniel, P.; Papernot, N. Making machine learning robust against adversarial inputs. *Commun. ACM* **2018**, *61*, 56–66. [CrossRef]
3. Stewart, J.; Sprivulis, P.; Dwivedi, G. Artificial intelligence and machine learning in emergency medicine. *Emerg. Med. Australas* **2018**, *30*, 870–874. [CrossRef] [PubMed]
4. Guo, J.; Yuan, X.; Zheng, X.; Xu, P.; Xiao, Y.; Liu, B. Retracted: Diagnosis labeling with disease-specific characteristics mining. *Artif. Intell Med.* **2018**, *90*, 25–33. [CrossRef] [PubMed]
5. Agarwal, N.; Singh, P.; Singh, N.; Singh, K.K.; Jain, R. Machine Learning Applications for IoT Healthcare. *Mach. Learn. Approaches Converg. IoT Blockchain* **2021**, 129–144. [CrossRef]
6. Siddesh, G.; Krutika, S.; Srinivasa, K.; Siddiqui, N. Healthcare Data Analytics Using Artificial Intelligence. In *Artificial Intelligence for Information Management: A Healthcare Perspective*; Springer: Berlin/Heidelberg, Germany, 2021; pp. 45–85.
7. da Costa, C.A.; Pasluosta, C.F.; Eskofier, B.; da Silva, D.B.; da Rosa Righi, R. Internet of Health Things: Toward intelligent vital signs monitoring in hospital wards. *Artif. Intell Med.* **2018**, *89*, 61–69. [CrossRef]
8. Zhang, Y.; Szolovits, P. Patient-specific learning in real time for adaptive monitoring in critical care. *J. Biomed. Inf.* **2008**, *41*, 452–460. [CrossRef]
9. Al-Ashmori, A.; Basri, S.B.; Dominic, P.; Capretz, L.F.; Muneer, A.; Balogun, A.O.; Gilal, A.R.; Ali, R.F. Classifications of Sustainable Factors in Blockchain Adoption: A Literature Review and Bibliometric Analysis. *Sustainability* **2022**, *14*, 5176. [CrossRef]
10. Saha, A.; Amin, R.; Kunal, S.; Vollala, S.; Dwivedi, S.K. Review on "Blockchain technology based medical healthcare system with privacy issues". *Secur. Priv.* **2019**, *2*, e83. [CrossRef]
11. Roehrs, A.; da Costa, C.A.; da Rosa Righi, R. OmniPHR: A distributed architecture model to integrate personal health records. *J. Biomed. Inf.* **2017**, *71*, 70–81. [CrossRef]
12. Zalewski, A.; Long, W.; Johnson, A.E.W.; Mark, R.G.; Lehman, L.H. Estimating Patient's Health State Using Latent Structure Inferred from Clinical Time Series and Text. *IEEE EMBS Int Conf Biomed. Health Inform.* **2017**, *2017*, 449–452. [CrossRef]
13. Chester, J.G.; Rudolph, J.L. Vital signs in older patients: Age-related changes. *J. Am. Med. Dir. Assoc.* **2011**, *12*, 337–343. [CrossRef]
14. Adewole, K.S.; Akintola, A.G.; Jimoh, R.G.; Mabayoje, M.A.; Jimoh, M.K.; Usman-Hamza, F.E.; Balogun, A.O.; Sangaiah, A.K.; Ameen, A.O. Cloud-based IoMT framework for cardiovascular disease prediction and diagnosis in personalized E-health care. In *Intelligent IoT Systems in Personalized Health Care*; Elsevier: Amsterdam, The Netherlands, 2021; pp. 105–145.
15. Abdulameer, T.H.; Ibrahim, A.A.; Mohammed, A.H. Design of health care monitoring system based on internet of thing (IOT). In Proceedings of the 2020 4th International Symposium on Multidisciplinary Studies and Innovative Technologies (ISMSIT), Istanbul, Turkey, 22–24 October 2020; pp. 1–6.
16. Aceto, G.; Persico, V.; Pescapé, A. Industry 4.0 and health: Internet of things, big data, and cloud computing for healthcare 4.0. *J. Ind. Inf. Integr.* **2020**, *18*, 100129. [CrossRef]
17. Afzal, M.R.; Nadkarni, A.; Niemet, L.; Houmsse, M.; Devgun, J.; Koppert, T.; Ferguson, K.; Mease, J.; Okabe, T.; Houmsse, M. Resource use and economic implications of remote monitoring with subcutaneous cardiac rhythm monitors. *Clin. Electrophysiol.* **2021**, *7*, 745–754. [CrossRef]
18. Banaee, H.; Ahmed, M.U.; Loutfi, A. Data Mining for Wearable Sensors in Health Monitoring Systems: A Review of Recent Trends and Challenges. *Sensors* **2013**, *13*, 17472–17500. [CrossRef]
19. Goldstein, B.A.; Pencina, M.J.; Montez-Rath, M.E.; Winkelmayer, W.C. Predicting mortality over different time horizons: Which data elements are needed? *J. Am. Med. Inform. Assoc.* **2017**, *24*, 176–181. [CrossRef]
20. Shashikumar, S.P.; Stanley, M.D.; Sadiq, I.; Li, Q.; Holder, A.; Clifford, G.D.; Nemati, S. Early sepsis detection in critical care patients using multiscale blood pressure and heart rate dynamics. *J. Electrocardiol.* **2017**, *50*, 739–743. [CrossRef]
21. Bose, E.L.; Clermont, G.; Chen, L.; Dubrawski, A.W.; Ren, D.; Hoffman, L.A.; Pinsky, M.R.; Hravnak, M. Cardiorespiratory instability in monitored step-down unit patients: Using cluster analysis to identify patterns of change. *J. Clin. Monit. Comput.* **2018**, *32*, 117–126. [CrossRef]
22. Azeez, D.; Ali, M.A.; Gan, K.B.; Saiboon, I. Comparison of adaptive neuro-fuzzy inference system and artificial neutral networks model to categorize patients in the emergency department. *Springerplus* **2013**, *2*, 416. [CrossRef]
23. Alaa, A.M.; Yoon, J.; Hu, S.; van der Schaar, M. Personalized Risk Scoring for Critical Care Prognosis Using Mixtures of Gaussian Processes. *IEEE Trans. Biomed. Eng.* **2018**, *65*, 207–218. [CrossRef]
24. Kong, G.; Xu, D.-L.; Yang, J.-B.; Yin, X.; Wang, T.; Jiang, B.; Hu, Y. Belief rule-based inference for predicting trauma outcome. *Knowl.-Based Syst.* **2015**, *95*, 35–44. [CrossRef]
25. Chi, S.; Li, X.; Tian, Y.; Li, J.; Kong, X.; Ding, K.; Weng, C.; Li, J. Semi-supervised learning to improve generalizability of risk prediction models. *J. Biomed. Inform.* **2019**, *92*, 103117. [CrossRef]
26. Kshirsagar, P.R.; Manoharan, H.; Alterazi, H.A.; Lee, H.-N.; Singh, D. Perception Exploration on Robustness Syndromes With Pre-processing Entities Using Machine Learning Algorithm. *Front. Public Health* **2022**, 1424. [CrossRef]
27. Kshirsagar, P.R.; Manoharan, H.; Selvarajan, S.; Althubiti, S.A.; Alenezi, F.; Srivastava, G.; Lin, J.C.-W. A Radical Safety Measure for Identifying Environmental Changes Using Machine Learning Algorithms. *Electronics* **2022**, *11*, 1950. [CrossRef]

28. Li, Q.; Campan, A.; Ren, A.; Eid, W.E. Automating and improving cardiovascular disease prediction using Machine learning and EMR data features from a regional healthcare system. *Int. J. Med. Inform.* **2022**, *163*, 104786. [CrossRef]
29. Alanazi, H.O.; Abdullah, A.H.; Qureshi, K.N. A Critical Review for Developing Accurate and Dynamic Predictive Models Using Machine Learning Methods in Medicine and Health Care. *J. Med. Syst* **2017**, *41*, 69. [CrossRef]
30. Xiao, C.; Choi, E.; Sun, J. Opportunities and challenges in developing deep learning models using electronic health records data: A systematic review. *J. Am. Med. Inform. Assoc.* **2018**, *25*, 1419–1428. [CrossRef]
31. Gnaneswar, B.; Jebarani, M.R.E. A review on prediction and diagnosis of heart failure. In Proceedings of the 2017 International Conference on Innovations in Information, Embedded and Communication Systems (ICIIECS), Coimbatore, India, 17–18 March 2017; pp. 1–3.
32. Kavakiotis, I.; Tsave, O.; Salifoglou, A.; Maglaveras, N.; Vlahavas, I.; Chouvarda, I. Machine Learning and Data Mining Methods in Diabetes Research. *Comput. Struct. Biotechnol. J.* **2017**, *15*, 104–116. [CrossRef]
33. Liberati, A.; Altman, D.G.; Tetzlaff, J.; Mulrow, C.; Gøtzsche, P.C.; Ioannidis, J.P.; Clarke, M.; Devereaux, P.J.; Kleijnen, J.; Moher, D. The PRISMA statement for reporting systematic reviews and meta-analyses of studies that evaluate health care interventions: Explanation and elaboration. *J. Clin. Epidemiol.* **2009**, *62*, e1–e34. [CrossRef]
34. Bhalla, N.; Jolly, P.; Formisano, N.; Estrela, P. Introduction to biosensors. *Essays Biochem* **2016**, *60*, 1–8. [CrossRef]
35. Yoo, E.H.; Lee, S.Y. Glucose biosensors: An overview of use in clinical practice. *Sensors* **2010**, *10*, 4558–4576. [CrossRef] [PubMed]
36. Liedberg, B.; Nylander, C.; Lunström, I. Surface plasmon resonance for gas detection and biosensing. *Sens. Actuators* **1983**, *4*, 299–304. [CrossRef]
37. Vestergaard, M.d.C.; Kerman, K.; Hsing, I.M.; Eiichi, T. *Nanobiosensors and Nanobioanalyses*; Springer: Tokyo, Japan, 2015; Volume 1, p. 379.
38. Narita, F.; Wang, Z.; Kurita, H.; Li, Z.; Shi, Y.; Jia, Y.; Soutis, C. A Review of Piezoelectric and Magnetostrictive Biosensor Materials for Detection of COVID-19 and Other Viruses. *Adv. Mater.* **2021**, *33*, e2005448. [CrossRef] [PubMed]
39. Pillai, S.; Upadhyay, A.; Sayson, D.; Nguyen, B.H.; Tran, S.D. Advances in medical wearable biosensors: Design, fabrication and materials strategies in healthcare monitoring. *Molecules* **2021**, *27*, 165. [CrossRef]
40. Lee, E.K.; Yoo, H.; Lee, C.H. Advanced Materials and Assembly Strategies for Wearable Biosensors: A Review. *Biosens. -Curr. Nov. Strateg. Biosensing* **2020**, 83–110. [CrossRef]
41. Mohankumar, P.; Ajayan, J.; Mohanraj, T.; Yasodharan, R. Recent developments in biosensors for healthcare and biomedical applications: A review. *Measurement* **2020**, *167*, 108293. [CrossRef]
42. Fennedy, K.; Srivastava, A.; Malacria, S.; Perrault, S.T. Towards a Unified and Efficient Command Selection Mechanism for Touch-Based Devices Using Soft Keyboard Hotkeys. *ACM Trans. Comput. -Hum. Interact. (TOCHI)* **2022**, *29*, 1–39. [CrossRef]
43. Steele, B.G.; Holt, L.; Belza, B.; Ferris, S.; Lakshminaryan, S.; Buchner, D.M. Quantitating physical activity in COPD using a triaxial accelerometer. *Chest* **2000**, *117*, 1359–1367. [CrossRef]
44. Belza, B.; Steele, B.G.; Hunziker, J.; Lakshminaryan, S.; Holt, L.; Buchner, D.M. Correlates of physical activity in chronic obstructive pulmonary disease. *Nurs Res.* **2001**, *50*, 195–202. [CrossRef]
45. Patel, S.; Park, H.; Bonato, P.; Chan, L.; Rodgers, M. A review of wearable sensors and systems with application in rehabilitation. *J. Neuroeng. Rehabil.* **2012**, *9*, 21. [CrossRef]
46. Nachiar, C.C.; Ambika, N.; Moulika, R.; Poovendran, R. Design of Cost-effective Wearable Sensors with integrated Health Monitoring System. In Proceedings of the 2020 Fourth International Conference on I-SMAC (IoT in Social, Mobile, Analytics and Cloud) (I-SMAC), Palladam, India, 7–9 October 2020; pp. 1289–1292.
47. Cappon, G.; Acciaroli, G.; Vettoretti, M.; Facchinetti, A.; Sparacino, G. Wearable Continuous Glucose Monitoring Sensors: A Revolution in Diabetes Treatment. *Electronics* **2017**, *6*, 65. [CrossRef]
48. Jin, X.; Li, G.; Xu, T.; Su, L.; Yan, D.; Zhang, X. Fully integrated flexible biosensor for wearable continuous glucose monitoring. *Biosens. Bioelectron.* **2022**, *196*, 113760. [CrossRef]
49. Liu, H.; Ge, J.; Ma, E.; Yang, L. *Advanced Biomaterials for Biosensor and Theranostics*; Academic Press: Cambridge, MA, USA, 2019; pp. 213–255.
50. Khalilian, A.; Khan, M.R.R.; Kang, S.-W. Highly sensitive and wide-dynamic-range side-polished fiber-optic taste sensor. *Sens. Actuators B: Chem.* **2017**, *249*, 700–707. [CrossRef]
51. Lee, J.; Kim, J.; Kim, S.; Min, D.H. Biosensors based on graphene oxide and its biomedical application. *Adv. Drug Deliv. Rev.* **2016**, *105*, 275–287. [CrossRef]
52. Dincer, C.; Bruch, R.; Kling, A.; Dittrich, P.S.; Urban, G.A. Multiplexed Point-of-Care Testing—xPOCT. *Trends Biotechnol.* **2017**, *35*, 728–742. [CrossRef]
53. Ahmad Tarar, A.; Mohammad, U.K.; Srivastava, S. Wearable Skin Sensors and Their Challenges: A Review of Transdermal, Optical, and Mechanical Sensors. *Biosensors* **2020**, *10*, 56. [CrossRef]
54. Busch-Vishniac, I. Trends in electromechanical transduction. *J. Acoust. Soc. Am.* **1998**, *103*, 2860. [CrossRef]
55. Rim, Y.S.; Bae, S.H.; Chen, H.; De Marco, N.; Yang, Y. Recent Progress in Materials and Devices toward Printable and Flexible Sensors. *Adv. Mater.* **2016**, *28*, 4415–4440. [CrossRef]
56. Fan, F.-R.; Tian, Z.-Q.; Lin Wang, Z. Flexible triboelectric generator. *Nano Energy* **2012**, *1*, 328–334. [CrossRef]

57. Heikenfeld, J.; Jajack, A.; Rogers, J.; Gutruf, P.; Tian, L.; Pan, T.; Li, R.; Khine, M.; Kim, J.; Wang, J.; et al. Wearable sensors: Modalities, challenges, and prospects. *Lab. Chip* **2018**, *18*, 217–248. [CrossRef]
58. Chen, H.; Xu, Y.; Zhang, J.; Wu, W.; Song, G. Enhanced stretchable graphene-based triboelectric nanogenerator via control of surface nanostructure. *Nano Energy* **2019**, *58*, 304–311. [CrossRef]
59. Tang, N.; Zhou, C.; Qu, D.; Fang, Y.; Zheng, Y.; Hu, W.; Jin, K.; Wu, W.; Duan, X.; Haick, H. A Highly Aligned Nanowire-Based Strain Sensor for Ultrasensitive Monitoring of Subtle Human Motion. *Small* **2020**, *16*, e2001363. [CrossRef]
60. Wang, S.; Bai, Y.; Yang, X.; Liu, L.; Li, L.; Lu, Q.; Li, T.; Zhang, T. Highly stretchable potentiometric ion sensor based on surface strain redistributed fiber for sweat monitoring. *Talanta* **2020**, *214*, 120869. [CrossRef]
61. Wang, C.; Li, X.; Gao, E.; Jian, M.; Xia, K.; Wang, Q.; Xu, Z.; Ren, T.; Zhang, Y. Carbonized Silk Fabric for Ultrastretchable, Highly Sensitive, and Wearable Strain Sensors. *Adv. Mater.* **2016**, *28*, 6640–6648. [CrossRef] [PubMed]
62. Yang, M.; Pan, J.; Xu, A.; Luo, L.; Cheng, D.; Cai, G.; Wang, J.; Tang, B.; Wang, X. Conductive Cotton Fabrics for Motion Sensing and Heating Applications. *Polymers* **2018**, *10*, 568. [CrossRef] [PubMed]
63. Bi, S.; Hou, L.; Zhao, H.; Zhu, L.; Lu, Y. Ultrasensitive and highly repeatable pen ink decorated cuprammonium rayon (cupra) fabrics for multifunctional sensors. *J. Mater. Chem. A* **2018**, *6*, 16556–16565. [CrossRef]
64. Ren, J.; Wang, C.; Zhang, X.; Carey, T.; Chen, K.; Yin, Y.; Torrisi, F. Environmentally-friendly conductive cotton fabric as flexible strain sensor based on hot press reduced graphene oxide. *Carbon* **2017**, *111*, 622–630. [CrossRef]
65. Liu, S.; Hu, M.; Yang, J. A facile way of fabricating flexible and conductive cotton fabric. *J. Mater. Chem. C* **2016**, *4*. [CrossRef]
66. Yang, S.; Li, C.; Chen, X.; Zhao, Y.; Zhang, H.; Wen, N.; Fan, Z.; Pan, L. Facile Fabrication of High-Performance Pen Ink-Decorated Textile Strain Sensors for Human Motion Detection. *ACS Appl. Mater. Interfaces* **2020**, *12*, 19874–19881. [CrossRef]
67. Ozioko, O.; Karipoth, P.; Hersh, M.; Dahiya, R. Wearable Assistive Tactile Communication Interface Based on Integrated Touch Sensors and Actuators. *IEEE Trans. Neural Syst. Rehabil. Eng.* **2020**, *28*, 1344–1352. [CrossRef]
68. Qi, K.; Wang, H.; You, X.; Tao, X.; Li, M.; Zhou, Y.; Zhang, Y.; He, J.; Shao, W.; Cui, S. Core-sheath nanofiber yarn for textile pressure sensor with high pressure sensitivity and spatial tactile acuity. *J. Colloid Interface Sci.* **2020**, *561*, 93–103. [CrossRef]
69. Yi, Q.; Najafikhoshnoo, S.; Das, P.; Noh, S.; Hoang, E.; Kim, T.; Esfandyarpour, R. All-3D-Printed, Flexible, and Hybrid Wearable Bioelectronic Tactile Sensors Using Biocompatible Nanocomposites for Health Monitoring. *Adv. Mater. Technol.* **2022**, *7*, 2101034. [CrossRef]
70. Biswas, S.; Misra, S. Designing of a prototype of e-health monitoring system. In Proceedings of the 2015 IEEE International Conference on Research in Computational Intelligence and Communication Networks (ICRCICN), Kolkata, India, 20–22 November 2015; pp. 267–272.
71. Rodrigues, J.G.P.; Kaiseler, M.; Aguiar, A.; Cunha, J.P.S.; Barros, J. A Mobile Sensing Approach to Stress Detection and Memory Activation for Public Bus Drivers. *IEEE Trans. Intell. Transp. Syst.* **2015**, *16*, 3294–3303. [CrossRef]
72. Nowshin, N.; Rashid, M.M.; Akhtar, T.; Akhtar, N. *Infrared Sensor Controlled Wheelchair for Physically Disabled People*; Springer: Cham, Switzerland, 2019; Volume 2, pp. 847–855.
73. Mulfari, D.; Celesti, A.; Fazio, M.; Villari, M. Human-Computer Interface Based on IoT Embedded Systems for Users with Disabilities. In Proceedings of the International Internet of Things Summit; Springer: Cham, Switzerland, 2015; pp. 376–383.
74. Bhatnagar, V.; Chandra, R.; Jain, V. IoT Based Alert System for Visually Impaired Persons. In Proceedings of the Emerging Technologies in Computer Engineering: Microservices in Big Data Analytics; Springer: Singapore, 2019; pp. 216–223.
75. Marques, G.; Pitarma, R. IAQ Evaluation Using an IoT CO2 Monitoring System for Enhanced Living Environments. In Proceedings of the World Conference on Information Systems and Technologies; Springer: Cham, Switzerland, 2018; pp. 1169–1177.
76. Abdelgawad, A.; Yelamarthi, K.; Khattab, A. IoT-Based Health Monitoring System for Active and Assisted Living. In Proceedings of the International Conference on Smart Objects and Technologies for Social Good; Springer: Cham, Switzerland, 2017; pp. 11–20.
77. Umasankar, Y.; Jalal, A.H.; Gonzalez, P.J.; Chowdhury, M.; Alfonso, A.; Bhansali, S. Wearable alcohol monitoring device with auto-calibration ability for high chemical specificity. In Proceedings of the 2016 IEEE 13th international conference on wearable and implantable body sensor networks (BSN), San Francisco, CA, USA, 14–17 June 2016; pp. 353–358.
78. Mohan, S.; Shubha, R. Non-invasive Analytics Based Smart System for Diabetes Monitoring. In Proceedings of the International Conference on IoT Technologies for HealthCare; Springer: Cham, Switzerland, 2018; pp. 88–98.
79. Alshamrani, M. IoT and artificial intelligence implementations for remote healthcare monitoring systems: A survey. *J. King Saud. Univ. -Comput. Inf. Sci.* **2022**, *34*, 4687–4701. [CrossRef]
80. Triantafyllidis, A.K.; Tsanas, A. Applications of Machine Learning in Real-Life Digital Health Interventions: Review of the Literature. *J. Med. Internet Res.* **2019**, *21*, e12286. [CrossRef]
81. Blasch, E.; Pham, T.; Chong, C.-Y.; Koch, W.; Leung, H.; Braines, D.; Abdelzaher, T. Machine learning/artificial intelligence for sensor data fusion–opportunities and challenges. *IEEE Aerosp. Electron. Syst. Mag.* **2021**, *36*, 80–93. [CrossRef]
82. Chui, K.T.; Lytras, M.D.; Visvizi, A.; Sarirete, A. An overview of artificial intelligence and big data analytics for smart healthcare: Requirements, applications, and challenges. *Artif. Intell. Big Data Anal. Smart Healthc.* **2021**, 243–254. [CrossRef]
83. Davenport, T.; Kalakota, R. The potential for artificial intelligence in healthcare. *Future Healthc. J.* **2019**, *6*, 94. [CrossRef]
84. Farrokhi, A.; Farahbakhsh, R.; Rezazadeh, J.; Minerva, R. Application of Internet of Things and artificial intelligence for smart fitness: A survey. *Comput. Netw.* **2021**, *189*, 107859. [CrossRef]

85. Hiran, K.K.; Jain, R.K.; Lakhwani, K.; Doshi, R. *Machine Learning: Master Supervised and Unsupervised Learning Algorithms with Real Examples (English Edition)*; BPB Publications: Noida, India, 2021.
86. Janiesch, C.; Zschech, P.; Heinrich, K. Machine learning and deep learning. *Electron. Mark.* **2021**, *31*, 685–695. [CrossRef]
87. Vats, V.K. *Machine Learning Enabled Vital Sign Monitoring System*; University of Windsor (Canada): Windsor, ON, Canada, 2019.
88. Das, S.; Dey, A.; Pal, A.; Roy, N. Applications of artificial intelligence in machine learning: Review and prospect. *Int. J. Comput. Appl.* **2015**, *115*, 31–41. [CrossRef]
89. Celin, S.; Vasanth, K. ECG signal classification using various machine learning techniques. *J. Med. Syst.* **2018**, *42*, 1–11. [CrossRef] [PubMed]
90. Alsariera, Y.A.; Balogun, A.O.; Adeyemo, V.E.; Tarawneh, O.H.; Mojeed, H.A. Intelligent tree-based ensemble approaches for phishing website detection. *J. Eng. Sci. Technol.* **2022**, *17*, 563–582.
91. Balogun, A.O.; Basri, S.; Capretz, L.F.; Mahamad, S.; Imam, A.A.; Almomani, M.A.; Adeyemo, V.E.; Alazzawi, A.K.; Bajeh, A.O.; Kumar, G. Software Defect Prediction Using Wrapper Feature Selection Based on Dynamic Re-Ranking Strategy. *Symmetry* **2021**, *13*, 2166. [CrossRef]
92. Balogun, A.O.; Basri, S.; Mahamad, S.; Capretz, L.F.; Imam, A.A.; Almomani, M.A.; Adeyemo, V.E.; Kumar, G. A novel rank aggregation-based hybrid multifilter wrapper feature selection method in software defect prediction. *Comput. Intell. Neurosci.* **2021**, *2021*. [CrossRef]
93. Balogun, A.; Oladele, R.; Mojeed, H.; Amin-Balogun, B.; Adeyemo, V.E.; Aro, T.O. Performance analysis of selected clustering techniques for software defects prediction. *Afr. J. Comput. ICT* **2019**, *12*, 30–42.
94. Muneer, A.; Taib, S.M.; Fati, S.M.; Balogun, A.O.; Aziz, I.A. A Hybrid deep learning-based unsupervised anomaly detection in high dimensional data. *Comput. Mater. Contin.* **2022**, *70*, 6073–6088. [CrossRef]
95. Oladepo, A.G.; Bajeh, A.O.; Balogun, A.O.; Mojeed, H.A.; Salman, A.A.; Bako, A.I. Heterogeneous Ensemble with Combined Dimensionality Reduction for Social Spam Detection. *Int. J. Interact. Mob. Technol.* **2021**, *15*, 84–103. [CrossRef]
96. Usman-Hamza, F.; Atte, A.; Balogun, A.; Mojeed, H.; Bajeh, A.; Adeyemo, V. Impact of feature selection on classification via clustering techniques in software defect prediction. *J. Comput. Sci. Its Appl.* **2019**, *26*. [CrossRef]
97. Wu, M.; Luo, J. Wearable technology applications in healthcare: A literature review. *Online J. Nurs. Inform.* **2019**, *23*. Available online: https://www.himss.org/resources/wearable-technology-applications-healthcare-literature-review (accessed on 2 September 2022).
98. Kiral-Kornek, I.; Roy, S.; Nurse, E.; Mashford, B.; Karoly, P.; Carroll, T.; Payne, D.; Saha, S.; Baldassano, S.; O'Brien, T. Epileptic seizure prediction using big data and deep learning: Toward a mobile system. *EBioMedicine* **2018**, *27*, 103–111. [CrossRef]
99. Usman, S.M.; Khalid, S.; Bashir, S. A deep learning based ensemble learning method for epileptic seizure prediction. *Comput. Biol. Med.* **2021**, *136*, 104710. [CrossRef]
100. Nejedly, P.; Kremen, V.; Sladky, V.; Nasseri, M.; Guragain, H.; Klimes, P.; Cimbalnik, J.; Varatharajah, Y.; Brinkmann, B.H.; Worrell, G.A. Deep-learning for seizure forecasting in canines with epilepsy. *J. Neural Eng.* **2019**, *16*, 036031. [CrossRef]
101. Nasseri, M.; Attia, T.P.; Joseph, B.; Gregg, N.M.; Nurse, E.S.; Viana, P.F.; Schulze-Bonhage, A.; Dümpelmann, M.; Worrell, G.; Freestone, D.R. Non-invasive wearable seizure detection using long–short-term memory networks with transfer learning. *J. Neural Eng.* **2021**, *18*, 056017. [CrossRef]
102. LeCun, Y.; Bengio, Y.; Hinton, G. Deep learning. *Nature* **2015**, *521*, 436–444. [CrossRef]
103. Jeon, H.; Lee, W.; Park, H.; Lee, H.J.; Kim, S.K.; Kim, H.B.; Jeon, B.; Park, K.S. Correction: Automatic Classification of Tremor Severity in Parkinson's Disease Using a Wearable Device. *Sensors* **2017**, *17*, 2067, Erratum in *Sensors* **2017**, *18*, 33. [CrossRef]
104. Koushik, C.; Choubey, S.B.; Choubey, A. Application of virtual reality systems to psychology and cognitive neuroscience research. In *Cognitive Informatics, Computer Modelling, and Cognitive Science*; Elsevier: Amsterdam, The Netherlands, 2020; pp. 133–147.
105. Greco, L.; Percannella, G.; Ritrovato, P.; Tortorella, F.; Vento, M. Trends in IoT based solutions for health care: Moving AI to the edge. *Pattern Recognit. Lett.* **2020**, *135*, 346–353. [CrossRef]
106. Tobore, I.; Li, J.; Yuhang, L.; Al-Handarish, Y.; Kandwal, A.; Nie, Z.; Wang, L. Deep learning intervention for health care challenges: Some biomedical domain considerations. *JMIR Mhealth Uhealth* **2019**, *7*, e11966. [CrossRef]
107. Guan, J. Artificial intelligence in healthcare and medicine: Promises, ethical challenges and governance. *Chin. Med. Sci. J.* **2019**, *34*, 76–83.
108. Sun, T.Q.; Medaglia, R. Mapping the challenges of Artificial Intelligence in the public sector: Evidence from public healthcare. *Gov. Inf. Q.* **2019**, *36*, 368–383. [CrossRef]
109. Thakare, V.; Khire, G.; Kumbhar, M. Artificial Intelligence (AI) And Internet Of Things (IoT) In Healthcare: Opportunities And Challenges. *SPAST Abstr.* **2021**, *107*, 7941. [CrossRef]
110. Kumar, G.; Basri, S.; Imam, A.A.; Khowaja, S.A.; Capretz, L.F.; Balogun, A.O. Data Harmonization for Heterogeneous Datasets: A Systematic Literature Review. *Appl. Sci.* **2021**, *11*, 8275. [CrossRef]
111. Reddy, S.; Allan, S.; Coghlan, S.; Cooper, P. A governance model for the application of AI in health care. *J. Am. Med. Inform. Assoc.* **2020**, *27*, 491–497. [CrossRef] [PubMed]
112. Nahavandi, D.; Alizadehsani, R.; Khosravi, A.; Acharya, U.R. Application of artificial intelligence in wearable devices: Opportunities and challenges. *Comput. Methods Programs Biomed.* **2022**, *213*, 106541. [CrossRef]

113. Mohanta, B.; Das, P.; Patnaik, S. Healthcare 5.0: A paradigm shift in digital healthcare system using artificial intelligence, IOT and 5G communication. In Proceedings of the 2019 International Conference on Applied Machine Learning (ICAML), Bhubaneswar, India, 25–26 May 2019; pp. 191–196.
114. Clarke, R. Regulatory alternatives for AI. *Comput. Law Secur. Rev.* **2019**, *35*, 398–409. [CrossRef]
115. Le Douarin, Y.; Traversino, Y.; Graciet, A.; Josseran, A.; Bili, A.B.; Blaise, L.; Chatellier, G.; Coulonjou, H.; Delval, C.; Detournay, B. Telemonitoring and experimentation in telemedicine for the improvement of healthcare pathways (ETAPES program). Sustainability beyond 2021: What type of organisational model and funding should be used? *Therapies* **2020**, *75*, 43–56. [CrossRef]
116. Akmal, A.; Greatbanks, R.; Foote, J. Lean thinking in healthcare–findings from a systematic literature network and bibliometric analysis. *Health Policy* **2020**, *124*, 615–627. [CrossRef]

MDPI
St. Alban-Anlage 66
4052 Basel
Switzerland
www.mdpi.com

Applied Sciences Editorial Office
E-mail: applsci@mdpi.com
www.mdpi.com/journal/applsci

www.ingramcontent.com/pod-product-compliance
Lightning Source LLC
Chambersburg PA
CBHW040757250926
51850CB00007BA/1014